OXFORD CONSTITUTIONAL T

Series editors:
Martin Loughlin, John P. McCormick, and

The Three Branches

OXFORD CONSTITUTIONAL THEORY

Series editors:

Martin Loughlin, John P. McCormick, and Neil Walker

One consequence of the increase in interest in constitutions and constitutional law in recent years is a growing innovative literature in constitutional theory. The aim of *Oxford Constitutional Theory* is to provide a showcase for the best of these theoretical reflections and a forum for further innovation in the field.

The new series will seek to establish itself as the primary point of reference for scholarly work in the subject by commissioning different types of study. The majority of the works published in the series will be monographs that advance new understandings of the subject. Well-conceived edited collections that bring a variety of perspectives and disciplinary approaches to bear on specific themes in constitutional thought will also be included. Further, in recognition of the fact that there is a great deal of pioneering literature originally written in languages other than English and with regard to non-anglophone constitutional traditions, the series will also seek to publish English translations of leading monographs in constitutional theory.

ALSO AVAILABLE IN THE SERIES

The Twilight of Constitutionalism?
Edited by Petra Dobner and Martin Loughlin

Beyond Constitutionalism
The Pluralist Structure of Postnational Law
Nico Krisch

The Constitutional State
N W Barber

Sovereignty's Promise
The State as Fiduciary
Evan Fox-Decent

Constitutional Fragments
Societal Constitutionalism and Globalization
Gunther Teubner

Constitutional Referendums
The Theory and Practice of Republican Deliberation
Stephen Tierney

Constituting Economic and Social Rights
Katharine G. Young

The Global Model of Constitutional Rights
Kai Möller

The Three Branches

A Comparative Model of Separation of Powers

Christoph Möllers

OXFORD
UNIVERSITY PRESS

OXFORD
UNIVERSITY PRESS

Great Clarendon Street, Oxford, OX2 6DP,
United Kingdom

Oxford University Press is a department of the University of Oxford.
It furthers the University's objective of excellence in research, scholarship,
and education by publishing worldwide. Oxford is a registered trade mark of
Oxford University Press in the UK and in certain other countries

First published 2013
First published in paperback 2015

Published in the United States of America by Oxford University Press
198 Madison Avenue, New York, NY 10016, United States of America

British Library Cataloguing in Publication Data
Data available

Library of Congress Cataloging in Publication Data
Data available

ISBN 978–0–19–960211–7 (Hbk.)
ISBN 978–0–19–873808–4 (Pbk.)

Acknowledgments

This book is the result of a decade of thinking about the topic of separation of powers that already resulted in two German books: a long Habilitation thesis (*Gewaltengliederung*, Mohr: Tübingen, 2005) and a shorter more comparative book (*Die Drei Gewalten*, Velbrück: Weilerswist 2008) that was the basis for this work. During this time many people contributed with insight, advice, critique, and language: Johannes Bethge; Hannah Birkenkötter; Hauke Brunkhorst; Frances Foley; Dieter Grimm; Nick Kumaroff; Andrej Lang; Oliver Lepsius; Isabelle Ley; Gerhard Möllers; Frank Nullmeyer; Eberhard Schmidt-Aßmann; Alexander Tischbirek; Joseph Weiler; Tim Wihl; and Rüdiger Wolfrum.

Contents

List of Abbreviations

ECHR	European Convention on Human Rights
ECtHR	European Court of Human Rights
ECJ	European Court of Justice
EP	European Parliament
EU	European Union
GATT	General Agreement on Tariffs and Trade
ICC	International Criminal Court
ILO	International Labour Organization
IOSCO	International Organization of Security Commissions
NATO	North Atlantic Treaty Organization
NGO	Non-governmental organization
OECD	Organization for Economic Co-operation and Development
TEU	Treaty of the European Union
TFEU	Treaty on the Functioning of the European Union
UN	United Nations
US	United States
WTO	World Trade Organization

'...in constitutional government the ultimate power cannot be left to the legislature or even to a supreme court, which is only the highest judicial interpreter of the constitution. Ultimate power is held by the three branches in a duly specified relation with one another with each responsible to the people.'

John Rawls, Political Liberalism

Introduction: Constitutional Theory and Political Philosophy

A chamber of the US Congress reserves the power to veto a naturalization, even if the candidate fulfils every statutory requirement to become an American citizen. Germany's Constitutional Court obliges parliament to pass a law regulating abortion more strictly. The European Commission issues directives to liberalize the energy markets of the EU member states. The Dispute Settlement Body of the WTO rules on whether the parliament of a democratic member state may introduce certain trade restrictions for environmental reasons.

Are such institutional mechanisms admissible? Do they even make sense? By what criteria should we decide? Analysis of positive law tells us only whether such arrangements conform to the legal system in question. This answer is important but not sufficient. If we intend to criticize and improve how decisions are made at the national and supranational levels, we need criteria beyond those of positive law.

The present study will attempt to develop such criteria. It will inquire how the decision-making responsibilities of courts, administrations, and parliaments should relate to one another in order to plausibly claim legitimacy. It will reconstruct the traditional notion of the separation of powers as a theory of legitimate decision-making and apply that theory comparatively to different national, European, and international legal issues. First, however, it must examine the disciplinary context of our enterprise.

INSTITUTIONAL BLINDNESS OF POLITICAL THEORY—LACK OF THEORY IN CONSTITUTIONAL LAW

Since the publication of John Rawls' *A Theory of Justice* in 1971, interest in normative political theory and systematic responses to the question of an appropriate political order has been growing throughout the world. The most significant contributions to this discussion have come from philosophy and the social sciences; less often from economics; some from law. The discussion has focused either on identifying reasons for certain political decisions, such as responses to economic inequality, inclusion of minorities, and justification of taxes, or, alternatively, on developing theoretical models of legitimacy. Interest has been less focused on concrete problems of legitimately *organizing* public action, and therefore in the question of what influence organizational and procedural arrangements should have on the justification of political decisions. It is true that organizational sociology has, since the 1930s, been pointing out the significance of organizational arrangements, both for business and public administration.[1] This kind of inquiry has been applied productively to economic methods such as game theory. A variant of game theory, the veto player approach, even addresses classical separation of powers themes.[2] Only very rarely, however, have these contributions affected normative political philosophy.

Legal scholars, especially in the civil law tradition, have long stood on the sidelines of such discussions. Though they played a considerable role in political theory from the era of the Atlantic revolution to the debates in French and German interwar constitutional scholarship, from the Federalists and Sieyès to Hans Kelsen, Léon Duguit, Raymond Carré de Malberg, and Carl Schmitt, their importance has declined with the rise of the judiciary in constitutional law. Preoccupied with interpreting and systematizing the rapidly growing and refined corpus of decisions of constitutional and international courts, contemporary constitutional scholarship is finding fewer links to contemporary political theory. To be sure, important exceptions to this rule can be seen in the serious dialogues between political theory and constitutional scholarship in the United States.[3] But for many reasons, not least the unique structure of the US presidential system, it seems problematic, though still all too common in comparative law, to generalize the American debates.[4]

This mutual ignorance of political theory and constitutional scholarship comes at a price. What constitutional scholarship lacks in theoretical insight, it compensates by focusing on actual institutional practices. The theory of constitutional law rarely concerns itself with theories of democracy. Yet it

---

[1] H. A. Simon, *Administrative Behavior [1947]* (New York: The Free Press, 4th ed 1997).

[2] G. Tsebelis, *Veto Players: How Political Institutions Work* (Princeton: Princeton University Press, 2002).

[3] See, eg, B. Ackerman, *We the People*, vol 1 (Cambridge: Harvard University Press, 1991); C. R. Sunstein, 'Interest Groups in American Public Law', 38 *Stanford Law Review* (1985), 29; P. P. Craig, *Public Law and Democracy in the United Kingdom and the United States of America* (Oxford: Oxford University Press, 1991).

[4] For some convincing American doubts concerning the relevance of American constitutional law see M. Tushnet, *Weak Courts, Strong Rights* (Princeton: Princeton University Press 2008), 18–19.

has very concrete ideas of how democracy can be organized. Simply put, the practice of democracy is to a large extent a practice of the law.[5] Political philosophy, in contrast, considers the justification of political power. But if it is true that political power plays out in the form of law, it would seem appropriate to combine legal concepts with political theory. Often questions of positive law appear too technical for political theory; problems of political theory too abstract for legal doctrine. Yet the weak, discursive links between normative political theory and jurisprudence do not sever the strong institutional links between political power and law. Rather, they impoverish the discourse, which remains trapped within its own issues.

Introducing the idea of separation of powers into these debates could serve as a transmission belt for the conversation between constitutional law and political theory and bring the two disciplines closer together—considering that the concept dates back to a time when law and political theory were not wholly distinct from each other.[6] Using this concept as a reference point might be both timelier than pre-modern teleological approaches which justify power through goals such as peace or welfare and more precise than social contract models.[7] These, from Hobbes to Rawls, conclude with the act of the establishment of government, but they are generally little concerned with the ensuing specifics of institution building.[8] In a similar way, much of contemporary legal philosophy tends to belittle considerations of procedure.[9] Combining the normative idea of liberty with the institutional preconditions of liberty—a project that the American constitutional fathers set out in the *Federalist Papers*—seems today to be an exceptional quest. Pursuing it, however, is as worthwhile today as it was back then.

In particular, the state of the legal debate on globalization shows just how urgent and necessary the intervention of a theoretically motivated and methodically open-minded constitutional scholarship actually is. Much of globalization takes place in the form of law. Indeed, legal form appears to be a key condition for globalization. Fundamental global legal issues prominently discussed in political theory, such as the conflict between trade and

---

[5] E. W. Böckenförde, 'Demokratie als Verfassungsprinzip' in J. Isensee and P. Kirchhof (eds.), *Handbuch des Staatsrechts*, vol I (Heidelberg: C. F. Müller, 1st ed 1987), § 22.

[6] See with regard to the conceptual history H. Fenske, 'Gewaltenteilung' in O. Brunner, W. Conze, and R. Koselleck (eds.), *Geschichtliche Grundbegriffe*, vol 3 (Stuttgart: Klett-Cotta, 1982), 923.

[7] Similar E. Carolan, *The New Separation of Powers* (Oxford: Oxford University Press, 2009), Chap. 1.

[8] See N. K. Komesar, *Imperfect Alternatives* (Chicago: University of Chicago Press, 1994), 35, for a similar critique of Rawls. For Rawls' idea of separated powers: T. Lieber, *Diskursive Vernunft und formelle Gleichheit* (Tübingen: Mohr, 2007).

[9] R. Dworkin, *Taking Rights Seriously* (London: Duckworth, 1977); J. Raz, *The Morality of Freedom* (Oxford: Clarendon Press, 1986).

environmental protection, rarely emulate the actual institutional practice of the globalized legal order. Rather, legal mechanisms reduce such conflicts to minor cases, precisely in order to prevent, for good or bad, any politicization of the issue in question.[10] If we want to understand and assess how the law deals with these kinds of contradiction, we must confront such procedural structures. Virtuous as they may be, refined legal procedures likewise contribute to the theoretical impoverishment of the legal discourse, for legally refined solutions tend to hide fundamental moral problems and political conflicts.

THE MODEL: ORGANIZATION AND LEGITIMACY

This book will therefore try to develop a systematic link between a model of normative political theory and the organization of public action, based on the idea of separated powers. It will explore the idea that constitutional orders acknowledge the contradictory claims of individual and democratic collective autonomy, and that a specific correlation between the three branches of government serves to express, mediate, and mitigate those claims. Linking the concept of separation of powers to normative theory is an old though somewhat forgotten enterprise. As far back as the theories of Kant and Rousseau, the separation of powers has been reconstructed from its origins in models of legitimacy.[11] Their common point of departure, the idea of individual and collective autonomy, will likewise guide the following study.

A concept that argues according to a theory of legitimacy may claim its validity from beyond the jurisdiction of one legal order. It may prove itself even for structures beyond the nation-state like the European Union or international organizations. Whereas political philosophy does not engage in specific institutional arguments, legal studies mostly limit themselves to questions of positive law in a particular legal system regarding the separation of powers principle. Comparing different legal systems, then, can only *describe* similarities and differences without evaluating them.[12] This is not enough. For it can be assumed that the common commitment of all democratic constitutional systems to an order that separates governmental powers into three branches is closely linked with their likewise common

[10] See N. Luhmann, *Legitimation durch Verfahren* (Darmstadt: Luchterhand, 1975), 121 for an unmatched analysis of court procedure.

[11] J.-J. Rousseau, *Contrat Social [1762]* (Paris: Gallimard, 1969), II/3; I. Kant, 'Metaphysik der Sitten, Rechtslehre [1797]', *Werke* [ed Weischedel] (Darmstadt: Wissenschaftliche Buchgesellschaft, 1983), § 45.

[12] See G. Frankenberg, 'Critical Comparisons: Re-thinking Comparative Law', *26 Harvard Law Review* (1985), 411, for a still valid critique.

basis of legitimacy. This empirically obvious connection between the political philosophy of constitutional democracies and the prevalence of the idea of separated powers needs systematic exploration.

In order to develop such a general normative concept of separated powers, theoretical and comparative work has to be done. We will have to devise and prove our normative concept in existing constitutional orders, namely the Basic Law of the Federal Republic of Germany; the Constitution of the United States; the French constitution; the constitutional system of the United Kingdom; other national orders; the law of the European Union; and some patterns of international institutional law. From the outset, we will apply the perspective of political philosophy to the procedural and organizational structures of these legal orders.

Characteristically, democratic states simultaneously protect individual and democratic self-determination.[13] The central systematic task of this book will be to advance a systematic connection between the protection of individual freedom and democratic self-determination on the one hand and, on the other, the organizational principle of a *trias politica* which is confusingly called by a variety of names: separation of powers; division of powers; or checks and balances. This book will argue firmly in favour of a *monistic* normative approach. It differs from models that combine various forms of legitimacy, for example through economic success, peacekeeping, or distributional justice, in a syncretistic manner.[14] Our exclusive concentration on individual and democratic self-determination, on freedom, does not rest on the assumption that other justificatory standards are irrelevant; clearly, they are. Rather, three reasons speak in favour of a monistic normative concept, limited to freedom, in the context of this book.

Firstly, procedures of self-determination seem necessary to both legitimately define and adequately specify other standards of legitimacy, such as justice, welfare, or efficiency. All democratic constitutions share this view: they both oblige public authorities to achieve certain objectives and set in place democratic procedures to identify these goals.

Secondly, output-based concepts of legitimacy create particular methodological problems for a piece of legal scholarship. *Legal scholarship cannot speak with the same authority about the factual conditions or outcomes of the law as it can with respect to its procedural and organizational issues.* Legal scholars share this limitation with Rawls' basic approach of normative political philosophy, for example. This limitation distinguishes both from the empirical strands of the political sciences. Furthermore, the analysis of legal institutions

---

[13] In this regard we will rely on the basic concepts of J. Habermas, *Between Facts and Norms* (Cambridge: MIT Press, 1996).

[14] F. Vilbert, *The Rise of the Unelected* (Cambridge: Cambridge University Press, 2007).

comprises its own corpus, which can be thoroughly measured against those empirical studies. Constitutional norms and judicial decisions are part of political practice, albeit one which is often difficult to decipher without knowing the structures of positive law. This is a plea for a moderate formalism[15] that is open to empirical insights about the law, though not necessarily exercised by legal scholars. We will come back to this point at the end of the introduction.

Thirdly and finally, a monistic normative approach also seems more productive in debates with other differing approaches. Its vices and virtues can be more easily evaluated, its limits better assessed. Here too, being consistent seems to be the 'greatest obligation of the philosopher'.[16]

The argument of this book runs on two different normative levels: it develops an argument from a theory of legitimacy, thereby operating on the level of political philosophy's theoretical normativity. Then, it applies this argument to legally constituted institutions, thereby operating on the level of the normativity of positive law. Both levels are distinct without being separable. When a constitutional text codifies 'democracy' or 'freedom', positive law refers to notions of political philosophy. In making this reference, however, it puts an element of philosophy in a concrete political and legal context and modifies its meaning. Therefore, the demand of political philosophy to determine the content of positive law seems dubious. The Platonic legacy of a jusnaturalistic philosopher's kingdom, in which philosophy stipulates general normative boundaries that shall be filled only by legislators, administrators, and courts, is not compatible with a democratic understanding of the law.[17] Such an approach may also overestimate the argumentative reach of philosophical and, especially moral arguments. Despite that, it is just as unconvincing to draw the methodological line between law and political philosophy in a positivistic manner and simply stick to some letter of the law. There are two reasons to look at the distinction between political theory and positive law as something necessary, but only relative: first, political theory must be interested in the conditions of institutionalizing its own standards. For this reason it has to shift its interests towards positive law and the conditions of its functioning. Secondly, it is evident that the methodological separation of normative theory and positive law cannot survive when positive law adopts concepts of political philosophy

---

[15] S. Fish, 'The Law Wishes to Have a Formal Existence', in S. Fish, *There's No Such Thing as Free Speech: And It's a Good Thing, Too* (Oxford: Oxford University Press, 1995), 141.

[16] I. Kant, 'Kritik der praktischen Vernunft [1788]', *Werke* vol 6 [ed. Weischedel] (Darmstadt: Wissenschaftliche Buchgesellschaft, 1983), 132.

[17] For a critique of constitutional review that argues on this theme in a different manner see: G. C. Christie, *Philosopher Kings? The Adjudication of Conflicting Human Rights and Social Values* (Oxford: Oxford University Press, 2012).

and thereby makes theoretical problems its own. This is particularly relevant with respect to the de-nationalization of legal orders. When national legal orders begin to influence and compare each other, when they attempt to agree upon common foundations or begin to be overarched by supra- and international legal spheres, the relationship between political theory and positive law changes.[18] Today, it is no longer plausible to trace the positive law at any place back to just one single national source.[19] It is becoming necessary to find a legal language that is more strongly theoretically motivated than the classical interpretations of national law. Such a language will not lead to a common legal system. It will be a contested language as well as a language of contestation. But the clear distinction between normative requirements of a philosophical level and positive obligations of the juridical level, though methodologically desirable, will blur more and more. Such a distinction is not equally plausible under all institutional conditions. 'Everything would be much easier, if the distinction between law and justice were a real distinction . . .'[20]

Finally, our approach provokes the question of how to resolve the basic methodological problem of every political theory that includes questions of internationalization: how to treat categories of the *state*. On the one hand, they appear badly strained as a result of new phenomena such as European integration. On the other hand, one cannot easily break free from a conceptual world that has accompanied us in principle since the beginning of modern politics. But with the distinction between individual and democratic self-determination and its institutional implementation into a concept of the separated powers, the achievements of democratic constitutional states could be transposed to levels beyond the state. The concept of self-determination may help to solve the problem of 'methodological nationalism'.[21]

Under the banners of self-determination, freedom, or autonomy, neo-liberals and anti-globalization champions of the welfare state, minority rights advocates, and Rousseauists can all come together. The only question is: who is the autonomous subject and how should the autonomy be organized? The conflict between individual and collective self-determination or, to put it another way, the conflict between liberalism and democracy does not and should not vanish through the construction of a constitution.

---

[18] See C. Möllers, 'Globalisierte Jurisprudenz', 79 *Archiv für Rechts- und Sozialphilosophie/Beiheft* (2001), 41.

[19] N. Krisch, *Beyond Constitutionalism* (Oxford: Oxford University Press), 69–103.

[20] J. Derrida, *Force de Loi* (Paris: Galilée, 1994).

[21] In any case, the problem is in most cases framed in a too simple manner, treating national and international politics as a zero-sum game. For a strong argument that even the normative ideal of cosmopolitanism needs the state and its form of politics: L. Ypi, *Global Justice and Avant-Garde Political Agency* (Oxford: Oxford University Press, 2012), Chap 3 and Part III.

It must instead be perpetuated as a political controversy within its framework.[22] It occurs in political disputes, for instance between paternalistic and economically liberal understandings of freedom, as well as in an institutional form. Separation of powers, according to the concept of this book, merges the contradiction between individual and democratic self-determination into the form of law.

STATE OF THE DISCUSSION

The contemporary academic discussion of the idea of separated powers is defined by a simple, powerful, and mistaken narrative: once upon a time, there was a 'classical' system of separated powers, in particular within the constitutional nation-states of Europe. Today this classical system has eroded. What we observe instead is the rise of institutional phenomena that have overcome the classical system: the rise of the unbound political executive;[23] the decline of parliamentarism;[24] the rise of the administrative state;[25] political parties;[26] the boom of technocratic agencies;[27] the proliferation of constitutional review;[28] the privatization of regulatory structures;[29] and the internationalization of national legal orders.[30]

There is no doubt that all these developments represent significant phenomena that challenge our idea of constitutional democracy. Yet the way these phenomena are often discussed against the background of separation of powers also tends to be misleading. The narrative of all the quoted accounts relies—in a remarkable and irritatingly homogeneous way—upon a canonical idea of separated powers that has, in fact, never existed.[31] All

---

[22] See eg C. Mouffe, *The Democratic Paradox* (London/New York: Verso, 2000).

[23] E. A. Posner and A. Vermeule, *The Executive Unbound* (Oxford: Oxford University, 2010), Chap. 2. They provide an American story that does not work in parliamentary systems.

[24] G. Agamben, *State of Exception* (Chicago: University of Chicago Press, 2005), 11–22; C. Schmitt, *Die geistesgeschichtliche Lage des heutigen Parlamentarismus [1923]* (Berlin: Duncker & Humblot, 7th ed 1991); C. Crouch, *Post-democracy* (Cambridge: Polity Press, 2004).

[25] Since J. Landis, *The Administrative Processs* (New Haven: Yale University Press, 1938), this is a recurrent theme. See E. Carolan, *The New Separation of Powers* (Oxford: Oxford University Press, 2009), 18–21, referring to 'pure' theories with scarce historical examples.

[26] D. Levinson and R. Pildes, 'Separation of Parties not Powers', *119 Harvard Law Review* (2006), 2311.

[27] F. Vilbert, *The Rise of the Unelected* (Cambridge: Cambridge University Press, 2007).

[28] A. Stone Sweet, *Governing with Judges* (Oxford: Oxford University Press, 2000); R. Hirshl, *Towards Juristocracy. The Origins and Consequences of the New Constitutionalism*, (Cambridge, Mass.: Harvard University Press, 2007).

[29] H. Schepel, *The Constitution of Private Governance* (Oxford: Hart, 2005).

[30] A.-M. Slaughter, *A New World Order* (Princeton: Princeton University Press, 2004).

[31] A. Stone Sweet, *Governing with Judges* (Oxford: Oxford University Press, 2000), 24, 114–15, 130, and elsewhere. This alleged traditional view concerns eg the role of statutory interpretation by courts. Stone Sweet talks about the 'the quasi-official myth of judges being slaves of the codes, prohibited from

these accounts underestimate this variety of modern constitutionalism and its normative as well as factual openness for different institutional solutions. On the one hand, the myth of a classical era of separated powers is evoked, on the other hand the fuzziness of the concept is an object of complaint.[32] The idea of a Golden Age of a classical separation tends to serve as an unquestioned background to a suggestive storyline. The historical case has never been made, however, because there never was an early and wonderful phase of European and American constitutionalism when parliaments were more powerful than they are today, private regulation was less relevant, and the supervision of independent agencies was not yet a critical governance issue. Instead of using such narratives, any approach to our problem has to provide complex and non-linear answers. It is no accident that reference to the separated powers concept often effectively raises negative connotations. In other words, the concept of separated powers regularly serves as a punching bag that contrasts with and describes deviations from institutional realities. Therefore we must carefully reconstruct what the idea of separated powers actually means and how this idea was put into effect in different traditions to show its normative and descriptive value for contemporary legal orders.

All in all, there seem to be two main problems with the contemporary academic debate on separation of powers: it dismisses a 'classical' model without elaborating it and claims to elaborate the concept but in fact only treats one of the three powers, in most cases either the executive or judicial branch.[33] Chapter 1 of this book will present some of the traditions that defy this assumption. At the very end of the book, a more systematic critique of some contemporary contributions will follow.

The ongoing discussion regarding the idea of constitutionalism is a second important issue in this book. For many observers, in particular those specializing in European and international law, constitutionalization

creatively interpreting or re-writing the laws', but this myth was never dominant in continental Europe, neither in France nor in Germany: J. Krynen, *L'emprise contemporaine des juges*, (Paris: Gallimard, 2011), 104, 191; R. Ogorek, *Richterkönig oder Subsumtionsautomat* (Frankfurt am Main: Klostermann, 1991).

[32] E. Carolan, *The New Separation of Powers* (Oxford: Oxford University Press, 2009), 77–9.

[33] More recent examples beyond those quoted in notes 23–30 are: R. Masterman, *The Separation of Powers in the Contemporary Constitution. Judicial Competence and Independence in the United Kingdom* (Cambridge: Cambridge University Press, 2011); D. J. Samuels and M. S. Shugart, *Presidents, Parties, and Prime Ministers. How the Separation of Powers affects Party Organization and Behaviour* (Cambridge: Cambridge University Press, 2011); P. Gerangelos, *The Separation of Powers and Legislative Interference in Judicial Process* (Oxford: Hart, 2009). E. Carolan, *The New Separation of Powers* (Oxford: Oxford University Press, 2009) is the only fully-fledged recent model of separation of powers, though centred on the administration. The book this account owes most to is, despite many differences, R. Bellamy, *Political Constitutionalism* (Cambridge: Cambridge University Press, 2007).

is synonymous with the legalization and judicialization of political power.[34] Such an account, however, does injustice to a concept that has always been about both the legalization of politics and the politicization of the law.[35] This means that a purely political concept of constitutionalism[36] is as deficient as a purely legal one. An important means of connecting legal and political constitutionalism—a key assumption of this book—is a model of separated powers that acknowledges the significance of both elements and identifies their proper place in a legitimate government structure. This is exactly what the epigraph by John Rawls refers to: purely legal and purely political constitutionalism both miss the very point of a constitution—to mutually reinforce the legal and the political systems and to protect their differences.[37] Therefore, separation of powers should not be understood as a pure instrument of restraining political power. It is also an instrument that constitutes this power. There is no legitimate structure of separated powers without a political lawmaker, but the idea of a 'political lawmaker' is in itself not a purely political one.[38]

CLAIMS AND METHODS: FOR A NEW CONCEPTUALISM
IN COMPARATIVE CONSTITUTIONAL LAW

This book's first and central claim is conceptual: it will try to make the case for a particular concept of separated powers that is derived from the idea of autonomy and seek to apply this concept to particular constellations of comparative constitutional law. Therefore, this is not a book on comparative law in a direct sense. The examples given here are neither new nor particularly original; the research draws neither on unknown cases nor at newly researched jurisdictions. They rather serve as illustrations for a way in which comparative law could be practised.

This entails a second claim, that comparative constitutional law needs a theoretical and normative framework beyond both empirical quantitative

---

[34] For the context: C. Schwöbel, 'Situating the Debate on Global Constitutionalism', 8 *International Journal of Constitutional Law* (2010), 611.

[35] C. Möllers, 'Pouvoir constituant—Constitution—Constitutionalisation', in A. v Bogdandy and J. Bast (eds.), *Principles of European Constitutional Law* (Oxford: Hart, 2nd rev ed, 2010), 169 (170–8).

[36] R. Bellamy *Political Constitutionalism* (Cambridge: Cambridge University Press, 2007).

[37] C. Möllers, 'Les Gardiennes d'une séparation: Les constitutions comme instruments de protection des différences entre le droit et la politique', *Ius Politicum* VII (2012), forthcoming.

[38] C. Möllers, 'Pouvoir constituant—Constitution—Constitutionalisation', in A. v Bogdandy and J. Bast (eds). *Principles of European Constitutional Law* (Oxford: Hart, 2nd rev ed, 2010), 169 (177–8); G. Gee and G. C. N. Webber, 'What is a Political Constitution?', *30 Oxford Journal of Legal Studies* (2010), 273 (294–9); a more general important contribution in the vein is S. Holmes, 'Precommitment and the Paradox of Democracy', in: *Passions and Constraints* (Chicago: The University of Chicago Press: 1995), 134–77.

research and individual comparative case analysis: it needs a *move to conceptualism.*

There is a methodological crisis in comparative constitutional law. To be sure, the method of comparison, if there is one, has always been highly problematic. This is a lesson we can draw from comparative literature, a discipline that, though not older than comparative law, has longer been aware of its own methodological troubles.[39] For a practice of reasoning as in both law and comparative literature, there is no purely quantitative solution to the question of how to conduct comparative studies.[40] If we take the judicial practice of courts seriously, and not as the pure deceit of a cryptically politicized system, it seems questionable to treat courts just as producers of some judicial output that can be compared quantitatively on a global level. The assumption that comparative constitutional law should adhere to the standards of 'Causal inference, arguably the ultimate goal of scientific inquiry'[41] seems to miss this normative point, and may therefore also miss the individualized practice of reason-giving in constitutional law, and sounds like a relapse into a pre-modern concept of legal research. The practice of constitutional law can hardly be reduced to such a purely quantitative approach. But does that mean, on the other hand, that we should just look at cases? Or even, in an amazingly self-referential move, at cases concerned with foreign materials and put comparative law into practice?[42] The rise of casebooks in comparative constitutional law is both a sign of a growing interest in the subject and of the Anglo-American tradition of doing law.[43] Both developments are welcome, but it still seems important to find other, more generalized ways to 'do' comparative law. One obvious problem of casebooks is the selection of cases. As long as some legal orders could serve as a kind of common language of comparative law, this seemed less problematic. US constitutional law has taken this role for a long time, but its relevance is rapidly declining without any legal order in sight that could fill its place.[44] It is the important insight of the quantitative branch of

---

[39] Just compare the portraits in H.-U. Gumbrecht, *Vom Leben und Sterben der großen Romanisten* (München: Hanser, 2002).

[40] A good impression of this is given by the portraits of comparative lawyers in A. Riles (ed.), *Rethinking the Masters of Comparative Law* (Oxford: Hart, 2001).

[41] R. Hirschl 'On the blurred methodological matrix in comparative constitutional law', in S. Choudry (ed.), *The Migration of Constitutional Ideas* (Cambridge: Cambridge University Press, 2006), 39 (65).

[42] For this discussion that seems a little bit out of proportion to the practice it describes, see V. Jackson, *Constitutional Engagement in a Transnational Era* (Oxford: Oxford University Press, 2009).

[43] Vicki C. Jackson and M. Tushnet, *Comparative Constitutional Law* (New York: Foundation Press, 2nd ed 2006); N. Dorsen, M. Rosenfeld, A. Sajo, and S. Baer, *Comparative Constitutionalism. Cases and Materials* (St. Paul: West, 2nd ed 2011).

[44] M. Tushnet, *Weak Courts, Strong Rights* (Princeton: Princeton University Press, 2008), 18–19.

constitutional comparison that the reference to some important legal orders as such won't do. A second problem of casebooks is their fixation with judicial law-making. If quantitative empirical comparison tends to ignore judicial reasoning, casebooks tend to take it as the whole of constitutional law. This fits well within a sometimes positive, sometimes negative confinement of contemporary constitutional scholarship to constitutional courts. But reducing it to judicial reasoning is not only problematic as such, it is especially unsatisfying for a theory of separated powers in which even constitutional courts can be understood only as one part of an institutional system.

This book's path may be called conceptual: it cannot claim to offer a solution to the methodological problems of comparative constitutional law, but it may develop an alternative approach to this kind of law that might complement others. Conceptualism endeavours to find a normative framework that can be understood as being implicit in different constitutional orders to make their similarities and differences more comprehensible. In other words, normative political theory and constitutional law are understood as in a relation of implicitness and explicitness in our model. But that does not mean that the implicit political theory does not allow far-ranging explicit varieties of different constitutional legal orders. The systematic connection between a normative argument from political theory and a phenomenon of comparative constitutional law cannot be strictly deductive, otherwise there would be nothing to compare. There must be some room for institutional variety as well as a justification for this variety: the freedom of a political organization to define its institutions. This also describes the limits of our concept. One important element of applying a concept must be the recognition of its boundaries. One important element of this book and one reason for its relative brevity is the fact that there are many institutional problems in constitutional law that can*not* be addressed by the concept of separated powers. It seems important to stress this somehow self-evident fact because there is the double danger of either conceptual defeatism, as presented by much of critical jurisprudence, or the conceptual overreach, as presented by much of modern jusnaturalism, that threatens every conceptual approach to constitutional law.

To make more understandable what we mean by conceptualism, we may refer to a passage in Hegel's philosophy of law: 'The basis of right is the *realm of spirit* in general and its precise location and point of departure is the *will*; the will is *free*, so that freedom constitutes its substance and destiny and the system of right is the realm of actualized freedom, the world of spirit produced from within itself as a second nature.'[45] Hegel's use of the

---

[45] G. W. F. Hegel, *Elements of the Philosophy of Right [1820]* (Cambridge: Cambridge University Press, 14th reprint 2010; translated by H. B. Nisbet), § 4, 35.

Aristotelian notion of a second nature to describe the law is relevant for us. Beforehand, it is important to see that this notion can be adapted without accepting any Hegelian myth of statehood. As read by an important branch of neo-pragmatist philosophy,[46] the concept of second nature refers to the need for a framework that does not strictly separate between natural and social phenomena and, therefore, does not evoke a methodological dichotomy between the conceptual and the empirical. For the law there is no sharp distinction between the facts and the law, but legal concepts are an important tool not only to justify but also to explain legal phenomena. The reference to a legal concept may be one possible answer to the question of how a legal system works. This kind of answer must not produce an overall uncritical account of a given legal practice. Moderate formalism is not necessarily affirmative, though a powerful strand of legal realist thinking has assumed so. On the contrary, only by developing a concept can we find a justified critical attitude to the institutional phenomena we are interested in.

Therefore, in addition to my first claim to make normative conceptual sense of the idea of separated powers and my second claim to use this sense for comparative constitutional law, there is a third claim in this book, the most demanding and perhaps least plausible one: it assumes that the prospect of a concept of separated powers derived from a model of constitutional legitimacy may explain some institutional developments of constitutional orders. To be sure, institutional developments do not just express patterns of legitimacy, of freedom as it is assumed in the Hegelian theory of law. But even given the fact that constitutional institutions depend on various political, economic, and social contexts, the question of their legitimate organization may be one of the factors that help to understand them. This claim is based on the pragmatist (and post-Hegelian) assumption that the distinction between normative and descriptive assumptions is only a relative one.[47] But it is directed against a legal pragmatist reading of this assumption that takes the scientific treatment of facts to be the only methodology of understanding the law. If the distinction between empirical and normative propositions is in fact blurred, it would be strange to treat everything as empirical propositions. Beyond the reference to a great philosopher, the idea of 'naturalizing' legal theory[48] also entails a reference to a rather outdated concept of 'nature' and to empirical science as the real form

---

[46] J. MacDowell, *Mind and World* (Cambridge, Mass.: Harvard University Press, 1994), 84–92; C. Halbig, 'Varieties of Nature in Hegel and McDowell', 14 *European Journal of Philosophy* (2006), 222; compare also the use of legal examples in R. Brandom, *Reason in Philosophy* (Cambridge, Mass.: Belknap, 2009), 84–92.

[47] H. Putnam, *The Collapse of the Fact/Value Dichotomy* (Cambridge, Mass.: Harvard University Press, 2002), 28–45.

[48] B. Leiter, *Naturalizing Jurisprudence* (Oxford: Oxford University Press, 2007), 183–199.

of explanatory practice.[49] Yet the bad reputation that concepts still have in legal theory, their critique as 'formalistic', seems no longer backed by much of the philosophical discussion.[50] Our study will attempt to put normative reasons to justify certain institutional structures of the democratic state to use as possible causes for their development. How such an explanation can function will be shown in the following analyses, but one example may illustrate the point. There may be many reasons for the development of independent administrative agencies: political, social, maybe it is the complexity of the regulated matters, as is often claimed though rarely proven by comparative empirical research.[51] But one reason among many may also be found in the structure of institutional legitimacy. In systems with a dual political legitimacy as in US Presidentialism, the political competition between Congress and the President may lead to a certain autonomy among administrative agencies, whereas systems with a monist legitimacy, including classical parliamentary governments, have a more plausible case for executive hierarchy.[52] As we will pursue neither historical nor sociological case studies, the reference to this explanatory element can only serve as a conceptual plea for further research. Still, the empirical fact of a certain institutional coherence in constitutional states expressed by their common structure of tripartite or separated government may at least make this plea more attractive. And it might be a more genuine contribution than the often repeated and quite empty explanation by reference to the growing complexity of the globalized world so common in legal research.

One important final implication that ties the normative to the descriptive lies in the answers to the question of what we can expect from constitutional institutions. As we have already seen, much of the contemporary discourse on separated powers presents a history of rise and fall without much of a historical background. One possible result of a more conceptual approach might lie in a more nuanced definition of what institutions do and should be able to achieve. The disappointment with regard to the deliberative quality of parliaments, a perpetual leitmotif since the late 18th century, might partly stem from a mistaken concept of parliamentarism. The thesis of the rising power of the executive, another evergreen that is more than a century old, may have to do with a definition of power that is in any case closer to executive action than to legislative programming of action. To be sure, this means neither that institutions do not change—the judiciary certainly does—nor that more or less normatively desirable moments may exist in

---

[49] W. V. O. Quine, 'Epistemology Naturalized', in E. Sosa and J. Kim (ed.), *Epistemology: An Anthology* (London: Blackwell, 2000), 292.

[50] M. Klatt, *Making the Law Explicit* (Oxford: Hart, 2008), Chapter 3.

[51] See footnote n. 27.   [52] See Chapter 3, I., 4.

the life of a constitutional polity. Still, this means we should try to avoid an intellectual scheme in which normative evaluations are explicitly pushed aside yet implicitly endorsed by means of historical or other pseudo-factual narratives.[53]

The argument of this book will progress in two parts, each consisting of two chapters. Chapter 1 looks comparatively at four possible concepts of separated powers. Chapter 2 develops a concept of separated powers which is applied to national legal problems in Chapter 3 and to international ones in Chapter 4.

---

[53] One example is E. A. Posner and A. Vermeule, *The Executive Unbound* (Oxford: Oxford University Press, 2010).

❧ 1 ❧

Division of Powers: Traditions and Meanings

I. THE TRADITIONAL DIVISION OF POWERS:
A COMPARATIVE SKETCH

Even the Vatican shares the idea of separated powers. Article 1, paragraph 1 of its constitution distinguishes the three powers, but also states: 'The Pope as the head of the Vatican state possesses the full extent of legislative, executive and judicial power.' This is an astonishing rule, which nevertheless has something in common with democratic constitutions: it connects the unity of the state with a trinity of powers. One obvious difference is that in democracies the source of this power lies in the people, whereas in Catholicism it stems from the *Vicarius Christi*. Another obvious difference is that in the Vatican there is just one person who holds all three powers. For the pioneers of the separation of powers theory, such an arrangement was the epitome of tyranny. Nonetheless, it remains remarkable that even a monocratic system would use the triadic notion. This is not necessarily an attempt to deceive.[1] Rather, a conceptual distinction of powers might prove valuable even in non-democratic systems, which would want to distinguish different forms of generating law, even if all of these remain under the control of one person.

One might wonder whether the trinity of the powers is the expression of a more general structure that can also be found in other contexts, in philosophy[2] or in the trinity of the Christian dogma.[3] Moreover, both the Vatican constitution and the separation of powers principle, which can be traced back to Greek antiquity,[4] demonstrate an astonishing continuity and breadth. Evidently, the concept of the separation of powers, along with its

---

[1] A semantic constitution: K. Loewenstein, *Political Power and the Governmental Process* (Chicago: University of Chicago Press, 1957), 203; G. Sartori, *Democratic Theory* (New York: Praeger, 1965), 150, 157.

[2] See R. Brandt, *D'Artagnan und die Urteilstafel* (München: dtv, 1998), 14, and the parallel to separation of powers in M. Walzer, *Interpretation and Social Criticism* (Cambridge, Mass.; Harvard University Press, 1987), 18–20.

[3] R. Kany, *Augustins Trinitätsdenken* (Tübingen: Mohr Siebeck, 2007), 23–8.

[4] Aristotle, polit. 1298 a–b. For practical application see M. H. Hansen, *Initiative und Entscheidung: Überlegungen über die Gewaltenteilung im Athen des 4. Jahrhunderts* (Konstanz: Universitätsverlag, 1983).

other manifestations—checks and balances, division of powers—was developed in order to highlight specific problems of political institutions and to solve them by means of organization. Herein lies its striking modernity. But all of this also seems to provide evidence of a high degree of conceptual arbitrariness. Since the institutional and political questions vary according to their constitutional orders, so do the suggested 'separation of powers' answers. To be more specific: in constitutional orders that distinguish between executive, legislative, and judicial institutions, institutional threats to the system can emerge from any of the three. In fact, in western legal systems we find a variety of separation of powers concepts, each of which is directed towards just one of these threats. We will therefore look at four different western constitutional traditions that may also prove relevant for other constitutional systems outside Europe and the United States.

1. Democratic doubts about courts: France

Two somewhat contradictory events connect France with the doctrine of separated powers: the publication of Montesquieu's *De l'Esprit des Lois* and the French Revolution. Along with Locke, Montesquieu is considered the founding father of the separation of powers doctrine. At the same time, his relevance for modern constitutionalism is widely disputed.[5] Montesquieu approaches political institutions with the eyes of a comparative observer. When he develops his ideas on the separation of powers in his reflections on the English governmental system,[6] he does so against the background of an understanding of constitutionalism that views a corporative society—the *societas civilis*—in its entirety, rather than one clearly distinct apparatus of state power.[7] Besides, his observations are often just that—observations without normative implications. Yet the protection of individual freedom is one central theme of his reflections, but this protection must adapt to present traditions and cultural contingencies, just as the 'laws' of the 'Esprit' are not categorically normative laws, but draw extensively from laws of nature. This approach may be qualified as 'old liberal', because it aims to protect individual freedom in a traditional feudal context. Only once one understands that Montesquieu categorically differentiates neither norms nor facts, neither public power nor private sphere, can one judge his contribution to political theory and appreciate its accuracy.

---

[5] For such doubts see C. Eisenman, 'L'Esprit des lois' et la séparation des pouvoirs', in *Mélanges Carré de Malberg* (Paris: Recueil Sirey, 1933), 163, 173.

[6] C. de Montesquieu, *De l'ésprit des lois* (1748), Ch VI, 2; XI, 1–7, 20.

[7] M. Riedel, 'Gesellschaft, bürgerliche' in O. Brunner, W. Conze, R. Koselleck (eds.), *Geschichtliche Grundbegriffe Vol 2* (Stuttgart: Klett-Cotta, 1975), 719, 738.

Montesquieu works with a concept of political freedom aligned more toward protecting from the uncertainties of arbitrary rule than toward political self-determination. He thereby only hints at a concept of democratic legislation in order to make it dependent upon the greatness of the body politic and condemn it with a view to the actual political potential of the aristocracy. All of this is unsatisfactory from the unhistorical perspective of our contemporary understanding of democracy. What is decisive, however, is Montesquieu's sensitivity to the specific functional conditions of institutions, such as when he distinguishes between the right to veto and the presence of a quorum. In this respect he was the first to develop explicitly the distinction between legislation, execution, and jurisdiction in a way that is still familiar today. He emphasizes that the three powers cannot be allowed to rest in the hands of one person or institution without being strictly separated from one another: the legislative branch, whose power is potentially unrestricted, must be restrained by the executive, whereas the executive power, being reduced to applying the law, should not be undermined by further interventions of the legislature.

The role of the courts in Montesquieu's theory is somewhat unclear. Commentators constantly cite, mantra-like, two canonized statements about the judge, who is the *bouche de la loi* and *en quelque façon nulle*. Both quotes seem to suggest that, for Montesquieu, the role of the courts can be disregarded. But this would be an astounding assertion, when one takes into account the fully detailed treatment of the courts in the text, the importance of the English model in the central passages, Montesquieu's interest in individual freedom, and, finally, the fact that he himself worked as a judge in a feudal court. Yet above all, Montesquieu was the first modern thinker to systematically include the courts in his reflections and thereby nominally establish the separation of powers as a *triad*.[8] A differing interpretation, therefore, seems more plausible:[9] Because Montesquieu's scheme does not demand any strict separation of the powers, but instead develops the freedom-ensuring effects of their institutional distance, it reserves a specific role for the courts. That is, they do not participate in the reciprocal control mechanisms of the two other powers. In fact, due to their political independence, which Montesquieu explicitly demands, they are institutional solitaries. As a result, they cannot represent a threat to freedom. They are for Montesquieu—in the subsequent words of Alexander Hamilton[10]—the 'least dangerous branch'. Montesquieu then provides concepts for the

---

[8] M. J. C. Vile, *Constitutionalism and the separation of powers* (Oxford: Clarendon Press, 1967), 88.

[9] R. Ogorek, 'De l'Esprit des *légendes*', 2 *Rechtshistorisches Journal* (1983), 277.

[10] Federalist Papers, No 78 (*Hamilton*).

doctrine of separated powers in a pre-democratic context and combines them with the concern of balancing ruling power with the protection of individual freedom. The theory is hardly original, as it takes its place within the long Aristotelian tradition of the subject, in which different constitutional forms have to be applied appropriately.[11] Yet Montesquieu's enduring influence may also suggest against the idea of juxtaposing pre-modern mixed constitutionalism with a strictly modern concept of divided powers.[12] As we shall see, strict separation has always been an exceptional concept. In any case, his approach remains impressive for its immense sensitivity to institutions. As a result, for Montesquieu and the entire pre-revolutionary discourse, the legislator remained the most dangerous power.

Even if the thoughts of Montesquieu arguably represent the most important European contribution to the constitutional system of the United States, their influence on the debates of the French Revolution seems less significant. It is here that we see the difficult relationship between popular sovereignty and separated powers.[13] The revolutionary self-empowerment of the third estate becoming the constituent National Assembly opened the way for an order of popular sovereignty as foreseen by Rousseau[14] and institutionalized by Sieyès: the democratic subject addresses itself through the representatives of the National Assembly, thereby laying a new foundation of political rule to bring about democratic discontinuity.[15] However, the political choice of the early revolutionaries was the constitutional monarchy, in which the office of the king changes from being an absolute monarch with a dynastic basis to become a special constitutional institution, from the King of France to the King of the French.[16] He thereby retained a role far older than the new constitution yet normatively derived from it. This contradiction was hard to resolve and finally consumed the office as well as its holder. Yet it is this spirit of early revolutionary constitutionalism in which the separation of powers was assigned a prominent role in the *Déclaration des Droits de l'homme et du citoyen*. As Article 16 states: 'Toute

---

[11] For this tradition see A. Ryklin, *Machtteilung. Geschichte der Mischverfassung* (Darmstadt: Wissenschaftliche Buchgesellschaft, 2006); for changes in this tradition see R. Bellamy, *Political Constitutionalism* (Cambridge: Cambridge University Press, 2007), 196–202.

[12] In this vein eg M. Hansen, 'The Mixed Constitution versus the Separation of Powers: Monarchical and Aristocratic Aspects of Modern Democracy', 31 *History of Political Thought* (2010), 509–31.

[13] See M. Troper, *La séparation des pouvoirs et l'histoire constitutionnelle française* (Paris: Pichon et Durand-Auzias, 1973), 130.

[14] J. Cohen, *Rousseau. A Free Community of Equals* (Oxford: Oxford University Press 2011), 135–7.

[15] H. Arendt, *On Revolution* (New York: Viking Press, 1963), 139.

[16] The moderate tradition before, during, and after this constitution, from Montesquieu to the doctrinaires, is depicted in A. Craiutu, *A Virtue for Courageous Minds. Moderation in French Political Thought 1748–1830* (Princeton: Princeton University Press, 2012).

société dans laquelle la garantie des droits n'est pas assurée, ni la séparation des pouvoirs déterminée, n'a point de constitution.' The concern expressed here can be found in line with Montesquieu. Yet it could not prevail during the Revolution and—to a certain extent—throughout the following history of French republican constitutionalism. Running counter to the idea was the historical experience of the Revolution with the *parlements*, the feudal courts, whose function was to protect feudal privileges against reform. Unlike other courts that judge cases, these feudal courts decided upon the legality of royal decisions on their own initiative.[17] If the abolition of feudal privileges and the assertion of normative civil equality were a central concern of the Revolution, then precisely such 'courts' were the ones to oppose it. Just as the rights to freedom of the *Déclaration* were not understood as claims that could be enforced in a court of law, but rather as political goals that mandated the democratic legislator, the historically inherited political distrust of the Revolution was directed against the courts more strongly than against any other power. This also stems from the Rousseauian concept of the people's sovereignty, in which the individual's sphere of freedom requires definition by the legislator.[18] It is interesting to see that courts do not play any role in the institutional reflections of Rousseau's *Contrat Social*. Within his concept of freedom, the democratic power of the state cannot pose a threat to individual freedom—in stark contrast to the situation on the other side of the Atlantic at that time. Indeed, the national legislator is the *condition* for the possibility of all freedoms, including individual freedom. Freedom arises not from the absence of the state or through the creation of state-antecedent or state-free spheres, but through its democratic constitution. The institutional form of freedom is the general democratic law, *la Loi, expression de la volonté générale*.[19] The general freedom is expressed through the republican equality of the act of legitimacy: '*un peuple libre obéit aux Lois, mais il n'obéit qu'aux Lois.*'[20] The constitutions of the self-radicalizing Revolution consistently subdue the other powers to the democratic legislative

---

[17] For the context see F. Furet, *La Révolution, tome I* (Paris: Hachette, 1988) 17, 22. For the *parlements* see J. Rogister, 'Parlementaires, sovereignty, and legal opposition in France under Louis XV: An Introduction', *Parliaments, Estates, and Representation* vol. 6:1 (1986), 25–32. For the distinctions between the *parlements* and other courts see A. de Tocqueville, 'De la democratie en Amérique [1835]', in *Œuvres* Ed. A. Jardin *Tome II* (Paris: Gallimard, 1992), 110.

[18] J.-J. Rousseau, *Contrat Social [1762]* (Paris: Gallimard, 1969), II/6. This corresponds with Kant's concept of law: I. Kant, 'Metaphysik der Sitten, Rechtslehre' in *Werke* [ed Weischedel] (Darmstadt: Wissenschaftliche Buchgesellschaft, 1983), Einleitung, § B.

[19] For a radical application of this idea in the constitution of the IIIrd Republic: R. Carré de Malberg, *La Loi, expression de la volonté générale* (Paris: Sirey, 1931; reprint: Paris: Economica, 1984); and the reading in É. Maulin, *La théorie de l'état de Carré de Malberg* (Paris: Presses Universitaires de France, 2003), 251–5.

[20] J.-J. Rousseau, 'Lettres écrites de la Montagne N 8', in *Œuvres Complètes Tome III* (Paris: Gallimard, 1969), 842.

power: they reinforce the personal responsibility of the government to the legislative and even introduce a legislative power to overturn court decisions.[21]

The significance of the separation of powers for French constitutional theory, particularly in its intellectual blossoming during the Third Republic, is a much-debated subject. Its contribution cannot be given due consideration here.[22] What remains important is that, to the present day, the Republican tradition is sceptical of judicial review of state action.[23] After Napoleon's decision to separate control of the administration from civil jurisprudence through a separate administrative body, the Conseil d'État, the long French liberal struggle for judicialization and the political independence of this institution ensued.[24] Even today the Prime Minister is formally the President of the Conseil d'État, and the Conseillers, regularly move between the Conseil and higher administrative offices. Tocqueville remarked that one could not explain the Conseil d'État to an American or English person.[25] Accordingly, modern French constitutional law started with constitutional review, late in the 20th century: the Conseil Constitutionnel of the Fifth Republic functioned more as an exclusive independent advisory organization, as a council, than as a court.[26] The self-image of the Conseil is becoming more court-like, and it now has the power to review questions addressed to it by the two high courts.[27] Yet, like a legislative organ, it still may intervene in the process of legislation before a law is publicly enacted. In this respect its procedure is reminiscent of the old *parlements* of the *Ancien Régime*. It remains remarkable for our purposes, however, that the original function given to the Conseil was to protect a certain concept of separation of powers: the Conseil should protect the strong presidentialism and governmentalism of the Fifth Republic, the idea of a rationalized democracy, from parliamentarian party politics. In this regard the Conseil served less as the guardian of the constitution—that is

---

[21] Troper, *La séparation des pouvoirs* (Paris: Pichon et Durand-Auzias, 1973), 165. This is illustrated by the constitution of the year One that never entered into power.

[22] A typical theme is Montesquieu's distinction between 'faculté de statuer' and 'faculté d'empêcher', see G. Glénard, 'La doctrine publiciste française et la faculté d'empêcher', 24 *Revue d'histoire des facultés de droit et de la science juridique* (2004), 99.

[23] M. Gauchet, *La Révolution des pouvoirs* (Paris: Gallimard, 1995), 55.

[24] J. Krynen, *L'emprise contemporaine des juges* (Paris: Gallimard, 2012), Chaps. 3–6.

[25] With regard to history see B. Pacteau, *Le conseil d'Etat e la fondation de la justice administrative française au XIXe siècle* (Paris: Presse Universitaire de France, 2003). For information on the personal history of the court members see B. Latour, *La Fabrique du Droit* (Paris: La Découverte, 2002), 137. For the quote see A. de Tocqueville, 'De la democratie en Amérique [1835]', in *Œuvres Ed. A. Jardin Tome II* (Paris: Gallimard, 1992), 116.

[26] D. Schnapper, *Une Sociologue au Conseil Constitutionel* (Paris: Éditions Gallimard, 2010), Chap. 3.

[27] D. Rousseau, *Droit de Contentieux Constitutionel* (Paris: Montchrestien, 9th ed 2010), 243–68.

the President's job—than as the guardian of presidential power against the parliament. Only since 1971 has the Conseil Constitutionnel acknowledged a legislative commitment to fundamental rights.[28] Finally, the Constitution establishes a special court for bringing indictments against members of the government.[29] All this demonstrates the fear that special interests could, with the help of a court that is not politically accountable, turn against the egalitarian democratic process.

This interpretation of republicanism has never been uncontroversial in France. It is opposed by a liberal constitutionalism going back as far as Montesquieu, to Necker, Mirabeau, Sieyès, Constant, and Tocqueville, which accords great intrinsic value to the freedom of the individual and its protection by courts, even vis-à-vis the democratic decision-making process.[30] The increasing significance of fundamental rights, not least through the European Convention on Human Rights, does its bit to strengthen the entire court system with respect to the political institutions. Nevertheless, the Republican legacy remains relevant to France and to our argument: it serves as a reminder that even the scope of individual rights requires definition in the democratic process. It also highlights the question of the courts' legitimacy in relation to democratically accountable bodies. Both are important challenges to any theory of separated powers.

2. Parliamentary fusion of powers: England

Before Montesquieu, John Locke formulated his model of separated powers.[31] The trisection of the powers in Locke's concept follows a distinctly different pattern than in Montesquieu. Locke differentiates between the legislative, executive, and federative powers, the latter concerning foreign policy. The judiciary remains outside his model. As with Hobbes, Locke's political theory stems from experience with the ongoing revolutionary crises in 17th century England, in which the relations between parliament and the monarchic executive were the crucial institutional issue. But as we shall see, the silence of Locke's concept with regard to the institution of courts has something to tell us.

---

[28]   Conseil Constitutionnel, Decision n 71–44 of 16 July 1971, a revolution with a short opinion of the court; see A. Stone Sweet, *The Birth of Judicial Politics in France* (New York: Oxford University Press, 1992).

[29]   Art. 68 of the French Constitution. For a critique O. Beaud, *Le sang contaminé. Essai critique sur la criminalisation de la responsabilité des gouvernants* (Paris: P.U.F., coll. «Béhémoth», 1999).

[30]   A. Craiutu, *A Virtue for Courageous Minds. Moderation in French Political Thought, 1748–1830* (Princeton: Princeton University Press, 2012). Important contemporary contributions are: M. Gauchet, *Révolution des pouvoirs*, (Paris: Gallimard, 1995); P. Ronsanvallon, *La contre-démocratie*, (Paris: Éditions du Seuil, 2006), III.

[31]   J. Locke, *Two Treatises of Government* (London: Black Swan, 1698), II, 143.

At least since the beginning of the 18th century, constitutional law in England has been developing in a long, continuous process in which certain institutional practices received the status of traditions or conventions. In this way constitutional history and constitutional law in England are interlocked much more closely than on the European continent.[32] The constitution is unwritten. There is no text to speak to its interpreters.[33] The classic doctrine of English constitutional law, which emerged at the end of the 19th century in the canonized account of Albert Venn Dicey, does not mention the separation of powers at all.[34] The leading organizational principle of classical English constitutional law is the sovereignty of the King in Parliament, later of the Parliament, whom no other public power can oppose.[35] In order to exercise sovereignty, both houses of Parliament and the crown must unite. As a result, the three powers all form part of Westminster, for the Cabinet and the Judicial Committee of the House of Lords have traditionally been special commissions of Parliament.[36] The House of Commons chooses the Prime Minister from their midst. The Judicial Committee was composed of members of the House of Lords.[37] Today the recent establishment of the UK Supreme Court symbolically underlines the personal independence of the Justices from the other political institutions. But the power to strike down a parliamentary statute remains absent. The Court cannot force Parliament to take action—its decisions remain formal suggestions.[38] As a result, as in France, but derived from a completely different tradition, a version of constitutional review with the power to repeal laws finds no place within the system. In France the democratic dignity of the parliamentary law stands in the way of constitutional review. In England it is the sovereign majesty of the joint decisions of the institution. Of course, both traditions have been

---

[32] F. W. Maitland, *The Constitutional History of England [1908]* (Cambridge: Cambridge University Press, 1961), 526.

[33] M. Foley, *The Silence of the Constitutions* (London: Routledge, 1989); D. Baranger, *Écrire la constitution non-écrite* (Paris: Presses Universitaires de France, 2008), 141–51.

[34] Compare A. V. Dicey, *Introduction to the Study of Law of the Constitution*, (London: Macmillan, 8th ed 1920). The reference to separation of powers serves as a political argument for institutional reform. For examples see M. J. C. Vile, *Constitutionalism and the separation of powers* (Oxford: Clarendon Press, 1967), 107.

[35] This is Blackstone's classical formula: W. Blackstone, *Commentaries on the Laws of England [1776]*, quoted after A. V. Dicey, *Introduction to the Study of Law of the Constitution*, (London: Macmillan, 8th ed 1920), 39–40.

[36] Standing Committee of the Supreme Legislature. See for citations M. J. C. Vile, *Constitutionalism and the separation of powers* (Oxford: Clarendon Press, 1967), 215.

[37] This has at no time inhibited a keen awareness for the significance of judicial independence, especially in Blackstone's work, see M. J. C. Vile, *Constitutionalism and the separation of powers* (Oxford: Clarendon Press, 1967), 103.

[38] As the recent terrorist cases have shown: *A (FC) and others; (X) FC and another v Secretary of State for the Home Department ('Belmarsh')*, [2004] UKHL 56.

forced to converge especially because of the rise of the European Convention of Human Rights, in Britain characteristically enshrined in the Human Rights Act of 1998.[39] Both traditions, however, have specific means to resist or at least slow down this process of convergence.

Civil freedoms are in no way excluded from this tradition. In fact, England was considered their homeland for most of the early modern era in Europe. The courts reviewed executive measures that interfered with the rights of the citizens on a case-by-case basis, if necessary according to unwritten rules that were generously extrapolated from general legal principles. In English common law, the courts developed the legal standards of review on their own in the form of a body of case law. As a result, courts may create their own legal cosmos, which decides social conflicts without the intervention of the legislature. The common law constitutes the private freedom of the subjects. In stark contrast to the revolutionary tradition in France, this approach resembles a pre-state concept of freedom established by Locke.[40] The absence of the courts from his concept of separated powers corresponds to his idea of natural freedom that is best protected and developed by institutions outside the governmental system. Property and bodily integrity are natural spheres, and the courts act as the agents of private self-determination, deciding over the proper allocation of these spheres. This is the core of the traditional English notion of the *rule of law*. In classical English constitutional law, the relation between the *rule of law*, whose standards claim validity beyond the positive law, and parliamentary sovereignty, whose traditional legitimacy also has its own claim to validity, is not considered a contradiction.[41] On the one hand, it is true that the earliest cases of courts drawing legal boundaries for the political power of the monarch are to be found in England.[42] On the other hand, to this day English law provides for no enforceable, judicial remedy to the actions of Parliament. Parliament is free to suspend standards of basic rights in a state of emergency and does so even today, as in the fight against terrorism. This dualism is also expressed in two lines of English legal theory: on one side from Hobbes through Bentham and Austin to H.L.A. Hart—we find a strict hierarchical theory of the validity of law, which recognizes only one state source of law. On the other hand is the common law tradition, as represented by Blackstone, in

---

[39] For the implications for the judicial power: R. Masterman, *The Separation of Powers in the Contemporary Constitution. Judicial Competence and Independence in the United Kingdom* (Cambridge: Cambridge University Press, 2011), 56–9 and *passim*.

[40] Traces of such a concept of freedom are also present in Kant's notion of republican freedom, the starting point of which is based upon private law.

[41] A. V. Dicey, *Introduction to the Study of Law of the Constitution* (London: Macmillan, 8th ed 1920), 402.

[42] See Judge Coke's famous 'Dr Bonham' Case, 8 Co. Rep., 113 b, *76 Eng. Rep. 644* (1610): J. W. Gough, *Fundamental Law in English Constitutional History* (Oxford: Clarendon Press, 1955), 12.

which there is no central source of law, but rather a spontaneous pre-state law-making process carried out by mutually monitoring courts.[43]

Around the end of the 19th century the basic distinction between the rule of law and parliamentary sovereignty lost much of its persuasiveness through the rise of administrative regulation.[44] Increasingly, the spheres of the common law regulation of property and parliamentary sovereignty are clashing with one another, for example in the fields of social and employment law or the regulation of railways. Understanding private property as a quasi-natural sphere becomes unconvincing, and, consequently, the division of labour between parliamentary sovereignty and the rule of law is called into question. This problem shapes the English discussion on the character of administrative law to the present day.[45] For, on the one hand, the control of administrative action is believed to be an excessive burden for the common law courts. On the other hand, the establishment of special courts to handle administrative law cases would challenge the classical English understanding of the courts' independence from the state administration. The cautionary example for both Dicey and modern authors is the French Conseil d'Etat, with its personnel coming from—and returning to—the administration.[46] In this context of growing welfare-state regulation, the executive becomes for the first time an ultimately unsolved problem for a system of separated powers. As its discretion widens continually through legislative delegations, the courts struggle more and more to control it. Moreover, the burgeoning bureaucracy undermines the internal coherence of both a government accountable to parliament and the government's subordinate administration.[47]

It appears that the English contribution to the separation of powers is more institutional than juridical.[48] As we have seen, Montesquieu invoked the English constitution as a model in his writings on the separation of powers. But what constitutes this model? It seems that the model character consisted in the dignity of institutions which—independent from or in opposition to the monarch—cultivated their own legitimate will: courts as well as parliament. The practice of a government accountable to a

---

[43] G. D. Postema, *Bentham and the Common law Tradition* (Oxford: Clarendon Press, 1986).

[44] M. Loughlin *Foundations of Public Law* (Oxford: Oxford University Press, 2011), 435–44.

[45] M. Loughlin, *Public Law and Political Theory* (Oxford: Clarendon Press, 1992), 153.

[46] A. V. Dicey, *Introduction to the Study of Law of the Constitution*, (London: Macmillan, 8th ed 1920), 396. Representing this position today is J. W. F. Allison, *A Continental Distinction in the Common Law* (Oxford: Clarendon Press, 1997), 136 (168–9).

[47] Two Commissions had already been set up to solve this issue: the Committee on Ministers' Powers (1929–1932) and the Committee in Administrative Tribunals and Enquiries (1957).

[48] For the contemporary and rather unsystematic use of the notion in British and Irish courts: E. Carolan, *The New Separation of Powers* (Oxford: Oxford University Press, 2009), 28–31.

parliament became a model for numerous democratic constitutional states. In this respect, it is precisely the institutional proximity of government and parliament, the parliamentary vote for the Prime Minister—and not their separation—which is the core of the English model. As Walter Bagehot, the great 19th century political commentator of the English system of government, put it: 'The English system, therefore, is not an absorption of the executive power by the legislative power; it is a fusion of the two.'[49] A second model invention is the establishment of a stable distinction between government and opposition, a phenomenon that has since become indispensable for parliamentary democracies, even though it plays almost no role in normative democratic theory to the present day.[50] However, these seminal institutional developments are not accompanied by any juridical discussion. Despite Locke, the separation of powers has not become a central theme of English constitutional law. Any form of judicial review of the relations between the political organs remains unknown in the English system. The political system has to solve its conflicts without this kind of legal support. Yet, if it is broached, the discussion is directed towards the courts,[51] although in a characteristically different way from the French discussions. In classical English constitutional law, the idea of separated powers protects the independence of the courts from the executive. A special regime of administrative law and administrative courts would threaten this independence. In France, the argument ran the other way: here the concept of separation of powers was introduced to protect the democratic mandate of the administration from individual interests, which are articulated through the courts.

3. The separation of powers as a mixed democracy: the United States

The American fighters for independence—unlike the French revolutionaries—could draw on generations of experience in the practice of government and administration. In a historically rare combination, they combined a sense for the practical problems of institutions with a wide knowledge of European political theory. This becomes obvious in the historical debate on separation of powers[52] that began before the conflict with the English and

---

[49] W. Bagehot, *The English Constitution [1867]* (Ithaca: Cornell University Press, 1966), 69.

[50] Compare the analysis in W. Jäger, 'Opposition', in O. Brunner, W. Conze, R. Koselleck (eds.), *Geschichtliche Grundbegriffe Band 4* (Stuttgart: Klett-Cotta, 1978), 469. Notable exceptions are Hegel and Marx, in W. Jäger, 'Opposition' at 495–502.

[51] See J. W. F. Allison, *A Continental Distinction in the Common Law* (Oxford: Clarendon Press, 1997), 158.

[52] G. Casper, *Separating Powers* (Cambridge: Harvard University Press, 1997), 1; M. P. Sharp, 'The Classical American Doctrine of "The Separation of Powers"', *3 University of Chicago Law Review* (1935), 385.

remained multifaceted until its end through the adoption of the US Constitution. The fathers of the Constitution had no unified concept of separated powers. Even in practical terms, there was much uncertainty over its implications after the enactment of the Constitution, including, for example, questions of protocol over how intensively the President and Congress should interact.[53] Today these discussions appear rather arcane. From a distance, however, and comparing them with the French revolutionary debates, certain features stand out. First, at least some of the American revolutionaries believed the notion of democratic self-determination to be no less radical and serious than the Jacobins did. For Thomas Jefferson in particular, democratic self-determination is always potentially revolutionary—so the revolution in principle never ends: 'The spirit of resistance to government is so valuable on certain occasions, that I wish it to be always kept alive . . . I like a little rebellion now and then.'[54] But the American constitutional model does not have any legal concept that enables the revolutionary will to fully merge with an institutional form. Whereas in France the democratic law assumes this function, in the US Constitution the form of the law is set out as well, but *law* is merely a technical legal term. To put it another way, from the point of view of the Founding Fathers and in sharp contrast to the French republican tradition, laws could clearly be a threat to freedom. The establishment of a democratically legitimate body politic therefore does not solve the problem of how to protect liberty. Behind this lies an understanding of freedom that is shaped by the English colonial power and judges individual freedom to be pre-legal, indeed even pre-social. This freedom may be better protected through democratic institutions in which the powers are separated than through other forms, but that does not abolish the permanence of the threat.

A comparative first glance at the question of who is the subject of legitimacy yields further characteristic differences: the expression *people*, with which the American Constitution *we the people* famously begins, diverges from both France and England. Unlike in England, democracy as self-rule is a central theme of the American tradition.[55] However, regardless of whether it was the *people* of the United States or the individual *peoples* of the member states that were meant, the word—unlike in French or German—also retains a plural meaning that preserves the idea of a heterogenous multitude. As late as in the mid-1990s the US Supreme Court was split over the question whether there really is one American people or just the

---

[53] S. Elkins, E. McKittrick, *The Age of Federalism*, (Oxford: Oxford University Press, 1993), 55.

[54] T. Jefferson, *Letter to Abigail Adams, February 22nd 1787.*

[55] For the ongoing importance of the English revolutionary tradition: M. Loughlin, *Foundations of Public Law* (Oxford: Oxford University Press, 2010) 280–1.

peoples of the separate states.[56] Individual persons, unlike in France, are not assimilated to make a new collective subject but remain in an assembly of individuals. For this reason, one crucial concern of American constitutional theory is the blockade of governmental action, not its facilitation. In this respect, the American constitutional tradition and Montesquieu's theory are closer to each other than they are to the tradition of the French Republic.

Therefore, the American revolutionaries were foremost concerned about the threat to freedom that resulted from democratic government itself. The most dangerous power, then, seemed to be the legislative.[57] This view was also the consequence of bad political experiences in the years between independence and the adoption of the US Constitution. The state parliaments developed dubious practices: they did not only enact laws, they also changed court judgments, outlawed individual citizens, deposed officials, and issued currencies.[58] In short, American constitutional history has a special experience—as does the English, but with quite different consequences—with a dictatorship of parliament.[59]

In the Founding Fathers' analysis, namely in the analysis of James Madison, such phenomena of a degenerating legislature do not express some kind of democratic weakness of the will. Instead, they result from an extraordinarily effective assertion of special interests with the help of the governmental powers. This intuition, which perceives every governmental action as potentially guided by special interests, thereby fundamentally delegitimizing government itself, has remained a major theme in American political theory to the present day.[60] Madison, though, did not believe the biased interest-led partisanship of the government to be inevitable.[61] His theory of separated powers in the *Federalist Papers* is a model of democratic process that serves the common good. To protect the government from being usurped by the specific interests of individuals, the various institutions must, on the one hand, be created through different mechanisms and by the multiplication of constituencies to resist usurpation while, on the other hand, keeping each other in check. This has become known as *checks and balances,* an idea to which the American principle of the separation of powers

---

[56] See the split Court in *US Term Limits, Inc v Thornton*, 514 US 779 (1995).

[57] Federalist Papers, No 10 (*Madison*).

[58] J. W. Bessette, *The Mild Voice of Reason* (Chicago: University of Chicago Press, 1994), 13.

[59] An example for a constitution that establishes a dominant legislative is the 1776 Constitution of Philadelphia, see M. J. C. Vile, *Constitutionalism and the separation of powers* (Oxford: Clarendon Press, 1967), 138 (145).

[60] D. Farber, P. Frickey, *Law and Public Choice* (Chicago: University of Chicago Press, 1991).

[61] See especially Federalist Papers, No 10 (*Madison*). C. R. Sunstein,'Interest Groups in American Public Law', 38 *Stanford Law Review* (1985), 29.

is all too often reduced to without including the conditional democratic element. The possibility of blockades, however, makes sense only when the different institutions draw upon distinct forms of democratic legitimacy. Therefore, both chambers of Congress and the President are elected in different procedures by different constituencies. Senators serve a period of six years in office, but the Senate is successively replenished by a third every two years. State assemblies elected US Senators until 1912. In this respect, the US Senate stands for two things: first, for the political interests of the members at the federal level, but also for a continuing process of decision-making that, instead of being radicalized by daily politics, is preserved and modulated by the long terms of office and the continuous replenishment of the institution. The two-year term of the Representatives and their proximity to the small constituencies, on the other hand, sets this house in a permanent state of electoral campaign and produces a much higher level of everyday politicization. The President, who is personally elected every four years, represents the *people* of the federal nation. Through bicameralism and Presidential veto power, these three institutions must congregate for a law to be passed. President and Senate must cooperate in appointing top officials and federal judges as well as ratifying international treaties. Madison thereby merged a theory of legitimacy with his practical grasp of institutions. The sheer functional capacity of America's constitutional institutions for at least two centuries demonstrates, a somewhat broken current political practice notwithstanding, that his achievement has had no parallel in history.

Where are the courts within this construction? In the early days of the American constitutional tradition, in fact, the courts seem to have been taken for granted. The judicial system was conceived at state level and represents a continuation of the Common Law court system of the English colonial period. However, even if they do hail from the colonial era, why were these courts not—like the *parlements,* the feudal courts in the French Revolution—perceived as threats to freedom? This question leads to the Anglo-Saxon concept of the law as a common law, which the American Revolution strangely left untouched. With the Declaration of Independence, the rather slow evolution of American idiosyncrasies of common law was accelerated but in principle, it has remained a unified body of law. Blackstone's *Commentaries*, the leading textbook of common law in the late 18th century, was an authoritative source of law even for the American revolutionaries. It also touches upon questions of separation of powers.[62] The significance of common law for the political system is often underestimated

---

[62] W. Blackstone, *Commentaries to the Laws of England I* (Oxford: Clarendon Press, 1765–1769), 149 (259).

or overlooked by foreigners.[63] It is nonetheless immense, since it entails a pre-political understanding of property, for instance. The courts regulate citizens' private agreements according to principles of common sense. They are not, however, part of the political system and they hardly ever touch upon the problems of the separation of powers, which interested the framers of the American Constitution. The pre-political understanding of the common law system has remained a central theme in the US system to the present day. It has also been the object of critical reflection for a whole range of legal theorists for over a hundred years.[64]

But even the framers were unable to restrict themselves to this concept of the courts. They established a federal jurisdiction in order to regulate the federal side of the Constitution. Federal courts were intended to facilitate the unification of the American legal system or to protect the states from the impositions of the central legislature. We will return to this later. But should the federal courts play a new role above and beyond this? Should they oversee the legislature to make sure it complies with the Constitution? The formative texts of the American Constitution are quite ambiguous on this point and the answer to this question is still much disputed.[65] At least one constitutional framer, Hamilton, certainly argues in favour of such a strong judiciary.[66] For contemporary American constitutional law, what rests on this historic question is the legitimacy of the federal High Court; the US Supreme Court. The historical texts that were important points of reference in drafting the Constitution remain authoritative for its interpretation. An unambiguous clarification, however, seems historically impossible. In any case, even giving a satisfactory, systematic answer to the question of whether courts should be able to control the legislature is insufficient. Rather, one has to remember that the Americans were also familiar with the English tradition of restraining the legislature by the courts. Courts protect individual freedoms in specific cases. But the federal structure creates a situation in which the federal court and the legislator can come into conflict with one another at a more fundamental level. Therefore, it seems inaccurate to hold that the American constitutional tradition was either for or against a constitutional review of democratic politics. To be sure, American constitutional scholarship has disputed this question from the very

---

[63] See, however, E. Fraenkel, *Das amerikanische Regierungssystem* (Opladen: Westdeutscher Verlag, 3rd ed 1976), 22; K. Llewellyn, 'American Common Law Tradition, and American Democracy', 1 *Journal of Law and Political Sociology* (1942), 14. For a rereading of American contemporary law: G. Calabresi, *A Common Law for the Age of Statutes* (Cambridge: Harvard University Press, 1982), 163; D. A. Strauss, 'Common Law Constitutional Interpretation', 63 *University of Chicago Law Review* (1996), 877.

[64] N. Duxbury, *Patterns of American Jurisprudence* (Oxford: Clarendon Press, 1995), 32.

[65] L. Kramer, 'Foreword: We the Court', 115 *Harvard Law Review* (2001), 5.

[66] *Federalist Papers*, No 81 (*Hamilton*).

beginning. The controversy cannot be separated from the question of which vision of the American republic one espouses: either a basically democratic one in which the central government intervenes little, the states rule themselves and the democratic process cannot be overpowered by judicial control, like the Party of Jefferson; or one with a national central government with strong regulatory powers and technocratic features, which also stands for strong judicial control of politics, ie the Party of Hamilton.[67]

For a long time, commentators have been wondering if the American constitutional system is dysfunctional.[68] Today the academic discussion of separation of powers in the United States draws the distinction between a formalistic understanding, which refers to the text of the Constitution, and a functional interpretation that allows for more flexibility and provides the legislature with a higher degree of discretion to distance itself from the model of the Founders.[69] As in England, the American perspective has, since the First World War, turned increasingly toward the power of the executive, whose apparatus is, in the opinion of many observers, slowly liberating itself from political and judicial control—a development whose compatibility with the American model of the separation of powers remains disputed.[70] We shall see that the distinction between formalism and functionalism is not very helpful.

As a result, we can point out three different and somewhat contradictory ideas underlying the American understanding of separated powers. First, there is the revolutionary idea of the democratic creation of a constitution. Secondly, there is an ultimately individualistic notion of freedom, expressed in the pre-revolutionary judicial system meant to protect private property without political interference. Thirdly, there is federalism. Separation of powers may be the only way to organize democratic decision-making to prevent it from falling into the hands of special interests, which were to the Federalists what the tyrant was to Montesquieu. But separation of powers may also be an instrument to prevent government from any action at all. Judicial review of federal legislative action does not seem to be a central

---

[67] For two cases that illustrate this conflict: *Marbury v Madison*, 5 US 137 (1803); *Stuart v Laird*, 1 Cranch (5 US) 299 (1803): B. Ackerman, *The Failure of the Founding Fathers* (Cambridge: Harvard University Press, 2005). Both judgments were delivered at a time when it was necessary to adjust the relation of the Court to the political majority. The judges, most of whom had been appointed by the then minority party, had to prove both their institutional determination as well as their political independence.

[68] W. Wilson, *Congressional Government: A Study in American Politics* (Boston, New York: Houghton Mifflin Co, 1885); B. Ackerman, 'The New Separation of Powers' 113 *Harvard Law Review* (2000), 634, both recommend a parliamentary system.

[69] P. F. Strauss, 'Formal and Functional Approaches to Separation of Powers Questions – A Foolish Inconsistency?', 72 *Cornell Law Review* (1987), 488; M. E. Magill, 'The Real Separation in Separation of Powers Law', 86 *Virginia Law Review* (2000), 1127 (1136).

[70] See Chapter 3, I., 4.

element of this original concept. It emerged in a slow process, which began over questions of federal jurisdiction, but whose legitimacy remains contested today.

The American Constitution uses the tradition of mixed government, but the mixture is a purely democratic one, combining different constituencies into a complicated system in which the relations between the branches depend, and this is crucial, as much on the tides of political power as on constitutional rules.[71] The contested issue of war powers is only one important example: the separation of war powers between Congress and the President remains contested,[72] and there is no constitutional rule and no judgment to solve this conflict. This form of political contestation between the powers is one possible solution to the problem of separated powers.[73] Separation of powers can be understood as a constitutional legal rule, but one important lesson of the American constitutional tradition is that this is not the only possible understanding: it may also be the abbreviation, for a contest between political and legal institutions that cannot be organized according to an over-arching rule.

4. The separation of powers in monarchist constitutionalism: Germany

German constitutional history has provided no comparable contribution to the theory of separated powers. The doctrines of Montesquieu quickly spread to Germany and met with criticism just as quickly.[74] Contemporary commentators regarded the balancing of different political powers as a risky proposition that underestimated and undermined the capabilities of the monarch. The pre-modern project of a proper education of the Prince was still considered, even at the end of the 18th century in Germany, a serious alternative to normative political theory.[75] As a result of the constitutional movement after 1800 the coexistence of the monarchical executive and popular representation merged into a dualist constitutional model, which

---

[71] The canonical statement of this dependence is *Youngstown Sheet & Tube Co v Sawyer* 343 US 579, 635 (Jackson, J., conc.): 'Presidential powers are not fixed but fluctuate depending upon their disjunction or conjunction with those of Congress.'

[72] Ph. Bobbitt, 'War Powers: An Essay on John Hart Ely's *War And Responsibility: Constitutional Lessons of Vietnam and Its Aftermath*', 92 *Michigan Law Review* (1994), 1364.

[73] For an application of the concept of legal pluralism also to the domestic US constitution:
D. Halberstam, 'Systems Pluralism and Institutional Pluralism in Constitutional Law: National, Supranational, and Global Governance', in M. Avbelj and J. Komárek (eds.) *Constitutional Pluralism in the European Union and Beyond*, 85–125. (Oxford: Hart Publishing, 2012).

[74] L. Pahlow, *Justiz und Verwaltung* (Goldbach: Keip, 2000).

[75] The most important example is C. G. Svarez, *Die Kronprinzenvorlesungen 1791/1792. Erster Teil: Staatsrecht. Zweiter Teil: Das positive preußische Recht.* Peter Krause (ed.), (Stuttgart-Bad Cannstatt: Fromann-Holzboog, 2000).

was typical for the German territories as for many other European states of the 19th century.[76] The executive had traditional privileges at its disposal, while the developing parliaments had the power to pass laws and the budget. The underlying model of separated powers was based on two distinct considerations:

The model served – in the sense of a literally understood *division* of powers – to immunise the representation of the people and the executive. This interpretation often had a detrimental effect on parliament if, for example, an entire political field remained out of parliamentary reach, such as foreign policy or the regulation of the military. But it also helped to protect the representation of the people from the impositions of the executive, for example through indemnity and immunity regulations, which (more or less) shielded members of parliament from political persecution. This dual function cannot, however, belie the fact that during the 19th century in Germany political conflicts between parliament and the monarch – unlike in England and France – consistently resolved themselves in favour of the monarch: from the Hanoverian to the Prussian constitutional conflicts, the executive would prevail every time.[77]

Secondly, alongside separation, the idea of balancing powers remained important in German constitutional thought. This concept was, however, almost always directed against an extension of parliamentary powers. Astonishingly, as early as the 1830s, the debate had been dominated by the fear of the dangers of a parliamentary dictatorship, even though no sign of this danger had ever manifested itself in German constitutional history.[78]

After the failed 1848 revolution the attention of constitutional politics shifted from the issue of popular sovereignty and its expression through the government's parliamentary responsibility to the particularly German concept of *Rechtsstaatlichkeit*, which is inaccurately identified as the notion of the 'rule of law'. Constitutionalism understood as *Rechtsstaatlichkeit* became a substitute for democracy.[79] The political demand for the *Rechtsstaat* led to the establishment of a system of comprehensive judicial control over administrative acts intruding on freedom and property. Such intrusions were not illegal per se, but they required a law passed by parliament, sanctioned by the monarch, and monitored by the courts. The law coupled the three otherwise strictly separated powers and required them to cooperate. In this regard, it is necessary to distinguish the German idea of the law from

---

[76] For a comparative analysis: M. Kirsch, *Monarch und Parlament im 19. Jahrhundert* (Göttingen: Vandenhoeck & Ruprecht, 1999).

[77] H. Boldt, *Deutsche Verfassungsgeschichte Band 2* (München: dtv, 1990), 106.

[78] H. Boldt, 'Parlamentarismustheorie', 19 *Der Staat* (1980), 385 (390–7).

[79] I. Maus, 'Entwicklung und Funktionswandel der Theorie des Bürgerlichen Rechtsstaats', in I. Maus, *Rechtstheorie und politische Theorie* (München: Fink, 1986), 11.

both the democratic French concept and Anglo-Saxon rule of law, which encompasses judicial review regardless of the existence of any formal legal basis.[80] The law according to the German idea of *Rechtsstaat* is an instrument through which the actions of the state are rendered rational and predictable. It is also a means to separate the sphere of the state from society. It is not the expression of democratic self-determination, but rather of the rule of a competent monarchic bureaucracy, in which the representatives of the people are merely involved. The law, in a strange adoption of the Kantian concept, regulates the relations between the personal spheres of individuals and the state, ie between natural and legal personalities. But inside the organization of the state other rules apply, which do not enjoy the status of laws, do not need parliamentary consent, and are not controlled by the courts.[81] The internal life of the monarchic executive remains unchecked, and the legal definition of this institution is peculiar, including the military, state schools, and prisons. As in the United States the German system is a dualist one, but unlike the American system the dualism is not purely democratic. The conflict between the executive and parliament in 19th-century Germany is a conflict between different forms of political legitimacy.

In a certain sense, the idea of a division between the executive and legislative branches outlasted the monarchy in Germany. A still common misunderstanding of the parliamentary system illustrates this. The defining element of English parliamentarianism, the dependence of the government on a parliamentary majority, became part of the Constitution of the Weimar Republic and the German Basic Law of 1949. If, however, the governmental power rests upon a majority in parliament, there is evidently no separation between this majority and the government. Both work intensively, albeit informally, with each other: bills are prepared on the political level of the ministerial bureaucracy; technical work on legislation becomes much less significant than its public debate; and one function of parliament is to provide the government with political personnel.[82] But it is fascinating to observe how the members of the Reichstag of the Weimar Republic after 1919 only reluctantly accepted this role of backing the government and how they perceived themselves as an institutionalized opposition to the execu-tive—and how they were also treated as an opposition by the bureaucracy

---

[80] L. Heuschling, *Etat de droit, Rechtsstaat, Rule of Law* (Paris: Dalloz, 2002).

[81] D. Jesch, *Gesetz und Verwaltung* (Tübingen: Mohr, 2nd ed 1968), 15.

[82] C. Schönberger, 'Die überholte Parlamentarisierung. Einflußgewinn und fehlende Herrschaftsfähigkeit des Reichstags im sich demokratisierenden Kaiserreich', 272 *Historische Zeitung* (2001), 623.

that remained in place after the revolution.[83] This slowly changed in the post-Second World War German Bundestag. But until today the political practice, appropriate for a parliamentary system, is often accompanied by criticism even of constitutional scholarship, which perceives the cooperation between the parliamentary majority and the government as a symptom of decline of the separation of powers.[84]

Behind the German pre-democratic interpretation of the separation of powers there emerges an apolitical concept of the executive as an entity whose actions are justified not through the political process but through expertise, an interpretation that Max Weber already strongly criticized during the First World War.[85] In this interpretation, governing is reduced to an enhanced form of administration. The legitimacy of the executive is based not on the political agenda of the responsible minister, but on the qualification of the bureaucracy. This vision is widespread in Germany even today, as is the call for 'experts' in politics, a practice that led to some damaging experiences for the Weimar Republic. It is true, though, that such an interpretation highlights an intrinsic problem of every system of separated powers: how to integrate the government into the separation of powers as a part of the executive, which is obliged to observe the laws even as it works to change them. We will return to this issue.

While political practice under the Basic Law still had to cope with the monarchic legacy, the Weimar Republic had already set a trend which would prevail in the Federal Republic and become the model for many other legal orders: a form of protection of basic rights through the courts, directed against the legislature. Theory and practice of the Weimar Republic, coming not least from a politically conservative distrust of the parliamentary legislature, slowly developed constitutional standards for restricting parliament through basic rights.[86] But there is at least one crucial difference to the American rights review that emerged in the second half of the 19th century: Perhaps for the first time the German courts understood rights not only as the rights of individuals, but also as objective norms, as values, which may even restrict the legislature when an individual is not immediately

[83] P.-C. Witt, 'Kontinuität und Diskontinuität im politischen System der Weimarer Republik', in G. A. Ritter (ed.), *Regierung, Bürokratie und Parlament in Preußen und Deutschland* (Düsseldorf: Droste, 1983), 117.

[84] I. v. Münch, 'Minister und Abgeordneter in einer Person: die andauernde Verhöhnung der Gewaltenteilung', *Neue Juristische Wochenschrift* (1998), 34.

[85] M. Weber, 'Regierung und Parlament im neugeordneten Deutschland [1918]', in J. Winckelmann (ed.), *Gesammelte Politische Schriften* (Tübingen: Mohr, 5th ed 1988), 306.

[86] P. Caldwell, *Popular Sovereignty and The Crisis of German Constitutional Law* (Durham: Duke University Press 1997), 145–70; M. Stolleis, 'Judicial Review, Administrative Review, and Constitutional Review in the Weimar Republic', 16 *ratio juris* (2003), 266.

affected.[87] During the making of the Basic Law in 1948/49, there was little dispute that the new constitutional order should be equipped with a strong constitutional jurisdiction. According to the founding fathers and mothers, constitutional review over politics was above all installed as an instrument against the dangers of totalitarianism. Democratic self-distrust stands at the origin of this strong form of constitutional review.

It is not without irony that this distrust of democracy generated precisely the intensive judicial control of the legislator that was favoured by the conservative enemies of parliamentary democracy in the Weimar Republic. The Basic Law established what is to date the most powerful and comprehensive form of constitutional review, setting substantial legal limits to the political process. Never before had a judicial interpretation of the supremacy of the constitution been so consistently institutionalized: everyone can challenge any act of the state which concerns his or her rights. Everyone has access to the Federal Constitutional Court. The Court established the basic right to a general freedom of action,[88] which protects any desired form of action against state intervention, such as feeding pigeons on public squares[89] and riding horses through public woods.[90] This construction triggers broad judicial review and provides individual plaintiffs with substantial means of intervening in the political process. These constitutional guarantees served thereafter as a model for those post-totalitarian societies which—like Germany's after the Second World War—did not trust their own democratic process:[91] Italy; Spain; Poland; Hungary; South Africa; Brazil; and Taiwan are all examples of this. And even international developments, as will be shown, relied upon comparable forms of judicialization.[92] Beyond the question of how such a strict constitutional review fits into a legitimate framework of separated powers, it is striking that the German system, after some initial doubts, came to be viewed, especially within German constitutional scholarship, as self-evident. The notion that a 'real' constitution requires a strong constitutional review still dominates the discourse in Germany[93] and finds some factual confirmation in the global

---

[87] Exemplary: R. Smend, 'Das Recht der freien Meinungsäußerung', 4 *Veröffentlichungen der Vereinigung Deutscher Staatsrechtslehrer* (1928), 44.

[88] German Constitutional Court, *Elfes*, BVerfGE 6, 32.

[89] German Constitutional Court, *Taubenfüttern*, BVerfGE 54, 263.

[90] German Constitutional Court, *Reiten im Walde*, BVerfGE 80, 137.

[91] P. Pasquino, 'What is Constitutional Adjudication about?' (NYU School of Law Working Paper, 2002), 3.

[92] Chap. 4

[93] For a critical account: M. Jestaedt, O. Lepsius, C. Möllers, C. Schönberger, *Das entgrenzte Gericht* (Frankfurt am Main: Suhrkamp, 2011).

spread of constitutional courts.[94] It is increasingly considered to be the norm, even though this form of judicialization had long been the comparative exception in democratic nation-states and in constitutional theory. The idea of judicial supremacy builds on an understanding of the constitution as a standard legal text to be interpreted by the courts. Revolutionary traditions, such as those in France or the United States, however, understand the Constitution at least also as a political document, a pledge that the citizens make *to themselves*, which the representatives of the people, the legislators, are primarily responsible to uphold. In the words of Franklin D. Roosevelt, the constitution is 'a layman's document, not a lawyers' contract'.[95] In this view, the promise of the constitutional text—including the basic rights—is not primarily a political goal to be attained by the democratic process. This idea of political constitutionalism never gained any relevance in the German context.

German constitutional scholarship after the Second World War did not add much relevance to the theory of separated powers. But the German constitutional court made wide use of the principle. As in America, a functional understanding of the separation of powers, the so-called *Funktionenordnung*, became central in Germany. In a much-cited quotation of the Federal Constitutional Court, the tripartite division of the powers should guarantee the 'best possible' decision by the organ that most adequately disposes of the personal, material, and organizational capacities.[96] This statement reminds us that the concept of separated powers may also be used as a feature to increase the effectiveness of public action instead of limiting it. If there is a primary, continuous line in the German constitutional tradition from the 19th century to today, though, it is its sheer unlimited trust in courts and judicial review. In characteristic contrast to an American political understanding of our principle, there is a strong tendency to define separation of powers as a legal and judicially enforceable rule.

5. Some federal additions

Two of the constitutional systems introduced here are federal orders: Germany and the United States. What ramifications does this fact have for the separation of powers? A look at these constitutional systems is of

---

[94] R. Hirshl, *Towards Juristocracy. The Origins and Consequences of the New Constitutionalism* (Cambridge, Mass.: Harvard University Press, 2004), Introduction.

[95] F. D. Roosevelt, *Address on Constitution Day*, Washington DC, 17 September 1937.

[96] Federal Constitutional Court, *Atomwaffenstationierung*, BVerfGE 68, 1 (86); *Südumfahrung Stendal*, BVerfGE 95, 1 (15); *Rechtschreibreform*, BVerfGE 98, 218 (251–2).

particular interest because they represent two basic models for the organization of the federal executive.[97]

The German federal system has remained largely unchanged in its basic structure since the foundation of the Kaiserreich in 1871. With the founding of the Reich, the founding states such as Bavaria, Saxony, and Prussia retained their entire tripartite organizational structures—the representative assembly of the people, the executive, and the courts. The Reich received a bicameral legislature: a representation of the royal state executives—the Federal Council (Bundesrat)—and a democratically elected parliament—the Reichstag. A single supreme court of the German Reich was responsible for the consistent implementation of the laws of the Reich. The Reich was primarily designed as a legislating entity under the political leadership of the Kaiser and the Chancellor. The implementation of the Reich's laws resided with the administration and the courts of the member states. This arrangement, linking Reich and states in what has been called 'executive federalism',[98] has survived in the German Federal Republic. It is a design in which the governments of the states participate in the legislative process at the federal level as members of the Federal Council (Bundesrat). The federal level is left with relatively few administrative responsibilities, but does pass laws, which are implemented by the states. Within Bismarck's concept, these links between the states and the Reich served, if nothing else, to prevent the democratic accountability of the Chancellor.[99] Today, whenever debating the German federal system, analysts inevitably deplore a similar effect. In fact, democratic responsibilities are difficult to determine when the Bundestag and the state governments in the Federal Council must agree upon a federal law that will subsequently be implemented by the state administrations. Conveniently, this construction has been able to make use of the already existing administrative structure without being compelled to create new administrative bodies for every new law of the Reich or of the Federation. When the states' administrations have to implement federal laws, it seems fitting to include them in the federal law-making process.

In the United States the trend went in the opposite direction. Here, too, there was initially a federal level without its own administration. In early US

---

[97] D. Halberstam, 'Comparative Federalism and the Issue of Commandeering', in K. Nicolaidis, R. Howse (eds.) *The Federal Vision* (Oxford: Oxford University Press, 2001), 213. For a different model: P. Dann, 'Federal Democracy in India and the European Union: Towards Transcontinental Comparison of Constitutional Law', 44 *Verfassung und Recht in Übersee* (2011), 160.

[98] E.-W. Böckenförde, 'Sozialer Bundesstaat und parlamentarische Demokratie', in J. Jekewitz (ed.), *Politik als gelebte Verfassung* (Opladen: Westdeutscher Verlag 1982), 182–99.

[99] The Chancellor of the Reich was almost always simultaneously Prussian Prime Minister, in this function a member of the Federal Council and in this function not accountable in Parliament; T. Nipperdey, *Deutsche Geschichte 1866–1918 Band II* (München: Beck, 1995), 92.

history the federal government made use of the member states to implement federal laws.[100] Over time, however, the federal and state levels
gradually separated. Since 1912 the members of the US Senate have been
elected directly by the people.[101] In this way they still represent the interests
of the states in the federal legislature, but unlike the members of the
German Federal Council, they are elected specifically to engage in politics
at the federal level. Otherwise, the two federal levels operate separately to a
large extent. Federal law is implemented by federal authorities, which are
reviewed by federal courts. All powers are restricted in principle to the law of
their own level. In its recent jurisprudence, the US Supreme Court has even
declared this separation to be required by the constitution.[102]

What do these two models tell us about the problem of separated powers?
In principle, federal constitutional systems, in contrast to unitary states, are
more power-separating. Not least because of this, the United States insisted
upon a federal structure for Germany after the Second World War. And
indeed, the connection between federalism and the separation of powers
results from the increased number of policymakers: the three powers are
duplicated within the federation, with greater possibilities for reciprocal
checks and balances. A positive relationship between the federal structure
and the separated powers is therefore based on a rule of law-inspired concept
of the limitation of powers, as well as on a democracy-inspired vision of the
proliferation of political participation. The more levels a constitutional order
has, the more possibilities it can provide for political participation. However,
the proliferation of levels can also restrict opportunities for democratic
participation in decision-making, particularly when the actions of different
levels can no longer be clearly ascribed to a specific democratic constituency.
As we already saw, democratic accountability may become unclear in a
federal system when actions of both levels are fused. Furthermore, the
participation of the German-type Federal Council in legislation looks like
a classic problem of separation of powers because an organ made up of
governmental executives is thereby granted authority to legislate.[103] At first
sight, the American model seems more convincing in this respect: for with
the strict separation of the levels, it adheres to the classic separation of
powers and a clear distribution of democratic responsibility.

---

[100] S. B. Prakash, 'Field Office Federalism', 79 *Virginia Law Review* (1993), 1957.

[101] C. H. Hoebeke, *The Road to Mass Democracy* (New Brunswick: Transaction Publishers, 1995).

[102] *Printz v United States*, 521 US 898 (1997).

[103] For the lack of the general public in the *Bundesrat*: D. Grimm, 'Die Gegenwartsprobleme der
Verfassungspolitik und der Beitrag der Politikwissenschaft', in *Die Zukunft der Verfassung* (Frankfurt am
Main: Suhrkamp, 1991), 336 (352).

In conclusion: the federal structure has an influence upon the configuration of the separation of powers. This influence does not, however, necessarily yield a positive effect. It is not correct to simply understand federalism as a vertical version of separation of powers. In a federal structure, the organization is more complex, with the different powers occurring in duplicate form. The levels can act for the most part separately, such as in the United States, or they can interact, such as in Germany and also in the European Union. For a more precise evaluation of these institutional options, however, we need a better grasp of what we understand by separation of powers itself. This brings us to a systematic record of the observations made thus far.

II. THE SEPARATION OF POWERS—FUNCTIONS AND MEANINGS OF A CONCEPT

The constitutional traditions so far presented seem disturbingly diverse. Is it possible and would it make sense to merge them into a common analytical framework? Any attempt to develop such a framework has to answer two preliminary questions: (1) which functions might different concepts of separated powers fulfil in a constitutional system? And (2) what concrete meaning could the invocation of separate powers have in a constitutional context?

1. What is it for: empowerment or limitation of government?

The different historical traditions we have analysed illustrate our concept's vast variety of possible interpretations. Moreover, the point of reference for the concept has slowly changed over time. Whereas Locke and Montesquieu were interested in the limitation of an absolute ruler,[104] the constitutional practitioners of the late 18th and 19th centuries were already working against more complex threats to freedom: threats not from tyrannical individuals, but from organized private interests and legitimate parts of the state structure, legislative assemblies (such as in the early American states), the administration (in the rise of bureaucracy since the late 19th century), or the courts (as in the French Republican tradition). The fact that the appeal for the separation of powers can potentially be directed against all three branches, although the concept is based on the differentiation into those three, seems to suggest that the concept has little, if any, systematic value.

---

[104] For a historic perspective, see M. Stolleis, 'Condere leges et interpretari. Gesetzgebungsmacht und Staatsbildung in der frühen Neuzeit', in M. Stolleis, *Staat und Staatsräson in der frühen Neuzeit* (Frankfurt am Main: Suhrkamp, 1990), 167.

At first glance, it begins to look like a placeholder, a blank cheque for the constitutional justification of political interests.

This irritation proves even more justified if we ask for possible functions of the concept. For Locke and Montesquieu the answer to this is unequivocal: separation of powers, directed against tyranny, serves to protect individual freedom. Even Montesquieu, however, was already conscious of the ambiguities of political power. As Hannah Arendt observed so pertinently:

> Power can be stopped and still be kept intact only by power, so that the principle of the separation of power not only provides a guarantee against the monopolization of power by one part of the government, but actually provides a kind of mechanism, built into every heart of government, through which new power is constantly generated, without, however, being able to overgrow and expand to the detriment of other centres or sources of power. Montesquieu's famous insight that even virtue stands in need of limitation and that even an excess of reason is undesirable occurs in his discussion of the nature of power; to him, virtue and reason were powers rather than mere faculties, so that their preservation and increase had to be subject to the same conditions which rule over the preservation and increase of power. Certainly it was not because he wanted less virtue and less reason that Montesquieu demanded their limitation. This side of the matter is usually overlooked because we think of the division of power only in terms of its separation in three branches of government.[105]

Only with the French Revolution would this consideration change from being a merely intellectual concern to becoming a fundamental, normative consideration. By challenging the feudal courts, the revolutionary concept of the separation of powers *facilitated* the establishment of a democratic public authority. If, in a traditional, pre-democratic understanding, the necessity of repressing sovereign power still took priority,[106] then it was during the French Revolution that a different reading first appeared. In this account, separation of powers and division of labour serves as an organizational instrument to enforce democratic decisions. Such an understanding, which recognizes the separation of powers as a means of organizing public authority under conditions of democracy, has remained important to this day as a 'functional' interpretation, eg in American and German constitutional law.[107] As developed by organizational theory, the improvement of the

---

[105] H. Arendt, *On Revolution [1963]* (New York: Penguin Books, 2006), 142–3.

[106] See the classical theories: Locke, *Two Treatises of Government* (London: Black Swan, 1698), II, 143; C. de Montesquieu, *De l'ésprit des lois* (1748), XI, 6; Federalist Papers, Nr. 47 *(Madison)*; I. Kant, 'Über den Gemeinspruch: Das mag in der Theorie richtig sein, taugt aber nicht für die Praxis [1793]', in: *Werke* [ed Weischedel] (Darmstadt: Wissenschaftliche Buchgesellschaft, 1983), B 26.

[107] This tendency can be found in K. Hesse, *Grundzüge des Verfassungsrechts* (Heidelberg: C. F. Müller, 20th ed 1995), para. 482; J. Korn, *The Power of Separation* (Princeton: Princeton University Press, 1996), 15.

organizational structure does not, or does not *only*, protect against the abuse of power, but rather increases the assertiveness of the organization.[108] Seen this way, separation of powers is a form of functional division of labour for the democratic state.

It is therefore no accident that the discourse on the function of separated powers shows a deep discrepancy, referring to both the empowerment of public authorities and its restraint. This is rarely made explicit in the literature and is instead regularly concealed in contingent formulae, such as references to the 'common good' or 'proper' organization.[109] However, there is much to be said for the argument that this discrepancy must first be explicitly recognized and brought to a head, so that the meaning of our concept can be properly reconstructed. Behind this discrepancy lurk different ideas of the relationship between individual freedom and public authority. The pre-democratic picture painted by Montesquieu of the moderation of political power through their separation emphatically underlined the primacy of individual freedom and saw the sovereign exercise of power as the potential threat. The idea of democratic empowerment, which followed in the wake of Revolutionary democratization, however, placed its trust in the effect of public action to guarantee freedom, not least against restrictions of individual freedom caused by other individuals. Freedom *from* and freedom *through* public authority are the alternatives which find expression in different concepts of the separation of powers.

This antagonism obviously corresponds to the old distinction between negative liberal freedom and positive republican freedom,[110] and it seems equally obvious that modern constitutional orders do not choose between these two as alternatives but try to combine them. For on the one hand it is clear that a purely negative concept of freedom does not actually benefit those people who lack the opportunities to seize it. On the other hand, any sweeping concept of positive freedom threatens the individualistic foundation for the legitimacy of public authority. In this way it is not difficult to recast political debates, such as that between a libertarian and a social-democratic understanding of the state, as well as theoretical ones such as

---

[108] An endorsement of this concept is N. W. Barber, 'Prelude to the Separation of Powers', 60 *Cambridge Law Journal* (2001), 59.

[109] This pale language is employed by the Federal Constitutional Court and treated favorably in constitutional scholarship: Federal Constitutional Court, *Nato Tactical Nuclear Weapons*, BVerfGE 68, 1 (86); *Highway Bill* 95, 1 (15); *Ortographic Rules* 98, 218 (251–2); agreeing H. Maurer, *Staatsrecht I* (München: Beck, 5th ed 2007), § 12, § 4.

[110] The distinction can be traced back to ancient sources. For a modern elaboration see I. Berlin, 'Two Concepts of Liberty', in Hardy (ed.), *Liberty* (Oxford: Oxford University Press, 5th ed 2005), 166; B. Constant, 'De la liberté des anciens comparée a celle des modernes (1819)', in Gauchet (ed.) *De la liberté chez les modernes* (Paris: Hachette/Pluriel, 1980), 491.

that between communitarianism and liberalism, as debates about either a positive or a negative concept of freedom. We will pursue this path further in Chapter 2, where we will see that the real nub of an appropriate reconstruction of the separation of powers doctrine consists precisely in *leaving open* this fundamental problem. At this point it suffices to remark that the concept of separation of powers is closely linked to these fundamental constitutional issues.

2. What does it mean: division, balance, or ban on usurpation?

Our analysis of different constitutional traditions has not only demonstrated that the idea of separation of powers is applicable to a whole range of governmental structures, but also that the concept is associated with completely different organizational principles. This is not least proven by the great inconsistency of a terminology that refers to balance, control, division, or separation. The concept of separation is not infrequently rejected precisely because it is not primarily invoked to demonstrate a division of the powers, but rather to analyse the relationship between them.[111] Expressions such as *checks and balances* constitute a different understanding without actually being systematically distinct from the concept of the separation of powers.

   Even though we cannot simply replace this historically evolved variety of terms and meanings by offering one 'correct' understanding, it appears that these different uses refer to real institutional problems. Constructing a unified, systematic understanding against this background is not easy, but also not impossible. Before we develop such a systematic concept in Chapter 2, the question as to what the expression of *separation of powers* denotes has to be readdressed. A closer look at the different traditions will help identify three basic meanings:[112] the first demands an organizational *division* of different parts of the polity. The second unfolds a precept of alternating *checks and balances* for all institutions or offices. Finally, the third assigns to the powers specific *tasks or functions* and prohibits the exercise of these functions through other powers.

a) The separation of powers as a precept for division

The simplest understanding of the separation of powers is the precept that the different functions carried out by a state should be organizationally

---

[111] L. H. Tribe, *American Constitutional Law* (New York: Foundation Press, 3rd ed 2000), 137.

[112] For alternative ways of systematization: M. J. C. Vile, *Constitutionalism* (Oxford: Clarendon Press, 1967), 12; B. Manin, 'Checks, balances and boundaries: The separation of powers in the constitutional debate of 1787', in B. Fontana (ed.), *The Invention of the Modern Republic* (Cambridge: Cambridge University Press, 1994), 27 (30).

divided from one another. As Locke and Montesquieu emphasized, wherever all state duties are concentrated within one institution, tyranny—the ultimate threat to individual freedom—is present as well. But apparently, this precept is not meant to lead to a complete dissolution or dissociation of the polity. Something must hold it all together, and that something must also connect the powers with one another. Different expressions for this unity are to be found in different constitutional traditions: in the Anglo-Saxon tradition it is termed *government* (even the Supreme Court is part of the US government); Germans and French speak of the *state*; and European integration created a 'Union'. These concepts can be legally relevant,[113] but for our focus it is more important that even the idea of the separation of powers presupposes some kind of unity. Categorical divisions are thereby ruled out. It is rather a question—as Carl Schmitt put it—of a differentiation of powers,[114] than of their division. But does this understanding that emphasizes internal differentiation still have its own value for modern constitutions, or does it merely document an old-fashioned, mechanistic idea?

At first sight, most constitutional orders appear to have one thing in common: All institutions or departments that are named in the constitution must be put in a position to independently carry out the duties assigned to them. The bodies must therefore have their own organizational apparatus available to them and they must be able to autonomously prepare their own decisions. The literal understanding of division can be translated into this concept of an autonomous internal structure of every power. Even in a parliamentary system, the parliament may not interfere in every political proposal prepared by the government—and the government cannot, by the same token, restrict the parliament's working routines, which are normally defined by internal rules. This necessity for every institution to work autonomously and have certain boundaries that demarcate their unity is an important factor in organizational theory.[115] These boundaries may, however, be constitutionally disputed, such as in conflicts between parliament and the executive over the provision of information, for instance in Germany in a parliamentary inquiry or in the US during the crisis of President Nixon.[116] In such cases, the executive regularly—and in some circumstances not unwarrantedly—refers to the separation of powers and

---

[113] C. Möllers, *Staat als Argument* (München: Beck, 2000).

[114] For the expression 'Gewaltenunterscheidung', see C. Schmitt, *Verfassungslehre* (München: Duncker & Humblot, 1928), 186.

[115] K. Weick, *Sensemaking in Organizations* (Thousand Oaks: Sage, 1995), 18–24, stresses the importance of identity construction in 'organizational sensemaking'.

[116] Federal Constitutional Court, *Flick-Untersuchungsausschuss*, BVerfGE 67, 100 (139); *Public Citizen v Department of Justice*, 491 US 440; *Nixon v Administrator of General Services*, 433 US 425 (443) (1977).

the right contained therein to a separate domain in which to prepare its decisions. This argument is both plausible and prone to misuse, and the examples show that the necessity to accept organizational boundaries must not lead us to the stipulation of categorical rules that protect these boundaries. In fact, courts in both orders only admitted rather limited restrictions to parliamentary control with regard to separation of powers.

For Montesquieu and Locke the idea of separation was less a matter of organizational distinction than of preventing personal unions between the legislature and the government. However, it is for precisely this issue that there is no consistent solution in modern constitutional states. Instead it is widely accepted that parliamentary democracy, in which the parliament elects a member from its own ranks to be the leader of the government, and presidential democracy, in which president and parliament are selected in separate elections and members of parliament do not appear in the cabinet, represent equally legitimate governmental forms. Evidently, it is more important that the executive and the legislative possess democratic legitimacy than whether this legitimacy arises from one or two electoral processes. In addition, in many cases the rules that prescribe relations between government and parliament are formally spelled out in constitutional texts and allow little room for further references to a constitutional principle of separated powers. In any case, cooperation between parliament and government seems to be necessary even in presidential systems.[117] Yet, it is quite a different story for the courts. As we shall see, acting independently of all the other state institutions seems to be a definitive feature of a legitimately operating court. A court that depends on other branches loses its institutional virtues and starts to resemble a subdivision of the administration.[118]

A strict division of the branches from one another is not a generally accepted implication of the separation of powers. Rather, the compartmentalization of the different powers is managed in various ways for different powers. A clear concept of division applies only to courts, for reasons we will elaborate in the next chapter. Only by systematically justifying our concept from the perspective of its legitimacy can we specify it any further.

b) The separation of powers as a precept for checks and balances
The idea of the division discussed before has rarely been highly valued.[119] More common but also less clear is a concept of separated powers that

---

[117] See Chapter 3, I., 1.   [118] See Chapter 2, III., 3.

[119] The German Federal Constitutional Court holds that the German constitution does not require a separation of powers, see *Gleichberechtigung*, BVerfGE 3, 225 (247). The US Supreme Court, too, formulates in a similar way, eg *Youngstown Sheet & Tube Co v Sawyer* 343 US 579 (635) (Jackson, J., conc.): 'While the Constitution diffuses power the better to secure liberty, it also contemplates that practice will

requires a balancing and reciprocal check among the powers. Exactly what should be balanced in this understanding is rarely made clear, but it seems to be Montesquieu's idea of mitigating power through power.[120] Through checks, the exercise of authority is modulated until a general balance is struck. This notion of *checks and balances* is a more concrete legacy of the ancient tradition of mixed constitutions.[121] If one compares the idea of balance with the understanding of separation discussed before, an ambiguous relationship emerges: in its weak sense the obligation to divide the powers is an obligation to distinguish them, but this distinction is a necessary condition for checking and balancing among them. But a strictly understood separation precludes all contact between these institutions. Still, checks are precisely this: institutional contacts among the institutions.[122]

The notion of checks on the powers is directed at different problems in various constitutional contexts. As shown above, the idea of *checks and balances* comes closest to the considerations of the American Federalists,[123] who sought to prevent the takeover of government by a certain social group (*faction*). In the jurisdiction of the US Supreme Court, by contrast, the idea of checks plays a rather unimpressive role. The formula is, of course, often referred to, but it does not, in comparison with the third meaning, which will soon be discussed, develop its own independent body of legal argument. Since the beginning of its jurisdiction, the German Constitutional Court has been committed to the concept of checks and explicitly prioritized it over the concept of separation. In this way, the German court extrapolated from the notion of balance a commitment to an effective parliamentary control on the executive through investigative committees.[124] But in contrast to that jurisprudence, a more literal reading of 'separation' has also served to limit precisely these checks.[125] Different, contradictory interpretations of the separation of powers come into conflict here within one and the same legal problem.

---

integrate the dispersed powers into a workable government. It enjoins upon its branches separateness but interdependence, autonomy but reciprocity.'

[120] C. Montesquieu, 'The Spirit of Laws [1748]', in *Complete Works, Vol 1* (London: T. Evans, 1777), 198–212.

[121] Origins go back to Polybius, *History*, 6.4.6–11.

[122] This has been rarely remarked, but: R. Bellamy, *Political Constitutionalism* (Cambridge: Cambridge University Press, 2007), 202–6; and the reference to J. Braithwaite, 'On Speaking Softly and carrying Big Sticks: Neglected Dimensions of a Republican Separation of Powers', 47 *University of Toronto Law Journal* (1997), 342–4.

[123] See G. S. Wood, *The Creation of the American Republic 1776–1787* (Chapel Hill: University of North Carolina Press, 1969), 441 (548).

[124] Federal Constitutional Court, *Untersuchungsgegenstand* and *Neue Heimat*, BVerfGE 49, 70 (85), 77, 1 (42).

[125] Federal Constitutional Court, *Flick-Untersuchungsausschuss*, BVerfGE 67, 100 (129, 139).

The notion of balance plays a very prominent role in the jurisdiction of the European Court of Justice.[126] Whereas the Court seldom uses traditional notions such as the separation of powers, it has developed the concept of 'Institutional Balance' with respect to the institutions of the European Union. This expresses the common assumption that conventional categories of constitutional theory simply cannot be applied to the EU. The EU functions differently than its member states, but not entirely so. Yet, with the expression 'balance', even the Court of Justice cannot but make reference to a state tradition. In fact, as will be shown in Chapter 4, the Court of Justice has most notably strengthened the position of the European Parliament with reference to institutional balance.[127] What can be established at present is that the Court creates an overriding concept by conjoining the distribution of power between member states and among Union organizations, the effect of which tends to strengthen the latter.

The understanding of separation of powers as a balanced regime of checks protects the mutual exchange between the institutions. This mutual exchange serves to restrain power by power, realizing an important rationale for the doctrine of separated powers. But the ambiguity of the balancing metaphor remains a problem as long as no overall concept provides any idea of what guise an ideal balance should ultimately take. As long as this is missing, the formula remains a well-meaning but rather arbitrary picture of a 'good' government.

c) Powers and branches: the separation of powers as a ban on the usurpation of power

Locke and Montesquieu had already recognized that the idea of separated powers must include two different aspects: the establishment of governmental institutions and the allocation of certain duties to these institutions. The common notions of power, *pouvoir*, and *Gewalt*, obscure this distinction since 'power' linguistically encompasses both the office holder—the King—as well as what he does: say, signing a death sentence. Every useful theory of the separation of powers, however, must define precisely this distinction, which also plays an important role in many modern constitutional texts. The first three articles of the US Constitution allocate the executive, legislative, and judicial powers to the President, Congress, and the Supreme Court respectively. The German Basic Law frames the allocation in a similar way, with Article 20, Paragraph 2, Sentence 2 distinguishing, just like the Constitution of the French Fifth Republic, between the institutions of the 'legislature, the executive power and the judicature'. Other Constitutions distribute this form over different articles like articles 43, 85, and 165 of the South African

Constitution. Such textual arrangements raise two questions that help us to approach this third, most difficult, and most important concept of separated powers. The first question is how to define and to distinguish among the legislative, executive, and judicial powers. The constitutional text typically provides no definitions at all. From this follows the second question: is the allocation of a power to a particular institution, to a governmental branch, exclusive? If this were the case, the guiding rule for the allocation of power would be a very strict one. Or is it a relative assignment, in which a given branch, like parliament, only regularly exercises a certain power though exceptions are common?

With the help of these questions we can plainly formulate the third concept of the separation of powers doctrine: the separation of powers imposes a prohibition against the exercise of a particular power by an institution to which this power has not been allocated; a *ban* on any functional usurpation of a power. Adjudicating this prohibition takes a central role in the case law of many constitutional courts. It constitutes what is practically the most relevant concept of the separation of powers.

Even though constitutions contain numerous broad and general provisions, which provide at least some orientation on how to properly assign a power to a certain institution, the recourse to more fundamental considerations may often remain necessary. But one standard solution to define the attribution of a power to a branch is the definition of a specific legal form by a constitution. A good example for that is the notion of a 'law' in the sense of a parliamentary statute. The procedure for passing a law is set forth in great detail in most constitutions. Making laws, however, is nothing else than the exercise of 'legislative power'. Hence, the legislative power is undeniably allocated to parliament. The same can be said of courts and the form of the judgment as the classical expression of the judicial power. In both cases, a legal form couples branches and powers.

Matters are not always so easy, however, mainly because the procedures laid out in constitutions are not always sufficient and often have to be completed by the legislature. To give one much disputed example: the legislature regulates only the bare bones of an issue and delegates the details to be filled in by the government by means of an executive order or decree. Does this decree constitute an illegitimate legislative act by the executive? Or, conversely, is the parliament of an EU member state usurping executive powers when it requires its own intensive, permanent involvement in the negotiations for a European directive? A court may order a whole, lengthy administrative procedure to be repeated. Or it simply repeats the procedure in the oral argument itself. Where, in these examples, is the difference between the functions of the courts and those of the administration; between the executive and the judicial power? The legislature may set up bodies that barely acknowledge the distinction between courts and administrative entities. Ultimately the place of the constitutional court within a system in which the powers are separated remains questionable: does a constitutional court issue anything other than, to use Hans Kelsen's term, 'negative legislation'?[128] And if it does, is it acting like a court in doing so?

These questions have to be discussed in what follows. But first, we must underline that understanding our concept as a ban on the usurpation of powers constitutes the most important as well as the most complicated of the three interpretations of separation of powers. For two reasons it is also more suited in order to develop a concept of separated powers than the others: the contradictions in rationales as well as in the meanings of the separation of powers can better be merged into a model which allocates certain powers to certain institutions. The third concept may even include the other two. For within this concept there is not only room for the conflicting ideas of the limitation of power and the empowerment of the democratic process but also for solving the antagonism between the separation of institutions and the reciprocal checks of these institutions. Secondly, using powers—legislative, executive, judicial—as the more general reference point facilitates the application of the concepts to more recent institutional developments and to non-state organizations, which like the EU have no head of state or, like most international organizations, no parliament.

III. SOME INTERIM CONCLUSIONS

At the end of this chapter, the reader may well have plenty of questions regarding the meaning and function of our concept.[129] Too many constitutional traditions from the same, liberal-democratic political origins seem to have generated widely differing understandings of separation of powers. Some of them are directed against the monocratic tyrant, some against the tyranny of parliament, some against the non-democratic rule of courts, or, most recently, against the dangers of public bureaucracies.

There is not even a theoretical consensus as to why the organization of a state needs a system of separated powers. Instead, we find opposing patterns of justification. One strand uses the concept to limit the power of the state; another applies it in order to enhance this power. The original motive was that restricting the power of the state protects the freedom of the individual. But later, constitutional democratic self-determination arrived on the scene.

---

[128] H. Kelsen, 'Wesen und Entwicklung der Staatsgerichtsbarkeit', 5 *Veröffentlichungen der Vereinigung der Deutschen Staatsrechtslehrer* 30 (1928), 87.

[129] This has often been remarked: E. Carolan, *The New Separation of Powers* (Oxford: Oxford University Press, 2009), 32.

For Kant, Rousseau, and the Federalists, separation of powers cannot be separated from the question of democratic legitimacy, indeed ultimately they are indistinguishable. A final ambiguity lies in the precise meaning of the principle. Our analysis has demonstrated that even within one legal system, different and not entirely consistent interpretations are applied. The concept may serve to literally separate powers, as a precept of reciprocal checks and balancing, or as a precept of the proper allocation of certain duties to certain institutions.

A final uncertainty has to be mentioned. It regards the legal status of the concept within different constitutional systems. In some systems, like in the English, there is neither a legal principle of separation of powers nor any corresponding constitutional review. The French Fifth Republic installed a more or less court-like institution first and foremost to protect a certain concept of separated powers. Other countries with a general system of constitutional review may see separation of powers primarily as a legal principle, as in Germany, or rather as a matter of political competition, as in the United States. As a result, even the question of whether the concept should be understood as a legal rule or a political mechanism remains open.

Separation of powers seems like 'an institutional vision in search of an ideal'.[130] But despite this variety of ambiguities, we have not arrived at this point empty-handed. We have carved out three propositions that will carry the argument forward into the next chapter. The first is the discovery that, even with all these variations, the constitutional orders we have examined share something in common, namely the simple fact that they differentiate three powers and identify them accordingly: legislative; executive; and judicial. Whether this is also the case with organizations such as the EU or the UN will require an additional inquiry in Chapter 4. The second is an insight, thus far only implicit, that emerges as another common feature: all considered constitutional orders are democracies and recognize basic rights. This fact will help us find a model of legitimacy appropriate to our concept of separated power. Finally, it seems plausible to pursue the last of the three models of separated powers—the ban on power usurpation—as the point of departure for our further inquiry.

---

[130] E. Carolan, *The New Separation of Powers* (Oxford: Oxford University Press, 2009), 44.

∽ 2 ∾

Self-determination as the Source
of Separated Powers

In this chapter, a normative concept of separated powers shall be developed. This concept will be derived from the notion of autonomy or self-determination—both individual and collective—as the central element of the justification of public authority (I). Each type of self-determination requires different forms of institutional protection through law (II). This approach will allow us to define criteria for the legislative, executive, and judicial function (III). In order to achieve these goals, however, a detour to the theory of legitimacy will be necessary. Thereafter, we can begin to devise a model of a legitimate separation of powers. The goal of this chapter is to establish a systematic connection between the idea of individual and collective self-determination and certain institutional features of public organization that can be understood as building blocks for a theory of separated powers.

I. SELF-DETERMINATION AS THE BASIC
CONCEPT OF LEGITIMACY

1. The concept of self-determination

How can public authority be justified? The question is an old one; the answer remains disputed. Nevertheless, a certain mode of justification has prevailed in modern times: public authority can be justified as a form of self-determination for its subjects. One might call this principle democracy, self-government, or freedom. To find acceptance, public authority must be traced back to the governed themselves.

This notion has replaced other models, namely those that sought justification for state action in order to achieve certain goals that would safeguard freedom, welfare, or efficiency. In modern social contract theories, such as in Hobbes', one can observe the shift from one concept to the other. The justification of public authority through a contractual act is based on the individual freedom of the contracting parties. But the contract still strives to attain a firmly defined goal, such as the security of the subjects.[1] Furthermore, the requirement of participation ends with this one act of consent. The contract does not have to be renewed. In this way, a monocratic order can be erected on the basis of voluntary consent.

In comparison with a static definition of goals, self-determination as the point of reference for our model of legitimacy has at least two comparative advantages: its *inclusivity* and its *procedural character*. The concept of self-determination is inclusive since it does not preclude other material justifications of public authority. A decision for self-government is not a decision against peace, welfare, the market, social security, or environmental protection, but rather *that* there has to be a decision on these goals and *how* this decision shall be taken. The goals may remain the same but they are treated as neither self-evident nor uncontested. In this sense, self-determination is also a procedural concept. This is not undisputed in itself, both as far as the social conditions for self-determination are concerned and with regard to the option of abolishing a regime of self-determination through a self-determined process. However, such criticism does not alter the fact that a regime of self-determination can be recognized by its procedure. 'Goal choice, no matter how elegantly executed, is no substitute for institutional choice.'[2] This seems even more reasonable when one accepts that the goal choice and goal preference are almost always contested. From this perspective, self-determination is also a response to the general contestation of normative rationales.[3] But even factual assumptions may be contested as such (does climate change exist?) as well as in their distinctiveness from normative questions,[4] and growing doubts over the possibility of undisputed knowledge or, in more abstract terms, over the categorical ability to discriminate between facts and judgments[5] may extend the scope of procedures of self-determination even beyond the political realm.

Only open procedures allow the constant *revision* of goals. Perhaps the most important practical justification for regimes that are built on the idea

---

[1] Though it is finally the liberty of the so secured people that is the aim; Q. Skinner, *Hobbes and Republican Liberty* (Cambridge: Cambridge University Press, 2008), 47–54.

[2] N. K. Komesar, *Law's Limits* (Cambridge: Cambridge University Press, 2001), 151.

[3] H. Kelsen, *Vom Wesen und Wert der Demokratie* (Tübingen: Mohr, 2nd ed 1929), 98.

[4] B. Latour, *Politiques de la Nature* (Paris: La Découverte, 1999), 50; J. Lentsch, P. Weingart (eds.), *The Politics of Scientific Advice: Institutional Design for Quality Assurance* (Cambridge: Cambridge University Press, 2011).

[5] See again H. Putnam, *The Collapse of the Fact/Value Dichotomy* (Cambridge: Harvard University Press, 2002); more cautiously: J. Habermas, *Wahrheit und Rechtfertigung* (Frankfurt am Main: Suhrkamp, 2004), 281.

of self-determination is their receptiveness to constant change.[6] Regimes of self-determination can respond to more than just changing circumstances. By distinguishing between government and opposition, for instance, they even allow for the possibility of fundamental revisions of former decisions without dismissing their institutional structure. For organizations that are not built on procedural legitimacy, such as the Catholic Church, such revisions are problematic. For them, every fundamental change may delegitimize not just the revised practice but the history of the entire institution.

Despite these arguments, self-determination is not undisputed as the basic principle for a model of public authority.[7] Even in democratic theory, reference to the justifying effect of the results or the simple functionality of public authority is common.[8] The legitimacy of political systems seems to be judged less on their ability to provide formalized mechanisms of self-determination as on their practical success, such as the guarantee of general welfare. In the words of Abraham Lincoln, democratic government is the combination of 'government by the people' with 'government for the people'.[9] This assumption, the idea of output-legitimacy, is emphasized particularly often with regard to the European and the international sphere.[10] Without a doubt, correlations between output, acceptance, and stability are undeniable—no regime can be explained solely by the power of the rulers or by the reasons that justify the rule.[11] But it is precisely here that this perspective also finds its limits for the argument of this book: it is not a matter of a *normative* argument to define sufficient patterns of stability or functionality.[12] On the contrary, a normative model of legitimacy makes at the outset no assertions about the survival of a regime. Even if there were a correlation between the normative reasons for a regime and its factual performance, this correlation could be established only if both parameters were defined independently of each other. This echoes the critique of syncretism made in this book's introduction. Moreover, the functional performance of an institutional regime, such as the level of prosperity it has achieved, is in many cases contested and once again

---

[6] J. Dewey, *The public and its problems* (Athens: Ohio University Press, 1954), 206–8; R. Posner, *Law, Pragmatism, and Democracy* (Cambridge, Mass.: Harvard University Press, 2003), 158.

[7] I. Shapiro, *The State of Democratic Theory* (Princeton: Princeton University Press, 2002).

[8] See D. Held, *Models of Democracy* (Oxford: Polity Press, 1987), 143.

[9] A. Lincoln, *The Gettysburg Address Government*, 19. XI. 1863.

[10] F. Scharpf, *Governing in Europe* (Oxford: Oxford University Press, 1999).

[11] See already D. Hume, 'On the First of Principles of Government (1741)', in *Political Essays* (1994), 16.

[12] See the observations with regard to output-legitimacy in H. Brunkhorst, *Solidarity* (Cambridge, Mass.: MIT Press, 2005), 140.

requires normative criteria: 'expectations of performance are shaped by a normative background.'[13]

Self-determination as a starting point for our model has, as we have seen, a variety of advantages. However, it is also very demanding. It assumes, first of all, its own possibility, and that means the ability to make decisions freely. One might take the view that liberal institutions imply only external freedom of action, the freedom to follow one's own will, without having to answer the question whether this will was freely formed.[14] But is it really meaningful to speak of freedom of action in this context? For without a free will, the concept of freedom of action just remains a purely physical absence of obstructions. This is surely not enough for the *justification* of a certain constitutional system. Here is not the place to make any contribution to the philosophical discussion of free will. Nonetheless, the problem must be integrated into our line of reasoning, and it is important to bring the perspective from constitutional theory into the picture. For a constitutional model of legitimacy through autonomy, it might be relevant to wonder if there is an *internal* relation between the structure of a legal system and the concept of free will.[15] For a concept of separated powers it will be important to allocate precisely requirements of reasoning and reason-giving into the institutional framework of a constitutional order.

Legal systems imply the free will of their subjects, but treat this will as an intersubjective, communicative capacity, not as a purely internal state. This can be observed in different areas of law: in the recognition of guilt; establishment of standards of responsibility and criteria for attributing responsibility in criminal and torts law; as well as in the constitutional protection of individual freedom.[16] All of these normative constructions presuppose a capacity that operates internally but is outwardly conveyed. The capacity to act freely is accepted or dismissed according to externally communicated behaviour.

Legal systems specify the notion of free will for the question of whether a person could plausibly have behaved differently in a certain context and, thus, whether that person should be held accountable for their behaviour.[17]

---

[13] P. Graf Kielmannsegg, 'Legitimität als analytische Kategorie', 12 Politische Vierteljahresschrift (1971), 393.

[14] For a brief account of this distinction see <http://plato.stanford.edu/entries/freewill/>; M. Pauen, *Grundprobleme der Philosophie des Geistes* (Frankfurt am Main: Fischer Taschenbuchverlag, 2001), 271.

[15] An attempt to make this case is C. Möllers, 'Willensfreiheit durch Verfassungsrecht' in E. Lampe, M. Pauen (eds.), *Willensfreiheit und rechtliche Ordnung* (Frankfurt am Main: Suhrkamp, 2007), 250.

[16] M. S. Moore, *Causation and Responsibility* (Oxford: Oxford University Press, 2009).

[17] E. Tugendhat, 'Der Begriff der Willensfreiheit', in E. Tugendhat, *Philosophische Aufsätze* (Frankfurt am Main: Suhrkamp, 1992), 334 (347).

On the one hand, the affirmation of accountability does not imply that said behaviour could be described only outside nomological categories. On the other hand, the question of whether someone could have acted differently ultimately cannot be verified through empirical evidence. It is necessarily a counterfactual, normative assumption, which can only be made plausible in a specific context for a specific person. The practice of law has presumably been dealing with this much longer than the philosophical discourse. Legal systems have been drawing upon notions of accountability, intention, or negligence for a comparatively long time in order to frame social expectations of individual behaviour. In this context, free will is the result of intersubjective normative expectations. Legal rules make use of artificial, constructed standards when they attribute the accountability of an actor.[18] Such legal standards seem, on the one hand, relatively immune to the tides of philosophical debates about free will. On the other hand, the practice of law seems to have anticipated a turn in philosophy towards a pragmatic understanding even of individual freedom as a form of social practice.[19] Hegel's insight that there is no concept of freedom and action without the inclusion of its own social and institutional context may be the most relevant philosophical reference to this approach.[20]

Liberal legal systems assume the possibility of self-determination at least as a refutable presumption. This presumption is nothing more than the decision by law to make a difference between an action and other events; to treat damage caused by a hailstorm differently from damage caused by a driver who runs a red light. But legal systems do not stop at this assumption. They institutionalize more intimate connections to what they reconstruct as individual will formation. This becomes more apparent when we understand the concept of free will with the practical possibility of giving reasons for one's actions.[21] If one accepts this understanding, then a 'practice of free will', understood as a practice of reasoned behaviour, can even be stimulated and prompted by legal rules. Legal systems can define standards of responsibility or do without them; they can establish a duty to give reasons or set up procedures in which one may—or must—express these reasons. They can create situations that are inclined towards individual reasoning, such as when they oblige us to justify our own behaviour and thereby not only clarify why we have a certain preference but exactly what this preference is.

---

[18] H. L. A. Hart and T. Honoré, *Causation in the Law* (Oxford: Clarendon, 2nd ed 1985).

[19] R. Brandom, 'Freedom and Constraint by Norms', 16 *American Philosophical Quarterly* (1977), 187–96.

[20] G. W. F. Hegel, *Elements of the Philosophy of Right* (Cambridge: University Press, 1991), §§ 14, 15, 142; R. Pippin, *Hegel's Practical Philosophy* (Cambridge: University Press, 2008), 147; M. Quante, *Die Wirklichkeit des Geistes* (Berlin: Suhrkamp, 2011), 204, 264 (337).

[21] See the next section; 2. Between will and justification: the institutional use of self-determination.

Self-determination in law, thus, may turn out to be self-determination *through* law.

A key situation, which both supposes and stimulates the practice of a free will, is the establishment of a democratic order. If our arguments were at first applied only to individual self-determination, they are not necessarily restricted to it. The differences between individual and democratic will formation must not be exaggerated at this fundamental level. Why not attribute will formation to a business, which, as a legal person, claims its own rights—or even to a large number of people who structure themselves as the people of a state?[22] It is precisely this last point that critics of democracy often call into question—not least by suggesting that a body of persons or a 'people' cannot have their own will, that this will is only a fictitious entity.[23] This objection, however, seems to reify the concept of free will and, at the same time, to assume that this reification would work at least for individual persons. But if one interprets free will as the normative construction of an attributed responsibility, as we do here for the context of a constitutional model only, then it may be acceptable that comparable conditions apply to a democratic will as they do to an individual one. Both may seem fictitious or, to be less demeaning, just normative. Then it seems possible to attribute the decision among different alternatives also to a collective unity, to a company, or to a government. This attribution is without doubt institutionally more demanding than it is on an individual level. It requires organizational provisions, procedures, and decision-rules, but these necessities do not make the attribution impossible. The possibility of individual or collective self-determination ultimately results from the choice of a certain normative system of attribution. The institutional implications of this choice will emerge once again when we return to the concept of separated powers.

2. Between will and justification: the institutional use of self-determination

If it is possible or indeed necessary to ascribe a free decision-making ability to individual persons, which legal procedure mechanisms can latch on to, a further problem arises. In a long and influential philosophical tradition, self-determination reveals itself in principle only in the form of rationally

---

[22] For more general observations regarding the treatment of objects as having a will or being ready for interpretation: M. Tamen, *Friends of interpretable Objects* (Cambridge, Mass., Harvard University Press, 2001), 76–116, (with some Kelsenian insights regarding the constitution of objects through law: 97, 114–15).

[23] A central source to this kind of critique is J. Bentham's critique of fictions, see eg, *An Introduction to the Principles of Morals and Legislation*, J. H. Burns, H. L. A. Hart (eds.), (Oxford: Oxford University Press, 4th ed 1998), 205–12.

justifiable action.[24] Freedom is the freedom to act rationally. Distance from causality and the plausibility of an alternative way of acting can be expressed only through rational action, for which there are reasons. Accordingly, in modern times we find the assertion—from Kant to Brandom—that free will is manifest only through the giving and receiving of reasons;[25] that freedom is nothing other than the possibility of rationality. In this way, a condition of rationality is included in the concept of the will.[26]

This common philosophical identification of freedom and reason has serious institutional implications. In the Kantian theory of law, it is its consistency with a principle of generalization that gives the law its validity. But whether this generality can be achieved only through a general, inclusive democratic procedure remains open, at least. It may also be established through the thought experiment of a well-informed and there-fore enlightened King who knows how to rationally generalize rules. In the Kantian account, a democratic vote is not necessarily required.[27] For Kant, democratic approval coincides with reason in the concept of free will. From an institutional perspective, however, reason may prevail at the expense of the democratic process. Even for Rousseau, the distinction between *volonté de tous* and *volonté générale* ultimately works to safeguard the reason of truly democratic procedures from the arbitrary nature of other political decisions, especially of majority rule.[28]

Therefore, it is not surprising that some of the most important institu-tional features of democratic systems today are not part of these classical democratic theories: majority rule and the distinction between government and opposition. The latter distinction allows for contradictory but equally

---

[24] Compare Charles Taylor, *Sources of the Self* (Cambridge: Harvard University Press, 1992), 363, re Aristotle (phronesis) 125–6. For an analysis of the debate before Kant see T.-A. Ramelow, 'Wille', in J. Ritter, K. Gründer, G. Gabriel (eds.), *Historisches Wörterbuch der Philosophie Vol 12* (Basel: Schwabe, 2004), 770; J. B. Schneewind, *The Invention of Autonomy* (Cambridge: Cambridge University Press, 1998).

[25] Analysing this connection with different approaches: R. B. Brandom, *Making it Explicit* (Cambridge, Mass.: Harvard University Press, 1994), 50; and in the same publication, 270 with the reference to Kant; D. Davidson, 'Actions, Reasons and Causes', in D. Davidson, *Essays on Actions and Events [1963]* (Oxford: Clarendon Press, 2001), 3.

[26] The Platonic Euthyphro (Plato, 'The Euthyphro', in *The Works of Plato Volume V* (Westbury: Prometheus Trust 1996), 5–23) is the source of the problem, and the philosophical answer tends to plead for rationality. Obviously there is a counter-tradition from the sophists to Nietzsche to Foucault. For the systematic problem in legal theory: K. Tuori, *Ratio and Voluntas: The Tension between Reason and Will in Law* (Farnham: Ashgate, 2009), 60–91.

[27] W. Kersting, *Kant über Recht* (Paderborn: Mentis, 2004), 96 (136); N. Urbinati, *Representative Democracy* (Chicago: The Universityof Chicago Press, 2006), 124–126; differently I. Maus, *Zur Aufklärung der Demokratietheorie* (Frankfurt am Main: Suhrkamp, 1992), 148.

[28] J.-J. Rousseau, *Contrat Social [1762]* (Paris: Gallimard, 1969), II/3, where he contrasts *volonté générale* and majoritarian decision-making. J. Cohen, *Rousseau. A Free Community of Equals* (Oxford: Oxford University Press, 2011), 74–5.

legitimate subsequent decisions in a political system, something impossible in classical democratic theory. Voluntarism, contingency, indeed the option of first deciding one way and then the other, are excluded as irrational.[29] For the classical democratic tradition up to Habermas and Rawls the identification between democracy and reasonableness remains strong. The contingency of decision-making and the necessity of conflict within democratic decisions are not appreciated as democratic virtues.

This emphasis continues to have problematic effects on democratic theory.[30] Many theories tend to leave no room at all for democratic voluntarism.[31] As we shall see, basic rights and human rights currently represent the most important tool for the limitation of democratic voluntarism and are even beginning to take on a role similar to the old ideal of a rational teleology of the state. Theories in the tradition of social contract models, such as those of Rawls and his successors, have similarly little room for democratic voluntarism. They remain distant to the majority rule.[32] Decision-making procedures serve only as a means of approaching the right decision. They justify themselves cognitively or as matter of practicality, not normatively.

Theories that stress political voluntarism show the opposite tendency. A strong concept of collective voluntarism inspired by a thinker like Carl Schmitt and a strong concept of individual preference that is still dominant in economic theory and basically inspired by David Hume[33] converge, despite all their other differences, in the assumption of pre-existing preferences open neither to rational deliberation[34] nor to any modification.[35] From the individualist perspective, collective decision-making is little more than a potentially distorted representation of individual decision-making. In this view, a collective decision-maker's claim to legitimacy seems like a misguided project from the outset. Rationality coincides with maximization

---

[29] It appears possible to meaningfully link a theory to this phenomenon that resorts to the minority as the starting point to conceptualize democracy: H. Kelsen, *Allgemeine Staatslehre* (Berlin: Springer, 1925), 322.

[30] For the most articulated analysis of this issue: C. Mouffe, *The Democratic Paradox* (London, New York: Verso, 2000), 80.

[31] See eg E. Carolan, *The New Separation of Powers* (Oxford: Oxford University Press, 2009), 104 and his concept of non-arbitrariness.

[32] J. Rawls, *A Theory of Justice* (Cambridge: Harvard University Press, 1971), 356; for a convincing counter-critique: R. Bellamy, *Political Constitutionalism* (Cambridge: Cambridge University Press, 2007), 225–30.

[33] D. Hume, *A Treatise of Human Nature* (New York: Oxford University Press, 1978), 265; E. Millgram, 'Was Hume a Humean?', 21 *Hume Studies* (1995), 75.

[34] R. Nozick, *Anarchy, State, and Utopia* (New York: Basic Books, 1974).

[35] G. J. Stigler, G. S. Becker, 'De Gustibus Non est Disputandum', 67 *American Economic Review* (1977), 76. For a critique: C. R. Sunstein, *Free Markets and Social Justice* (New York: Oxford University Press, 1997), 14; H. Albert, *Marktsoziologie und Entscheidungslogik* (Tübingen: Mohr Siebeck, 1998), 29, 240.

of individual utility. From the perspective of an absolute concept of democratic will, on the other hand, in which the political preference is essentially an existentialist idea, democratic decisions are understood effectively as the epitome of the irrational or anti-rational.[36] In this account, human rights become reasonable, rationalistic restrictions of politics. Hence a concept of the political realm emerges which can think only in categories of unjustifiable hostility.[37] When the scope of democratic decision-making is constantly restricted by arguments of rationality and commitments to human rights, then politics can ultimately be found only where reason clearly has no more room. Democratic will vents itself only violently—through war.

a) Legitimate limits of rational deliberation

Yet how can we define a sustainable relationship between the rational and the voluntaristic element of self-determination that does not require giving one up at the expense of the other? Or is it inevitable that every normative model of legitimacy merges political decision-making into mere procedural *rationality*? This seems at least to be the assumption in a common interpretation of the theory of deliberative democracy, an interpretation that is albeit more common in legal than in political theory. This interpretation assigns a justifying effect to the non-public conversations of democratically unaccountable executive experts.[38] Jürgen Habermas' democratic theory, which aims to some extent to solve precisely this problem, will now be discussed in more detail on our way towards understanding the institutional implication of the problem.

At first sight we might state: deliberation, that is to say the rationalizing exchange of reasons and counter reasons, has a complementary relationship to democratic decision-making: the open debate of personal preferences informs collective decision-making and improves its cognitive capacities.[39] The result of a democratic election defines the specific terms, not to mention the burden of justification, for democratic deliberation after an election with the following election in mind.[40] Furthermore, deliberation also has cognitive functions: it ensures that we know what we are voting on in the first place. Through deliberation, the participants mutually inform

---

[36] P. Kahn, 'Speaking Law to Power: Popular Sovereignty, Human Rights, and the New International Order', 1 *Chicago Journal of International Law* (2000), 1.

[37] C. Schmitt, *Der Begriff des Politischen [1932]* (Berlin: Duncker & Humblot, 1963), 26.

[38] A.-M. Slaughter, *A New World Order* (Princeton: Princeton University Press, 2004).

[39] For the essential considerations of this issue E. Burke, 'Speech to the Electors of Bristol (3. November 1774)', in D. Bromwich (ed.), *On Empire Liberty and Reform. Speeches and Letters of Edmund Burke* (New Haven: Yale University Press, 2000), 39 (45).

[40] C. Lafont, 'Is the ideal of a deliberative democracy coherent?', in S. Besson; J. L. Marti, *Deliberative Democracy and its discontents* (Aldershot u.a.: Ashgate, 2006), 3.

each other of the content and meaning of their own decision-making process and that of others.[41] The rational discourse not only provides the justification of the decision; it already identifies what is decided upon. In this way a complementary relationship develops between the voluntarism of the decision and the rationality-forming deliberation.[42]

This solution seems plausible in its results, but too simple in its theoretical construction and too undifferentiated for a theory of the organization of public authority. For it remains unclear to what extent the decision-making process can withdraw itself from a rationalizing discourse without losing its claim to legitimacy. The basic proposition of deliberative theory—that any claim to legitimacy must justify itself in an intersubjective discourse—is derived from a theory-of-truth line of reasoning concerning the conditions for the possibility of rationality as such.[43] Discourse theory, under the overarching heading of 'recognition', has adopted this model for the question of the legitimacy of political decisions.[44] This theory does indeed further distinguish between the justification of normative arguments and the truth of descriptive, empirically verifiable principles,[45] but it does not differentiate between the rationality of deliberation and the generation of democratic legitimacy. We might say that in this model the equal vote is merely an instrument for the purposes of the rational debate, not the other way around.[46] Or, to put it more categorically: *the use of self-determination may require the ability to provide a justification, but the protection of self-determination must also protect against the duty to constantly provide a justification.* An example from constitutional law may illustrate the point: it would be wrong to make the protection of free speech and free assembly subject to the condition that speech and assembly contribute to a rational democratic deliberation.[47] Such a condition would exclude some from the enjoyment of basic rights from the outset.

---

[41] For this aspect, see B. Manin, *Principes Du Gouvernement Représentatif* (Paris: Flammarion, 1995), 277–9, who considers this aspect to be distinct, even contrary to deliberation.

[42] J. Habermas, *Between Naturalism and Religion* (Cambridge: Polity Press, 2008), 91.

[43] J. Habermas, 'Wahrheitstheorien', in J. Habermas, *Vorstudien und Ergänzungen zur Theorie des kommunikativen Handelns* (Frankfurt am Main: Suhrkamp, 1983), 127.

[44] This provenance of the theory is rarely observed, but see F. Jullien, *De l'Universel* (Paris: Points Essai, 2010).

[45] J. Habermas, 'Rightness versus truth: On the sense of normative validity in moral judgments and norms', in J. Habermas, *Truth and justification* (Cambridge: MIT Press, 2003), 237.

[46] C. Möllers, 'Expressive versus repräsentative Demokratie', in R. Kreide (ed.), *Internationale Verrechtlichung und Demokratie* (Frankfurt am Main: Campus, 2007), 160.

[47] That is the unfortunate holding of some German constitutional decisions: Federal Constitutional Court, *Love Parade*, BVerfG NJW 2001, 2459.

But then again, how do we properly reconstruct the relationship between rationality and voluntarism for our institutional problem? From the practical constitutionalist perspective chosen here—a perspective that has to solve the question of how and to what extent theoretical considerations should or should not be put into legal form—the following approach may appear appropriate.

Firstly we need to distinguish the *protected possibility* of a decision-making process from the *actual* decision-making. The possibility of making a decision—within our specified tradition of thought—is not different from the ability to give and take reasons in a form of procedural rationality. However, this possibility is not always realized: many of our actions are not rational decisions. And whether an action actually is may be subject to dispute. That leads us to a normative presumption: we presume the possibility of rational will-formation and decision-making for all members of a political community as a general rule that can be rebutted. The reason for this rule is not only a matter of practicality—that the faculty of free will cannot be a matter of discussion for each decision that requires it, such as with every daily purchase that requires the free decision to enter into a contract. Even more important is the fact that such a general assumption as a part of mutual recognition is constitutive for a community, which is based upon self-determination. The faculty of free will represents a general and reciprocal assumption, which is not subjected to any demanding criteria, because of the incalculable implications this may have for everybody concerned. Excessively demanding criteria for the recognition of rational decision-making ability could lead to disenfranchisement of parts of the community, which would undercut the equality of the participants—an equality already included in the recognition of self-determination.[48]

Such a general rule presuming the faculty of free will and the rationality of every member of the community is, in fact, explicitly or implicitly observed in all liberal legal orders. At the age of consent, nobody has to pass a test to make use of his basic rights or to close a contract. Assuming the ability to give and take reason is an expression of the rational element of the concept of will. But recognizing a decision for which no reasons have been provided, in contrast, implies approval of the voluntaristic element in the legal practice of individual and collective self-determination.

With that, we take a second step: the faculty of free will *can* be examined under certain circumstances. The question, then, is: when and under what circumstances should we require specific reasons for a certain decision and

---

[48] W. Sadurski, *Equality and Legitimacy* (Oxford: Oxford University Press 2008), 77–92; W. Heun, 'Freiheit und Gleichheit', in D. Merten; H.-J. Papier (eds.), *Handbuch der Grundrechte Band II/1* (Heidelberg: Müller, 2006), § 34, sect. II.

not simply be satisfied with the presumption for the general ability to make a rational decision? Who decides upon the terms and modalities of this procedural arrangement? In which cases is a mere 'I want' sufficient, and when is a rational deliberation required? There is no universally valid answer to such questions, but we will see that the concept of separated powers relates to them. From the perspective of equality it should be obvious, however, that the obligation to reason-giving itself requires particular reasons. We will develop more precise criteria in the second section of this chapter.

b) Self-determination through public authority

If we accept self-determination as the key element of legitimate public authority, then the question arises as to why we must make the detour to public authority at all in order to facilitate self-determination. In fact, democracy is sometimes identified with the absence of public authority; with statelessness.[49] At least a perfect state of democracy could be seen as the final goal for any form of government or as the factual identification of the rulers and the ruled.[50] As we will see now, however, it is more appropriate to describe democracy as the rule of the ruled, and thereby recognize the necessity of public authority even in a democracy.[51] This seems, in fact, necessary if one accepts the need for collective decisions. It is true that collective decisions, at least consensual ones, do not in themselves exercise any public authority, just as the form of the contract presupposes consensus, thereby representing an instrument for the exercise of freedom, a fact that is much emphasized in economic theory.[52] But this point loses at least some of its value in the case of an unequal distribution of power between the contracting parties.[53] And it seems to fall apart at the very latest when there is no actual consensus: not only when someone does not agree, but also when someone who did agree changes his or her mind. In such a case, only a legally enforceable contract—as opposed to a mere agreement— would be of use to the other party. Hence, even contracts need some system of public authority. Therefore, the need for collective decisions, and thus of

---

[49] The idea of the coming death of the state is a heritage of early German idealism: *Ältestes Systemprogramm des deutschen Idealismus* (1796/97).

[50] See C. Schmitt, *Verfassungslehre* (München: Duncker & Humblot, 1928), 235.

[51] C. Möllers, 'Der parlamentarische Bundesstaat', in J. Aulehner (ed.), *Föderalismus* (Stuttgart: Boorberg, 1997), 81, 97; also see H. Brunkhorst, *Solidarität* (Frankfurt am Main: Suhrkamp, 2002), 98. Similar already H. Kelsen, *Allgemeine Staatslehre* (Berlin: Springer, 1925), 321.

[52] For a critique see A. Tschentscher, 'Der Konsensbegriff in Vertrags-und Diskurstheorien', *34 Rechtstheorie* (2002), 43.

[53] An analysis of problematic forms of consent is D. Beeham, *The Legitimacy of Power* (Macmillan: London, 1991), 90–7.

public authority, is suggested not only by Hobbesian civil war scenarios. In this respect, public authority is merely one mode of power, and power will inevitably occur in one form or another. In establishing market-based rights, for instance, there is likewise a need for enforceable decision mechanisms. This speaks in favour of collective decisions. Although it is true that one can think of spontaneous regulations, which emerge without such mechanisms,[54] these phenomena cannot fully replace organized collective decisions.

The need for collective decisions leads to the conclusion that a political system based on self-determination, like a democratic order, cannot be identified with the absence of public authority. And even public authority according to the principles of self-determination has to override the will of certain subjects, thereby constantly calling its own legitimacy into question. As a result, even the best system of self-determination includes excesses.[55] Every democratic system violates the self-determination of its subjects in certain cases, as many post-modern criticisms of liberal constitutionalism remind us. But it is also true that this insight is vulnerable to two forms of misuse. There is, on the one hand, the unattainable promise of a system without any public authority by theories of radical democracy.[56] There is also the authoritarian justification of violations of self-determination by a general reference to the abstract inevitability of public authority.[57] However, the insight in the inevitability of public authority can only remind us to keep looking for better means for its organization.

II. SELF-DETERMINATION THROUGH LAW

1. *The relationship between individual and collective self-determination*

Self-determination can take place both in individuals and collectives. Both forms of self-determination can be differentiated but not separated. Every collective decision-maker, be it a people or an interest group, effectively depends upon the individual members who constitute it. This link is also significant in the context of a theory of *legitimacy*: a claim to recognition made by a collective act of self-determination should not be recognized without due consideration of the participating individuals' decision-making processes. This does not preclude the possibility that individual decision-making can fundamentally change within the moulds of collective

---

[54] R. Ellickson, *Order without Law* (Cambridge: Harvard University Press, 1991).

[55] It might be added that the distinction between democracy and populism is necessarily instable, see E. Laclau, *On Populist Reason* (London/New York: Verso, 2005), 157.

[56] eg M. Abensour, *La Démocratie contre l'État* (Paris: Éditions du Féln, 2004).

[57] I. Shapiro, *The State of Democratic Theory* (Princeton: Princeton University Press, 2004), Chap 2 is a careful critique of domination.

self-determination, or even that an individual contribution can be ignored as a result, for instance through majority rule. It does follow, though, that no collective decision-making is conceivable that is not somehow linked to individual decision-making.

Reconstructing the inverse relationship is more difficult. At first, it seems possible that the formation of an individual political will can take place independently of any collective will formation. Our discussion of the concept of a free will, however, has already shown that, when put so simply, this is not the whole truth. For the constitution of an individual political preference cannot in any case be *effectively* articulated—and indeed cannot in fact be constituted—outside a social context. By there were only one human being, then their consciousness would structure itself according to different categories. This becomes particularly apparent when we consider the practice of law. Individual self-determination is legally articulated, as will be further illustrated, in the form of rights. A right is a social institution: it is directed towards others and requires social mechanisms for its implementation. One of Kant's points in his definition of law is that the right, though it takes the subject as its point of departure, can be understood only as an externalization, that is, as a social phenomenon between different persons.[58] This descriptive insight, however, should not be confused with the question of justification: even though the individual will is formed through social communication, its claim to recognition does not depend in the same way on its connection to a collective will as it does vice versa. To put it differently, no expression of a collective or political will can be recognized as legitimate if it is not linked to any individual person who supports or constitutes this collective will. But the expression of an individual will always deserves some degree of recognition, although not to such an extent as to necessarily overcome other competing individual claims. There is hence a justificatory asymmetry between individual and collective will.

How should we reconstruct this asymmetry? Once again it seems useful to distinguish between the general capacity of rational will formation and the actual formation of will. The former can be described as *personality*. Individual and collective will formations initially differ from each other insofar as personality can be recognized only in individuals. Only expressions by individuals can readily count as an act of self-determination, insofar as we assume their rational capacities. Precisely because we attribute to individuals the ability to give reasons for their behaviour, it is not required

---

[58] This is often misunderstood because philosophy of law and moral philosophy are confused, eg in E. Carolan, *The New Separation of Powers* (Oxford: Oxford University Press, 2009), 98–9. I. Kant, 'Metaphysik der Sitten, Rechtslehre [1797]', in *Werke* [ed Weischedel] (Darmstadt: Wissenschaftliche Buchgesellschaft, 1983), Introduction § B.

to always justify it. In saying this, we make a paradoxical move: we attribute a pre-social characteristic to the individual—an attribution, which is itself a social act.

Acts of collective will formation, by contrast, cannot so readily claim to be valid. Collectives do not in the same way *necessarily* enjoy recognition as individual persons do, or to be more precise: particular expressions are comprehensible as acts of a legitimate collective self-determination only if they are traceable to individual acts. A plausible reconstruction of a collective will formation to a majority of individual acts of self-determination is *democratic* when certain criteria are fulfilled. On what this plausibility is based will be discussed further. Ultimately, the greater permanence of individual self-determination may be rooted in the physicality of individuals, in them having a body and, therefore, a physical boundary, which renders individual will-formation a more reliable phenomenon. The bond between individual personality and the body is more stable than the bond to supra-individual institutions.

2. The equal status of individual and collective self-determination

Individual personality is the source of both individual and collective self-determination.[59] But we have to be careful which institutional implications to draw from this insight. As we shall now see, the dependence of collective self-determination on individual personality does not result in a normative supremacy of individual over collective self-determination. Rather both are—this being Habermas' fundamental insight—normatively of equal rank, albeit not normatively co-original, as he puts it in his rather romantic terminology.[60] This assumption is widely contested by individualist and collectivist models of politics. But even the recognition of individual personality developed above does not force us to accept a rule that prioritizes individual over collective self-determination on an institutional level.[61]

This follows already from the possibility of a legitimate conflict between autonomous individuals. There can be no determinate and enforceable rule for the resolution of such a conflict that is actually accepted by both individuals, otherwise there would be no conflict. One approach of political theory is to refer to *potential* instead of *actual* consent and thereby to use an

---

[59] It seems to me that the main problem with the model in E. Carolan, *The New Separation of Powers* (Oxford: Oxford University Press, 2009), is that he does not distinguish between these two levels of individual autonomy, so that his reference to individual liberty leads rather arbitrarily to an institutional plea for administrative independence.

[60] J. Habermas, *Between Facts and Norms* (Cambridge: MIT Press, 1996), 103.

[61] D. von der Pfordten, 'Normativer Individualismus', *58 Zeitschrift für philosophische Forschung* (2004), 321 (338).

idealized or normative version of individual consent in order to save normative individualism. But this approach is not possible for a model that seeks to solve an institutional problem. An actual conflict between two persons can be resolved only supra-individually. Precisely because the coordination of several persons is concerned, there cannot be a general supremacy of actual individual over collective self-determination. Does it then follow inversely that collective self-determination takes priority over individual? Again, no. The exclusion of only one individual from the process of collective self-determination may take away the legitimacy of the whole process; its character as an act of self-determination.[62] If one vote does not count, no vote counts. In this respect both forms of self-determination presuppose individual personality without implying any normative hierarchy between them.

This entwined and complex normative relationship, the equal status of democratic and individual self-determination on an individual, personal basis, is nicely illustrated by the practice of democratic constitution-making. Democratic constitutions define the act of their creation—mostly contrary to all historical plausibility[63] and nonetheless for good reason—as an act of democratic self-empowerment. Preambles in constitutions frequently invoke a *pre-state (!), individual (!)* freedom. Yet it does not follow from this invocation that individual self-determination is constantly prioritized over democratic decisions. That this is not the case shows the act of constitution-making itself which precisely formulates the esteem for individual freedom in the context of a *collective* act. With the collective act of democratic constitution-making, a system of protecting individual rights and making democratic decisions is put into place without stipulating an abstract rule of priority between both.

The assumption of a normative equality between individual and democratic self-determination provokes widespread objections. Some argue it has a potentially totalitarian effect; for one because it grants at least relative priority to democratic decisions; for another because it argues in a purely procedural fashion.[64] Limits on individual self-determination seem on this account to be ubiquitous, but what limits are there for democratic self-determination?

---

[62] Jürgen Habermas, *Between Facts and Norms* (Cambridge: MIT Press, 1996), 110.

[63] K. v. Beyme, *Die verfassunggebende Gewalt des Volkes* (Tübingen: Mohr, 1968); J. Elster, 'Deliberation and Constitution Making', in J. Elster (ed.), *Deliberative Democracy* (Cambridge: Cambridge University Press, 1998), 97.

[64] For a categorical critique of procedural models of legitimacy, see D. v. d. Pfordten, 'Rechtsethische Rechtfertigung—material oder prozedural?', in L. Schulz (ed.), *Verantwortung zwischen materialer und prozeduraler Zurechnung* (Stuttgart: Steiner, 2000), 17 (25, 32); A. Gutmann / D. Thompson, 'Deliberative democracy beyond process', 10 *Journal of Political Philosophy* 2 (2002), 153.

One limitation lies in the idea of individual personality itself. Democratic decisions may not block the conditions for the formation of individual free will. A democratic decision loses any claim to legitimacy when it excludes even a single member of the democratic community. Just when this is the case is, admittedly, a matter of debate. We will turn again to this question in the next section with an inquiry into the idea of human dignity and Hannah Arendt's concept of a right to rights. But it must already be admitted that these limitations will turn out to be rather narrow. They do not remove the suspicion that authoritarian structures could, under the conditions of this concept, make a claim to legitimacy. What can, for instance, be said about the rights of minorities infringed by a democratic decision? It is true that our approach provides no guarantees whatsoever against injustice or certain curtailments of freedom. Rather, minority rights, like all other rights when they are at the expense of other legal positions, must vindicate themselves. Constitutional theory cannot prevent problematic or even unjust decisions. It can only serve as a reminder that all decisions concerning the self-determination of others require democratic justification. Even the justification for the protection of an individual claim to self-determination finds no basis in the nature of the individual themselves as long as their exercise of freedom affects others. However, this is no point against institutional solutions in more concrete levels of argument that are yet to be considered, such as the definition of subjective rights and the distinction between statutory law and constitutional law that may give protection against majoritarian decisions.

a) Individual and democratic legitimacy

How can individual and democratic self-determination be legally institutionalized and protected? Legal systems must justify themselves through the protection of individual and democratic self-determination. This presupposes corresponding procedures, which can claim *individual and democratic legitimacy*. Through the reconstruction of these two forms of legitimacy we will finally be able to explain the specific qualities of legislative and judicial institutions in a system of separated powers.

b) Individual legitimacy

Public authority justifies itself by reference to the self-determination of its subjects. An act of individual self-determination, however, requires no further justification. Any concept of 'individual' legitimacy, therefore, seems at first sight counter-intuitive. It seems more plausible to define the relation between individual self-determination and public authority as a purely negative one so that individual legitimacy can emerge only in the absence of public authority. But this assumption is insufficient. The relationship between individual legitimacy and self-determination proves itself to be more complicated for two reasons: first of all, because restrictions on freedom can also conceivably come from other citizens, not only from the state. If these citizens can also invoke individual self-determination, however, more than the retreat of public authority is necessary to protect their individual freedom. Secondly, some freedoms, such as property, cannot function without public authority. The state cannot simply withdraw here. Rather, a legal system must create mechanisms to allow the practice of freedom in the form of property. At this point, the above arguments against the identification of democratic rule with the absence of public authority can be reiterated.[65] In both cases, the absence of public authority cannot simply be equated with the protection of self-determination.

Social mechanisms such as markets or even families are not constructs in which public authority is simply absent. However, at the same time one of the biggest challenges for a constitutional theory that originates from the idea of self-determination is the question of to what extent these examples have to be understood as *exceptions*. For if it were the rule that private individuals represented the threat to freedom whereas government only enabled freedom, this would fundamentally call into question the distinction between individual freedom and public authority itself. We therefore need a more refined concept.

Individual legitimacy is created by procedural mechanisms, through which public authority facilitates or protects individual self-determination. To do this, it is not sufficient to establish material standards for the distribution of freedom, such as the organization of property or other subjective rights. Rather, mechanisms are necessary that help to implement these norms. The relation between individual self-determination and subjective rights underlines this result: subjective rights are general rules that protect the individual self-determination of all people by defining spheres of entitlement, for instance property as such. Without subjective rights there would be no individual legitimacy. In this sense, subjective rights also include the claim to the fulfilment of a contract against a private person and the claim to public enforcement of said right against the state. At the same time, however, subjective rights are *general* provisions that reflect the attribution of freedom in the whole legal order. The general scope of these rights potentially affects everybody.

Thus, we see an ambiguity in the expression 'subjective right' that has to be clarified.[66] On the one hand, there is the general rule that defines a

---

[65] See Chapter 2, I., 2b.

[66] Two important sources for such a clarification are W. N. Hohfeld, 'Some fundamental legal conceptions as applied in judicial reasoning', *23 Yale Law Journal* (1913), 16; G. W. F. Hegel, *Elements of the philosophy of right* (Cambridge: Cambridge University Press 1991), § 38.

certain sphere of freedom for the whole political community. This rule requires democratic legitimacy. For example, the general petition for freedom of speech is a political demand that must be anchored in a democratic law or in the constitution. 'Individual self-determination', meanwhile, refers to a strictly personal action by a specific individual person in a specific context: my right to demonstrate tomorrow in front of the Brandenburg Gate, for example. The protection of this specific claim creates individual legitimacy. This claim is just my individual matter and not a question of the whole democratic polity. The legal mechanisms that take care of this individual claim and sort out its specific context and scope may claim what we shall call individual legitimacy.

How can such claims of individual self-determination be institutionally protected? What do we need to create individual legitimacy? To answer this question, we must take into account another consideration: an individual person will turn to the legal system with a matter in the first place only when the realization of his demand, his wish, has been impeded, when something has obstructed the actualization of his intentions. Otherwise, the question of possible help from the legal system would not come up, and neither would the question of individual legitimacy. This has important implications: most actions never come into contact with the legal system.[67] An action will only be claimed as protected by a right when its realization is uncertain and when legal institutions can take this impediment away. In temporal terms, a mechanism that protects a specific act of individual self-determination, therefore, always responds *retrospectively* to it. The law deals with the protected action *in retrospect* and on the initiative of the actor.

The action to be protected must refer to an individualized event. Otherwise, there is the danger that the person externalized his own right at the expense of others. For this reason, I am entitled to my right to demonstrate only in a certain place at a certain time, and not to the general right or somebody else's right.[68] Obviously, the distinction between individual and collective self-determination is fluid. If the police arrest someone, at first only that person's own legal sphere will be affected, but potentially also that of their children, or if they are an opposition candidate for political office, perhaps the sphere of political rights of the voters or their party. As in the public/private distinction, we are dealing with matters of degree. And in order to make plausible use of such distinctions, we will have to establish institutional mechanisms. Finally, the guarantee of a procedure that protects individual claims will not entail that this individual claim is ultimately

---

[67] For the everyday relevance of law: W. M. Reisman, *Law in Brief Encounters* (New Haven/London: Yale University Press, 1999).

[68] As we shall see, there are exceptions to this, but only for specific justificatory reasons.

upheld. Otherwise there would be a general rule of priority in favour of individual legitimacy, which, as we discussed above, cannot be accepted.

If we concede that the individual claim to self-determination is decided upon the initiative of the individual, the question arises as to which criteria should be applied in order to accept or reject this claim. Only a democratic decision can serve as the basis for the distribution of individual spheres of freedom. Obviously, it is clear that a liberal legal system has a general default rule in favour of individual freedom, so that the individual gets his right if there is no democratic rule restricting it.[69] For in this case, there is no conflict at all between individual and democratic self-determination. Whatever is not prohibited is permitted. Nothing other than a democratically sanctioned rule can abridge individual self-determination.

But can a system protecting individual legitimacy simply accept individual concerns as they are expressed? Or else must it ask for evidence and justification with respect to our considerations of will formation?[70] First, one must acknowledge—as shown above—that all those participating in the legal system are in a position to make free decisions. This implies, secondly, that the system has to acknowledge a specific individual expression without any need of justification or proof that the expression has been voiced freely. Certainly, legal norms can also influence individual will formation.[71] Prohibitions, and also social views that have themselves been induced by law, can have an influence upon whether a certain person has a certain preference or not. What follows from the general rule of recognition, however, is that the result of this influence is attributed to the person. Norms create subjective rights as institutionally secured spheres. They also protect and influence the individual use of freedom, for example by creating incentives to make a certain decision. Norms can, after all, stimulate a practice of freedom, as we have seen. But despite all that, a specific act of individual self-determination has to be treated by the legal system as being independent from this influence, as an act of their own freedom.

And yet, there may still be some need for self-explanation on the side of the person claiming an individual right. But having to justify one's case mainly serves to demonstrate the fact that one has a case at all. Reasons are necessary on the part of the claimant in order to identify and individualize the demand. Precisely the description of a demand as an individual concern, as exclusively or primarily relating to one's own sphere, requires

---

[69] This rule seems, amazingly enough, to be the invention of a Frenchman: E. J. Sieyès, 'An essay on privileges', in E. J. Sieyès: *Political writings* (Indianapolis: Hackett, 2003), 68.

[70] See Chapter 2, I., 2.

[71] L. Lessig, 'The New Chicago School', *27 Journal of Legal Studies* (1998), 66; C. Sunstein, 'On the Expressive Function of Law', *144 U. Pennsylvania Law Review* (1995–1996), 2021.

explanation. This need for explanation is cognitive, not normative. The same is, as we shall see, not true for the acts of a public authority, however. There is an obligation of justification on its part when an individual demand is to be judged by a court. This also serves the cognitive function to individualize the issue at stake. It is primarily a normative justification, however: the restriction of an individual sphere of freedom in the name of a general rule needs a justifying explanation which shows the connection between the democratically defined general rule and the specific situation to which it is applied.

In conclusion: legal procedures are justified by what we call *individual legitimacy* when they concern a specific individual claim to self-determination on the initiative of the entitled, and judged according to the standards of a democratic rule. Such procedures receive their prime justification from the person who initiates it. Their will is carried through the procedure. But individual legitimacy depends only on the procedure itself, not the success of the petitioner. Otherwise, individual legitimacy would have to guarantee every individual claim at the expense of the other members of the community. It is not difficult to recognize the basic structure of a *judicial* procedure behind the concept of individual legitimacy.

c) Democratic legitimacy

Which criteria does democratic legitimacy require? How does it work? Unlike individual self-determination, the legal system cannot take the existence of democratic self-determination for granted. As we have seen, every individual expression of the will must be taken seriously as a self-determined act and is therefore entitled to an individualized procedure. But unlike individual self-determination, the recognition of collective expressions of the will requires a specific justification to be considered democratic and, therefore, legitimate. Certain criteria must be fulfilled: *all* members of a community must potentially have the *same* opportunity to contribute to the expression. These criteria originate once again from the reference to personality as the argument's foundation. Personality has the benefit of being *equally* ascribed to *all* participants. If consensus for a decision is not possible—and it is only because consensus is normally not possible that public authority is at all necessary—then the majority rule makes equally distributed decision-making possible.[72] Democratic decisions are the decisions of the ruled, not just decisions through which they have had the opportunity to express their view. *All* questions are to be decided upon

---

[72] W. Sadurski, *Equality and Legitimacy* (Oxford: Oxford University Press, 2008), 277–92. For a short critique of a unanimity rule: I. Shapiro, *The State of Democratic Theory* (Princeton: Princeton University Press, 2004), 16–19.

equally by *all* members: democratic universality in the sense of all decisions' need for legitimacy; democratic equality in the sense of an equal opportunity of participation; and democratic responsibility in the sense of a legally framed sanctioning mechanism are the minimum criteria for a collective will formation to qualify as democratic.[73]

But how do voluntaristic and rational elements relate to one another within the democratic process? Even though a democratic will is composed of individual contributions, it is nonetheless clear that these contributions make reference to a distinct, collective form of self-determination, and that both—the individual contributions and the collective form of self-determination—mutually constitute and define each other. The programme of the party I vote for and the state of political debate in my community shape my political opinion just as I help to shape the discourse through my participation. We might wonder whether these processes, as deliberative democratic theory conceives them, truly have the function to provide reasons and counter-reasons for a certain position, or whether their purpose is really to provide an opportunity to introduce certain positions so that they become identifiable. In any case a mechanism is required through which an independent, democratic will formation can take place. It is important in this regard to provide for procedures in which conflicting individual positions find common ground. The process of democratic decision-making is therefore constituted by, but also distinct from, a simple aggregation of individual decisions.[74] Rather, the process of political will formation already occurs at the democratic level. This raises the question of how far democratic will formation can or should assume an identity separate from the individual contributions that constitute it.

This problem can be nicely illustrated by the issue of the temporal frequency with which the democratic will is gauged, that is, the question of how often democratic elections should take place. We might first think that we should, for the sake of legitimacy, hold elections as often as possible, with only practical considerations requiring a minimum length of the term of office or legislature. But this assumption seems premature. For evidently the process of will formation needs a certain internal stabilization. Just as we do not ascribe a strong independent will to someone who permanently casts doubt upon his own opinion or constantly changes his views, it is also not the case that the democratic claim to legitimacy emerges through seamless

---

[73] For such a minimal account see C. Möllers, *Demokratie—Zumutungen und Versprechen* (Berlin: Wagenbach, 3rd ed 2012), 15–26.

[74] For a short and concentrated overview of this debate see J. Elster, 'Introduction', in J. Bohman, W. Rehg (eds.): *Deliberative Democracy* (Cambridge: Cambridge University Press, 1998), 3.

feedback to surveys or elections.[75] Conversely, however, the necessary independence of the democratic level from fresh acts of legitimacy has its limits. Although it is common in deliberative democratic theory to think of democratic representation as constant, idealized deliberation, this seems hardly possible without giving up the actual reference of the political process to its egalitarian foundation. Like every individual action, democratic legitimacy requires a break; an interruption of the expected course of action. As Hannah Arendt has stressed,[76] political action arises through disruptions of the anticipated course of events. Such turning points are, even beyond all questions of legitimacy, one of the greatest functional achievements of democratic systems. They allow for self-correction. Indeed, the system makes it legitimately possible through a change of government to condemn all previous democratic actions as wrong. Neither a too concentrated temporal timeframe nor complete independence from the individual sources of legitimacy is therefore appropriate as such. A specific election cycle is not deducible. It requires a democratic decision itself.

The same ambiguity applies to the question of the unity or diversity of the democratic subject. The need for a single democratic subject is often derived from the concept of democratic representation—indeed French constitutional law is an example. But the successful multiplication of democratic subjects in federal constitutional systems shows that this conclusion is not imperative.[77] If individuals simultaneously belong to different levels of polities it becomes necessary to organize these overlapping democratic subjects, eg the people of the municipality, the state, and the federation. We will analyse this problem while looking at the international level in Chapter 4. This experience with democratic federalism also entails an argument against excessive expectations of social cohesion among democratic subjects. Examples as different as India and Switzerland show that democratic systems can be quite heterogenous with regard to language, religion, and wealth, while problems stemming from these differences are not better solved by an authoritarian system of government.[78] We will have a closer look at this question while discussing the European Parliament.

---

[75] That is one reason why the web-driven idea of liquid feedback does not seem unproblematic for the design of democratic procedures.

[76] H. Arendt, 'Introduction into Politics', in *The Promise of Politics* (New York: Schocken, 2005), 93.

[77] Christoph Möllers, 'Multi-Level Democracy', 24 *Ratio Juris* (2011), 247.

[78] An empirically informed critique of the idea that divided societies could not introduce democracy is in I. Shapiro, *The State of Democratic Theory* (Princeton: Princeton University Press, 2004), Chap. 4.

Moreover, the question arises of *who should be included* in the *democratic subject*.[79] Democratic universality correlates with the members of a collective subject, but in modern states the members of the community, the citizens, are not identical with those that are subjected to the exercise of public authority in the community. Non-citizen residents have no right to vote, yet are subjected to multiple legal obligations such as paying taxes. From a democratic point of view, we might argue that it is up to the democratic community to define its own membership. Every democratic community is free to develop a certain identity to which not everyone belongs. But what is the justification for extending the public authority to non-members? First, we might argue that non-members voluntarily enter into the territory. In doing so they accept the prospect of living without the right to political membership in favour of other advantages for their own lives. Secondly, we may point out that certain exclusions from the democratic process are required to stabilize the process. As with the question of temporality, however, here too is a certain ambivalence to be accepted: a democratic will capable of making decisions presupposes—as is the case with the individual—that the democratic subject has arrived at a certain level of institutional identity. This identity, however, changes with the voluntary admission of new members. It does not follow from this insight that this identity ought to be renounced, but it does follow that this identity is subject to constant change and further development, so that the congruence between those who rule and the ruled does not erode.

How can we resolve this ambivalence? First, it seems necessary to acknowledge that the argument from democratic theory should replace the democratic decision. There is no universal rule of democratic inclusion and no universal democratic subject but rather a variety of such subjects, namely as peoples of democratic states, but also as part-peoples of states and communities.[80] An existing democratic subject must, however—as for all other questions—decide the issue of membership on its own.[81] In the legal systems examined here this insight finds expression in the fact that the democratic legislator decides upon questions of national citizenship.[82] Non-members, however, must have at least subjective individual, ie non-political, rights at their disposal when confronted with the public authority,

---

[79] With a comprehensive analysis of the concept of democratic citizenship: H. Brunkhorst, *Solidarität* (Frankfurt am Main: Suhrkamp, 2002), 79.

[80] A theoretical analysis is I. Roellecke, *Gerechte Einwanderungs-und Staatsangehörigkeitskriterien* (Baden-Baden: Nomos, 1999).

[81] For an examination of the normative character of citizenship: H. Brunkhorst, *Solidarity* (Cambridge: MIT Press, 2005), 167.

[82] For German law: Federal Constitutional Court, *Ausländerwahlrecht I*, BVerfGE 83, 37, 52. For US law art. I sec. 8 cl. 3 US Constitution.

for the arguments which may justify a certain degree of exclusion from democratic membership do not hold for individual rights. In addition, individual rights may consolidate and become an important step on the way to full democratic membership, such as through protection against discrimination in democratic participation rights. The process of citizens' rights in the EU shows such an evolutionary pattern.[83]

Democratic self-determination is also general. It may not exclude any topic, lest it turn into a sectoralized heteronomy. From this, it follows that democratic decisions require an institutional forum with general powers. If decisions concern the distribution of freedom across the whole political community, they should not be allocated to various institutions, even if each of these separately meets democratic standards. Every departmentalization of decision-making poses a threat to democratic legitimacy, because competing spheres of freedom cannot be balanced against each other and because institutionally insulated political disputes tend to become one-sided and even radicalized.[84] As a consequence that is incompatible with the idea of democratic legitimacy, preferential treatment of special interests may arise, particularly if only certain interests are involved in a decision-making process that affects everyone. The democratic process requires an institutional locus of universal competence.

Democratic legitimacy's relation to law reveals a characteristic difference from individual legitimacy. A collective act constitutes an expression of the democratic will only when it results from a process that has respected the democracy-constituting standards we have just identified. These rules form part of the legal system. Unlike individual will, the legal order does not presuppose a democratic will because that will can emerge only in some institutional form. This has many implications, one of which is important for the temporal structure of democratic decisions within a constitutional system. We have seen that an individual preference is already completed and even impeded before it encounters the law. Hence, the legal order adopts a *retrospective* view of this preference. A democratic decision, in contrast, finds expression only through legal institutional channels. Of course, revolutionary actions, populist upheavals, public demonstrations, or organized actions of civil society against an authoritarian regime may occur that have a perfect claim to political legitimacy. But within the framework of an already established constitutional order the democratic character of a decision

---

[83] A sceptical perspective towards the development of con-federative structures in the EU is C. Schönberger, *Unionsbürger* (Tübingen: Mohr-Siebeck, 2005).

[84] For this aspect in more detail, see: C. R. Sunstein, 'Deliberative Trouble, Why Groups go to Extremes', 110 *Yale Law Journal* (2000), 71, 85, whose approach is based on a deliberative theory of democracy and informed by Federalist ideas.

must be expressed by an egalitarian political community, and the constitution of this community depends on constitutional standards. To be sure, protests and political actions must be allowed to make a democratic system possible, but they are strictly speaking not expressions of a democratic will. As a democratic will is formed through procedures, there is no strictly democratically legitimate decision outside the legal order, because only formal procedures can actually guarantee the chance of the kind of equal participation that we may call democratic. For this reason, the legal form of democratic legitimacy has a temporal structure that differs from that of individual legitimacy. As democratic legitimacy is produced in the form of law, its legal expression is forward-looking, *prospective*. It aims at designing the future.

Finally, to make any sense of the idea of democratic will-*formation*, the content of the democratic decision must ultimately be left open by the procedure that constitutes the democratic subject. The democratic legitimacy of the substance of a specific decision is therefore—unlike the case of individual legitimacy—not based on the application of a rule. This entails an argument in favor of a very limited legalization of democratic procedures. The democratic process depends on a consensus on the procedure, but also on dissent on the merits.[85] This significance of conflicts for a democracy is sometimes underestimated. But it is obvious that the whole democratic procedure would be useless under the condition of a perpetual consensus. The democratic process is fundamentally called into question through an excess of consensus or even the appearance of such.[86] The striving for consensus, harmony, or integration potentially leads to a de-democratization, when political conflicts remain, but are no longer openly debated.

Legal procedures are democratically legitimate if they express the will of all members of the subject of legitimacy in a general, equal, forward-looking way. In addition, democratic will formation must gain independence from the individual contributions by which it is constituted. The institutional conditions for legitimate *legislation* have already been suggested here.

d) Limitations of democratic power: the 'right to have rights' as the right to a procedure

If the general scope of subjective rights must be defined democratically, one might wonder if there are protective limits to this power of definition. A technical answer could refer to the supremacy of the constitution, which limits the democratic process by protecting basic rights. This reference does not solve the underlying theoretical problem, however.

---

[85] M. Neves, *Zwischen Themis und Leviathan: Eine schwierige Beziehung* (Baden-Baden: Nomos, 2000), 108.

[86] See C. Mouffe, 'For an Agonistic Public Sphere', in O. Enwezor (ed.), *Democracy Unrealized* (Ostfildern: Hatje Cantz Verlag, 2002), 87.

Respect for each individual capacity to form a free will is both a precondition for individual, and a consequence of, democratic self-determination. Some substantial restrictions on democratic decisions result from this insight, which may help to define a basic status of each individual in a legal order. This definition is not one of the central topics of this study, but it has some ramifications for the concept of separated powers. What might help us to get a brief glance of these ramifications is what Hannah Arendt famously called a 'right to rights'.[87] For instance, the absolute prohibition of torture can be justified in this way, because torture reduces a person to his body, thereby denying him the ability to make a decision and to claim a right. Torture equates persons with non-persons.

In the context of our search for a concept of separated powers, however, *procedural* guarantees are more relevant than substantial restrictions. A procedure through which a person can bring up restrictions of his or her rights conveys individual legitimacy. In the following section we will explain why judicial review corresponds to this type of legitimacy. The institutional guarantee of such a procedure, therefore, belongs to the minimum standard for the protection of rights against the democratic process. The claim to such a procedure is inalienable as long as the legal order recognizes individual personality. Nobody can lose this procedural right, even by committing serious wrongdoings. Otherwise, the sanction on, for example, a terrorist assassinator, would have to be the complete loss of his status of a person protected by law. In fact, after 9/11 the exclusion of terrorists from any judicial review was a standard procedure in many democratic states. From our point of view this means nothing less than an exclusion from the community of legal persons; a loss of the right to have rights.[88] There are many reasons why this is unacceptable and undermines what we would define as a minimal standard.[89] If the exclusion from independent review were justified, there would no longer be any reason to treat terrorists according to any rules at all. Denying legal personality does not just imply abridging some rights. It negates the possibility of having any rights at all by means of a procedure. It would as a matter of coherence not even be clear why not dispossess or kill such persons, a consequence that

---

[87] For her this right consists of the right to membership in a political community: H. Arendt, 'Es gibt nur ein einziges Menschenrecht', 4 *Die Wandlung* (1949), 754 (760).

[88] K. Scheppele, 'The migration of anti-constitutional ideas: the post-globalization of public law and the international state of emergency', in S. Choudry (ed.), *The Migration of Constitutional Ideas* (Cambridge: Cambridge University Press, 2006), 347 (362–71); T. Stahlberg, H. Lahmann, 'Humpty-Dumpty, the War on Terror, and the Power of Preventive Detention in the United States, Israel and Europe', 59 *The American Journal of Comparative Law* (2011), 1051.

[89] A consistent argument from autonomy is developed in A. Walen, 'A unified theory of detention, with application to preventive detention of suspected terrorists', 70 *Maryland Law Journal* (2011), 871.

is realized by the politics of targeted killings. But even if a complete loss of rights were an appropriate legal sanction, such an extreme sanction, if it were not to hit anybody by some institutional accident, could be imposed only after some kind of procedure, which for its part would presuppose acceptance of some rights-based status.

The relevance of this consideration is obvious in the fight against terrorism, especially by the United States. Having people arrested solely by reference to presumable danger without any due process is incompatible with any legal system that claims to respect individual self-determination. The US Supreme Court seems to share this basic insight.[90] As a result, the court recognizes a general right to such a procedure, irrespective of the nationality of the claimant. The question of which standards of judicial independence are sufficient within a military context remains widely contested, however.[91] As we shall see, the establishment of politically independent courts is a centerpiece of the procedural recognition of individual personality, irrespective of their belonging to a certain democratic community. In conclusion: the right to rights requires a procedure to independently review infringements of freedom.

3. Law and politics

At some point, individual and democratic legitimacy—procedures of individual and collective self-determination—may conflict with or contradict one other. But their procedural mechanisms are designed to deal with such problems. The definition of these mechanisms, as will be shown, is the central task of a doctrine of separated powers, which recognizes both forms of legitimacy to an equal degree.[92] It is at this point important to understand, however, that both forms of legitimacy are not only equally valuable, but mutually dependent and reinforcing. The justificatory capacities of individual and democratic procedures do not operate at the expense of one another. Democratic and individual legitimacy do not play in a zero sum game. The democratic process can claim legitimacy only if the rules that guarantee equal participation are observed.[93] Inversely, the scope of individual liberties needs a democratic procedure because it potentially

---

[90] At least a benevolent reading supports this assumption: *Hamdi v Rumsfeld*, 542 U.S. 507 (2004). Cf., eg, G. R. Stone, 'National security v. civil liberties', *95 California Law Review* (2007), 2203.

[91] *Boumediene v Bush*, 128 U.S. S.C. 2229 (2008); cf. H. H. Koh, 'The case against military commissions', *96 American Journal of International Law* (2002), 337.

[92] J. Habermas, 'On the internal relation between the rule of law and democracy', in J. Habermas, *The Inclusion of the Other* (Cambridge: MIT Press, 1998), 253–64.

[93] See above p. 71–76.

concerns everybody.[94] As a result, any act of public authority must live up to both modes of legitimacy. No binding decision may refer *only* to *one* mode. Public action cannot renounce its commitment to individual rights just because of its democratic legitimacy. By the same token, the appeal to an individual right cannot replace a democratic definition of its scope.[95] In terms of constitutional theory, this insight defines the relation between *law and politics*. The political process ends with the democratic creation of a law. This decision receives its legitimacy through the observance of constitutional rules. Vice-versa, constitutional law receives its legitimacy by opening itself to change through a democratic, political process. Legitimate law is, in a democracy, politically alterable law. These considerations enable us to establish a more systematic coherence in the above criteria for individual and democratic procedures. The two types of legitimacy reveal three distinct institutional features that are crucial for the subsequent development of a model of separated powers.

As a first feature, there is the *scope* of the decisions: individual legitimacy emerges by reference to individual right-holders in an exclusive context defined in time and space. An individual right is asserted not as such, but with regard to a specific act. The issue at stake is not the general right to demonstrate (which would be a political demand) but the possibility of holding a specific demonstration at a defined time and place; it is not about a 'liberal' employment law but about the specific right to keep one's job. By contrast, democratic decisions are *inclusive*. They potentially affect everybody; they create general spheres of freedom and obligation between all members of a democratic community.

The second feature concerns the *temporal orientation*.[96] The legal protection of individual freedom establishes a retrospective relationship between the legal system and the asserted act of individual self-determination. This act is acknowledged by the law, but not created by it. The law addresses such a matter when the realization of self-determination has already been inhibited. By contrast, democratic decisions function *prospectively*; they are constituted through the legal system. Democratic decisions aspire to bring future change.

Thirdly, there is a difference with regard to the *degree of legalization* itself. Here, an important asymmetry within the legal system emerges. The scope

---

[94] See above p. 68–69.

[95] For a critique even with regard to the right to self-ownership: L. Ypi, 'Self-Ownership and the State: A Democratic Critique', *Ratio (new series)* (2011), 91; for the international context: Chapter 4, Introduction.

[96] G. Husserl, *Recht und Zeit* (Frankfurt am Main: Klostermann, 1955), 55; H. Hofmann, *Das Recht des Rechts, das Recht der Herrschaft und die Einheit der Verfassung* (Berlin: Duncker & Humblot, 1998), 43; F. Ost, *Le Temps du Droit* (Paris: Éditions Odile Jacob, 1999) 71–5, 165–74.

of individual self-determination in the process of individual legitimacy must be conclusively defined through law. The state can claim legitimacy for its decisions only once it has given the individual 'his due' in a manner defined by law. The democratic will formation, on the other hand, must be kept open through law. Otherwise, we could not speak of a democratic process in the first place. Only the democratic procedures shall be defined through law, not the content of the democratic decision.

These three criteria are interconnected. They build a continuous scale, not cleanly separable poles. The demand for law does not always concern either potentially everybody in general or one individual in a specific situation, nor can every decision be either entirely politicized or completely determined by law. Rather, there must also be middle-range decisions, which connect democratic and individual legitimacy, thereby making democratic decisions concrete without immediately affecting only one individual. In this way, the more clearly individual self-determination is affected, the more a scale develops on which the law becomes more and more determinate. This scale also has a temporal dimension—from the future-orientated democratic decision to the retrospective judgment of a single case. Here, one can discern the path of a law-making circle from the legislature, through the executive, to the judicial decision of a single case. Personal autonomy appears as a driver of legitimacy on both ends of this scale: once among members of the political community, once among individuals.

III. THE THREE POWERS: A MODEL FROM LEGITIMACY

1. *Law-making as reference point*

These considerations will finally lead us now into a concept of the three powers. Before that, we still need to respond to one more preliminary question: what is the common reference point of the three powers and what function is fulfilled by their tripartite organization? In traditional theories of the separation of powers the first question was answered semantically with reference to the exercise of 'power' or 'force', *pouvoir*, *Gewalt*. The three powers yield power. But this answer is too unspecific for many reasons, even if we concede that all powers exercise public authority. First, other parts of society—which do not belong to the state—can also exercise power.[97] Secondly, the concept of power seems underdetermined. It evades a more accurate description of the factors at work. Finally, we would not even know how to assess methodologically different quantities of power.

---

[97] Foucault seems to misunderstand the techniques of legal power when he identifies sovereignty and law. But much of the older private law tradition did not need political sovereignty to define the way power is yielded.

These objections call for a different concept: in a legal model of separated powers, the task of the three branches is not the exercise of power, but the *creation of law.*[98] For, contrary to the Weberian concept of public authority as the equivalent to the state monopoly on legitimate power, the state and other public authorities certainly do not have a monopoly on physical violence and not at all on other forms of sometimes legitimate power such as economic power. But public authorities may claim, if not a monopoly, at least a central role in the creation of legal standards.[99] This is perhaps best illustrated by the case of the European Union, which has neither army nor police force, yet acts as a law-making machine that depends *completely* upon external national enforcement mechanisms. A rejoinder to this example could be that public authority cannot assert itself without a physical monopoly on violence; in the case of the EU the monopoly on physical power of the member states. But this would lead us to a concept of political authority which explained authority purely in terms of unilateral command, rather than at least partly in terms of acceptance.[100]

On the other hand, conceptualizing the three powers as mere agents of law-making sounds quite formalistic. We may think of the role of a head of government, particularly in foreign policy, in which the creation of legal norms is still the exception—or we might think of political pressure sustained by the military or the police or just by a prime minister who also acts as the party boss. Clearly, the state also exercises power with instruments other than law. We might call this informal state action. Should we dismiss such action from our inquiry into the separation of powers? The following differentiations might help describe our take on the problem.

Many areas of the informal exercise of political power aim to produce legally relevant decisions and are thereby also covered by a concept that relates separation of powers to law-making. Most political exchange between the electorate, parliament, and government is informal, and we will soon see that one key function of a working system of separated powers is to *protect* such areas of political informality from juridification.[101] But informality becomes more questionable when it is no longer directed towards and does not result in a legally formalized decision, for in this case the state exercises a form of power which is opaque, difficult to oppose, and for which there is no form of procedural accountability. This is the case

---

[98] The following arguments are based on Hans Kelsen and Adolf Merkl.

[99] Similarly understanding the power monopoly on the basis of Kelsen as the power to make law: M. Troper, 'Le monopole de la contrainte légitime—Légitimité et legalité dans l'Etat moderne', in H. Haller (ed.), *Festschrift Winkler* (Wien, New York: Springer, 1997), 1195.

[100] H.L.A. Hart, *The Concept of Law* (Oxford: Oxford University Press 2nd ed 1994), 50–78.

[101] See Chapter 2, III, 2.

of a political official threatening unspecific 'sanctions'. However, the legal system may apply rules that limit this kind of malevolent informality. For example: a coalition agreement between political parties to form a government with a specific programme is not a sufficient legal basis to abridge a fundamental right. A parliamentary statute is required. It may then cause a certain uneasiness that this parliamentary law is not 'genuinely' made in parliament, but merely represents the implementation of the coalition agreement. The connection of these different layers of informal and formal decisions, however, is part of a democratic system in which political parties are responsible for the merits of the political process. What success the relevant actors have in keeping decisions in the right forum, such as parliament, is therefore not necessarily an issue for the law but for the institutional self-confidence of the actors, such as in the case of a parliamentary majority vis-à-vis its government.

Perhaps the most important mechanism to reformalize this kind of problematic informality is the protection of rights by courts. Clearly, informal action potentially curtails subjective rights, such as the discriminatory remark by a government spokesperson against a certain minority, or police threats of violence. But when they are interpreted as an abridgment, such actions may be subject to judicial review. In this case they are reformalized and reintroduced into the legal system. Separation of powers, though focused on the formal side of law-making, has to take both into account: the protection of a formless political process and the institutional option to reformalize informal political or even private power.[102]

There is a *second objection* to our assumption that the concept of separated powers refers to law-making powers: it seems rather uncommon to think of all three powers as law-*makers*. Do courts make law or do they merely apply the law? The continental legal tradition has established a distinction between making and applying the law that is theoretically rooted in the difference between will and action.[103] The enacted 'willed' law is applied and enforced by the monarch and thereby becomes 'real'. The legislature wills; the executive acts. This distinction is influential to the present day, in everyday legal language as well as in legal theory.[104] This dichotomy, however, is incapable of conceiving a coherent distinction between administration and

---

[102] See Introduction.

[103] This is quite explicit in classical democratic theory: J.-J. Rousseau, *Contrat Social [1762]* (Paris: Gallimard, 1969), III/1; I. Kant, 'Metaphysik der Sitten, Rechtslehre', *Werke* [ed Weischedel] (Darmstadt: Wissenschaftliche Buchgesellschaft, 1983), § 45–6.

[104] See, for example, K. Günther, *Der Sinn für Angemessenheit* (Frankfurt am Main: Suhrkamp, 1992). Not explicitly, but in principle: R. Alexy, *Theorie der juristischen Argumentation* (Frankfurt am Main: Suhrkamp, 1983), 261.

court, which both only 'apply' the law;[105] an assumption that seems less than convincing and methodically rather naive for both. It presupposes that the application of a general norm to a case is effectively self-explanatory and requires no personal contribution from the 'applier'. But the practice of adjudicating does not work like a logical syllogism[106] which is simply only true or false. This we have known since Kant's conception of the power to judge[107]—underlined by both American Legal Realism and the German *Freirechtsschule*.[108] Precisely these parts of the legal system that interest us, namely organizational and procedural questions, are omitted in such an account. If a general rule were to determine its own application, procedural rules would be useless, as it would be irrelevant who decides. If, on the contrary, the structure of procedure has any significance for the content of the decision, substantial legal norms cannot by themselves transport their own standards of application. Therefore the application of a legal norm in a certain situation should be understood as a form of making new law.[109] Courts and administrations make law. This is, by the way, one of the very few fundamental insights that both Legal Realism and Kelsenian Formalism share.

Giving up the categorical distinction between law-making and applying the law does not suggest that legal rules have no determining effect. There exists no absolute hiatus between rule and rule application, as critics of democratic constitutional systems from Schmitt to Agamben have claimed in a sort of vulgar deconstruction.[110] The mere fact that a constitutional rule may first prompt somebody to assert his right illustrates this well enough. There is no doubt that norms are not, in a strict sense, determinate. The standard complaint about legal indeterminacy seems strange though, given the fact that its negation—determinacy—not only seems impossible, but would mean the end of what we call a system of legal decision-making. Determinacy of law would be a computational phenomenon, not an ideal of

---

[105] The problem is rarely addressed, so it is not surprising that it is made clear in the context of a critique of the distinction between law-making and law-application discourses: T. Lieber, *Diskursive Vernunft und formelle Gleichheit* (Tübingen: Mohr, 2007), 206–7.

[106] See the detailed analysis regarding the parallel between judgment and legal operationalization of S. Meder, *Urteilen* (Frankfurt am Main: Klostermann, 1999), 131.

[107] I. Kant, *Kritik der Urteilskraft*, in *Werke* [ed. Weischedel] (Darmstadt: Wissenschaftliche Buchgesellschaft, 1983).

[108] An example is C. Schmitt, *Gesetz und Urteil* (Berlin: Liebmann, 1912).

[109] Seminal for this insight: A. Merkl, *Die Lehre von der Rechtskraft entwickelt aus dem Rechtsbegriff* (Leipzig: Deuticke, 1923), 81.

[110] Examples: C. Schmitt, *Gesetz und Urteil* (Berlin: Liebmann, 1912); G. Agamben, *Ausnahmezustand* (Frankfurt am Main: Suhrkamp, 2004). More differentiated: J. Derrida, 'Force of Law', in *Deconstruction and the possibility of justice* (New York: Routledge, 1992), 3–67.

a rule of law. In any case, we have seen that if norms were determinate we would not need the whole law-producing apparatus we are interested in here. The question of a legitimate system of separated powers stems from the fact that norms are ambiguous and their implementation requires a complex system of reviews and controls. This insight, however, is not identical with any fundamental scepticism of the possibility of legal meaning as such; a scepticism that seems to have more adherents in critical legal theory today than in the general philosophical theory of meaning.[111] It is true that texts do not have an immanent meaning, as formalist lawyers often seem to assume. The meaning ascribed to a legal text emerges from a practice of interpretation which the text cannot itself determine. But that does not mean that the law is not capable of stabilizing such practices through process, the training of legal practitioners, or even sanctions.[112] How intensively the use of the law is shaped by legal texts is gauged quite differently in different legal systems.[113] But this does not as a result absolutely question the binding force of norm texts on the one hand without denying that the practice of administrations and courts generates new, more specific legal commitments on the other. Courts and administrations are bound by law, and they also make new law. In this way all three powers function as generators of law, though in different forms shaped by the type of legitimacy they claim. This will now allow us to typify the three traditional powers—legislative, judicial, and executive—from the perspective of a theory of legitimacy.

2. The legislature

If we apply our preliminary considerations to a traditional pattern of separation of powers, it becomes clear that the *legislature* institutes democratic legitimacy by articulating an autonomous democratic self-determination. The legislature initiates and organizes a democratic decision-making process that generates general, future-orientated legal decisions. The parliament is the institutional manifestation of this model in democratic states. Parliaments are organized in a variety of ways in different legal systems. They have a variety of decision-making processes and are elected in similarly varied ways. This illustrates the open understanding of democracy, which

---

[111] See M. Klatt, *Making the Law Explicit* (Oxford: Hart, 2008), 278.

[112] L. Wittgenstein, *Philosophische Untersuchungen* (Oxford: Blackwell, 1953), § 201. For the need to establish sanctions to render this distinction plausible: R. B. Brandom, *Making it Explicit* (Cambridge: Harvard University Press, 1994), 42. But for the limited relevance of Wittgenstein for the legal debate: S. Hershovitz, 'Wittgenstein on Rules: The Phantom Menace', 22 *Oxford Journal of Legal Studies* (2002), 619.

[113] D. N. McCormick and R. Summers (eds.), *Interpreting Statutes* (Aldershot: Dartmouth, 1991); J. Goldsworthy (ed.), *Interpreting Constitutions* (Oxford: Oxford University Press, 2006).

allows for very different mechanisms beyond the indicated minimum standard. However, it neither excludes a comparative perspective nor prevents us from taking a closer look at some common features of parliamentarism.

Why are legislatures organized as *assemblies that meet in public*? Why would a general election not create enough legitimacy by just producing a single person as the legislator? We will take the need for democratic will formation as a starting point in examining the organization of the legislative power. It means—as we saw before—that the democratic will cannot be treated as a given, but has to be produced in a certain legal procedure. This includes the establishment of a contingency to decide one way or the other that serves precisely as the *formation* of the democratic will. A key function of the parliamentary process must therefore consist of voicing alternatives to the decided course of action and, thereby, clarifying the decision that is ultimately reached. In this way, the parliamentary process records that a different decision could have been made. A parliamentary legislature, in contrast to a single legislator, thereby also serves to document the differing minority opinions. This formal establishment of political alternatives can also affect subsequent elections.

Consequently, a serious exchange of rational arguments in parliament is not necessarily required. The status of parliamentary debate remains much disputed in constitutional theory, both over whether it is normatively required or even actually takes place.[114] But high demands on the level of the rationality of parliamentary deliberation regularly provoke disappointment and, eventually, tend to delegitimize parliamentarism.[115] According to the more voluntaristic interpretation of democratic self-determination we arrived at above, the debate is less a matter of rational deliberation than public documentation of political alternatives. The public presence of these alternatives allows us to speak of a democratic decision.

One central feature of the legislature consists in the very limited, yet constituent significance of the law for its functioning. Law ensures the democratic character of the legislative by providing rules for its creation and for parliamentary decision-making. There must be an electoral franchise according to standards of equal freedom, majority rule, and certain minority rights for the opposition. Beyond this, however, the legal standards must retreat and give space to the democratic will formation. This leads to a situation in which the rules that actually organize the parliamentary process are in many cases not legal rules, but rather internal conventions that can be

---

[114] J. W. Bessette, *The Mild Voice of Reason* (Chicago: University of Chicago Press, 1994); K. v. Beyme, *Der Gesetzgeber* (Opladen: Westdeutscher Verlag, 1997).

[115] See A. v. Bogdandy, 'Parlamentarismus in Europa: eine Verfalls-oder Erfolgsgeschichte?', *130 Archiv des Öffentlichen Rechts* (2005), 445.

changed or ignored at anytime. The functioning of these rules rests upon the same respect of the majority for the minority and the insight that today's majority may very well turn into tomorrow's minority.[116]

However, if the legislative decision-making process must be open in its results, what about other features of legislative law-making we have identified, such as its general scope and its future-orientation? Should these features enjoy the status of constitutional obligations that bind the legislator, or are they just weak normative suggestions? The former would, in fact, contradict the logic of democratic self-determination. The requirement of the 'generality of law' is frequently interpreted as a legal demand, and laws that address only one person are, as a result, constitutionally prohibited in some legal orders.[117] But democratic legislation cannot solely produce general codifications. The legislator must be allowed to regulate fragmented problems and details that concern particular parts of society. Comparative law shows that the requirement of generality is difficult to legalize.[118] This would turn a constitutional ideal against the necessary openness of the democratic process to compromise. The legislature *must* be authorized to make general decisions but does not *have* to make general decisions. The form of the law, not the universal content, is what counts.

Despite this, these features of legislative action are not just terminological gimmicks. This is demonstrated by the fact that many constitutional systems are familiar with written restrictions to retroactive or single-case legislation. Laws that directly address a specific individual or regulate one single issue are often seen as constitutionally problematic. The same goes for laws that retroactively address terminated issues. A law condemning a particular person X to a prison sentence would most probably be prohibited in many constitutional orders.[119] But, as we will see, such phenomena are often more precisely framed as a matter of basic rights than as a problem of separated powers.

So what is still acceptable from a separation of powers point of view? If we cannot construct a simple rule or a clear line, there is at least a general obligation of the legislative to make decisions that need the other powers, the executive and the judicial branch, for further implementation. Self-executive laws seem dubious. The legislature must not pre-empt the

---

[116] That such rules can be a threat to the majority rule can be seen in the US Senate: see Senate Rule XXII concerning the so-called 'filibuster'.

[117] H. Hofmann, 'Das Postulat der Allgemeinheit des Gesetzes', in C. Starck (ed.), *Die Allgemeinheit des Gesetzes* (Göttingen: Vandenhoeck & Ruprecht, 1987), 9.

[118] C. Möllers, *Gewaltengliederung* (Tübingen: Mohr Siebeck, 2005), 107.

[119] Such laws, so-called 'private bills', used to be quite common in the Anglo-Saxon legal tradition. See M. Weber, *Wirtschaft und Gesellschaft*, (Tübingen: Mohr, 5th ed 1980), 499.

decision-making contributions of the other powers. If a legislator delivers a criminal sentence to a single person, this circumvents the individualizing effects of the prosecution and court procedure. Such a constellation is problematic because the democratic will, the common form of expression of all citizens, takes on the case of a single individual. In such a case the legislature selects a rule for one person that excludes everybody else from its effect. This means that there is no general justification even if there was a general procedure. That this soft standard of generality cannot be understood too strictly is underlined by another argument: legislatures can regulate too specifically, but they can also regulate too generally. If legislative rules are too specific they ignore the contributions of the other branches and curtail individual freedom, as shown. If the legislature regulates too generally, on the other hand, it cedes too much of its power to the other branches and adds too little democratic legitimacy to the whole decision-making process.[120]

The necessity to keep the democratic will formation open casts doubt upon mechanisms in which the legislature is subject to permanent and formalized external control beyond judicial review. Such mechanisms are becoming more common in many constitutional systems. They are part of contemporary ideas of governance[121] that endorse, for instance, auditing procedures.[122] However, whether the practical necessity and the effects of a democratic law can genuinely be assessed by technocratic means seems questionable.[123] From the perspective of democratic legitimacy, it is not convincing to overrun the legislative with additional procedures, which restrict the openness of its decision-making process. 'Norm review councils' and similar institutions seem redundant as well as undemocratic, because their standard of review can hardly escape the political preferences that backed (or opposed) the law under review.

Nonetheless, to fulfil its task the legislative must also be able to establish an internal division of labour and features of specialization. As the legislature is potentially responsible for every general political decision, this ability constitutes one of the main problems of parliamentary organization, for democratic legitimacy can be claimed only by the legislator as a whole: single members of parliament or groups of members or committees are, indeed, directly elected, but only the plenum can claim democratic

---

[120] See Chapter 3, I., 2.

[121] C. Möllers, 'European Governance—Meaning and Value of a Concept', 43 *Common Market Law Review* (2006), 314–33 (314–16).

[122] M. Power, *The Audit Society* (New York: Oxford University Press, 1999).

[123] For a critical assessment of the German case: P. Blum, Wege zu besserer Gesetzgebung. Gutachten für den 65. Deutschen Juristentag, *Verhandlungen des 65. Deutschen Juristentages. Gutachten. Volume 1.* (München: C.H. Beck, 2004).

legitimacy. Only all the parliamentarians serve as a representation of the democratic subject. But what can they all do together? As John Stuart Mill remarked: 'there is a distinction between the function of making laws, for which a numerous popular assembly is radically unfit, and that of getting good laws made, which is its proper duty, and cannot satisfactorily be fulfilled by any other authority.'[124]

Therefore, the legislature's informal contact with the executive and its proximity to lobbyists seem unobjectionable in principle. The legislative does not have to be the place where laws are actually written. It should be the place, however, where the social demand for regulation and the technical expertise of lobbies and the executive arrive at an egalitarian and public political process. Nevertheless, problems remain because the production of laws and the political and technical cognitive ability of the legislature can become too far separated from each other. The internal organization into committees is therefore particularly important and must be determined by the legislature itself. However, the danger is always present that committees could take control and form informal, sectoralized centers of power without adequate legitimacy. It is most pronounced within the US system,[125] but can likewise be clearly observed in the European Parliament.[126] Only critical vigilance from the outside, by the electoral public, can restrict such asymmetries. A constitutional rule beyond the formal decision-making right of the majority of the plenum would be undemocratic. The internal organization of the legislative should remain its very own affair.

Another form of democratic legislation is conceivable and, indeed, is practised in many democracies—*the plebiscite*. From a standpoint of democratic theory, the problem with plebiscites lies in the fact that they do not allow for the same level of independence in democratic will formation as the parliamentary procedure. Plebiscites lack an institutional arena where a decision can be debated, modified, and compared with others. This leads to the question-answer structure of the plebiscite and the problem of who is authorized to pose the question in the first place. This structure privileges those who take the initiative in making a decision, which is not the case in a parliamentary procedure. Moreover, plebiscites do not allow for compromise. Instead, they intensify the politicization of the issue. This is not a loss in itself, but it requires the procedure to be embedded in a representative

---

[124] Quoted in W. Wilson, *Congressional Government: A Study in American Politics* (Boston, New York: Houghton Mifflin Co, 1885), 115.

[125] For an impressive description of the Congressional Committees see W. Wilson, *Congressional Government: A Study in American Politics* (Boston, New York: Houghton Mifflin Co, 1885).

[126] J. von Achenbach, *Das Mitentscheidungsverfahren des Art. 294 AEUV als demokratisches Gesetzgebungsverfahren der Europäischen Union, insbesondere im Bereich der Biomedizin und Humanbiotechnologie* (Heidelberg: Diss. jur., 2012), 172 (240).

structure. This is nothing unusual. The US, Switzerland, and France—all old democratic traditions—use plebiscites. All the same, in these systems, parliamentary legislation remains crucial to the legislative process, thus giving evidence of the primacy of an independent democratic will formation. One may recognize a certain mistrust of the independence of democratic self-determination in the institution of the plebiscite. Plebiscites seem to express a specific understanding of democratic freedom that gives greater weight to individual contributions than the representative system. This distrust is not convincing as a matter of theory, but it has to be respected. It may be especially appropriate in political systems in which the electoral process does not lead to palpable political change, as in Switzerland. As we shall see in Chapter 4, plebiscites are especially appropriate in situations in which the parliamentary process is also subject to specific institutional limitations, as in the case of parliamentary treaty-ratifications.[127]

When the legislative claim to democratic legitimacy results from its compliance with certain egalitarian rules, the question arises of who should guarantee this compliance. The rules designing the legislative process must be enforced even against the legislature, unless constitutional traditions are perceived as sufficient, as has long been the case in Great Britain. Protecting the legislative process from itself is therefore an important rationale for a judicially enforceable supremacy of constitutional law. Against the background of this insight, we will subsequently discuss constitutional review regarding the separation of powers in Chapter 3.[128]

3. The judiciary

Judicial law-making is located at the other end of our legitimacy spectrum. The judiciary is expected to make individualized decisions that derive their justification from an individual claim to self-determination. Therefore, the decisions of the judiciary are based on the initiative and the will of the individual—the judiciary neither forms its own institutional will nor does it act upon its own initiative. This stipulation captures the astoundingly consistent form, from a historical as well as from a comparative perspective, of decision-making by courts.[129] Courts adjudicate individualized cases on external initiative, retrospectively. Judicial decision-making requires

[127] See Chapter 4, II., 4.

[128] See Chapter 3, II.

[129] For a comparative analysis of judicial practice: M. Cappelletti, *The Judicial Process in Comparative Perspective* (Oxford: Clarendon Press, 1989), 30; M. Shapiro, *Courts* (Chicago: University of Chicago Press, 1981), 1, 28. The retrospective orientation of judicial law-making has been stressed by L. L. Fuller, *The Morality of Law* (New Haven: Yale University Press, rev. ed., 1964), 55–8.

independence from the political process. At the same time, the sole basis of judicial decision is the law.

Traditionally, in continental legal systems at least, the legitimacy of the courts is founded on their commitment to legal standards. This consideration also has its—albeit somewhat limited—worth in the model developed here. It is true that 'the law' should be the only basis for judicial decision-making; that courts should not construct their own institutional preferences. This reference, however, is obviously not enough to fully understand and justify the features of judicial decision-making. Otherwise we would not have to distinguish at all between courts and the executive, which is also bound by the law. Precisely because we cannot be sure how intensively legal provisions determine decisions, the claim to legitimacy needs complementary considerations to become fully plausible, through an individualizing judicial procedure. This procedure shall ensure that the self-determination of the plaintiff can be transformed into legitimacy of the court. But do our criteria in fact provide a proper description of judicial activity? Do courts really adjudicate individual cases retrospectively on the basis of the law?

The temporal structure lends itself most readily to our description of judicial decision-making. Courts invariably rule on an external initiative and thus on a situation which has already occurred. We must emphasize the significance of this often neglected standard, particularly in contrast to theories that derive the legitimacy of courts purely from their commitment to previously defined legal standards. The peculiarity of this feature is rarely observed: by organizing a court system, a state establishes a whole apparatus that becomes active only when someone decides to make use of it. But if the action of the court is permissible only in this case—no plaintiff, no judge—then the legitimacy of judicial decision-making cannot be understood without recourse to the individual autonomy of the plaintiff. To be sure, there are courts—such as the US Supreme Court—which have the discretionary authority to take on cases as they please. This invites us to look for its political agenda. But even then it remains true that the chosen case could be chosen only because a plaintiff had brought it to court.

Normally, courts adjudicate completed events retrospectively. By contrast, procedural law regularly makes any judicial intervention in ongoing issues difficult for the claimant. In harmony with the logic of legitimacy set out here, courts rule on injunctions only if and to the extent that there would otherwise be no proper recourse for the plaintiff. Only the threat of an irreparable loss entitles the court to intervene in these cases. This form of injunctive relief is especially problematic with respect to complaints filed against the executive. In this constellation, instead of controlling the executive's decision, the judiciary threatens to *replace* it.[130] Therefore it is no accident that this form of recourse is exceptional in most legal systems.[131] The closer the judiciary intervenes in and replaces an ongoing executive decision-making process, the weaker its claim to legitimacy becomes.

The pure commitment of the courts to the law is initially ensured by their political independence. This is a very old organizational feature that remains essentially undisputed, though its concrete implication for the organization of a court system varies widely, referring to different features, from the appointment procedure to the organization of the court system. Nonetheless, the idea that courts adjudicate only on the basis of legal norms has been subjected to methodological critique for more than a century.[132] The critiques of textualism and judicial independence mutually reinforce each other. Obviously nobody can rule out the possibility that judges actually do adjudicate based on their own political or other preferences.[133] Legal history is full of examples of politically biased courts. The question remains what these examples can tell us. To begin with, how the court ought to adjudicate a case remains contested, otherwise there would be no case. It is therefore difficult to determine where the law ends and where political bias begins. This is especially true for constitutional law, which explicitly serves as a medium to express and to formulate political conflicts. As a result, empirical studies seeking to demonstrate the presence of political bias tend to struggle methodically with the role of legal reasons in their own argument.[134] Secondly, legal norms often allow for discretion in judicial decision-making. As a consequence, a politicized judge who blurs the distinction between law and politics, thereby endangering the legitimacy of both, is a threat to every constitutional system.[135] But there is no legal instrument to completely eliminate this threat. On the contrary, efforts to uncover the alleged politicization of the judiciary may even become a self-fulfilling prophecy, as the discussion in the United States suggests.[136] To be sure, courts are not

---

[130] See further, Chapter 3, III.

[131] For a comparative analysis of injunctive relief against administrative acts: G. Knoll, *Grundzüge eines europäischen Standards für den einstweiligen Rechtsschutz gegen Verwaltungsakte* (Berlin: Duncker & Humblot, 2002).

[132] This is the same argument as to the critique of textualism: Chapter 2, III., 1.

[133] For references, especially regarding the conservative judiciary in Germany, see D. Simon, *Die Unabhängigkeit des Richters* (Darmstadt: Wiss, Buchgesellschaft, 1975), 41, 104.

[134] I. Schulz-Schaeffer, 'Rechtsdogmatik als Gegenstand der Rechtssoziologie', 25 *Zeitschrift für Rechtssoziologie* (2004), 141; C. Möllers, 'Why there is no Governing with Judges', Manuscript (2012).

[135] M. Neves, *Verfassung und Positivität des Rechts in der peripheren Moderne* (Berlin: Duncker & Humblot, 1992).

[136] For an overview, see M. Kelman, *A Guide to Critical Legal Studies* (Cambridge: Harvard University Press, 1987).

case-solving automats, as has always been accepted even in the European continental tradition.[137] Significantly, however, in a power-separated system they are required to give reasons for all decisions exclusively by referring to legal arguments. It is this formal obligation that leads not to determinate decisions but to a form of legal reasoning that can generate a distinct logic beyond the political process. The fact that courts are not accountable to the political process does not contradict that legal rules are open to different interpretations. Rather, it is a consequence of the fact. To make sense of this interpretory task, the court is required to look at the case, not the political rule-maker. The alleged circle that courts may only apply the law, but that the law is only what courts proclaim it to be is at a closer look not a circle at all.[138] What we call 'law' is defined less by the idea of a determinate norm than by the form of the judicial procedure that works in a very specific way. It is the concept of law that is characterized by this procedural form.

But do courts decide on individualized issues? There are a variety of individualizing mechanisms in the judicial processes. The plaintiff is required to submit a well-defined complaint. The substantiation of a charge identifies and individualizes a specific issue. The entire process, from the hearing of the parties to the individual justification of the judgment, suggests that the judgment is meant to be a ruling for this one single issue only. Niklas Luhmann interpreted this form of individualization as a mechanism designed to prevent the politicization of judicial decision-making. The procedure indicates to the losing party that the decision was only about its own specific problem, which can hence neither be generalized nor politicized.[139] The party is prevented from turning its claim into a general issue. This is a functional, perhaps cynical, yet persuasive characterization of the judicial procedure, which is also compatible with a normative justification: courts should narrow the scope of their reasoning, first in order to engage intensively with the concerns of the plaintiff, and secondly to leave room for the democratic process and thus for the participation of those persons who did not participate in the judicial procedure. To individualize decisions is to prevent the plaintiff from externalizing his or her problem.[140] Tocqueville has already described this phenomenon precisely:

> If the judge had been empowered to contest the laws on the ground of theoretical generalities, if he had been enabled to open an attack or to pass a censure on the legislator, he would have played a prominent part in the

---

[137] This is the problematic basic assumption in much of Alec Stone Sweet, Governing with Judges. Constitutional Politics in Europe (Oxford: Oxford University Press, 2000), eg, p. 115.

[138] O. W. Holmes, 'The Path of the Law', 10 *Harvard Law Review* (1897), 457–78.

[139] N. Luhmann, *Legitimation durch Verfahren* (Darmstadt: Luchterhand, 1975), 121.

[140] The second aspect has been elaborated by C. R. Sunstein, *One Case at a Time* (Cambridge: Harvard University Press, 1999), 24.

political sphere; and as the champion or the antagonist of a party, he would have arrayed the hostile passions of the nation in the conflict. But when a judge contests a law applied to some particular case in an obscure proceeding, the importance of his attack is concealed from the public gaze, his decision bears upon the interest of an individual, and if the law is slighted it is only collaterally.[141]

We will see later how far this model is compatible with the special case of constitutional review.[142] But constitutional review is not the only challenge to our model: courts in the Anglo-Saxon legal realm have created an entire body of uncodified private law, the Common Law, without reference to or application of any statute.[143] Other high courts are expected to deliver more general rulings that give orientation to a multitude of future cases.

At the heart of Common Law rule-making lies the idea of a private property system which evolves best in the context of judicial coordination of two-party relationships, without the intervention of a political legislator. The law applied by the courts consists of other judgments; of precedents. In continental law such as in Germany or France, rulings of higher courts do not function very differently, even though they have no formal binding effect and the techniques of legal reasoning are different.[144] In any case, judicial precedence does not fit our scheme. It provides reasons that are *not* completely individualized yet remain applicable to other cases. How do we treat this certainly unexceptional phenomenon?[145]

Normal courts—as distinct from constitutional courts—tend to distinguish between two considerations: the scope of their rulings in a particular case and the legal principles they apply to the case. The whole professionalization of law, the making of an academic legal doctrine, rests precisely on this distinction. Distinguishing cases is impossible without some legal expertise on the one hand but, on the other, also requires the coexistence of judicial law-making and its individualizing effect.

Nevertheless, the question remains: how to assess the legitimacy of judicial law-making and the complementary lack of democratic legitimacy for judicial rules? To be sure, there is no generally satisfying solution to this problem. It can be solved more convincingly for some fields of law than for others. Various legal systems distinguish between the private law judge who

---

[141] A. de Tocqueville, 'Democracy in America [1835]' (Stilwell, KS: Digireads.com, 2007), 80–81.

[142] See Chapter 3, II.

[143] R. C. van Caenegem, *Judges, Legislators & Professors* (Cambridge: Cambridge University Press, 1987).

[144] S. Vogenauer, 'Sources of Law and Legal Method in Comparative Law', in Reimann;
R. Zimmermann (eds.), *Oxford Handbook of Comparative Law* (Oxford: Oxford University Press, 2006), 894–5.

[145] C. Schönberger, 'Höchstrichterliche Rechtsfindung und Auslegung gerichtlicher Entscheidungen', 71 *Veröffentlichungen der Vereinigung der Deutschen Staatsrechtslehrer* (2012), 296 (302 11).

is non-political and decides according to an internal logic of private law, and the public law, which has been created by the political rule-maker.[146] The true point of this highly problematic distinction is that the settlement of a legal dispute which exclusively concerns the spheres of two persons requires no further external, political justification, at least as long as the two persons are equally socially powerful. The idea at the very root of the judicial procedure, of voluntary mediation between equal parties, appears in this context.[147] If the judicial process concerns only the relation between two persons, a democratic rule may not be required for an independent judge to find a legitimate solution. This model makes some sense for individually negotiated contracts but is flawed in many other instances, for example in the context of power inequalities between contractual partners—employer and employee or landlord and tenant—or regarding the impact of the system of property rights on public interests. To be sure, private law is not apolitical. Legal questions, however, have a different scope and affect different levels of social inequality and therefore require different standards, which should be decided upon in democratic procedures. The more exclusive the matter under conditions of equal social power, the more persuasively judicial law-making can claim legitimacy.

In addition, courts are often asked to decide cases for which the legislator has refused to make rules. Legislative silence is legitimate, as long as the legislator observes and reacts to judicial decisions. Assuming the existence of a constitutional obligation of the legislator to make laws may be problematic in another respect.[148] This is also the reason why even Common Law systems provide plenty of illustration for political decision-making in the field of allegedly apolitical private law, as in consumer-protection or labour law on the one hand, and in the subsistence of legal areas not regulated by the democratic legislator, eg classical contract law. As a result, some areas of law have a better justification for judicial law-making than others do. In any case, the legislator must be able to correct a settled judicial practice.

How is it finally possible for a court to violate the principle of separation of powers? According to the concept developed here, not even fatuous, nonsensical, or anomalous interpretations of a statute or a precedent violate the separation of powers principle. Interpretive activism is often understood as a legislative activity of courts and considered a violation of an allegedly classical concept of separated powers. A court that reinterprets a statute seems to act like a legislator. This conclusion, however, is based on a fallacy:

---

[146] H. Hofmann, *Das Recht des Rechts, das Recht der Herrschaft und die Einheit der Verfassung* (Berlin: Duncker & Humblot, 1998).

[147] M. Shapiro, *Courts* (Chicago: University of Chicago Press, 1981), Chap. 1.

[148] See Chapter 3, II.

the idea of separated powers is a procedural principle. It does not provide any material standards for statutory interpretation. The nonsensical interpretation of a law or of a constitutional provision by a court may violate that law or the constitution for various reasons, but such an interpretation does not constitute a violation of any understanding of separated powers as long as the court still acts as a court within a judicial procedure. A violation of our principle can occur only if a court overrides procedural standards, by deciding without a plaintiff or intervening without cause in ongoing executive or legislative affairs. Interestingly, this view is generally not shared by constitutional courts, which, when a lower court has engaged in an anomalous legal interpretation, tend to declare this interpretation to be a breach of the principle of separated powers. Theoretically, this view is barely tenable. The difference between legislating and adjudicating is a procedural one. As a useful instrument to gain jurisdiction, however, this approach reaps institutional benefits: it expands the scope of constitutional review into the field of statutory interpretation. This is especially relevant in systems with specialized constitutional courts that are not empowered to review statutory legal questions. This move is equally important in certain federal systems in which constitutional courts may only apply federal law but use the separation of powers argument to review the jurisprudence of state law by state courts.[149]

The individualization of conflicts in judicial proceedings contributes significantly to the protection of individual rights. This is perhaps best illustrated by a branch of law that, at first sight, seems to have the opposite effect: criminal law. It would be a misconception to assume that the criminal procedure is only a means to protect state interest or the interests of actual or possible victims of crimes. Those interests could be protected much more efficiently and without any judicial procedure just with a completely administrative security apparatus. The primary function of criminal procedure is to protect the rights of the defendant: establishing his or her guilt is perhaps the purest example of what we have called individualization. The court's sentence refers to a specific event; one single action committed by one person in an exactly defined spatio-temporal context. Though leading to a sanction if guilt has been established, the procedure is most respectful of individual personality and deeds. The judicial criminal procedure acknowledges the defendant as a free person,[150] and allegations of any misconduct

---

[149] This is what happened in *Bush v Gore*, 531 US 98 (2000) when the majority struck down the decision of a state court concerning state law with regard to separation of powers.

[150] This is noted by G. W. F. Hegel, *Grundlinien der Philosophie des Rechts [1821]* (Frankfurt am Main: Suhrkamp, 2006), § 100.

require the exact identification of both the defendant's ability to act and the action under review.[151]

4. *The mysterious executive*

Within the present model, there seems to be no place for the executive, though it is traditionally labelled as the *second* power. It cannot be mapped onto either of the two types of legitimacy realized by the legislative and the judiciary. Yet the executive power assumes a *central* position, in the literal sense of the word, between the two other branches of government. It fills the gaps in regulatory scope, temporal orientation, and degree of juridification that emerge between the two poles of legislative and judicial law-making. The executive must mediate between and connect the two modes of legitimacy. Therefore, it is hardly surprising that legal scholarship has always struggled to grasp the concept of the executive and prefers to define it negatively as the part of the state that is neither the legislative nor the judiciary.[152] Furthermore, it is telling that there are openly contradictory ideals of executive action. On the one hand, constitutional theorists who assume a priority of politics over law like to see the executive as a regulating and therefore quasi-legislative entity. The opposite approach, which stresses the importance of the legalization of political action, places the executive close to the courts.[153] Different strategies of legal or political constitutionalism find their foothold in the concept of the executive.

The impression of ambivalence grows further when one considers the range of different operations assigned to the executive. On the one hand, there is the head of the government and the cabinet: acting politically; initiating legislation; and leading foreign affairs. On the other hand, there is the multitude of low-ranking officials making insulated decisions on defined questions without much (if any) discretion. A conceptual response to this diversity is the distinction between the political *government* and the law-bound *administration*. However, these terms do not explain where to draw the line between the two or how their common features are to be understood. Most constitutions employ a consistent concept of the

---

[151] See for this aspect in light of international human rights protection, Chapter 4, II., 4.

[152] eg N. W. Barber, 'Prelude to the Separation of Powers', 60 *Cambridge Law Journal* (2001), 59 (87), attempts to define the executive as 'profitless'.

[153] On the one hand, C. Schmitt, 'Legalität und Legitimität' [1932], in *Verfassungsrechtliche Aufsätze* (Berlin: Duncker & Humblot, 1958), 263; on the other hand, Kelsen, *Allgemeine Staatslehre* (Berlin: Springer, 1925), 244.

executive and do not draw a categorical line between government and administration.[154]

Our theoretical framework leads to a different approach: the legislative and the judiciary alone cannot satisfy the demand for law of an intermediary scope and temporal orientation; for rules which concern neither one individual party nor the entire democratic community; or for decisions that are taken neither to solve a past conflict nor to implement a programme for the future. The function of the executive is therefore to mediate continually between democratic and individual self-determination. The much-disputed question of where to draw the line between political government and law-bound administration—and how to identify the relation between the two— must be phrased differently.[155] Instead of a clear line, we have within the executive organization a gradual and continual process of concretizing law-making. This continuity is realized by the definition of a gradually narrowing scope of responsibilities and a corresponding de-politicization and legalization of executive decisions. As the executive distances itself from the political leadership and more organizational levels come between government and an individual official, rules defining the scope of executive action grow stricter and law-making comes closer to the legal sphere of individual citizens; to their individual claim to self-determination. Ministries, governmental departments, or directorates of the European Commission are typically occupied with proposing legislative acts and implementing already enacted laws through secondary regulations, ie decrees and executive orders. By contrast, officials in a municipal administration, for instance, fulfil a variety of tasks that most directly affect the legal spheres of individual citizens.

The more individualized the decisions of the executive are, the narrower the framework of legal rules becomes that the executive has to follow. This is why courts in all democratic constitutional states, in both the Common Law and continental traditions, have developed certain unwritten standards for decisions of the executive that concern individual rights.[156] The Anglo-American tradition frames this in the distinction between executive rule-making and adjudication. These standards include the right to be heard by the administrator before a decision is made and the right to get reasons for the decision. These procedural requirements do not apply equally to the political leadership of the executive branch.

---

[154] For two counter-examples see art. 20 of the French Constitution of the Fifth Republic—for the terminology see E. Zoller, *Droit constitutionnel* (Paris: Presses Universitaires de France, 2nd ed 1999), para. 235—and the Swedish Constitution chapter 1, arts. 6 and 8, chapters 6 and 7.

[155] H. D. Jarass, *Politik und Bürokratie als Elemente der Gewaltenteilung* (München: Beck, 1975).

[156] For comparative references see C. Möllers, *Gewaltengliederung* (Tübingen: Mohr Siebeck, 2005), 117.

A closer look at the temporal structure of executive decisions illustrates what is meant by the *central* position of this branch. Whilst the judiciary rules retrospectively and the legislative prospectively, the executive must concentrate on the present realization of law. In fact, the enforcement of a legal norm can be interpreted as the very moment in time in which norm and its implementation coincide. The executive does not restrict itself to such (effectively quite rare) acts of enforcement, but it does temporally center itself on them. This occurs in the *post-legislative* implementation of norms by way of rule-making as well as in the *ante-judicial* acts of administrative self-regulation, which are often a procedural condition for access to judicial review of an administrative act.

Since the late 19th century, the executive has often been justified by its expertise vis-à-vis the other powers. The executive claim to expertise plays an important role, for instance, in Germany before the First World War, in the American debate since the 1920s, and also in the discourse surrounding the legitimacy of the European Commission.[157] The concept centered on the idea of self-determination developed here cannot simply accept this justification as such. In democratic constitutionalism, expertise cannot be taken as a basis or as an uncontested criterion. While expert opinion must be available to every branch of government, it cannot substitute the legitimacy of one of them.[158] Nonetheless, there is a valid point in the alleged connection between the executive and expertise, and thus between standards of action beyond politics or law. Though the legislative and the judiciary likewise make use of expert advice, two organizational features of the executive make this branch particularly open to the use of expertise.

First, the executive branch is able to develop forms of internal specialization by creating a departmental structure. Second the administration can act upon its own initiative and, therefore, develop expertise. Each of the other two branches lacks at least one of these features for reasons that guarantee their legitimacy. The legislature has to make general decisions. That limits its ability to specialize. Instead, the legislature has to apply different expert discourses to a political pattern. Furthermore, it acts with an eye to the future, therefore making decisions with only limited access to empirical knowledge and expertise.[159] The judiciary is specialized to a certain degree in some legal systems, for example continental Europe. But

---

[157] Influential in the US: J. Landis, *The Administrative Processs* (New Haven: Yale University Press, 1938). For the process of European integration, see: G.-D. Majone, *Regulating Europe* (London: Routledge, 1996), 9.

[158] A. Voßkuhle, 'Sachverständige Beratung des Staates', in J. Isensee and P. Kirchhof (eds.), *Handbuch des Staatsrechts Vol III* (Heidelberg: C.F. Müller, 3rd ed 2005), § 43.

[159] The following distinctions may get lost in a unified concept of administrative accountability: E. Carolan, *The New Separation of Powers* (Oxford: Oxford University Press, 2009), 149–52.

as courts do not have the ability to initiate their own procedures the judiciary is restricted in collecting expert knowledge. Courts demand this kind of knowledge for specific problems in a given case. However, the judicial system is not able to systematically store, process, and integrate expert knowledge on a larger scale. Therefore, expertise as a canon of decisional standards, which is independent from both politics and law, should be allocated to the one power that takes its legitimacy less obviously from one of both. It is precisely the relative distance from our two modes of legitimacy which allows for the continuity of the executive organization and, thereby, for the possibility of structured contact with expertise. Because of this organizational continuity of the executive bureaucracy, 'the state' is in some authoritarian traditions identified solely with the executive, not with the legislature or the courts.[160] From our point of view, precisely the opposite is correct: the state is a form of organizing competing claims of individual and democratic self-determination whose sources are particularly far removed from the executive. The executive is legitimized by its incorporation into the two legitimatory mechanisms, its equal commitment to democracy and individual freedom.

The executive is expected to make legislative standards concrete through rules and regulations and, later, through more specific decisions when faced with more individual concerns. This sequence usually requires a *hierarchical* structure of the administrative organization. But hierarchy should *not* be understood as a structure in which the head of the executive determines every single decision of the lower level. There would be no need at all for a hierarchy if the central office itself were supposed to make all the decisions. The intervention of a head of government in a specific administrative procedure, such as in the approval of a merger or the naturalization of a foreign citizen, always leaves the impression of an improper politicization of a decision which should be determined solely by legal criteria. If such a decision deviated from the administrative practice, it could even violate standards of equal protection. This kind of governmental intervention does not create more democratic legitimacy, but rather the suspicion of a possible discrimination by the political process. Ideally, different hierarchical levels of the executive should make decisions falling only within the scope of their respective responsibilities without interference from higher levels. That does not mean the lower levels are independent. They have to act in accordance with the medium-range standards that are determined by the higher level, but not on the basis of specific orders relating to individual cases.

---

[160] This point of view is particularly prevalent in Germany and in France: C. Möllers, *Staat als Argument* (München: Beck, 2000); D. Bates, 'Political Unity and the Spirit of the Law: Juridical Concepts of the State in the Late Third Republic', *28 French Historical Studies* (2005), 69.

The executive mission to mediate between the other branches involves a specific familiarity with expertise and facts, as we have seen. To make the most of this, in all legal systems the executive has its own discretion for decision-making, a space for judgement, which is not completely determined by law.[161] Unlike all court rulings, many executive decisions claim a discretionary space; a specific will formation.[162] This is justified by the temporal and factual proximity to a specific problem as well as its differentiated hierarchy and political accountability. The democratic executive should not be immunized from political standards to the same extent as the judiciary.[163] Both the implemented legislative standard itself and the margin of discretion, which has been created by this standard, may be filled with political preferences if done in a non-discriminatory manner. Yet it would be wrong to completely equate the decision-making of the political legislative with executive discretion for two reasons. First, executive discretion emerges in democratic systems due to a political decision either of the democratic legislator[164] or the democratically elected head of the executive. Hence, the allocation of executive discretion is the *result* of a democratic decision-making process; it is derived from a political process. Secondly, not all cases of executive discretion can be seen as political ones, particularly when the executive makes specific decisions that affect just one person. Such decisions are limited in scope and very much determined by factual considerations. Here, executive discretion serves instead to make the executive sensitive to the circumstances of a specific situation.[165]

We have seen that our understanding of hierarchy describes a structure in which the legal obligations of administrators become more concrete as the executive's action more closely approaches a citizen's individual legal sphere. Hierarchy does not refer to a picture of the executive as a large pyramid,[166] at the head of which is the head of government. Such a concept might be an accurate description of some centralistic states like France, for

---

[161] For a comparative approach see R. Brinktrine, *Verwaltungsermessen in Deutschland und England* (Heidelberg: C.F. Müller, 1998).

[162] For the concept of will in this context see N. Achterberg, *Probleme der Funktionenlehre* (München: Beck, 1970), 150.

[163] A. Merkl, *Allgemeines Verwaltungsrecht* (Wien: Springer, 1927), 336. For the US see H. Finer, 'Administrative Responsibility in Democratic Government', 1 *Public Administration Review* (1941), 335.

[164] This is not true for a monarchy, in which the dynastical legitimacy is identified with the executive. For the German tradition see T. Ellwein, *Das Erbe der Monarchie in der deutschen Staatskrise* (München: Isar Verlag, 1954).

[165] Good reasons for executive discretion can be found in E. Carolan, *The New Separation of Powers* (Oxford: Oxford University Press, 2009), 130–4.

[166] For a critique of the concept: F. Ost, M. van der Kerchove, *De la pyramide au réseau* (Brussels: Facultés universitaires Saint-Louis, 2002).

example.[167] It is certainly not true for countries with a strong corporatist tradition or federal systems such as Germany or the US. An official in Germany who grants a building permission in a city is bound by the city's local ordinance issued by the municipal council, by federal planning law, and by state building regulations. Additionally, this official is subject to the directions of the mayor and the oversight structure of the state over the city. Finally, in many circumstances, EU regulations may also be relevant. In some cases, even international law may be directly applicable. In granting a building permission, the administrator applies the law of at least three public authorities that are accountable to the respective people of the federation, the regional, and the local community. The administrator is part of the municipal administration, incorporated into an official hierarchy and subject to a variety of norms, which also establish a hierarchical dependence on those who created these norms. His or her decision is legally bound; uncertainty over how to act is fairly limited.[168] In this example, there is no sign whatsoever of a straight, hierarchically constructed pyramid of administrative organization.

5. Electing and appointing officers

How do we fit the creation of officers into our tripartite scheme?[169] This is not necessarily an executive or a judicial task. Instead, responsibility for the appointment depends on the scope of the responsibilities of the office. In this respect, there is no categorical difference between the appointment power and the law-making power. The power to appoint an officer might effectively wield more influence than the power to make a law. A rule for the legitimate appointment of officers must take into account what scope of functions the office in question will have.

In this respect, the appointment is characterized by the same institutional logic of legitimacy developed above for law-making: both adhere to a principle of gradual individualization. Institutions with all-encompassing powers, such as the parliament, or the people appoint all-encompassing offices. The appointment process raises the same issue we discussed previously with regard to the proper level of parliamentary involvement: should parliament have the power to appoint civil servants below government level?

---

[167] With regard to the French administrative agencies, one would have to qualify this statement even here. See Y. Gaudemet, O. Gohin (eds.), *La République decentralisé* (Paris: LGDJ, 2004).

[168] For this function of hierarchies see N. Luhmann, *Organisation und Entscheidung* (Opladen: Westdeutscher Verlag, 2000), 322.

[169] An interesting differing approach is in E. Carolan, *The New Separation of Powers* (Oxford: Oxford University Press, 2009), 164–7.

In parliamentary systems the legislature elects the head of government and both institutions cooperate otherwise. The aspiration for more influence on the side of the parliament is typically limited, however, simply because the parliamentary majority and government are politically connected as a result of the parliamentary responsibility of the government and all its officials. Thus there is no real institutional need for allowing the legislature to appoint specialized lower level executives in a parliamentary system. In a presidential system, by contrast, the legislature and the president are legitimately separated. On the one hand, the logic of the system does not necessarily require any parliamentary influence on the appointment of executive officers; on the other, there is a much more pressing political need for parliament to exert some influence. But even in this context it seems problematic when a political body with legislative power is empowered to pick officers under the governmental level who are responsible for implementing this legislation. Again, the general political process does not seem suited to taking care of too-specific decisions.

In a comparative perspective, the procedures for the appointment of judges are regulated in a greater variety of ways. In some systems the idea of separation of powers is understood to require that the judiciary builds a system of co-optation, in which only judges can appoint judges.[170] In others, judges are appointed by the ministry of justice, in still others by the parliament or by parliamentary commissions, and in some they are elected directly by the people.[171] As long as judicial independence is guaranteed after the appointment, no particular mode of appointment seems to stand out as the best, though some additional points need to be made. Judicial co-optation or self-recruitment, like every other purely internal appointment procedure, evokes mistrust. Such a procedure tends to produce incestuous structures, as the only people who decide upon the appointment belong to the organization itself. The risk of losing all critical distance from its own practice and developing a form of corporatist spirit is obvious. Direct and parliamentary elections tend to politicize the selection process, so that the depoliticizing function of the judicial process is called into question. On the one hand, these considerations may suggest that the executive should appoint judges. On the other, different concepts of the function of the law seem to be lurking in the background. Especially at the state level in the

---

[170] Spain and Romania are points in case.

[171] F. Kübler, 'Demokratische Justiz?', in R. M. Kiesow, R. Ogorek, S. Simits (eds.), *Festschrift für Dieter Simon zum 70. Geburtstag* (Frankfurt am Main: Klostermann, 2005), 349–50, who distinguishes aptly between a democratic and a bureaucratic model of judicial appointments. For an overview on the different appointment procedures in established and new democracies and transitional states as well as on the international level see the articles in K. Malleson, P. H. Russell (eds.), *Appointing Judges in an Age of Judicial Power* (Toronto: University of Toronto Press, 2006).

United States, the pursuit of justice is a highly political issue, and there is a direct career path from the criminal justice system into politics. This seems acceptable if one applies a strong notion of democratic legitimacy to all three branches. But if there are differences, and especially if criminal justice provides procedures that are exemplary for the notion of individual legitimacy[172] as it has been developed here, the results could be unsound. While the content of criminal law must be defined by the legislature, its implementation should not depend on the outcome of democratic elections.

The significance of the right of appointment ultimately depends on the extent to which this right is linked to the power to dismiss the office holder: 'Once an officer is appointed, it is only the authority that can remove him, and not the authority that appointed him, that he must fear and, in the performance of his functions, obey.'[173] From this it follows that officials whose appointment requires direct democratic legitimacy must be dismissible, whereas officials in whom political influence is undesirable do not have to be dismissible. The independence of the judicial branch is either ensured through the limitlessness or the lack of renewability of the term of office. The re-electability of judges provided for in the European treaties, in contrast, is not sufficient to guarantee judicial independence. In the executive branch, life terms may also guarantee a certain degree of political independence that is to some extent desirable for subordinate officials and strengthens their obligation to the law,[174] while a government must have a limited mandate.

6. *Excessive legitimacy: political parties and objective basic rights*

Both modes of legitimacy may exceed their limits of appropriateness. Political parties do not belong to the narrow defined subject matter of a concept of separated powers.[175] Yet the point is often made that political parties are one element to undermine a 'classical' idea of separated powers. But in addition to the fact that this traditional idea is a myth, it is clear that this argument may cut both ways. A particular system of separated powers may change the way political parties organize themselves: ' . . . parties rarely reunite what constitutions divide.'[176] In any case, if political parties deserve

---

[172] See Chap. 2, III., 3.

[173] *Bowsher v Synar*, 478 U.S. 714, 726 (1986), referring to the lower court.

[174] For a comparative assessment: C. Möllers, 'Politik und Verwaltung', in A. v. Bogdandy, P-M. Huber, S. Cassese (eds.), *Ius Publicum Europaeum*, vol. V (Heidelberg: C. F. Müller, 2012), § 94.

[175] D. Levinson, R. Pildes, 'Separation of Parties not Powers', *119 Harvard Law Review* (2006), 2311; E. Carolan, *The New Separation of Powers* (Oxford: Oxford University Press, 2009), 41–2.

[176] D. J. Samuels and M. S. Shugart, *Presidents, Parties, and Prime Ministers. How the Separation of Powers affects Party Organization and Behaviour* (Cambridge: Cambridge University Press, 2011), 251.

at least brief consideration in this account, it is not only because of their great practical importance but also because a look at them may teach us something about our model of legitimacy. Political parties give structure to democratic will-formation, a process that takes two directions. Through political programs as well as through the nomination of persons, parties develop systems of collective preferences that are reflected in parliament and in government. Conversely, legislative decisions, such as electoral and campaign finance laws, influence the structure of the party system. Between the internal political process within parties and the democratic vote for a certain party, incongruities tend to emerge.[177] Parties may be more radical than their voters, so that voters may have difficulties to find a party that reflects their preferences. Still, there is no institutional alternative to political parties in democratic systems.

In our model the place of parties is above all in the legislative process. We have seen how critical explicit political alternatives are in the legislative process. Programmatic distinctions, such as between 'right' and 'left', serve to crystallize different possible courses of action. That also means that parliament and government are the powers in which parties should primarily be located. Parties connect government and parliament and this bridge conforms with a legitimate organization of powers, as we shall see.[178] A decision regarding a democratic statute serves as both the expression and the conclusion of the democratic process.[179] In contrast, the post-legislative cycle of the implementation of laws on different administrative and judicial levels requires patterns of legitimacy not equally open to legitimate influence by political parties. Especially, decisions regarding an individualized legal sphere cannot be taken legitimately with the help of criteria derived from a general democratic process. Of course, there might be a left-wing bias against a building permit or a right-wing rejection of a citizen's naturalization. Political opinions do not stop at the legislative level. But the question is whether reference to such political leanings is legitimate on all levels of the law-making cycle. As we have seen in the discussion of the executive branch, there might also be room for political criteria within executive discretion, filling a gap a democratic statute intentionally leaves open. But it is also obvious that this legitimate use of political preferences has strict limits from the perspective of the addressed individual persons and their right to equal treatment. Equality here means that political preferences

---

[177] For a good illustration: A. O. Hirschman, *Exit, Voice, and Loyalty* (Cambridge, Mass: Harvard University Press, 1970), 62.

[178] D. Grimm, 'Die Politischen Parteien', in D. Grimm, *Die Zukunft der Verfassung* (Frankfurt am Main: Suhrkamp, 3rd ed 2002), 265 (283).

[179] See Chapter 2, III., 2.

cannot lead to different rationales for comparable decisions. A defined institutional limit, however, at which the influence of parties should end, is difficult to ascertain. In any case, political influence should fade out while passing through the executive branch. It is legitimate at the top, therefore the apex of government should be politically appointed. It becomes problematic at the bottom end.[180]

There is no doubt that the political influence of parties, for many reasons and to differing extents in different political systems, does not stop where it should. Parties tend to overly politicize executive and judicial appointments or to micro-manage statutory interpretation. This is an excess of democratic legitimacy, in which democratic mechanisms gain an effect that crosses over into areas to which they no longer have a legitimate claim.

There is a corresponding excess of individual legitimacy that typically finds its expression in a broad interpretation of fundamental rights. One example is the so-called objective interpretation of basic rights typical of, but not limited to, German constitutional law.[181] As we have seen, individual legitimacy is generated through the individual use of subjective rights. Basic rights are an especially strong form of such rights, as they bind the legislator, and can be subject to review by constitutional courts.[182] In an objective interpretation rights gain a normative meaning beyond the individual concrete claim of a person. One example is the constitutional case law regarding abortion in Germany. The German Federal Constitutional Court declared a liberal regulation of abortion to be a violation of the right to life in a procedure in which neither the representative of a pregnant woman nor of an unborn child participated. The objective reading of a basic right was used to review a statute without any specific procedural connection to an individual complaint.[183] There are many methodological problems with such an interpretation of basic rights that need not concern us here. What is crucial is the fact that an objective interpretation of a basic right opens the scope of this right to cases in which no individual and concrete piece of individual freedom has been abridged. This example of an objective interpretation has to be distinguished from the much disputed private law effect of constitutional rights. Individual rights are not limited to public law constellations, and individual legitimacy also concerns private and criminal law.

---

[180] See Chapter 2, III, 4.

[181] R.Wahl, 'Die objektiv-rechtliche Dimension der Grundrechte im internationalen Vergleich', in D. Merten, H.-J. Papier (eds.), *Handbuch der Grundrechte* (Heidelberg: C. F. Müller, 2004), § 19; W. Heun, 'Verfassungsrecht und einfaches Recht—Verfassungsgerichtsbarkeit und Fachgerichtsbarkeit', 61 *Veröffentlichung der Vereinigung der Deutschen Staatsrechtslehrer* (2002), 80 (92).

[182] See Chapter 2, II.

[183] BVerfGE 39, 1, 88, 203.

Therefore, applying basic rights to problems of private law is of no concern as long as there is a connection between the evocation of the rights and an individualized sphere of freedom. The problem begins when this connection is missing. Rights become 'values' that no specific individual is ready to claim. The same structural problem arises here as in the case of political parties, though from the other direction. In the first example, the influence of political parties collectivizes decisions over individuals. In the second, individual rights become values and restrict the political process without an expression of individual legitimacy behind them.

IV. IS THERE A NORMATIVE HIERARCHY AMONG THE BRANCHES? THE RULE OF CONTINUOUS CONCRETIZATION

Is there a hierarchical relation among the three branches or how else could we reconstruct their relation?

First, it seems appropriate to think of the relation of the branches as a *cyclic* structure. The executive implements legislative decisions—hence, manifestations of democratic self-determination—across many different levels of bureaucratic organization, making them more and more specific and legally determined until they directly address one citizen and his or her individual legal sphere. The courts retrospectively assess this application as a potential obstacle to individual self-determination. At this point, with a judicial decision, a law-making cycle comes to an end. A new cycle may begin. Many elements of law-making do not go full cycle. This reconstruction speaks against the widespread notion of a hierarchy between the powers.[184] On the one hand, such a hierarchy is assumed by an alleged supremacy of the legislative because the legislature is entitled to define standards that bind the executive and the courts. On the other hand, one might argue that courts are supreme as they have the power to make a final decision. This ambivalence is especially characteristic in classical English constitutional theory, which juxtaposes parliamentary sovereignty and the rule of law.[185]

Still, a hierarchy among the branches cannot be established in a plausible manner. It is more convincing to understand the temporally and materially tiered mechanisms of concretization among the powers as an institutional solution, which precisely tries to *avoid* any hierarchy and instead assigns different incommensurable tasks that cannot be described in any relation of supremacy or subordination. It seems pointless to construct a hierarchy

---

[184] Again pronounced by Rousseau and Kant among others.

[185] But see Chapter 2, III, 6.

between the enactment of a general rule and the final decision on the content of this rule in a specific case, because there is no common element that could justify this hierarchy. As a matter of sheer influence we cannot compare the breadth of a legislative rule with the depth, ie concrete and final intrusion into individual matters, of a judicial decision. A formulation from Kant's 'Rechtslehre' may make this point: although he admittedly considered the legislative to be the highest power, Kant stated that the legislative was 'irreprehensible', the executive 'irresistible', and the judiciary 'irreversible'.[186] In this way, the legislative claim is set against specific attributes of the other powers, to which the legislature cannot gain legitimate access.

This reconstruction does not yet have concrete implications for the organizational relationship between the powers. The contested relationship between the legislative and the executive illustrates this. Both the political dependence of the government on parliament in a parliamentary system and its separation in a presidential system are accepted as legitimate forms of democratic constitutionalism. We will explore this further in the next chapter. On the other hand, it is not disputed that the judiciary has to be strictly separated from the other powers, for democratic constitutional systems generally provide for independent judicial decisions. But why is judicial law-making categorically separated from the other powers, while the same cannot be said for the legislative and executive branches?

It would be theoretically conceivable and practically feasible to set up administrative tribunals, which, as a part of the executive, monitor its actions and decide solely according to legal standards. In fact, administrative jurisdiction in France and Germany developed this way, most famously in the Napoleonic Conseil d'État.[187] The categorical distinction between such tribunals and a 'genuine' judiciary actually delayed and obstructed the opportunity to monitor the administration in the English legal system.[188] Nonetheless, from the perspective of a theory of legitimacy, the judicial process is only justified to the extent of the request of the plaintiff. This requires decisions to be made in a place that is organizationally distant from the areas of political power.

What we have developed so far could be framed as a *Rule of Continuous Concretization*. Our model allocates a certain scope of law-making to certain procedures carried out by specific branches. The relationship among the branches, and within the multi-faceted executive, may be best described by a

---

[186] I. Kant, 'Metaphysik der Sitten, Einteilung der Rechtslehre (1797)', *Werke* [ed. Weischedel] (Darmstadt: Wissenschaftliche Buchgesellschaft, 1983), B.

[187] See n. 78.

[188] For England, see once more M. Loughlin, *Public Law and Political Theory* (Oxford: Oxford University Press, 2003), 153.

need for continuous concretization. The legislature should not block contributions by the other branches by making over-detailed rules, the executive should not skip levels of hierarchies through politicized interventions, and the judiciary should respect the decision-making process in the other branches before it intervenes. Rather than talking about balance or control, one might understand this rule as an instrument to let all different parts of a system of separated powers contribute to the process of law-making in their own specific procedural way.

V. SOME CONCLUSIONS

In this chapter we have tried to derive a workable concept of separated powers from the idea of self-determination. The springboard for our line of argument was individual personality. On its basis, the two modes of individual and democratic self-determination proved to be of equal value: the 'only human right'[189] of freedom constitutes both an individual sphere of freedom and a right to participation in the democratic process. Both forms of self-determination must therefore be guaranteed through law within a community of free and equal individuals. Only a legal system, which facilitates and guarantees both forms of self-determination, can claim legitimacy. But individual and democratic self-determination both require different mechanisms of organization: the protection of individual freedom requires a procedural context that judges individualized actions solely on the basis of legal standards in order to remove an existing obstacle to individual freedom. Decisions that fulfil these procedural requirements and were initiated by the affected individual enjoy *individual legitimacy.* Conversely, an all-inclusive open and egalitarian decision-making process creates a democratic will that claims *democratic legitimacy.* Criteria of legal determination, the scope of the decisions, and their temporal orientation helped develop a legitimate system of organized powers. This system ascribes democratic legitimacy to the legislative power and individual legitimacy to the judiciary.

Models of political theory may be mirrored in this institutional distinction in a way that allows space for practical contradictions. The liberal-individualistic notion of stable, individual preferences has its institutional equivalent in the courts. The republican-Rousseauist idea of collective self-determination finds its institutional reality in the legislator. But recognizing both political ideas as equally necessary and mutually reinforcing is at the core of our interpretation of separated powers. The question of a correct understanding of freedom, of the relationship between the individual and the

---

[189] I. Kant, 'Metaphysik der Sitten, Einteilung der Rechtslehre (1797)', *Werke* [ed. Weischedel] (Darmstadt: Wissenschaftliche Buchgesellschaft, 1983), B.

democratic community, remains fundamentally open. The institutional division of labor between the powers is called upon to answer this question for each individual case anew. Decision-making claims, namely between courts and legislators, persistently continue to be contested.

In order to arbitrate between general legislative and individualized judicial law-making, another power is required, which mediates between both poles: the executive. Executive action can have both a legislative as well as a judicial character. Crucial, however, is the unique task of the executive to continuously implement future-orientated, general, and political decisions to more concrete constellations and, therefore, link these decisions to the retrospective, individual, and law-based decision-making mechanism of the judiciary. Hence, the ratio of the separation of powers in democratic constitutional states is not the repression and facilitation of political power, but rather the organization of a model of law-making in which individual and democratic matters of self-determination gain equal recognition.

3

Problems of Separated Powers
in the Constitutional State

The principles developed in Chapter 2 allow us to consider some more specific legal issues of the separation of powers in contemporary constitutional states. Three topics will be addressed: the relation between parliament and government (I.), constitutional review by courts (II.), and the limits of judicial review of the administration (III.).

I. PARLIAMENT AND GOVERNMENT

Political relations between government and parliament in democratic states have been subject to criticism since as early as the 19th century. This criticism found that the close cooperation between the parliamentary majority and the government in parliamentary systems could not be reconciled with the idea of a power-sharing *division* of powers (1.). But, on the other hand, parliamentary delegation of legislative powers to the government attracts criticism as a form of legislative surrender (2.) and seems to require other institutional devices to control the government (3.). Finally, the increasing independence of a technocratic executive from government and parliament requires a deeper analysis from the perspective of the concept of separated powers (4.).

1. *Presidentialism or parliamentarism?*

Government and parliament are, according to our concept, functionally related.[1] Both can claim a general democratic legitimacy. Both enjoy, unlike courts and subordinate executive authorities, comprehensive powers and substantially unlimited scope of action. Both are ideally subject to very few

---

[1] Similiarities between the two and the common feature of cooperation between governments and parliaments are likewise stressed in the excellent comparative accounts of R. Albert, 'The Fusion of Presidentialism and Parliamentarism', *57 American Journal of Constitutional Law* (2009), 531; R. Albert, 'Presidential Values in Parliamentary Democracies', *8 International Journal of Constitutional Law* (2010), 207.

procedural rules and accordingly make decisions that are future-orientated.[2] Nonetheless, government and parliament are organized very differently: one as a hierarchical apex of an administrative organization; the other as a deliberative assembly. Whether parliament and government stand in institutional contrast to one another, or whether they mainly cooperate with each other, depends on the design of the specific constitutional structure. In parliamentary systems, government and parliament owe their legitimacy to the same electoral act. In presidential systems they are legitimized by different independent elections. In parliamentary systems the process of law-making issues from the joint exercise of power by the government and the parliamentary majority. The parliament is the legislative institution by virtue of its organization as a public assembly. But the government also contributes to legislation in many ways, not only in that members of the government are also members of parliament, but also because technical details of legislation are resolved within governmental organizations. Even a governmental right to legislative initiative—which is part of many constitutions—does not pose a problem from this perspective, as long as the parliament may in principle still pass laws without the involvement of the government.[3] From the perspective set forth here, this cooperation between the two branches is a perfectly appropriate mechanism for a democratic decision-making process.

Whether these assumptions are also valid in the context of presidential systems with a directly elected head of state is a more difficult question. A glance at American constitutional law does, however, reveal similar mechanisms. Members of Congress cooperate with the president in producing legislative proposals. In American constitutional practice the law is also mainly conceived as a common political project undertaken by the initiating congressmen (*sponsors*) and the president. The negative equivalent of the governmental right of initiative in parliamentary systems is the presidential right to veto legislation. Of course, the presidentialist institutional arrangement leaves much more room for political conflicts between the two branches, which may in turn lead to political blockade, just as the Federalist individualistic political concept envisioned: when in doubt, there should be no legislation.[4]

Another form of conflict, in this case between the president and the parliamentary accountable prime minister, appears in the presidential system

---

[2] See Chapter 2, III., 2.

[3] Mill, for example, opposed a parliamentary right of initiative. See Pitkin's analysis: H. F. Pitkin, *The Concept of Representation* (Berkeley: University of California Press, 1967), 63–4. For a reconstruction of Rousseau's account on governmental initiative: J. Cohen, *Rousseau. A Free Community of Equals* (Oxford: Oxford University Press, 2011), 172–4.

[4] See Chapter 1, I., 3.

of the Fifth French Republic in times of cohabitation. Following negative experiences with the parliamentary decision-making process in the Third and the Fourth Republics, the strong position of the president and a remarkable weakening of parliament—quite similar to the constitution of the Weimar Republic[5]—was expected to improve the overall decision-making ability of the political system. However, both the expectation of the original authors of the French constitution and the newly amended reduction of the presidential period in office to five years[6] seem to demonstrate two things: a need for the unification of the electoral cycles and the homogenization of the democratic decision-making process between the parliamentary government and the president.

In fact, the French system of a parliamentary government and a powerful president chosen by the people turns out to be a highly problematic structure.[7] The lack of political accountability of the French president has been much criticized.[8] This so-called 'semi-presidentialism' has been introduced in various new constitutional systems in Eastern Europe, such as in Croatia, Romania, and Russia, as well as in Latin-America and Africa[9]—probably because it not only constitutes a compromise between the American presidential system and the parliamentarianism, which is predominant in Europe, but also a compromise between the parliamentary and the executive factions during the constitution-making process. But as a result, such a system plays right into the hands of authoritarian presidentialism, particularly under conditions of an unstable political party landscape. One reason seems to be that the powers of the office of the president—not unlike in the Weimar Republic—relieve the pressure on parliament to form majorities capable of producing decisions. There is always a reserve power.[10] In addition to that, the president has strong institutional incentives to inhibit the parliamentary ability to organize a majority because the weaker the

[5] C. Skach, *Borrowing Constitutional Designs* (Princeton: Princeton University Press, 2005), 4–11.

[6] For an analysis of the quinquennat, see L. Jaume, 'Le gaulisme et la crise de l'Etat', 8 *Modern and Contemporary France* (2000), 7.

[7] See for this aspect: C. Skach, 'The "newest" separation of powers: Semipresidentialism', 5 *International Journal of Constitutional Law* (2007), 93 (104); for a comparable empirical result: D. J. Samuels, M. S. Shugart, *Presidents, Parties, and Prime Ministers. How the Separation of Powers affects Party Organization and Behaviour* (Cambridge: Cambridge University Press, 2011), 255–7.

[8] M.-C. Ponthoreau, 'Pour une réforme de la responsabilité politique du Président de la République française', in O. Beaud, J.-M. Blanquer (eds.), *La résponsabilité des gouvernants* (Paris: Descartes et Cie, 1999), 301.

[9] For Africa's problematic turn to authoritarian presidentialism: H. Kwasi Prempeh, 'Africa's "constitutionalism revival": False start or new dawn?', 5 *International Journal of Constitutional Law* (2007), 469 (497).

[10] A historical analysis is M. Stürmer, *Koalition und Opposition in der Weimarer Republik 1924–1928* (Düsseldorf: Droste, 1967).

parliament is, the stronger the president becomes. Therefore, the president who regularly has the right to dissolve parliament will use this instrument to destabilize the parliamentary political process. As a consequence, different from the American system of pure presidentialism, there are not two independent power structures but finally only one. And unlike a parliamentary system there is less of a mutual dependence between government and parliament. Instead, parliament depends very much on the president.

These observations demonstrate again the more general point. The common concept of a necessary contrast between parliament and government as a requirement of separation of powers is misguided, even though certain systems do favour conflicts between both. In the parliamentary system, close cooperation between government and the parliamentary majority is indeed necessary to facilitate the realization of the democratic will expressed through the act of voting. If the constitution requires the president and parliament to originate from different elections, starker political contrasts emerge, but these also tend to bring about a more cooperative legislative process.

Is the relationship between parliament and the government then completely free of problems from the perspective of our model? In fact, it appears that the balance of power between government and parliament tends to favour the government. The facility of mobilizing the public through the media and the pressure for political unity within the governmental camp plays into the hands of the more versatile and visible government. But the question of exactly how the decision-making process between government and parliament in a parliamentary system unfolds is difficult to answer empirically, as it plays out on an informal level that is difficult to observe. And when we look at a powerful head of a parliamentary government we must not forget that part of his power had to be won by compromising with different factions of his majority. Responding to this informality with legal devices seems dubious. At least our concept of separated powers requires respect for the informality of the democratic decision-making process.[11]

The relationship between parliament and government has always been a particularly popular subject in separation of powers theory—but from the perspective offered here it is a rather fruitless topic. Ultimately, cooperation between parliament and the government is no threat to a sensibly understood organization of powers. It is prevalent even in presidential systems of government. The distinction between the parliamentary and the presidential system, which is often seen as central, appears to be similarly

---

[11] See Chapter 2, III., 2.

overestimated.[12] In both systems, informal structures of cooperation dominate in parties and in programmes and are ultimately expressed in the form of legislation. The choice between both systems is based on an understanding of what is meant by democracy and whether we prefer to express the democratic decision-making process through one or through several electoral acts. The multiplication of democratic cycles in presidential systems leads to more competition for legitimacy among the institutions; a practice alien to parliamentary systems. We shall see that this has important implications for parliamentary controls and administrative organization.[13] But there is no rule according to which one system is preferable to the other.

2. Delegations: the empowerment of the executive through the legislative

In 1936 Carl Schmitt, the National Socialist German constitutional theorist, declared the end of the epoch of parliamentary legislation.[14] As evidence for his assumption, he pointed not to totalitarian states like Germany and Italy but above all to the remaining democracies of Great Britain, France, and the United States. All of them had created broad legislative delegations since the end of the First World War, which authorized governments to enact general, legislative rulings—acts or decrees—without further involvement of the parliaments. Large parts of the legal system, in particular laws on the wartime economy, consisted of executive rulings or delegated legislation, which were formulated without any parliamentary contribution. It was not unusual to authorize the administration to set 'appropriate' or 'reasonable' prices for certain goods. However, in none of the democratic states did parliament formally relinquish and completely surrender the right to legislate to the government, in contrast to German constitutional history with the enactment of the *Ermächtigungsgesetz* of 1933.[15] In the United States, in 1935, the Supreme Court had annulled two laws for being unconstitutional because of overly far-reaching and vague delegation.[16] The rule, developed by the US Supreme Court from the separation of powers, that the legislator is limited in the extent to which he may cede powers to the administration,

---

[12] Differently J. J. Linz, A. Valenzuela (eds.), *The Failure of Presidential Democracy* (Baltimore: Johns Hopkins University Press, 1994). For a contemporary critique: F. Lehoucq, 'Constitutional Design and Democratic Performance in Latin America', *38 Verfassung und Recht in Übersee* (2005), 370.

[13] See later in this chapter I., 4.

[14] C. Schmitt, 'Vergleichender Überblick über die neueste Entwicklung des Problems der gesetzgeberischen Ermächtigungen (Legislative Delegationen)', in: *6 Zeitschrift für ausländisches öffentliches Recht und Völkerrecht* (1936), 252.

[15] German Law of 23 March 1933, RGBl. I (1933), 141.

[16] *Panama Refining Company v Ryan* 293 U.S. 388 (1935); *A. L. A. Schechter Poultry Corporation v U.S.* 295 U.S. 495 (1935). Compare also *Carter v Carter Coal Co.*, 298 U.S. 238, 310 (1936).

was termed the *nondelegation doctrine*. However, whether these decisions had any long-term impact is uncertain. Even after the Second World War, the significant uncertainty as to the limits of legal empowerment of the executive proved a problematic factor in many legal systems. After the experience of the Enabling Act, the German Basic Law sought to limit the practice of delegation by a constitutional rule. Accordingly, Article 80, Paragraph 1, Clause 2 of the Basic Law expressly stipulates that a law which authorizes the federal government to enact a legal decree may not be arbitrarily open but must determine the 'content, purpose and extent' of this decree.[17]

Before we analyse delegations based on our concept of separated powers, a historical note seems due: legislative delegations were the result of increasing state activity. They appeared on the scene when, at the end of the 19th century, nation states systematically assumed social and economic regulatory responsibilities and began to expand their administrative organizations.[18] Delegations are therefore not symptoms of decline but seem rather to depend upon the degree of state regulation. And even though the state today cedes many tasks to private bodies, the issue of delegations hardly disappears. On the contrary, the law of privatized markets has more legal rules than in a state monopoly, which—like the telecommunications and the energy laws—are supervised by authorities with extensive regulatory powers.[19]

But how do we assess delegations against the backdrop of the concept set forth here? How should we evaluate a case in which the legislator leaves it to the executive to ensure, for example, the 'security of food transport' without providing more specifics? On the one hand, by delegating, the legislature cedes part of its own authority to the executive. In extreme cases the legislator authorizes the government and the administration to enact far-reaching, future-orientated regulations. In such an instance, the legislator transforms the executive into a quasi-legislature[20] and forgoes his own legislative duty in favour of a branch that is organized and justified in a very different way. This is often interpreted as legislative surrender. This

[17] These strict conditions for delegation proved to be exceptional even in continental Europe, for a comparison: A. v. Bogdandy, *Gubernative Rechtsetzung* (Tübingen: Mohr-Siebeck, 2000). For an overview of the German practice: J. Saurer, *Die Funktionen der Rechtsverordnung* (Berlin: Duncker & Humblot, 2005).

[18] S. Cassese, 'Die Entfaltung des Verwaltungsstaates in Europa', in A. v. Bogdandy, S. Cassese, P. M. Huber (eds.), *Ius Publicum Europaeum Vol. II* (Heidelberg: C.F. Müller, 2010), 19; M. Stolleis, 'Die Entstehung des Interventionsstaats und das öffentliche Recht', *11 Zeitschrift für neuere Rechtsgeschichte* (1989), 129 (143).

[19] I. Walden, *Telecommunications Law and Regulation* (Oxford: Oxford University Press, 3rd rev. ed, 2009) 192–7.

[20] This notion already surfaces in the early case law of the US Supreme Court: *Yick Wo v Hopkins* 118 U.S. 355, 371 (1886).

description, however, seems incomplete for several reasons. First, there is no general rule as to how intensively parliament should regulate, which issues parliament should decide upon on its own, and how much parliament should leave to the executive. If a parliament rules too generally and unspecifically, we are faced with the problem of delegation. But, as we have seen, there may also be instances in which parliaments regulate excessively. In many constitutional systems parliament is denied the power to regulate the rights of a single individual, as this would constitute a discriminatory act. But even the legislative enactment of practically important details, e.g., emissions standards or curricula for public education, does not necessarily lead to a better or more legitimate regulation. In a system of separated powers the executive should have the possibility to apply and to adjust the political standards set by parliament to a particular set of facts. The ideal parliamentary statute is located somewhere between a too general and a too specific regulation: political questions should be decided by parliament; technical questions should be left to the executive. However, where to draw the line is a political question in itself. But if these assumptions are correct, then parliament should have some discretion as to the proper extent of delegation.

Therefore, it is dubious to stipulate an ideal delegatory division of labour in the constitution and to vest a constitutional court with the power to review such a rule. Still, some legal systems provide for such an arrangement, as is demonstrated by the above-mentioned German rule, as well as the former *nondelegation doctrine* of the US Supreme Court. Yet, it seems hard to accept the proposition that such a limit is properly drawn in the form of a constitutional rule. This is because the borderline between political parliamentary decision and executive implementation is always politically contested, and because different limits of delegation may be appropriate for different regulatory fields, from police law to environmental law or competition law. We have parliamentary procedures precisely because there is no such rule. This is the difference between the Kantian ideal of a general law and the constitutional practice of democratic self-determination.

From this angle, delegations are no longer synonymous to parliamentary self-abdication but seem rather to be a democratic standard solution for the problem of how a political program is best realized through the executive. Here, the executive serves as the implementation machine of parliament.[21] From the perspective of the legislator, broad delegations are often the best tool for attaining certain goals. The constitutional review must factor in these circumstances, otherwise constitutional courts risk paternalistically

---

[21] Empirically: D. Epstein, S. O'Halloran, *Delegating Powers* (Cambridge: Cambridge University Press, 1999), 18.

protecting the legislature from its own will. To put it differently: a constitutional definition of the limitations on delegation is constantly at risk of overturning a specific democratic decision for the sake of an abstract democratic ideal. For constitutional courts it is difficult to develop limits of delegation in a reasonable and predictable way, that is, to develop a truly workable rule. According to Germany's Constitutional Court, parliament is required to decide the 'principal' issues of the regulation itself—clearly not a readily applicable legal criterion.[22] The same goes for definitions of constitutional courts in India, South Africa, Canada, and the European Court of Justice.[23]

So is that all there is to say about the limits of delegation? A look at our concept may help us to find a more satisfying answer. As we have seen, there can be no general rule about what the legislature is required to decide on its own and what it may cede to the executive. Such a rule would contradict the necessary openness of the political process. But it is possible to draw some boundaries for the democratic process: the legislator, on the one hand, is exclusively empowered and required to define the distribution of freedom in a legal system.[24] On the other hand, the legislator is not allowed to intervene in specific individual legal cases, in the absence of an intermediary executive process of concretization. From both these poles, it is possible to devise criteria, mainly inspired by basic rights, for the boundaries of delegation. At any rate, the legislator is not entitled to limit himself to regulating the 'security of food transport' in our example above, for it remains entirely unclear in whose rights and in what manner the executive is hereby entitled to intervene. This suggests that substantial criteria for the boundaries of delegation should be derived from the perspective of the addressee of the regulation. The addressee has to know what the legislative rule means for the exertion of his or her own liberties. Consequently, parliament should lay out any intervention into rights and thereby make it predictable. While it seems unpromising to constrain delegations as such according to a non-delegation rule, the legislative act of delegating ensures that the courts review other constitutional standards, such as basic rights, procedural

---

[22] For criticism of this formula in German scholarship: M. Kloepfer, 'Der Vorbehalt des Gesetzes im Wandel', *Juristenzeitung* (1984), 685; W. Cremer, 'Art. 80 Abs. 1 S. 2 GG und Parlamentsvorbehalt', 122 *Archiv des öffentlichen Rechts* (1997), 248.

[23] Supreme Court of India, *Rajnarain Singh v Chairman, Patna Administration Committee, Patna,* 1955 S. C. R. 290, pp. 298–302; Constitutional Court of South Africa, *The Executive Council of the Western Cape Legislature and Others v The President of the RSA and Others* (1995), CCT 27/95, (10) BCLR 1289 (CC), paras. 51, 136, 142, 204–7; Supreme Court of Canada, *In Re George Edwin Gray,* [1918] S.C.R. 150, p. 157, distinguishing between delegation and abdication; European Court of Justice, *Smoke Flavorings,* Case C-66/04, European Court Reports 2005, I-10553, paras. 48–50.

[24] See Chapter 2.

standards of administrative action, and issues of federal competences, more intensively.[25] Finally, the delegation law may be interpreted in the light of constitutional standards. Admittedly, this solution does not solve all of the problems of the legislative process. Sometimes open-ended and indeterminate parliamentary laws are not the expression of a legislative willingness to shape public policy but rather a form of avoiding decision-making in the form of a compromise formula. But even in such cases, courts seem better capable of protecting individual rights than of improving the legislative process.

In conclusion: legislative delegation is not necessarily tantamount to the surrender of the democratic legislator to the executive power. It must be seen as a legislative instrument for implementing democratic decisions, which allows parliament to take advantage of the capabilities of the executive organization. The formulation of constitutional, judicially reviewable limits to delegation is dubious because in a democratic system there can be no general rule as to what should be decided by the legislator as a political issue and what should not. Instead, other rules such as basic rights or federal powers serve as limits to delegation. They provide the courts with the opportunity to review executive actions more closely.

3. Parliamentary control of the executive

The control of the executive is one of the most significant duties of every parliament. But what does *control* actually mean? In all democratic systems parliaments assume the role of the legislature; in parliamentary systems they also elect the government. But both powers are hardly covered by the term 'control'[26]—the notion of control makes better sense as a retrospective procedure, through which governmental action is assessed and judged according to certain political or legal standards. In other words, for parliament to exercise control over the government, the government must have already acted. Neither legislation nor the election of government represents a form of control in this more specific sense. The idea of control does not, as a result, fit neatly into the model of parliamentary action developed here, because control is retrospective and addresses specific issues. It rather resembles judicial action.[27] It is no coincidence that parliamentary committees of inquiry are reminiscent of courts.

---

[25] C. R. Sunstein, 'Nondelegation Canons', *67 University of Chicago Law Review* (2000), 315.

[26] The word 'control' derives from the French term 'contreroller' meaning 'to keep a copy of a roll of accounts': A. Stevenson (ed.), *Oxford Dictionary of English*, entry 'control *noun*' (Oxford: Oxford University Press, 2010), Oxford Reference Online, 7 July 2012.

[27] See Chapter 2, III., 3.

But parliaments possess full democratic legitimacy only when they decide *in pleno*, as they are only elected and representative as a whole.[28] Therefore, parliamentary control must monitor the executive implementation of parliamentary law with regard *to its own* parliamentary *tasks*. This has two implications, Parliamentary control has to aim at improving existing legislation and the performance of the government with a view to future elections. Parliament does not control the implementation of a statute because it does a better implementation job than the executive—it does not—but rather to learn from this control for the purposes of future political processes in and outside parliament. The central function of parliamentary control is the preparation of future democratic decision-making by informing itself and the public. Control mechanisms address the public, which responds to the informing and educative effects of the control process in one way or another. It also addresses the decision-making of parliament, which, as a consequence, enacts laws or imposes sanctions on the government, not least through budgetary decisions. For this reason, parliamentary control is a matter not of judicial, but rather of political judgement. Also, in a parliamentary system it is a task carried out by the opposition, not the majority, which is responsible for the government in office.

What follows from this? As a first consequence, parliaments must have access to all proceedings initiated by government. The practice of withholding information from parliament must remain a rare exception requiring strong normative justification. This concept of parliamentary control includes not only committees of inquiry but also the parliamentary right to question the government, in response to which an accountable executive must provide proper answers to parliament and, via parliament, to the general public. Again, it will practically be a matter of the opposition to make use of these rights. This also means that the majority should not have the power to intervene in this process of parliamentary control.

If parliamentary control is understood as an instrument to prepare and inform democratic decision-making, then other forms of parliamentary control that do not further this purpose become problematic. This is particularly true for cases in which parliament tries to take formal control over the implementation of already-enacted laws. In these instances, parliaments try to act as a sort of co-executive; a function they are neither designed nor suited for. An important example of this is parliamentary participation in executive rule-making.[29] Such arrangements are often viewed as enhancing the democratic legitimacy of the executive branch

---

[28] See Chapter 2, III., 2.

[29] See with respect to this aspect: Federal Constitutional Court, *Mehrdeutige Meinungsäußerungen*, BVerfGE 114, 196.

through parliamentary participation. But under a system of separated powers, not every form of parliamentary participation increases democratic legitimacy, especially when only a committee is involved. As we saw in the last sub-chapter on delegation, the legislator must be free to regulate in a detailed manner. But once the legislator has passed on this opportunity and authorized the executive to implement the legislation, further legislative involvement changes its meaning. In such a case, the legislator first uses the executive by providing a broad mandate for implementing the statute, only to subsequently interfere with that implementation in a particular case. The completed legislative process is thereby repoliticized in the context of applying the law to a particular case. The legislator encroaches upon another sphere.

This problem is nicely illustrated by two well-known cases from the US and Switzerland. In a famous case, Mr Chadha, a Kenyan citizen, had acquired the legal right to become a naturalized American.[30] The applicable legal regulations, however, required approval by the House of Representatives for each individual candidate before immigration authorities commenced the naturalization process. The House of Representatives struck a handful of candidates, including Chadha, off the list prepared by the executive. Chadha could not become an American citizen. He filed a lawsuit and won. The Supreme Court established that there had been a violation of the principle of the separation of powers because the House of Representatives had not restricted itself to the business of legislation.[31] The political legislator had interfered in a single case in the context of statutory implementation. As a consequence, a subjective right in an individual case was violated, with the result that there was no regular judicial protection available against the decision. This structure is particularly problematic for an individually affected citizen. But also when a parliament changes a certain environmental standard *ad hoc*, the question remains why the political majority has limited the decision to a particular case instead of having reached a decision that covers all similar subsequent cases.

A second example is the cantonal practice in Switzerland regarding the naturalization of citizens by plebiscite. Under this procedure, the citizens of a certain municipality receive a list with candidates for naturalization and vote on them. The Swiss Federal Court declared this practice unconstitutional because it violated the rule of law.[32] More specifically, as the form

---

[30] *INS v Chadha*, 462 U.S. 919 (1983).

[31] Interestingly, while the majority held the veto to be a legislative action (952), Justice Powell in his concurring opinion argued that the House of Representatives had usurped judicial powers (959–67). Justice White dissented. In his opinion, a congressional veto may usurp executive powers, but the veto in question did not (998–1003).

[32] See BGE 129 I 232 (235).

of the plebiscite does not allow for individual hearings and reason-giving it is not well suited to defining individual rights in an individual case.

In other problematic cases, parliaments dispatch individual members to supervisory bodies of the executive.[33] But if members of parliament sit on the supervisory board of executive bodies, their otherwise strong democratic legitimacy does not carry over to these structures. For one thing, only the plenum possesses such legitimacy, and for another, such bodies are not publicly assembled, deliberative institutions. They remain administrative bodies, even if partly occupied by parliamentarians. Such bodies must be distinguished from parliamentary committees, in which decisions of the plenum are discussed and prepared. In the American system, the relevant committees of Congress sometimes act like hierarchical superior authorities toward the executive agencies.[34] In this way, the obscure nexuses of power among particular committees, executive agencies, and the regulated parties concerned no longer display any of the organizational qualities associated with parliament.[35]

Parliamentary control is therefore best understood as a right to comprehensive information relating to all executive actions. This right is necessary for the legislator to make and correct decisions, and for the legislator and the public to make a political assessment of the achievements of the executive and of parliament itself, which provided the executive with legislative functions. This form of control should, however, be strictly distinguished from any intervention of parliamentary bodies into the implementation of enacted laws. In such instances, parliaments no longer have a valid claim to democratic legitimacy. They assume instead the position of a superior executive authority, though different from the real executive, neither bound by laws nor under judicial control.

4. Agencies: independent administrative action

In the modern age, administrative agencies are the epitome of unchecked state power. As we have set forth, both poles of executive law-making—politicized government and legally bound individual decision—are usually linked with each other through an hierarchical administrative organization. But independent administrative agencies emerged in democratic states as

---

[33] For Germany, see § 5 para. 1 of the Telecommunications Act regarding the Federal Network Agency.

[34] For details, see F. Kauser, W. Oleszek, T. Tatelmann (Congressional Research Service), *Congressional Oversight Manual*, Document RL 30240, June 10, 2011.

[35] See for this aspect already W. Wilson, *Congressional Government [1885]* (New Brunswick: Transaction Publishers, 2002), 74.

early as the late 19th century.[36] In this constellation, the legislator charges a specialized authority with a particular task, for example the regulation of a certain market. The agency sets rules and adjudicates particular cases in a quasi-judicial procedure. The leadership of the agency is exempted from government supervision. It has been outsourced from the executive hierarchy and is thus politically independent.

Such agencies do not fit within any classic model of separated powers. Consequently, they are often seen as a fourth branch that unites all three powers under one roof[37] but also as a new form of administrative tyranny.[38] This powerful narrative, however, is too simple. The fact that the executive issues rules and adjudicates individual cases is, as we have seen, nothing special, as long as the executive rules have a parliamentary basis and the individual decisions are subject to judicial review. The question remains, however, of how we justify the fact that such agencies are not tied to the democratic responsibility of the general executive, as they are no longer subject to the guidance of the democratically accountable government.

The basis for such a justification can neither be a critique of the executive hierarchy nor a reference to the agencies' expertise. Doubts over the performance of hierarchies have dogged the discussion of administrative law for some time.[39] But even though the governmental leadership, as we shall soon see, cannot know everything about subordinate authorities, the assumption that the political planning and programming of lower executive levels is fundamentally deficient or even impossible does not appear to be accurate:[40] as we have seen, the point of executive hierarchy is not to enable government to intervene in every single case,[41] but rather possibly to define general guidelines for implementing parliamentary laws. Hierarchies institute a normative relationship in which the possibility of intervening, not the actual intervention, is the crucial point. This forms the basis of political accountability. It is exactly for this reason that the

---

[36] S. Skowronek, *Building a new American State* (Cambridge: Cambridge University Press, 1982), 165; O. Lepsius, *Verwaltungsrecht unter dem Common Law* (Tübingen: Mohr Siebeck, 1997), 68.

[37] P. Strauss, 'The Place of Agencies in Government: Separation of Powers and the Fourth Branch', 84 *Columbia Law Review* (1984), 573.

[38] For this criticism: T. J. Lowi, *The End of Liberalism* (New York: Norton, 2nd ed 1979), 97.

[39] See for example E. C. Page, *Political Authority and Bureaucratic Power* (New York: Harvester Wheatsheaf, 2nd ed 1992). For examples from the recent debate in Germany: H.-H. Trute, 'Die demokratische Legitimation der Verwaltung', in W. Hoffmann-Riem, E. Schmidt-Aßmann, A. Voßkuhle (eds.), *Grundlagen des Verwaltungsrechts* (München: Beck, 2006), § 6.

[40] J. P. Olsen, 'Maybe it is Time to Rediscover Bureaucracy', 16 *Journal of Public Administration Research and Theory* (2006), 1–24.

[41] See Chapter 2, III., 4.

abolishment of hierarchical responsibility was not acceptable for the British constitutional system in the 1990s and had to be recalled.[42]

There is a more influential justification for independent agencies than the critique of hierarchy: the alleged necessity of integrating non-political expertise into the executive. Today, however, the belief in technocratic solutions that was particularly prevalent during the spread of agencies during the New Deal has lost much of its appeal.[43] Meanwhile, we tend to discuss the political elements of scientific research rather than the possibility of substituting science for politics.[44] One actual example on the international level is the UN-associated International Panel on Climate Change,[45] in which political critique is not completely substituted by scientific review. In any case, politically independent authorities tend to form structures of political interests and dependencies, which depart from the norms and standards of their self-generated expertise.[46]

For these reasons it could be more persuasive to explain and assess the phenomenon of independent administrative units from within our perspective of legitimacy. Maybe there are legitimate reasons why the democratic legislator should have the authority to create decision-making structures that are independent from the general electoral cycles.[47] Such a decision may be based on the insight that the reaction times of the legislative cycle are too fast or too slow to address certain issues. It is in this context in which the notion of expertise is appropriately placed. Administrative independence creates a distinct form of problem-solving capacity and a distinct organizational memory. If we conceptualize the whole constitutional system as a form of a cyclical self-commitment, then the duration of democratic commitment cycles may vary without necessarily correlating with a decrease in democratic legitimacy.[48] As long as such decisions retain a sufficient link

---

[42] A. Tomkins, 'The Struggle to Delimit Executive Power in Britain', in P. Craig, A. Tomkins (eds.), *The Executive and Public Law* (Oxford: Oxford University Press, 2006), 16 (24–37).

[43] P. H. Irons, *The New Deal Lawyers* (Princeton: Princeton University Press, 1982).

[44] B. Latour, *Politiques de la Nature* (Paris: Éd. la Découverte, 1999), 50; P. Weingart, *Die Stunde der Wahrheit?* (Weilerswist: Velbrück Wissenschaft, 2001).

[45] P. Edwards, S. Schneider, 'Self-Governance and Peer Review in Science-for-Policy: The Case of the IPCC Second Assessment Report', in C. Miller, P. Edwards (eds.), *Changing the Atmosphere: Expert Knowledge and Environmental Governance* (Cambridge: MIT Press, 2001), 219–46; B. Bolin, *A History of the Science and Politics of Climate Change* (Cambridge: Cambridge University Press, 2007), 126.

[46] On the issue of agency capture: R. Steinberg, *Politik und Verwaltungsorganisation* (Baden-Baden: Nomos, 1979), 122.

[47] H.-H. Trute, 'Regulierung—am Beispiel des Telekommunikationsrechts', in C.F. Eberle (ed.), *Der Wandel des Staates vor den Herausforderungen der Gegenwart: Festschrift für W. Brohm* (München: Beck, 2002), 169 (184).

[48] To the duration of cyclical self-commitment: J.G. March, J. P. Olsen, *Democratic Governance* (New York: Free Press, 1995), 116.

with the general political process through the democratic decision that established the agency, such a rationale appears convincing.[49] This rationale is generally recognized for the organization of the central banking system, which is politically independent in almost all democratic legal systems.[50] It also appears sensible in situations in which certain institutional incentives prevent the executive from pursuing the common good. This is the case when the state does business in a market it also regulates. The independence of the regulatory body ensures the independence of the decision-making process in such a scenario. Regulatory agencies for privatized markets with powerful state enterprises are a classic example.[51] In quite a different sense, the same rationale is of significance in the context of the European Union. In Article 17 (1) of the Treaty on the European Union, the European Commission is obliged to promote the 'general interest of the Union'. The underlying idea of this provision is that the member states are not neutral caretakers of European matters but rather tend to discriminate against each other in the pursuit of national interests. It should not come as a surprise against this background that the European Commission aims at establishing independent agencies to gain control over the implementation of European law in the member states.[52] This solution is certainly not unproblematic for any constitutional order because, as a general instrument, such an approach tends to delegitimize the order itself by implying that the regular executive is not capable of properly applying the law. According to our rationale, independent executives are acceptable only as exceptional institutions.

But the most important reason for the establishment of independent agencies is a political competition between different sources of legitimacy within a constitutional system. Many apparently 'independent' agencies are, upon closer scrutiny, relatively autonomous at best. In fact, it is very difficult to assess and compare degrees of administrative independence. The determinacy of statutory standards; appointment procedures; the structure of the

---

[49] For a classical analysis along these lines in which the US system serves as an example for Germany, see F. W. Scharpf, *Die politischen Kosten des Rechtsstaats* (Tübingen: Mohr Siebeck, 1970), 14, 59.

[50] R. M. Lastra, G. P. Miller, 'Central Bank Independence in Ordinary and Extraordinary Times', in J. Kleinemann (ed.), *Central Bank Independence* (The Hague: Kluwer Law International, 2001), 31–50. For a historical perspective on the US Federal Reserve System, and the Central Banks of England, France, Germany, and Italy, see G. Toniolo (ed.), *Central Banks' Independence in Historical Perspective* (Berlin: de Gruyter, 1988).

[51] M. Lombard, 'Warum bedient man sich im Bereich der Wirtschaft unabhängiger Behörden?', in J. Masing, G. Marcou, *Unabhängige Regulierungsbehörden* (Tübingen: Mohr Siebeck, 2010), 143 (154). In Germany the Federal Network Agency (Bundesnetzagentur) is regulating the electricity, gas, and telecommunication markets as well as postal services and railroads.

[52] On the 'complete independence' of the authorities responsible for monitoring the processing of personal data outside the public sector, see: European Court of Justice, *Commission v Germany*, Case C-518/07, European Court Reports 2010, I-01885.

agency (particularly at the top); procedural rules; and budgetary autonomy are all relevant factors. One important feature of this autonomy is the increased accountability towards institutions other than the government.[53] Being accountable to more than one institution tends to widen the discretion of the agency because a twofold control mechanism may be less coherent and strict.

The most prominent examples for such a competition come from presidential systems like the US or other constitutional orders with a dualist model of legitimacy like the system of the European Union. In the United States, Congress claims authority over agencies subordinated to the president.[54] In the EU, the European Commission and the member states compete for the control of the EU administration. In these settings, the struggle for control of one actor impacts the ability to control another one. In both systems, notwithstanding their differences, it is possible to observe both the struggle for control of the administration and the spread of an agency system.[55] While the internal organization of the agencies in each, and between both, legal systems differs considerably, they have in common the institutionally unsettled issue of who is the master of the administration.

There is another 'bottom-up'-type of legitimacy conflict that serves to justify a particular form of agency independence. Continental European systems of corporatism commonly display such decision-making structures, which are hardly democratically legitimate: for example, when the public self-administration of doctors is entitled to enter into agreements with health insurance companies that also affect patients' interests.[56] The association of doctors is conceived as a public authority whose legitimacy stems from doctors' obligatory membership. In this model of self-administration,[57] the standard top-down legitimacy generated through statutory regulation and governmental supervision is replaced by the ascendant string of legitimacy of an incorporated professional community. The inherent risk of such an arrangement is that the administration works at the expense of third parties, which only participate in the general democratic process without being represented in these self-administrating structures. Such an arrangement clearly limits the control exercised by the general democratic process.

---

[53] C. Möllers, 'Globalisierte Verwaltungen zwischen Verselbständigung und Übervernetzung', in M. Schulte, R. Stichweh (eds.), *Weltrecht* (Berlin: Duncker & Humblot, 2007).

[54] R. Cushman, *The independent regulatory commissions (1941)* (New York: Octagon Books, 1972), 37.

[55] R. Caranta, M. Andenas, D. Fairgrive (eds.), *Independent Administrative Authorities* (Lonson: British Institute of International and Comparative Law, 2004).

[56] See for Germany: E. Schmidt-Aßmann, *Grundrechtspositionen und -fragen im öffentlichen Gesundheitswesen* (Berlin: de Gruyter, 2001).

[57] E. T. Emde, *Die demokratische Legitimation der funktionalen Selbstverwaltung* (Berlin: Duncker & Humblot, 1991).

Administrative independence becomes an instrument for the externalization of control patterns.

For a long time, it was assumed that independent agencies were an unstoppable trend expressing the failure of traditional models of democratic legitimacy according to which parliament and government are responsible for the programming of the subordinate administration.[58] In the great narrative of the parliamentary democratic state's decline, agencies have taken on their own prominent role. The trend towards independence was supposed to come from the United States, across the European Union, and arrive in many nation-states all over the world. And yet this alleged trend of the president's waning political control over the administration is not even evident in the US. On the contrary, in America a process towards tighter presidential control of the administration has been perceptible since at least the 1980s.[59] As a matter of fact, at the European level many administrative units are currently emerging, but it would be too simple to deduce a high degree of political autonomy merely from their labelling as 'agencies'.[60] For the constitutional states in general, it is not possible to show that there has been a general trend toward autonomous administrative agencies.

II. CONSTITUTIONAL REVIEW

1. *Constitutional supremacy and constitutional review*

Constitutions are the supreme norms in legal systems. They establish political institutions and define the procedures by which these institutions interact with each other and make laws and rules. Constitutions contain the law of law-making.[61] But if the constitution is to be the supreme law of the land, more is required than a norm called 'the constitution', containing rules that claim to be at the top of the hierarchy of norms. The supremacy of constitutional law needs different institutional backups.

If it is possible to amend a constitution the same way as a normal law can be altered, the constitution will function no differently from such a law and can be amended or abandoned during any regular legislative action. The constitution remains just an organizational statute—such as many 19th

---

[58] See for a recent affirmative depiction of this alleged development: F. Vilbert, *The Rise of the Unelected* (Cambridge: Cambridge University Press, 2007).

[59] E. Kagan, 'Presidential Administration', *114 Harvard Law Review* (2001), 2245; L. Lessig, C. Sunstein, 'The President and the Administration', *94 Columbia Law Review* (1994), 1, 5–6.

[60] D. Curtin, *Executive power of the European Union* (Oxford: Oxford University Press, 2009), 146–165, 172–176.

[61] H. Kelsen, *Allgemeine Staatslehre* (Berlin: Springer, 1925), 248.

century constitutions were.[62] Even if a constitutional amendment required a more demanding procedure, one could speak meaningfully of constitutional supremacy only if there were an institution that reviewed compliance with the constitution. One, though not the only possibility[63] of organizing such a control is establishing a constitutional court that is entitled to review democratic statutes, be it in the form of a specialized court or one function of the highest court of the judicial system.

The institution of constitutional courts is by no means self-evident. The power to repeal laws emerged slowly.[64] The US Supreme Court, often identified as the first constitutional court, was at first only the highest court for the review of federal law. Whether the court was originally supposed to have the authority to examine the laws of the federal government against the constitution is as historically contested[65] as the question of when the court actually started the practice of constitutional review. Other old democratic systems still only very hesitantly recognize a judicially enforceable supremacy of the constitution, for example England or the Netherlands,[66] or have designed a limited constitutional jurisdiction, which functions rather as a political advisory body with processes similar to those of a court, such as in France.[67] It is not a mere historical incident that the idea to protect the democratic process by a court gained particular influence in post-totalitarian and post-authoritarian democracies. Germany, Italy, Spain, Poland, Hungary, and South Africa all established a strong specialized constitutional jurisdiction.[68] The negative political experiences of these countries motivated them to bind the democratic legislator to legally enforceable, substantial rules.

As we have noted, in the old revolutionary constitutional traditions the constitution was understood as a political document.[69] Its content was realized by political action. The political institutions and the public had to

---

[62] R. Wahl, 'Der Vorrang der Verfassung', 20 *Der Staat* (1981), 485.

[63] C. S. Nino, *The Constitution of Deliberative Democracy* (New Haven: Yale University Press, 1996), 187–216.

[64] D. Grimm, 'Constitutional Adjudication and Democracy', in M. Andenas (ed.), *Judicial Review in International Perspective* (Den Haag: Kluwer, 2000), 103 (108–9).

[65] Sceptical: L. Kramer, *The People Themselves* (Oxford: Oxford University Press, 2004).

[66] Compare Article 120 of the Constitution of the Netherlands, which excludes judicial review.

[67] D. Rousseau, *Droit de Contentieux Constitutionel* (Paris: Montchrestien, 9th ed 2010), 47–9.

[68] C. Thornhill, *A Sociology of Constitutions* (Cambridge: Cambridge University Press, 2011), 327–71; P. Pasquino, 'Constitutional Adjudication and democracy', in *11 Ratio Juris* (1997), 28; for the important Asian cases: T. Ginsburg, *Judicial Review in New Democracies* (Cambridge: Cambridge University Press, 2003), 90–105.

[69] To this tradition: C. Möllers, 'Pouvoir Constituant—Constitution—Constitutionalisation', in A. v. Bogdandy, J. Bast (eds.), *Principles of European Constitutional Law* (London: Hart, 2nd rev. ed, 2010), 169–203 (171–3).

come to an agreement on the meaning of the constitution time and again. Defining what the constitution meant could not be delegated to a court. And even in our age of widespread constitutional review it seems important to remember the fact that there can be no clear-cut hierarchy between the judicial interpretation of the constitution and the interpretation of the democratic legislator. In fact, the legislator always acts as the first interpreter of the constitution.[70]

The problem of any form of constitutional review with respect to our concept of separated powers is obvious: a politically independent court, which adjudicates individualized cases through an exclusive judicial procedure, has the power to suspend laws and to make decisions of a scope that would typically require democratic legitimacy. Is it defensible that democratic outcomes are produced by an exclusive court procedure directed towards individual legitimacy? Or does the establishment of constitutional review contravene the very idea of separated powers? And, though it may be legal, is it not an illegitimate institution? To resolve these issues we will have to consider the different tasks of constitutional courts. In any case, it is clear that the power of a court to repeal democratic laws always raises the issue of its democratic legitimacy, even though the judicial process is not actually geared towards this form of legitimacy.[71] Like all other courts, constitutional courts are expected to justify their decisions as purely juridical judgments. But this is especially difficult because constitutional texts are particularly open and in need of interpretation and because the repeal of a democratic statute is normally politically contested. Still, avoiding any appearance of political partisanship remains crucial for the legitimacy of constitutional courts.

2. *Constitutional courts as guardians of the democratic process*

The legislative claim to democratic legitimacy requires observance of certain rules, for example respect for egalitarian suffrage. Therefore, the democratic legislator is not free to set the rules that define the democratic process and create its own legitimacy.[72] This insight provides a first, albeit limited justification of constitutional jurisdiction: it may be needed to ensure the democratic legitimacy of the legislature.[73]

---

[70] For this term, see P. Kirchhof, 'Demokratischer Rechtsstaat—Staatsform der Zugehörigen', in J. Isensee, P. Kirchhof (eds.), *Handbuch des Staatsrechts Band*, vol. IX (Heidelberg: C. F. Müller, 1997), § 221, sect. 77.

[71] See Chapter 2, III., 3.

[72] Seminal for this concept of judicial review: J. H. Ely, *Democracy and Distrust* (Cambridge, Mass.: Harvard University Press, 1980), 73.

[73] M. Troper, 'The Logic of Justification of Judicial Review', 1 *International Constitutional Law* (2003), 99 (109).

Some legal systems—such as the German and the French—introduce special kinds of legal procedures for this purpose. In these constellations, not every individual citizen is entitled to initiate constitutional review of the democratic process, at least so long as the rules in question do not affect individual participatory rights such as the right to vote. Only certain constitutional institutions or the parliamentary opposition may trigger this type of review.[74] The idea underpinning this restriction is that even access to constitutional review of democratic procedures requires a special legitimacy. This legitimacy arises, for example, from the special status of a certain number of members of parliament. Such a process is similar to a court procedure, but it departs to some extent from the judicial function as understood here because the process does not revolve around individualized issues and individual rights, but rather around general issues that inevitably acquire a political dimension. This is not typical of courts. It is therefore no coincidence that Anglo-Saxon legal systems, which take the relationship between court procedure and protection of individual rights particularly seriously, are unfamiliar with such special constitutional procedures and do not make any distinction between 'high courts' and 'constitutional courts'.[75] Aberrations from traditional court procedure to accommodate political affairs have been regarded in the Anglo-Saxon tradition as an encroachment on the independence of the courts.[76] By contrast, the French tradition has no issues with the establishment of special entities for the review of state activity.[77] The Kelsenian concept of specialized constitutional courts, now globally the most common form of constitutional review, stands between the two: it allows for special procedures for questions of state organization, as in France. But, as in the United States, it is centred on the decision of individual cases, like an ordinary court, and unlike the original Conseil Constitutionnel in France, which acted as an advisory body and operated within the legislative process, before the law came into effect.[78] These peculiarities of the French system of constitutional review, which separate the constitutional court from the ordinary courts, are not hard to defend for the reasons mentioned above. But at least one question remains: to what extent does a democratic process require or is capable of bearing legally defined rules to define itself? Or, conversely, how much scope should there be—or not be—for informal democratic practices that are not under

---

[74] See E-J. Sieyès, *Du jury constitutionnaire* (1795), thereto M. Gauchet, *Révolution des pouvoirs* (Paris: Gallimard, 1995), 159–86.

[75] Explicitly: *Raines v Byrd*, 521 U.S. 811 (1997). Generally, the common law system seems to be procedurally more formalist and more conservative. Against this backdrop, the seminal critique in A. Chayes, 'The Role of the Judge in Public Law Litigation', 89 *Harvard Law Review*, 1281 (1976).

[76] See Chapter 1, I., 2.   [77] See Chapter 1, I., 1.   [78] Chapter 1.

constitutional review? A modest answer could be that the less a legal system trusts democratic traditions and the self-determined rules of the democratic legislative, the more plausible establishing court-like constitutional review seems to become.

This soft answer indicates that the explanatory power of models that defend constitutional review as a protector of the democratic process is limited to very specific constitutional contexts. One case in point is John H. Ely's famous theory of representation reinforcement targeted at the US Supreme Court.[79] This model, in which the court protects 'insulated minorities' from exclusion from the political process, might well explain and justify some of the court's interventions in electoral legislation. But it would be problematic to generalize this argument and to simply extend it to other jurisdictions: Ely's argument depends on the existence of a majoritarian electoral system, as well as a very specific social structure in which a minority cannot gain political traction within the formal power structures.[80] The argument does not work equally for other systems that do not have these features. What does representation reinforcement actually mean in a proportional electoral system? And how do we cope with minorities that are not as insulated?

Assigning courts the role of the guardian of democracy involves a more general risk. It is an unresolved question to what extent the democratic process is a rule-abiding procedure or, to the contrary, to what extent every democratic order is required to constantly change and adjust its own understanding of democracy while performing the democratic process. Should democracy adhere to a constitutionally defined and judicially enforceable democratic ideal, as some theorists and even some constitutional courts seem to assume?[81] Or do democracies rather function like a ship constantly repaired while at sea,[82] which would suggest that no Archimedian point of judicial review exists. The constitutional definition of a certain concept of democracy by a court is, in principle, dangerous—and possibly quite undemocratic. The US Supreme Court's decision concerning campaign financing is an example, though the majority claimed not to be interpreting a democratic principle but the First Amendment.[83] The decision was characterized by the clash of two competing concepts of democracy: on the one hand, the idea of an open marketplace in which everybody freely participates; on the other, the idea of democratic republican equality

---

[79] J. H. Ely, *Democracy and Distrust* (Cambridge, Mass.: Harvard University Press, 1980).

[80] I. Shapiro, *The State of Democratic Theory* (Princeton: Princeton University Press, 2004), 65–8.

[81] Germany is a case in point.

[82] This image stems from O. Neurath, Protokollsätze, *3 Erkenntnis* (1922/23), 204–14 (206).

[83] *Citizens United v Federal Election Commission*, 558 U.S. 50 (2010).

in which no one should have privileged access to the political process on the basis of wealth or social power. If a court is to provide a constitutional solution to this problem, it must define the democratic process in a far-reaching way, and exclude the democratic process from defining what it means by 'democracy'. As we have seen, some may argue that this is precisely the task of a constitutional court; that the democratic process has a claim to be democratic only after a court has provided such a definition. In any case, however, the result is judicial implementation of a contested understanding of democracy that cannot be changed by a democratic decision.

3. Constitutional courts as guardians of a federal polity

Federal systems require rules that govern the relationship between the law at the federal and at the state level. A critical task of the federal institutions is to ensure the consistent implementation of federal law in all constituent states. A federal law which is implemented only in Uttar Pradesh, but not in Kashmir, in Massachusetts but not Alabama, loses its claim to validity. Not only has the federal government a genuine interest in this claim. It is also important to those states wishing to implement the law but concerned over being disadvantaged if other states refuse to do so. A central federal court, though not necessarily a constitutional one, is required to monitor the uniform application of federal rules. However, the institution of a constitutional court becomes necessary if and to the extent that the division of powers between the federal and the state level is subject to judicial review. This judicial power seems crucial for the whole federal construction. As Oliver Holmes put it, 'I do not think the United States would come to an end if we lost our power to declare an Act of Congress void. I do think the Union would be imperilled if we could not make that declaration as to the laws of the several States.'[84] The power for such a form of review is typical of constitutional courts; indeed many constitutional courts came into existence only because a federal constitutional system had been established.[85]

For our concept of separated powers, the following, not unproblematic constellation seems to be typical: a constitutional court invalidates a democratic decision taken at the federal or state level because the acting level lacked the required constitutional power to legislate. At first glance, this seems to be a special case of the democracy-preserving review discussed

[84] O. W. Holmes, 'Law and the Court [1913]', *The Collected Legal Papers* (New York, 1920), 291 (295–6).

[85] O. Beaud, 'De quelque particularités de la justice constitutionelle dans un système federal', in C. Grewe, O. Jouanjan, E. Maulin, P. Wachsmann (eds.), *La notion de la 'justice constitutionelle'* (Paris: Dalloz, 2005), 49.

above. For if we understand a federation as a covenant between the people of different states constituting the foundation for a new, common political level from which a common democratic subject emerges,[86] then the distribution of authority between the people of the states and those of the federal level forms part of the democratic rules of the game. We need a politically independent authority to protect these rules.

But the problem is not solved that simply. Competence provisions in federal constitutions are often designed in a teleological form, which makes judicial review more difficult. This becomes particularly clear when we consider the example of economic competences as the authority over the domestic market in the European Treaties: the *interstate commerce* clause in the US Constitution or the 'Law of the Economy' clause in the German Basic Law. All these powers aim at a certain market-driven politically dynamic development of the federal level to bring the constituent states closer together. It is therefore not surprising that such norms regularly demand the additional condition that the enactment of a federal law requires a practical or economic *necessity*: the federal level is entitled to regulate only if this regulation is 'necessary' for preserving or enhancing the economic unity of the federation. Finally, if the federal institutions intend to pass a law that affects state powers, that law normally requires the approval of some kind of majority of the constituent states, be it because their governments or their representatives are represented in the legislature, or just because political majorities are hard to find at the federal level against a majority of the constituent states. If the states operate within and through the federal level, then in many cases decisions of the federal government may also be supported by a majority of the states.

All these circumstances cast some doubts on the legitimacy of a constitutional court to review federal rules. First, the federal powers are not defined by unequivocal rules of procedure, but rather by teleological principles which refer to political and social necessities and are replete with factual assumptions and political evaluations. Secondly, in such constellations the court has to review a democratic statute, which is typically backed by a majority of both levels, and has to review it in the light of a federal covenant that is designed to further unite the federation. To take a comparative example from a private law corporation: in the case of a contested issue of interpretation regarding a sales contract between two parties, it is not sufficient for a court to only take into consideration the legal position of one of the two parties to the lawsuit. In the case of a contract on the basis of

---

[86] O. Beaud, *Théorie de la Fédération* (Paris: Presses Universitaires de France, 2008); A. R. Greber, *Die vorpositiven Grundlagen des Bundesstaates* (Basel: Helbing & Lichtenhahn, 2000); see also C. Schönberger, 'Die Europäische Union als Bund', *129 Archiv des öffentlichen Rechts* (2004), 81.

which a number of parties founded a corporation, the claim to legitimacy of a decision of the executive body of the corporation, which is carried by the overwhelming majority of the shareholders, seems superior to the dissenting vote of a single shareholder. So even if the corporation, like a federation, was founded on the unanimous consensus of all its founders, the so-founded corporation starts to gain autonomy; the autonomy it was founded for in the first place. But this autonomy includes a development; a certain departure from the original contract and from the need for consensus among all founding parties. We will have another look at this structural phenomenon when we discuss international organizations.[87]

This raises the question of whether constitutional review is the best mechanism for the control of federal powers. Federal provisions are politically contentious norms with a universal scope that require practical political judgements for their interpretation. Unlike other constitutional norms, competence rules define the jurisdictions of two democratic systems. Finally, the question at which level an issue should be regulated is typically intertwined with the purely political question of how the issue should be regulated, if at all. The decision to establish a welfare system is hardly separable from a preference in favour of centralization. Gun control in the US can be effective only if regulated by the federal government. The political decision in favour of such controls is also a decision in favour of the federal level—and vice versa.[88] Under ordinary circumstances, such decisions should be made by the legislative. But this solution brings its own problems. The difficulty with such an arrangement is that deciding how to distribute competences would lie entirely in the hands of the federal legislator. This means that no constitutional competence rules at all would be necessary. Such a political understanding of competency norms is unfamiliar to some constitutional orders like the German one, in which issues of federal competencies are resolved through intensive constitutional interpretation by the court.[89] This is quite different in constitutional systems in which the constituent states have much greater political autonomy and the question of federalism remains politically contested. In the United States, Canada, and the European Union, the court mostly respects the federal legislator's claims to have power to regulate—unlike legislative decisions at the state level because the latter may compromise federal unity. The European Court of Justice has repealed legislative decisions at the European level for a lack of competence in only a very few cases.[90] The US Supreme Court has

---

[87] Chapter 4.

[88] *Printz v United States*, 521 U.S. 898 (1997) (Scalia, J.).

[89] S. Oeter, *Integration und Subsidiarität im deutschen Bundesstaatsrecht* (Tübingen: Mohr 1998).

[90] European Court of Justice, *Tobacco*, Case C-376/98, 2000, I-8419, paras. 84–5.

refrained from doing so for quite a while, although in recent times it has done so more frequently.[91] The development in the US, however, has been the target of much academic criticism and tends to split the court into two political factions.

What follows from all of this? First, there is no general rule as to when the authority to define federal powers should be assigned to a constitutional court. From the point of view of the separation of powers, there is a strong argument to be made in favour of assigning this power to the legislator at the federal level. A complete juridification of federal powers by means of constitutional review is probably desirable only when the distribution of authority is no longer fundamentally politically disputed—as it continues to be in the EU and the US—but is broadly centralized, as is the case in Germany. A second important factor is the constitutional amendment procedure. Federal systems have to constantly adjust to changes in society. If constitutional amendments are mostly uncontested and the constitutional amendment procedure is easily met, then it would seem less problematic to put the amended rules under stricter constitutional scrutiny. This is the case in Germany, where the democratic constitution-making power can react to the court by amending the federal rules.[92] If amending the constitution is difficult and the issue is politically contested it is helpful, perhaps even necessary, to ventilate the necessary adjustments of the federal order through normal legislation. This would also mean having a constitutional review of federal powers with less scrutiny. In this case, constitutional review should be limited to repealing completely implausible forms of exercised authority and otherwise respecting the democratic legislative process at the federal level.

4. *Constitutional courts as protectors of basic rights*

The protection of basic rights is the most significant and most debated function of constitutional courts. From the perspective of separation of powers, it may also be the most questionable one. In a constitution, basic rights define the fundamental legal position of individuals. They oblige the democratic legislator to create and/or protect a particular sphere of freedom. It is therefore widely accepted that basic rights should be subject to review by a constitutional court and that they may serve as liberal trumps

---

[91]   *United States v Lopez*, 515 U.S. 549, 556 (1995); *United States v Morrison*, 529 U.S. 598 (2000).

[92]   For an overview of the numerous constitutional amendments in Germany since 1949 that favoured the distribution of decision-making powers to the federal level: A. Busch, 'Das oft geänderte Grundgesetz', in W. Merkel, A. Busch (eds.), *Demokratie in Ost und West* (Frankfurt am Main: Suhrkamp, 1999), 549 (555). The last two federal reforms have started a reversal of this trend.

against the legislator.[93] However, in most democratic constitutional states this institutional protection of basic rights was only established in a slow and inchoate way. It took the US Supreme Court almost a century after Marbury vs Madison to repeal federal laws for the violation of basic rights.[94] The French Conseil Constitutionnel did so for the first time in 1972 and even today remains hesitant to invoke basic rights against a democratic statute.[95] This hesitation in no way represents a misreading of the revolutionary basic rights catalogues. In France these rights were, as we have seen, designed as political demands made upon the legislator,[96] while the fathers of the US Constitution's Bill of Rights intended that the rights laid down would be enforced by courts against Congress.[97] Some of the reasons for these conceptual differences have been explained already.[98] The establishment of subjective rights requires democratic legitimacy, for rights define a *general* rule for the distribution of freedom, which has a potential effect on everyone. Basic rights do not necessarily create a lawless zone free of the exercise of public authority. They may instead define legislative burdens of justification or even depend on some kind of state intervention, as in the case of private property that depends on the establishment of a legal system.[99] No constitutional court is required, however, to protect basic rights in individual cases. Regular courts may exercise this function as well. But how can we assess basic rights protection vis-à-vis the legislator, which is typical of constitutional courts?

The repeal of a democratic statute infringing upon a basic right poses an especially problematic case for the legitimacy of judicial action. The court adjudicates an individual claim expressed in an exclusive procedure—but with the effect of voiding a statute that concerns the whole democratic community. In an ideal situation, the division of labour between the branches would work differently. The distribution of freedom designed by the legislator would be implemented by ordinary courts as a legal rule and would, consequently, ensure a comprehensive protection of individual rights. But is the protection of individual rights from the democratic majority not the first and foremost task of a constitutional court? This is a

[93] R. Dworkin, 'Rights as Trumps', in J. Waldron (ed.), *Theories of Rights* (New York: Oxford University Press, 1984), 153–67.

[94] This occured during the Lochner era, in wich the Court relied on the right to freedom of contract to annul progressive social legislation. See e.g., Adair v. United States, 208 U.S. 161 (1908).

[95] Conseil Constitutionel, no 71-44 DC, 16 June 1971.

[96] See Chapter 1, I., 1.

[97] D. Currie, *The Constitution in Congress: The Federalist Period 1789–1801* (Chicago: University of Chicago Press, 1997), 111.

[98] See Chapter 2, II., 1.

[99] On the concept of right from a legal realist perspective: W. Hohfeld, 'Some Fundamental Legal Conceptions As Applied In Judicial Reasoning', 23 *Yale Law Journal* (1917), 16.

common perception. The problem with this assumption is that it seems rather impossible to determine the scope of a sphere of freedom solely on the basis of the interests of the individual concerned, exactly because this individual's idea of freedom potentially affects the freedom of everybody else. This insight also has implications for the individualized decision-making procedure of a constitutional court. In a procedure to which a plaintiff has privileged access, the court decides upon the general distribution of freedom on an absolutely minimalist textual basis.

This problem seems less pressing with regard to the legal conflicts between a single citizen and the state. If the freedom of an imprisoned person who has been arrested by the police is at stake, the court has to define a relatively exclusive legal relation between the person and the state. The problem also seems less pressing if the basic right can be interpreted as a clear-cut rule whose interpretation is relatively little contested. This may be the case with certain elements of American First Amendment law.

The legitimacy problem becomes more serious in cases in which the definition of the right concerns legal relations between more persons, for example, if two parties in a legal dispute can claim basic rights. As a matter of legitimacy, in such constellations the decision of the case is effectively a legislative decision regarding two spheres of freedom that enjoy equal constitutional protection. As a matter of methodology, this will tend to happen in constitutional systems that apply a balancing approach to basic rights rather than in those that categorically define spheres of non-intervention by the state. As a critique of the German balancing doctrine aptly put it, in a balancing approach nobody has rights that are defined independently from the community of everybody else.[100] Balancing tests like the different versions of the principle of proportionality[101] seem like legislative procedures in disguise, as they have to accept different preferences and decide among them. The idea that balancing could be rationalized, as proposed by an important strand of legal theory,[102] reminds us of the idea that we have tried to criticize above; that democratic procedures can be rationalized.[103] This is not the place to examine the merits of this debate, but if the model of rational balancing were right, the question of which rights are explicitly protected by a specific constitution and which are not would be completely irrelevant. Legal academia and courts in different jurisdictions

---

[100] B. Rusteberg, Grundrechtsdogmatik als Schlüssel zum Verhältnis von Gemeinschaft und Individuum, in Junge Wissenschaft im Öffentlichen Rechte.V. (ed.), *Kollektivität—Öffentliches Recht zwischen Gruppeninteresse und Gemeinwohl*(Baden-Baden: Nomos, 2012), 15–32.

[101] For a good comparative analysis: A. Stone Sweet, J. Matthews, 'Proportionality Balancing and Global Constitutionalism', *47 Columbia Journal of Transnational Law (2008)*, 72, 111–59.

[102] R. Alexy, *A Theory of Constitutional Rights* (Oxford: Oxford University Press, 2002), 369–87.

[103] Chapter 2, III., 2.

have come up with many subtle but diverging solutions for this type of case. Yet, if the issues at stake affect a great number of people a democratically legitimate decision is required; one which a court cannot provide.

In many cases, it is possible to accommodate these conflicts in a pragmatic way. For one, constitutional courts try to avoid the annulment of a law if it is possible to interpret the law in a way consistent with the basic right. Even in the case of an interpretation of the statute consistent with the constitution, however, the legislator's array of possible reactions is reduced: if a court decides not to annul a law regulating the right to assembly but interprets the law in a way consistent with the constitutional right to assembly to preserve the law, the consequence may be that the legislator is legally obliged to observe the judicial interpretation from that point on.[104] The problem is less urgent in legal systems in which the high court also serves as a constitutional court (US, Israel), as compared to systems with a specialized constitutional court, which interpret only constitutional, not statutory law (Germany, Spain, Poland). For in the latter systems, the court's interpretation receives constitutional status as a whole and thus binds the legislator more intensively. Everything these courts utter is necessarily constitutional law, whereas the decisions of supreme courts may also be framed as interpretations of the statutory rules in place.[105] Of course, in order to defuse the legitimacy problem constitutional courts still attempt, in accordance with their judicial function, to limit and individualize the scope of their decisions through an appropriate rationale.[106] But this is not always successful, as the political outrage caused by decisions protecting basic rights shows.[107] Finally, a lasting change in the social distribution of freedom, empirical studies presume, does not result from such verdicts alone. It comes about only when there is a politically enforceable legislative will to put the judicial concept of freedom into effect and to systematically enforce it through the administration.[108]

---

[104] An institutional dialogue is institutionalized by the override clause in section 33 of the Canadian Charter of Rights and Freedoms. For convincing doubts that such a dialogue could create legitimacy for the court because the ideal of deliberation does not apply to courts: L. B. Tremlay, 'The legitimacy of judicial review: The limits of dialogue between courts and legislatures', ICON 3 (2005), 617 (638–44).

[105] For a comparative analysis of the very different effects of the courts' decisions: W. Heun, 'Rechtliche Wirkungen verfassungsgerichtlicher Entscheidungen', in C. Starck (ed.), *Fortschritte der Verfassungsgerichtsbarkeit II* (Baden-Baden: Nomos, 2006), 173.

[106] Again C. R. Sunstein, *One Case at a Time* (Cambridge, Mass.: Harvard University Press, 1999), 24.

[107] *Brown v Board of Education*, 347 U.S. 483 (1954); Federal Constitutional Court, *Kruzifix*, BVerfGE 93, 1.

[108] See with regard to the US Supreme Court: G. Rosenberg, *The Hollow Hope* (Chicago: University of Chicago, 1991); M. Tushnet, *Weak Courts, Strong Rights* (Princeton: Princeton University Press, 2008), Part II.

Against this background, one doctrinal peculiarity that can be found in different jurisdictions, from Germany to the European Court of Human Rights, is especially disturbing: constitutional duties of the legislator to protect.[109] This construction deduces a legislative obligation to act for the protection of the basic right, thereby restricting the basic rights of others. There may be much said against the merits of legal argument that takes rights to justify the abridgement of individual freedom. For us it is more relevant to look at the considerable implications for the procedural role of a constitutional court in a system of separated powers. To provide another, already mentioned, German example: when, after reunification, a cross-party majority in the Bundestag passed a liberal law concerning abortion, a qualified number of members of parliament challenged the law in the Federal Constitutional Court. As a result of the protective duties doctrine, these members were entitled to request that the legislator be placed under an obligation to protect basic rights, even though they had no claim of their own.[110] But if a legislative omission constitutes a violation of a constitutional duty to protect, as the German constitutional court held with regard to the legislative 'omission' not to penalize abortion,[111] then the constitutional court effectively assumes the right of legislative initiative. In such cases, the court does not, as envisaged, intervene at the end but at the beginning of the law-making cycle. The members of parliament are turned into the admin-istrators of the constitutional court's interpretation of individual freedom. A democratic minority brings a case to the court to repeal a democratic majority decision in the name of an individual right it does not have. If the legitimacy of the court is based either on individual concerns or on the protection of democratic processes, then, in this constellation, the court lacks both.

What follows from these considerations? To be sure, the democratic decision to institutionalize constitutional review as such deserves respect. It would not be very democratic to deny the constitution maker the option to introduce constitutional review into a constitutional order. Therefore, the cases in which a court has reinvented itself as a constitutional court, as in Israel and the United States, may be the most spectacular and problematic, but they are also quite exceptional: in most constitutional systems,

---

[109] For a comparative analysis between Europe and the US, see D. Grimm, *The protective function of the state*, in G. Nolte (ed.), *European and US Constitutionalism* (Cambridge: Cambridge University Press, 2005), 137–55; F. Michelman, *The protective function of the state in the United States and Europe: the constitutional question*, in G. Nolte (ed.), *European and US Constitutionalism* (Cambridge: Cambridge University Press, 2005), 156–80. For a critique from the perspective of the separation of powers: W. Heun, *Funktionell-rechtliche Schranken der Verfassungsgerichtsbarkeit* (Baden-Baden: Nomos, 1992), 43.

[110] Federal Constitutional Court, *Schwangerschaftsabbruch II*, BVerfGE 88, 203.

[111] Federal Constitutional Court, *Schwangerschaftsabbruch II*, BVerfGE 88, 203.

constitutional review has been explicitly introduced. The literature about judicial revolutions is relevant only to very few states.[112]

As claimed in the Introduction, the purpose of our model of separated powers cannot be to delegitimize democratic decisions in the name of a one-size-fits-all model. One of the main problems of theories of political constitutionalism (one that makes them look rather unpolitical) denying the legitimacy of constitutional review in general is that they do not accept the diversity of institutional designs in different constitutional systems.[113] In our view, a theory of separated powers makes no immediate contribution to the interpretation of basic rights, but it illuminates the procedural aspect of different understandings of individual rights. The separation of powers concept laid down here is not capable of providing sufficient criteria to determine whether a basic right was violated or not. Nonetheless, certain consequences arise from our approach. To start with, we can establish that it is precisely the protection of basic rights against the legislator that raises the most urgent questions with regard to the legitimacy of constitutional review. This is because in such a constellation it is an individual concern that triggers a decision of general scope in an exclusive procedure. The notion that there are a defined number of basic rights which the court must enforce is not only methodically naive and blind to institutional limits, but also fairly undemocratic. Moreover, we have seen that this deficit becomes more acute under some specific circumstances, i.e., with specialized constitutional courts rather than supreme courts that also practise constitutional review. Finally, it is more acute under a balancing approach that simulates a legislative process in a judicial procedure. It is more acute when individual persons in a case are entitled to base their interests on different basic rights. It is the most acute with regard to constitutional duties to protect.

5. The theoretical debate: constitutional courts between moral and political constitutionalism

The question of constitutional review has become one of the main battle-grounds of constitutional theory. The two main fronts are constituted on the one hand by the critical stance of political constitutionalism,[114] which sees a global rise of constitutional courts taking political decisions with a special

---

[112] A. Stone Sweet, *Governing with Judges. Constitutional Politics in Europe* (Oxford: Oxford University Press 2000), 109–13.

[113] See, e.g., R. Bellamy, *Political Constitutionalism* (Cambridge: Cambridge University Press, 2007), 260; J. Waldron, 'The Core of the Case against Judicial Review', 115 *Yale Law Journal* (2006), 1346 (1406), claiming that 'rights-based judicial review is inappropriate for reasonably democratic societies'.

[114] M. Tushnet, *Taking the Constitution Away From The Courts* (Princeton: Princeton University Press, 1999).

agenda. On the other hand, we find an affirmative position that identifies constitutionalism with a strong, even moralistic reading of basic rights to be implemented by judges as moral experts.[115]

For our institutional approach, this debate seems too general, too abstract, and, on both sides, not sufficiently respectful of the democratic process. First, it has to be stressed that institutional differences between courts and legislatures matter. Judicial procedures allow for a specific perspective on rights, filtered through the individual experience with a specific event.[116] A constitution that wants to stress this perspective at the expense of the democratic community may introduce constitutional review, perhaps as a matter of democratic self-doubt. In any case, whatever the legitimacy of a constitutional court may be, it not does seem possible merely to substitute a judicial interpretation with a legislative interpretation of a right.[117] These two cannot be substituted because the legislature will produce a rule on the distribution of freedoms, whilst the court will produce a ruling on a case whose implementation works in a completely different manner. The idea that rights are contested and that, therefore, the legislator should make the decision regarding rights[118] makes use of an equivocation in the meaning of 'right'. But what is meant: a distributive rule or a decision about a concrete claim? We must concede that this distinction becomes blurry when courts are established that produce quasi-legislative rules to solve an individual case. This is the reason why constitutional review is not just endorsed here. On the other hand, however, it remains far from clear whether the legislature would be willing or able to honour this distinction by actually making such rules. As we have seen, much depends on the way courts and legislatures understand constitutional rights. This, again, reduces the likelihood that there could be one correct theory of constitutional review for all legal orders. In any case, the institutional alternative to constitutional review lies in the interpretation of basic rights through regular courts, which apply the rules of the constitution and of the normal legislator without being entitled to declare the latter void in the name of the first.

Secondly, it is no accident that much of the general discourse on constitutional review has been conducted by legal philosophers who tend to generalize their experiences ad hoc with a particular legal order, be it the

---

[115] See, e.g., Dworkin's depiction of the idealized judicial figure of Hercules: R. Dworkin, *Taking Rights Seriously* (Cambridge: Harvard University Press, 1977), 105; see also R. Alexy, *A Theory of Constitutional Rights* (Oxford: Oxford University Press, 2002), 86–92.

[116] This distinction is downplayed in M. Tushnet, *Weak Courts, Strong Rights* (Princeton: Princeton University Press, 2008), 91–6.

[117] J. Waldron, 'The Core of the Case against Judicial Review', *115 Yale Law Journal* (2006), 1346 (1406).

[118] J. Waldron, 'The Core of the Case against Judicial Review', *115 Yale Law Journal* (2006), 1346.

American[119] or the German[120]. But as long as rights work differently in different legal systems this claim to a universal legal argument does not help. But the same is true for the critique of constitutional review. After all, in most constitutional systems, constitutional review has been set up through an explicit decision by a democratic constitution-maker. Oft-quoted cases of judicial self-empowerment are as exceptional as examples of a judicial government.[121] If constitutions tie legal and political procedures together, there is no easy solution for constitutional theory that reduces constitutionalism to just one of its two necessary elements.

6. *Conclusion: constitutional courts as hybrids*

Finally, while much of the Anglo-American literature has focused its interest on Supreme Courts, Specialized Constitutional Courts are globally the institutional rule. Specialized Constitutional Courts may be understood best as hybrid entities that are neither appropriately described as courts nor as purely political actors. Such courts, created in an openly political process and equipped with particular procedural rules, may not be appropriately described as agents of judicial politics, as they adhere neither to a political agenda nor stick to a judicial procedure. At first glance, constitutional courts try to define rules that bind the political process. That is meant by the formula of a judicialization of politics. But if one looks at the very important relation between constitutional courts and other lower courts, one may well find that constitutional courts produce a very specific form of politicization of the legal argument. If civil and criminal law courts are obliged to implement a basic rights jurisprudence by a constitutional court, they are asked to apply constitutional law; a kind of legal reasoning that is less formalist, less textual, less technical, closer to political theory, and therefore in a certain sense more political and more general.[122] The constitutionalization of the court system is then also a form of *politicization of the judiciary*. And finally, we have already noted that, when constitutional courts constrain the majoritarian political process by protecting the rights of the political opposition inside and outside the formal political process, they may even *politicize the political process*, meaning that they

---

[119] R. Dworkin, *Taking Rights Seriously* (Cambridge: Harvard University Press, 1977); R. Dworkin, *Law's Empire* (Cambridge: Harvard University Press, 1986). The arguments developed in both of Dworkin's seminal books are almost exclusively based on US case law.

[120] R. Alexy, *A Theory of Constitutional Rights* (Oxford: Oxford University Press 2002), Alexy's theory of constitutional rights relies essentially on German cases.

[121] C. Möllers, 'Why there is no Governing with Judges', Manuscript 2012.

[122] This case is made in a comparative manner in D. Robertson, *The Judge as a Political Theorist* (Princeton, Princeton University Press, 2010).

open up the space of political alternatives and political discourse. Therefore, a specific problem of some constitutional courts may lie in the fact that they are not excessively but insufficiently politicized. To be sure, it is obviously problematic when a court like the US Supreme Court tends to make decisions in which the justices are split into partisan factions. It may, indeed, be more plausible to have such questions decided by a parliament. But there is also an opposite problem: there are constitutional courts like the German one that argue in a widely self-referential fashion, re-interpreting their own decisions with little reference to the political context or other specificities of a case, in order to secure its legitimacy as a truly judicial organ. The legitimacy of these courts suffers from a lack of political and institutional sensitivity towards the political process. They try to act as if they are normal courts that decide conflicts between two insulated parties but they are not.

These phenomena indicate that constitutional courts are hybrid institutions that are misunderstood by being pressed into either one of two schemes: the judicial court scheme or the scheme of majoritarian power politics. As it is the central function of constitutions to bridge the relation between law and politics in a way that protects the differences between them, constitutional courts cannot be categorized by reference to only one of these two. Taking such a perspective does not necessarily mean to be less critical of constitutional review; it might just open up a different perspective in which constitutional review is seen as a form of its own, whose critique has to be more specific.

III. LIMITS OF JUDICIAL CONTROL
OF THE ADMINISTRATION

We will, finally, take a glance at judicial control of the administration. This is an important historical achievement; an institutional expression of respect for citizens' rights. But can it also become a problem if there is too much or too intensive protection of rights as against the administration? This question once again juxtaposes our two types of legitimacy. On the one hand, the individual self-determination of a citizen affected by an administrative decision; on the other hand, the democratic legitimacy of the administration resting upon legislative delegation, which may restrict individual freedom, more or less directly, in the name and on behalf of other citizens' interests. What are the limits of the judicial control of the administration? This issue touches upon a rather technical, relatively complicated area of administrative law. For this reason, we will only look at three specific risks implied by judicial control of the administration.

1. Standards of review

The first problem concerns the question of how intensively courts should be allowed to review the legality of an administrative decision. As has been shown, it is one of the responsibilities of the executive to apply the law in a specific situation, to realize the aims of the law but also to imply non-legal standards, as far as the law allows—for instance to look at the effectiveness and the costs of a measure.[123] In this case, the administration has a discretion that may even help to protect individual rights if it helps to realize the cognitive advantages of administrative action. An example in point is the discretion of the police as to whether they should intervene in the case of a petty offence. Another consequence of administrative discretion is a limitation on judicial review. A court does not have the power to decide which of two legally permissible decisions is more efficient. Initially, this poses a dilemma: if the legislator were to bind the administration solely to standards of efficiency, then the courts would lack virtually any standard for judicial control. It is also for this reason that restrictions of freedom require a legislative basis. On the other hand, if the court were to thoroughly review an administrative decision in its entirety, this review would suppress the special capabilities of the administrative procedure. For it seems impossible to entirely rehearse and reproduce them in court. The case of public exams may help to illustrate the point. All participants have the right to an exam procedure ensuring equal opportunity. It is not possible, however, to review in court all aspects of the exam in a way that readjusts the equality of opportunities of those who sued and those who did not sue and therefore did not appear in court. Even the complete repetition of the exam would have a distorting effect. In such cases, instead of remedying the lack of equal protection, judicial review may even threaten to distort it.

As a result, the judicial reconstruction of every aspect of an administrative decision seems far from an ideal solution to the problem of judicial review. Administrative discretion can help protect freedoms and cannot be completely reproduced in court. It is up to the legislator to determine the extent to which this discretion is permissible and, in certain circumstances, this legislative decision may require justification in terms of the relevant basic rights. But beyond the realm of judicial control, there is no 'natural' administrative room for discretion, only a politically constituted one. In addition, many administrative decisions affect the competing rights of different citizens. In this case, the protection of a right is not a simple argument for a strict judicial review triggered by a plaintiff, for example, if a building contractor seeks a planning permit against which the neighbour

---

[123] See Chapter 2, III., 4.

brings a lawsuit, or if several persons apply for a public assignment, such as a grant or an official position. In such cases, the allocation of freedom to one person is only possible at the expense of another. This demonstrates that strict judicial review of administrative actions does not necessarily result in greater individual freedom. The standard of review remains best understood as the result of a legislative decision to create a certain standard.

2. The temporality of judicial review

A second problem associated with the judicial review of administration actions concerns the temporal structure of the decision. In an ideal situation, the court reviews a finalized administrative act. As we have seen, the organizational autonomy of all institutions requires that the branches do not anticipate the action of the other branches; that they respect their respective internal decision-making process.[124] Nonetheless, many legal systems know forms of provisional legal protection in which judicial review does not require a final administrative decision. From the perspective of legitimacy these forms of judicial review are acceptable only in the case of a sufficiently concrete danger that an individual right could be finally lost or that the conditions for individual self-determination threaten to disappear as time elapses. An example is granting permission for a political demonstration at a certain time.

Again, it is important to stress that the extension of judicial review may be a problem for any legitimate freedom-preserving state action. It is not some etatist concept of a functional public administration that implies a strict standard of justification for injunctive interventions of courts into administrative actions. It is rather the insight that the autonomy of administrative action, and the need for some protection of the administrative decision-making process, follows from the democratic legitimacy of the legislative decisions that are implemented by the administration, as well as from its own direct democratic legitimacy. The positive freedom of those whose decisions are represented and implemented defines such a burden of justification. It is for these reasons highly problematic when, as in the German case, injunctive relief in administrative litigation has become the rule, instead of remaining the exception.

3. Access to courts and public interest litigation

The third problem concerns the issue of access to the courts. Who is actually entitled to initiate the judicial review of administrative activity? One answer

---

[124] See Chapter 2, III., 1.

would be: all whose rights are affected by the administration. But does this entitlement extend to citizens who just take an interest in the administration abiding by the rules? Granting derivative rights of action to interested citizens could help better control the administration. This option has been discussed for quite a while, particularly within environmental law, as environmental pollution—and certainly not air pollution and climate change—typically do not affect individual rights. For this reason, many legal systems define the legal entitlement for bringing an action more broadly. As such, organizations that demonstrate a concern, or simply anyone, are entitled to take legal action.

Is there a problem with such a generous notion of standing? Whilst the introduction of further rights of action is often controversial as a matter of policy, it is not regarded as a problem of the separation of powers in most legal orders. The exception is the United States where the Supreme Court found a general standing rule to violate the separation of powers. The legislator had laid down a broad standing provision that entitled everyone to bring a legal action against the decision of an authority to put certain types of animals or plants under protection. The Supreme Court declared that the courts only serve to protect individual rights and that they were not independent supervisory authorities for the administration.[125] If everyone were entitled to take legal action and the administration were confronted with an undefined number of controlling agents, the tasks of the courts would unduly expand into the domain of the administration. This decision has remained controversial, not least because the concept of 'individual right' is difficult to define in this context. If the legislator provides the opportunity to bring a legal action, then the legal provision constitutes a subjective right as such—albeit not a substantial one; one that defines a certain sphere of freedom, though indeed a procedural right. But the question of what constitutes a subjective right and what does not remains a legislative matter. The Supreme Court claimed to be protecting the administration from the courts but by making this claim the court interfered with a legislative decision.

On the basis of the standards used here, a broad definition of standing is unobjectionable, for the courts act in the cases they always should: retrospectively, individualizing and on the basis of a legal standard, though both

---

[125] *Lujan v Defenders of Wildlife*, 504 U.S. 555 (1991). For an overview over the discussion: R. J. Pierce Jr, 'Lujan v. Defenders of Wildlife: Standing as a Judicially Imposed Limit on Legislative Power', *42 Duke Law Journal* (1992–1993), 1170. A more recent decision is *Massachusetts v EPA*, 549 U.S. 497 (2007). The separation of powers concept of the majority is prepared by A. Scalia, 'The Doctrine of Standing as an Essential Element of Separation of Powers', *17 Suffolk University Law Review* (1983), 881.

the US court and others have seemed to be rather restrictive.[126] Still, the courts have to take care that those entitled to bring a legal action have already had an opportunity to articulate their interests during the administrative procedure and before the administrative decision. Otherwise, the administration would be confronted in the court procedure with interests or arguments that it could not factor into its original decision. Out of the three complexes mentioned, this one seems to be the least difficult to defend.

From this point of view the phenomenon of public interest litigation does not seem to be too problematic. If there is no natural realm of liberty but only politically defined spheres of individual freedom, as we assume in this model, it is obvious that the legislator is free to define new connections between individual action and the protection of the common good. Public interest litigation therefore only becomes dubious if it is widely initiated by the courts themselves. In this case courts may even claim to act on their own initiative. The combination of judicial independence and self-initiative looks indeed like an institutional nightmare in which one branch of government has final powers to decide, while completely insulated from individual as from democratic initiative. To be sure, as we know from Indian constitutional law, there may be cases of such a flagrant violation of human rights that the intervention of a court may be the only morally permissible solution. But instead of finding a further constitutional justification for such an intervention, it seems more plausible to concede that this kind of argument ends at this point. In cases of moral emergency, procedural arguments from constitutional theory lose their appeal.

4. Conclusion: courts and administrations

In all three examples, we witness a certain procedural assimilation between the activities of the administration and of the courts; between administrative and judicial law-making. If courts were permitted to rule by the same standards as the administration, at almost the same time, and initiated by anyone, then the differences between court and administration would begin to blur. This assimilation corresponds with the general trend toward employing courts as permanent moderators of administrative action, and therefore not as a final, individual-related, corrective, retrospective decision-making body. This development can be in the interest of the citizens because it makes legal protection more predictable, and thus in every respect cheaper

---

[126] A critique in: L Berat, 'The Constitutional Court of South-Africa and jurisdictional questions: In the Interest of Justice?', 3 *International Journal of Constitutional Law* (2005), 39.

and quicker.[127] It may also come out that courts are better able to implement legislative programmes than public administrations. From the perspective of the individual plaintiff, however, it also raises serious issues that can be formulated as a problem of individual legitimacy. Procedural structures that turn the courts into moderators, which guide the administrative process without making a conclusive and final decision, confront the individual plaintiff with a potentially changing governmental justification for restricting his individual freedom.[128] The court ceases to function as an institution operating only on the basis of legal standards with an independent distance to the administration and assumes the role of a cooperative partner that helps the administration remain inside the legal system by providing the legal basis and reasons for administrative actions, if not even as the better regulator that stands on the side of the state. An example is the practice that entitles the administration to provide supplemental reasons for a specific administrative action during a pending case before the court. Although the administration initially justified the administrative action that constituted an interference with individual rights on impermissible grounds, the court gives the administration an opportunity to modify the original justification within the court procedure to make the interference legal. In this case, legal protection of the citizen is directed at a moving target and ultimately comes to nothing because the court and the administration lack sufficient distance. From the point of view of our model of legitimacy, this substitution of the rationale for administrative action is particularly problematic because it affords no opportunity to review the intrusion of the individual as it actually occurred. Though the court is in this way not hierarchically integrated into the administration—that would violate its independence—, it is embedded in a horizontal structure of cooperation. This horizontal structure formally preserves the judicial power of the final judgment, but the judiciary and the administration become, from the perspective of the justice-seeking citizen, almost indistinguishable.

The legitimacies of judicial and executive law-making, however, depend critically on the institutional distinction between both. The separation of powers protects the organizational and procedural features of each power as distinct from others. The configuration of administrative action should be determined neither by the degree of the administrative commitment to law nor by court-like procedure. Therefore, any form of complete judicial review

---

[127] For a further analysis: A. Tschentscher, 'Indienstnahme der Gerichte für die Effizienz der Verwaltung', in M. Demel et al (eds.), *Funktionen und Kontrolle der Gewalten* (Stuttgart: Boorberg, 2001), 165.

[128] This is the basic argument in A. Chayes, 'The Role of the Judge in Public Law Litigation', *89 Harvard Law Review*, 1281 (1976); an argument that has had to accept a de-individualizing idea of judicial law-making.

of the administration is not ideal. On the other hand, the judicial procedure should not be organized in a way in which the court dwindles to merely facilitating administrative activity.

IV. CONCLUSION

The development of the concept of separated powers at the end of Chapter 2 laid out some foundations for a systematic reconstruction. We saw that the distinction between democratic and individual law-making mechanisms required a differentiation of the law-making procedures that helped norma-tively reconstruct the traditional triadic distinction of the public powers. One of the aims of Chapter 3 was to demonstrate that such a model may help develop more concrete arguments, though it can by no means solve all the problems of the separation of powers in a democratic constitutional system.

Contrary to the frequent presumption of an antagonism between parlia-ment and government, our reconstruction emphasized the significance of a positive relationship between the two, which are connected by a common accountability to the whole democratic subject. Their relationship should ideally be considered not as a separation but rather a division of labour, which must be organized in a way that enables both to preserve their different sources of legitimacy. The parliament, as legislator, has extensive powers to shape and design the legal order and, for the purpose of legisla-tion, has equally extensive rights of information against the executive. In principle, the parliament is free to decide how to use the executive to carry out legislative programmes and what degree of executive discretion and decision-making powers it should allow. Once parliament passes a law, this framework changes. Parliamentary interventions in the implementation of the law tend to disturb the legitimate relationship between the legislative and the executive branch.

With regard to the relationship between the legislative and the judiciary, it was important to take a closer look at constitutional courts whose power to repeal democratic laws appears thoroughly problematic from the perspec-tive of our model. It is, however, appropriate to differentiate between various functions of constitutional courts. On the one hand, constitutional courts oversee the application of democracy-enabling rules. They thereby protect the legislative claim to democratic legitimacy. Furthermore, consti-tutional courts may operate as guardians of a federal system of power. But in this function they are exposed to competing legitimacy claims of parliaments at the federal level and that of the constituent states. Finally, they are instated as the protector of basic rights against the legislator. This last function was the most difficult to defend: while organizing subjective spheres of freedom is a legislative task, the constitutional court challenges the legislative framework in an exclusive and unaccountable procedure.

Regarding the relationship between the executive and the judiciary, our topic was the judicial powers to review administrative action. The definition of standards of review is a legislative task. The legislator determines what degree of judicial review, with respect to which parties, is exercised in legal actions against the administration. Doubts arise particularly over procedures that assimilate the different procedural contributions of the administration and the courts, thereby endangering their specific contributions to the legitimacy of the whole system.

⚭ 4 ⚭

Separation of Powers Beyond the State

I. INTRODUCTION: THE INTERNATIONALIZATION
OF LAW, AN ANALYSIS FROM LEGITIMACY

How do phenomena discussed under headings like multi-level governance, internationalization, or transnationalization of law fit into our concept of separated powers?[1] Our preliminary point of reference is once again the distinction between individual and democratic self-determination. In the process of internationalization, the borders between constitutional states are opened to the individual exercise of freedom and supranational organizations begin to develop their own regulatory powers. The evolution of international organizations is typically characterized by initially tight governmental supervision which then tends to loosen, while the institutions of the organization gain more independence and may even begin to set enforceable rules for citizens—the European Union is the prime, if quite unusual, example.

Why, from the perspective of legitimacy, do we need supranational regulatory levels at all? The internationalization of law is often simply interpreted as a loss of legitimacy;[2] sometimes, on the other hand, as a victory for freedom.[3] Both interpretations rely, yet again exclusively, on a democratic or an individual concept of freedom. By contrast, if we take the claim seriously that both forms of self-determination stand on an equal footing,[4] a different reconstruction emerges.

---

[1] For an overview over the problem of democratic legitimacy in international law: E. Stein, 'International Law and Democracy: No Love at First Sight', *95 American Journal of International Law* (2001), 489; A. v. Bogdandy, 'Globalization and Europe: How to Square Democracy, Globalization, and International Law,' *15 European Journal of International Law* (2004), 885. With a perspective beyond matters of international law: H. Brunkhorst, *Solidarity. From Civic Friendship to a Global Legal Community* (Cambridge: MIT Press, 2005).

[2] J.-M. Guéhenno, *The End of Nation-state* (Minneapolis/London: University of Minnesota Press, 1995).

[3] E.-U. Petersmann, *Constitutional Functions and Constitutional Problems of International Economic Law* (Fribourg: University Press, 1991).

[4] See Chapter 2, II.

In a hypothetical democratic country A, the guarantee of individual freedom is limited to the national borders. The reason for this limitation is the scope of the democratic legislator who is responsible for protecting and restricting individual freedom. The situation is the same in democratic country B. This limitation of subjective freedom due to national boundaries seems arbitrary from the perspective of the individual subject. It is the result of a fact that lacks any normative justification. But the democratic subject cannot determine the boundaries of its powers vis-à-vis other nation-states. This becomes crucial with regard to the possibility of exercising freedom transnationally. The legislator of A is entitled to extend the exercise of freedom granted to his compatriots to citizens of another country. The legislator of A will usually make the decision to open up the border mutually with the legislator of country B. A and B will do so in the form of a treaty under international law. The regulation may go as far as granting citizens a subjective, enforceable right to transnational trade between A and B. The use and enjoyment of such transnational subjective rights leads to further mutual exchanges between the societies of A and B. As a result of regular trade and travel, the citizens of both states who engage in transnational trade are increasingly subjected to each other's national legal systems. They are required to pay taxes there and respect the other country's environmental standards.

This raises questions. First, is it possible that the national rules of A are being abused to covertly curb transnational freedoms, that is, to discriminate against foreigners from B? The supposedly general environmental standards of A may be formulated and applied in a way that actually inhibits foreign competition. Secondly, a new legitimacy problem emerges if and to the extent that decisions from A also affect citizens from B and vice-versa because not all those affected are involved in the democratic decision-making process. We have already examined this question above.[5] The legitimacy challenge gains a new quality, moreover, if transnational trade between B and A is explicitly politically desired and legally protected in both countries. In this case, the legal obligations and indirect, informal consequences take effect in both directions, namely in the form of exports and imports: citizens from A are regulated in B (and vice-versa) and transnational trade originating from B has consequences in A (and vice-versa), such as for environmental protection laws and markets in A and B.

One important reason for a discriminatory structure and application of rules by one country against citizens of the other lies in the fact that the law-making institutions are democratically accountable only to the citizens of

---

[5] See Chapter 2, II., 2.

their respective countries. One possible solution to this dilemma is the establishment of a common, central regulatory level. At this point, the issue of separated of powers enters the picture. In economic terminology, the externalities of the transnational exercise of freedom[6] require democratic regulation[7]—much as in a purely national context, in which a democratic law is required to define the scope of subjective rights.[8]

This reconstruction makes clear that arguments that generally favour the lower level of regulation over the higher one, based on proximity to citizens or the idea of subsidiarity, tend to fall short.[9] They underestimate the propensity of spatially or politically 'close' structures of regulation to engage in discriminatory practices. Such proximity tends to favour historically evolved relations over abstract arguments for freedom.[10] It is no coincidence that in federal systems the struggle against all forms of discrimination has often been led by the upper level. This is true not only for the fight against economic discrimination through the creation of standardized markets but also for social discrimination against women or minorities. The regulatory distance facilitates the application of abstract standards of equality. This, as we shall see, is definitely not a blanket argument for centralization, but it illustrates the fact that centralization is not a technocratic end in itself. It may be a response to legitimate claims to self-determination. Establishing international regulatory levels may broaden the scope of national, democratic, decision-making processes.

But—this is the decisive question of this chapter—how do organizations located on a regulatory level beyond the state acquire their legitimacy? The two classic answers are: democratic legitimacy through the participation of democratic state governments and individual legitimacy through international courts. Both of these answers raise further questions, for themselves and also in relation to one another.

---

[6] From two very different perspectives: J. Trachtman, 'Regulatory Competition and Regulatory Jurisdiction', in *Journal of International Economic Law* (2000), 331 (337); J. Habermas, 'Hat die Konstitutionalisierung des Völkerrechts noch eine Chance?', in J. Habermas, *Der gespaltene Westen* (Frankfurt am Main: Suhrkamp, 2004), 113 (175).

[7] G. Majone, 'The European Union between Social Policy and Social Regulation', 31 *Journal of Common Market Studies* (1993), 153.

[8] See Chapter 2, II.

[9] Particularly significant with respect to the European level: C. Calliess, *Subsidiaritäts - und Solidaritätsprinzip in der Europäischen Union* (Baden-Baden: Nomos, 2nd ed 1999). A convincing inverse critique of its centralizing effects is G. Davies, 'Subsidiarity, the wrong idea, in the wrong time, at the wrong place', 43 *Common Market Law Review* (2006), 63.

[10] J. Tully, *Strange Multiplicity. Constitutionalism in an age of diversity* (Cambridge: Cambridge University Press, 1995), ignores this problem as well as the rich traditions of western constitutional, especially federal, traditions to include diversity.

1. Democratic legitimacy through intergovernmental cooperation

The still most common answer to the quest for legitimacy of supranational regulatory levels involves the participation of state democratic governments. This was for a long time the central paradigm of European integration[11] and is still of critical importance, both for the legitimacy of international organizations and their legality because the central source of international law remains the mutual commitment of sovereign states.[12] It is also true, however, that this transfer of legitimacy is flawed in many respects. The following paradox emerges: the closer a supranational organization is monitored by its member states, the better it is legitimized, but the more the proper purpose of the organization becomes unclear. If the formation of a supranational organization should be about more than mere multilateral coordination,[13] then it must gain independence from its individual members. Yet it is precisely this independence that endangers its democratic legitimacy derived from member states.[14] Moreover, intergovernmental decision-making processes within an international organization do not meet democratic standards even if only democratic governments are involved.

To begin with, the mandate of the member state and the authority of the organization lack democratic coherence.[15] This is a problem similarly discussed with regard to the legitimacy of federal upper legislative chambers in national constitutional orders.[16] The representatives of democratic states are elected solely to make political decisions that address their own constituencies. As representatives in international organizations, however, they also directly influence the politics of other states and vice versa. The intergovernmental negotiating table constantly creates heteronomy, which does not disappear only because a consensus is required. In an intergovernmental negotiating situation, all participators must give in to other interests. This means that national democratic accountability and supranational regulatory

---

[11] Thoroughly laid out by M. Kaufmann, *Europäische Integration und Demokratieprinzip* (Baden-Baden: Nomos, 1997).

[12] A careful defence in: J. L. Cohen, 'Sovereignty in the Context of Globalization: A Constitutional Pluralist Perspective', in S. Besson, J. Tasioulas (eds.), *The Philosophy of International Law* (Oxford: Oxford University Press, 2010), 261.

[13] For an essentially sceptical view from the perspective of economic analysis: J. Goldsmith, E. Posner, *The Limits of International Law* (Oxford: Oxford University Press, 2005).

[14] J. Klabbers, *An Introduction into International Institutional Law* (Cambridge: Cambridge University Press, 2nd ed 2009), 12–13.

[15] M. Zürn, 'Globalizing Interests—An Introduction', in: M. Zürn, G. Walter (eds.), *Globalizing Interests, Pressure Groups and Denationalization* (Albany: State University of New York Press, 200), 1–37.

[16] H. Pollmann, *Repräsentation und Organschaft* (Berlin: Duncker & Humblot, 1969).

authority fall apart. Furthermore, the decision-making process in intergovernmental bodies is deficient. The compromises reached on the supranational level by government representatives who explicitly represent the interests of their own states are not necessarily favourable to the common good of the whole supranational level. The European Union is a case in point.

Moreover, decision-making rules in such organizations do not follow the standard of democratic equality.[17] From the perspective of national democratic legitimacy, it would appear preferable to make decisions in international organizations unanimously. This is the only way to avoid the derogation of the national democratic subject. Unanimity is therefore common in classic international organizations, but it has its limits if and to the extent that the organization needs to make decisions. If we accept the need for majority decisions, the issue of weighted voting arises: weighting votes according to the standard of *democratic equality*—that is according to the number of inhabitants of the participating states—appears hardly feasible, for in that case we could just abandon negotiations between states and immediately call a general vote on the supranational level. Such an arrangement would effectively remove the co-decision-making rights of small states. According to the standard of *sovereign equality*, all states have the same number of votes. This way, the political weight and the number of affected citizens is completely set aside. As a result, in international and European law conciliatory vote-weightings are common, without meeting either of the two standards.[18]

Furthermore, the actions of the intergovernmental institutions neither face much publicity nor political ruptures. As we have seen, one of the practical achievements of democratic systems is that all past actions are subject to political challenge and may be undone through a change of the majority, while the system itself remains unquestioned.[19] The institutional discontinuity—the pinnacle of political action[20]—contributes significantly to the legitimacy and the problem-solving capacity of democracies. This feature is lacking in supranational organizations, in which governments continually carry on the work while being exchanged only little by little through national electoral processes. The organization turns into a steady bureaucratic continuity without any political break.

---

[17] See Chapter 2, II., 2.

[18] H. G. Schermers, 'Weighted Voting', in: R. Bernhardt (ed.), *Encyclopaedia of Public International Law Vol. IV* (Amsterdam: Elsevier, 2000), 1446.

[19] See Chapter 2, II. 2.

[20] Once again: H. Arendt, 'Introduction into Politics', in H. Arendt, *The Promise of Politics* (New York: Random House, 2005), 93.

Finally, although intergovernmental institutions are ultimately run by governments, they may make quasi-legislative decisions. Their decisions are generally not subject to change or to amendments by a member state parliament. At best, the parliament is entitled to a wholesale rejection of the decision in the ratification procedure.

It is certainly possible to respond to all these defects by pointing to the gain in democratic autonomy that is achieved through common decision-making procedures.[21] Through common decisions, the states involved expand their scope of action. Should that not compensate for the lack of legitimacy in intergovernmental structures? Is it not a legitimate part of the democratic agenda of a state to cooperate with other states, and does this preference not make good on the institutional flaws of intergovernmentalism? Not necessarily. This is because the problem and its alleged compensation seem incommensurable. On the one hand, the insufficient legitimacy of intergovernmentalism provides no definite argument against internationalization. If a democratic community is ready to cooperate it should not be stopped by such considerations. Again, there is no point in arguing against a democratic practice in the name of democratic theory. In any case, the decision in favour of internationalization itself requires democratic legitimacy. The concept of 'expanding' the scope of action remains plausible only if both sides agree, but even then it would still display the procedural defects outlined above. In other words, nothing in legitimacy theory disapproves of subjects, be it persons, be it states, reciprocally expanding their scope for action through negotiations and agreements. If such negotiations are carried out not by individuals but by representatives, however, the problems described above arise.

It therefore follows that the democratic legitimacy of intergovernmental institutions is deficient even if all participating governments—which is usually not the case—are democratic. This normative judgement is consistent with the factual observation that standard-setting powers among international organizations that do not require unanimous decisions still remain the exception.[22] It is true that there are examples of a substantial quantitative increase in international law-making.[23] But overall, the dominant choice is either unanimity rule or recourse to soft, non-compulsory rules. The absence of a global or even a European democratic subject pushes international rule-making in the direction of intergovernmental decision-making. Here, as we have seen, the following paradox emerges: on the one

---

[21] I owe thanks to Christoph Schönberger for pointing my attention to this aspect.

[22] J. Klabbers, *An Introduction into International Institutional Law* (Cambridge: Cambridge University Press, 2002), 217.

[23] To the example of the UN Security Council, see Chapter 4, IV., 2.

hand, *only* national democratic processes are capable of providing the international level with political legitimacy. On the other hand, rectifying the resulting legitimacy deficiencies requires law-making procedures that are independent of their national bases. This is why intergovernmental structures are not simply expendable, despite the defects just described.

2. Individual legitimacy through juridification

Many international regimes directly or indirectly expand individual persons' scope of action beyond state boundaries. Critiques of economic and legal globalization often deny that the empowerment of individual transnational action has an intrinsic value. This view is in turn a reaction to another reduction, according to which the benefit of international law does not lie in an increase in freedom but in an increase in economic welfare or a functional gain in the ability to act. This concept is often discussed under the heading of 'output-legitimacy'.[24] But it is far from clear why the distribution of options to act transnationally should be justified only in such functional terms. Instead, reinterpreting these phenomena into our model of legitimacy seems possible: transnational subjective rights bestow individual legitimacy as long as they are protected by procedures, which meet the criteria developed above.[25] At the international level, a growing number of decision-making structures function, by and large, according to such standards. The judicial procedural model has been flourishing in the supranational law of European integration, in world trade law, in human rights protection, in international criminal adjudication, and even in matters of general public international. This boom raises the question of how bringing all these newly emerging tribunals into line with one another might be possible.[26] Pending closer examination,[27] however, it seems that there are fewer fundamental objections to these decision-making structures than to intergovernmental action.

In the academic discussion, the proliferation of international courts and tribunals is often viewed favourably as part of a process of 'constitutionaliza-tion'[28] of international law. At first sight, this is plausible if, as a result, individual subjects are procedurally recognized in international law; subjects who in classical international law vanished behind the legal personality of

---

[24] F. Scharpf, *Governing in Europe* (Oxford: Oxford University Press, 1999), 7–22.

[25] See Chapter 2, III, 3.

[26] J. L. Charney, 'Is International Law Threatened by Multiple International Tribunals?', 271 *Recueil des Cours* (1998), 101.

[27] For this aspect with regard to the WTO see this Chapter IV., 3.

[28] For a critique, see Outlook, in this work.

the state. This seems particularly convincing in the case of elemental human rights violations[29] whose protection overrides matters of democratic procedure precisely because respect for the former is the precondition for the latter.[30] But before we take a closer look at some of these procedures and their specific problems, a prior question has to be addressed. One deficiency may not lie in the juridification of international relations itself but rather in the asynchrony between juridification and democratization, and in a too narrow concept of what constitutionalization of international law should mean.

3. Asynchronies in the development of legitimacy mechanisms

In the internationalization of law, the judicial, individually legitimized procedural model faces fewer institutional challenges than the legislative, democratic model does. There are practical reasons for this concerning the transferability of the two types of procedure to levels beyond the state but also conceptual reasons regarding the different relationships—discussed above—between law and individual self-determination on the one hand and democracy on the other. An individual subject acting on the transnational level, be it a multinational enterprise or a migrant worker, is more readily available than an international democratic subject; a constituency beyond the state. It is easier to establish an international court than an international parliament.[31] This asymmetry is well illustrated by the course of European integration.

Central issues concerning the legitimacy of legal internationalization arise from this asymmetrical development. We have seen that democratic and individual legitimacy are mutually reinforcing.[32] The legitimacy of judicial decisions hinges upon the individualizing procedural structure *and* the democratic approval of the law subsequently applied by the courts. This interconnection is missing at the regulatory levels beyond the state. The law applied by international courts or court-like institutions is negotiated intergovernmentally and legislated in the form of an international consensus. It suffers from the deficits outlined above. By virtue of their universality and intractability, these international standards are more akin to constitutional

---

[29] A. Fischer-Lescano, *Globalverfassung* (Weilerswist: Velbrück Wissenschaft, 2005).

[30] See Chapter 2.

[31] See as an artistic illustration the 'inflatable' parliament that 'can be dropped in any grounds and then unfolds itself': P. Sloterdijk, G. Mueller von der Hagen, 'Instant Democracy: The Pneumatic Parliament', in B. Latour, P. Weibel (eds.), *Making Things Public: Atmospheres of Democracy* (Cambridge, Mass.: MIT Press, 2005).

[32] See Chapter 2.

rules than to statutory ones. What they lack is a legislative process that accompanies and checks the international judiciaries[33] and provides political alternatives.[34]

In addition, judicial and quasi-judicial international law-making favours certain regulatory subjects and goals. The logic of juridification is not neutral with regard to different political issues. Repealing a trade restriction requires less justification and is practically easier than imposing an environmental standard even if the former has profound political implications. Normatively, this phenomenon is a consequence of the asymmetry discussed above between positive and negative freedom:[35] liberalization creates negative freedom by removing existing rules. The indirect implications of such a decision for the environment, or the labour market, concern matters that are hardly as easy for a court to grasp in the form of an individual legal position. This correlation can be well observed in European integration, which was plunged into crisis at the very moment the dismantling of barriers to the common market was completed and the European institutions had to act as positive regulators.[36] For this reason, the goals of quasi-judicial supranational organizations tend to be liberal and to stress individual concerns. Moreover, they are inclined to privilege those kinds of freedom typically relied upon in a transnational context; freedoms that can be used transnationally. These tend to be freedom of contract, of property, and of profession rather than freedom of expression or the right to bodily integrity.

Obviously, one can frame all of these critical points as social or political questions, as critiques of globalization do.[37] More interesting for our context is the insight that the logic of legitimacy works differently than both the economic praise and political criticism of globalization seem to assume. It is simply not possible to assess the legitimacy of globalization in terms of either pure loss or gain. The basis for its logic of legitimacy is that in globalization the transnational, individual use of freedom operates much faster than the complementary and necessary democratic process does. As we have seen, this is related to the fact that protecting the individual use of freedom is institutionally easier than organizing democratic self-determination. The former requires individual subjects, who plan to operate in the transnational realm on the one hand, and easily institutionalized court-like bodies on the other. By contrast, transnational democracy instead requires a

---

[33] Likewise with regard to the WTO: A. v. Bogdandy, 'Law and Politics in the WTO—Strategies to Cope with a Deficient Relationship', 5 *Max-Planck Yearbook of United Nations Law* (2001), 609.

[34] I. Ley, *Opposition im Völkerrecht* (Manuscript on file with the author, 2012).

[35] See Chapter 2, II., 1.

[36] See this Chapter, III.

[37] See the excellent overview in C. Leggewie, *Die Globalisierung und ihre Gegner* (München: Beck, 2003).

corresponding transnational democratic society, something that is institutionally and culturally much more demanding. Mere cooperation among democratic governments is not sufficient to generate this level of democratic legitimacy.

The process of globalization is thus closely associated with gains in individual freedom. One might object that, in fact, only few profit from these gains; but for one thing this is not clear, for those who do not operate in the transnational realm may gain from transnationalization because they profit from improved general welfare; but for another, this is in a certain sense true of every formal gain in individual freedom. Even the protection of freedom of expression at the national level effectively privileges those who possess the ability for political articulation. From the perspective of our model of legitimacy, internationalization results from the fact that, in a globalized world, it is no longer plausible to justify national restrictions on the individual exercise of freedom. To organize the transnational exercise of freedom democratically, supranational organizations are set up, which in turn can be only partially democratically legitimized. Between these two levels, however, a competition for legitimacy arises, which looks—not by accident—like the state pursuing a social democratic political project at the national level against the liberal individual at the supranational level.[38] This competition will continue as long as democratic identities fail to evolve at the level beyond the state. This dilemma cannot be solved but could be mitigated, by institutional devices. This requires a closer analysis of the functioning of power-separation of both the national and the international level.

II. THE INTERNATIONALIZED CONSTITUTIONAL STATE

Globalization is not simply a social phenomenon that descends upon the democratic nation-state. Rather, many but not all states are significant instigators of globalization.[39] Even the fact that almost the complete territorial organization of the globe consists of states implies globalization.[40] At the same time, the results of globalized law-making are constantly affecting national constitutional systems and must be legally processed by them. An examination of the separation of powers in the process of internalization must therefore begin with national constitutional systems and their development.

[38] W. Streeck and K. Thelen, 'Introduction: Institutional Change in Advanced Political Economies', in W. Streeck, K. A. Thelen (eds.), *Beyond Continuity*, (Oxford: Oxford University Press, 2005), 1–39.

[39] J. W. Meyer, G. M. Thomas, 'The Expansion of the State', *Annual Review of Sociology* 10 (1984), 461–82; compare Luhmann's analysis in *Die Politik der Gesellschaft* (Frankfurt am Main: Suhrkamp, 2000), 224.

[40] B. Badie, *L'État importé* (Paris: Fayard, 1992).

1. Separation of powers in foreign affairs

The finely balanced system of state separation of powers only works domestically. It was designed for domestic policy, whereas for a long time foreign relations were part of a particular area of government in which constitutional rules had no relevant role to play.[41] But the deficient structure of constitutional law of foreign relations has more than a historical-political basis. Practical demands on the development of international law worked in the same direction: international law has traditionally developed through state consensus. A state is required to enter the stage with a defined political will. Its internal pluralization in different institutions, parties, and procedures cannot, or only in a very limited manner, be reflected externally. Foreign policy power has to be centralized, and this centralization comes at the expense of parliamentary and judicial accountability. The state must enter into negotiations with other states ready to take on commitments. In terms of the temporal structure of decision-making, this means that the inclusion of other parts of the polity into the making of these commitments will often come too late.

The legal effect of many formal international commitments, mostly in the form of international treaties, resembles those of democratic statutes. They create duties that bind the state as a whole. Such duties require some kind of democratic legitimacy. In reality, however, international commitments mostly develop, for reasons already mentioned, only with the retrospective approval of parliaments and without any judicial review. National parliaments approve international commitments retrospectively, at a point when they can no longer change their content. The approval does not result from an open decision-making process. Similarly, courts check the decision only once the executive has already at least politically committed to other states. For this reason, instances of national constitutional courts repealing an international commitment are rare.[42]

From the perspective of our model, foreign policy seems doubly deficient even if its practice is not necessarily unconstitutional. The division of labour between the three powers is not designed for foreign commitments. The executive is privileged over the legislative and the judiciary. Solutions for this deficiency must be implemented at the different levels concerned, including that of the nation-state. In the following, we will introduce three

---

[41] M. Troper, 'Les rélations exterieur dans la constitution de l'an III', in *La Théorie, Le Droit, L'État* (Paris: P.U.F., 2001), 129.

[42] In the US, for example, not one of the hundreds of treaties ratified by the United States has been struck down by the Supreme Court as unconstitutional. R. Levin, P. Chen, 'Rethinking the Constitution-treaty relationship', *10 Journal of International Constitutional Law* (2012), 242 (248).

institutional arrangements, which, short of providing a complete solution, could at least mitigate the problem.

2. Parliamentarization

How can we extend parliamentary participation in the formation of foreign commitments beyond mere approval? The answer is not straightforward, for parliaments ideally generate legitimacy through *ex ante* actions. As we have seen, the legislature is a future-facing power.[43] In addition, the government is situated in a context of negotiation, which requires sufficient room for political discretion. It is a feature of parliamentary systems, in which the government enjoys the confidence of the parliamentary majority, that a parliamentary mandate that defines the governmental space to negotiate from the outset seems artificial and threatens to weaken the negotiation position of the entire polity.[44] Moreover, experiences with the involvement of national parliaments in the context of European integration have not been exactly encouraging. In reality, parliaments cannot or do not want to be involved too intimately in a negotiating process: majorities tend to back their own government; minorities cannot claim decision-making powers.[45] In accordance with our reflections on the notion of parliamentary control, it seems reasonable that the first and foremost right of the minority would be the right to complete information.[46] Some parliaments lack both an advanced culture of interest in international legal developments and the necessary institutional self-awareness for such a culture to develop.

Nonetheless, it might be helpful to free ourselves from classical concepts of parliamentary involvement in foreign affairs and vest parliaments with the power to clearly define the governmental mandate in international negotiations from the outset.[47] In the process of international negotiation, this seems at least to be the only moment in which parliaments are capable of generating specific parliamentary legitimacy in the context of foreign policy matters. As a result, we would have more democratic legitimacy for new

---

[43] See Chapter 2, III., 2.

[44] Though there might be instances in which an anterior self-commitment strengthens the position of the negotiating state: Thomas C. Schelling, *The Strategy of Conflict* (Cambridge, Mass., Harvard University Press 1960).

[45] R. Halfmann, *Entwicklungen des deutschen Staatsorganisationsrechts im Kraftfeld der europäischen Integration* (Berlin: Duncker & Humblot, 2000), 147; P. Kiiver, *National Parliaments in the European Union: A Critical View on EU Constitution-building* (The Hague: Kluwer Law International, 2006).

[46] See Chapter 3.

[47] Those forms of commitment do not always or necessarily weaken the state's negotiation position. Self-commitment may also have the opposite effect: T. Schelling, *The Strategy of Conflict* (Cambridge: Harvard University Press, 1960).

international commitments. Giving parliament the power to define a mandate *ex ante* also suggests that the political interests between the parliamentary majority and government differ. As we have seen, normally there is no such conflict in a parliamentary system, the majority and the government form a political unity. This is why relevant parliamentary control is control by the opposition, by means of access to governmental information.[48] However, this consideration also indicates more precisely why, as a matter of legitimacy, a parliamentary *ex ante* mandate could be helpful: not to split majority and government but to allow for the issue to be publicly debated before it is negotiated in the international sphere. The procedural implications are more relevant than the substantial ones. The parliamentarization of foreign relations may have beneficial knock-on effects for public debate. An example is the establishment of the World Trade Organization in 1994–95, which was intensely debated in America but practically ignored by the public in Europe.

American constitutional law demonstrates how strong parliamentary involvement can be, albeit in a presidential system. The US Senate grants the president a carefully defined and temporally restricted mandate entitling him to agree to a treaty without additional parliamentary approval.[49] Apparently, the real threat of a congressional rejection does not weaken the US negotiating position, though one must concede that its strength stems not mainly from its institutional organization but from its political clout. It is, in fact, the unknown democratic element in the US that diplomacy must always take into account, ever since the precursor of the WTO—the International Trade Organization—fell apart in 1947 after the US Senate rejected it.

A specific problem with parliamentary involvement in this context springs from the dynamic character of international agreements and the autonomous law-making of international organizations. How can parliaments participate here? In 2002, with the approval of the German government, NATO changed its strategy and authorized military operations outside the alliance's territory. This represents a serious change to the mission of the German forces. Nevertheless, Germany's constitutional court denied the Bundestag the right to co-decision-making because the change of strategy constituted an unwritten update within the practice of the organization, not

---

[48] See Chapter 3, I.

[49] For an analysis of the so-called Fast Track Authority, since 2002 also called the Trade Promotion Authority, delegated from Congress to the President: H. H. Koh, 'The Fast Track and United States Trade Policy', 18 *Brooklyn Journal of International Law* (1992), 143; H. Shapiro, L. Brainard, 'Trade Promotion Authority formerly known as Fast Track: Building Common Ground on Trade Demands more than a Name Change', 35 *George Washington International Law Review* (2003), 1.

a formal amendment of the North Atlantic Treaty.[50] Such a line of argument not only disregards the dynamic character of international treaties. It would also be rather unusual—and rightly so—as a matter of domestic constitutional law. Domestic law courts regularly judge whether parliament should be involved in a decision, and they apply substantial, not formal, criteria to justify this judgment. International regimes change incrementally on the basis of agreements made at a certain point. On the level of international law there is, unlike in the European Union, almost no independent judicial supervision of the limits of power of international organizations.[51] Therefore, national courts should at least ensure that national parliaments are involved when international organizations internally reformulate their missions. It is obviously difficult to define operable limits for these kinds of cases. But this is nothing unusual in constitutional law. And it is equally clear that these limits will be drawn differently for different constitutional orders. This could create practical problems within the organization. Obviously, matters of legitimacy and matters of functionality do not always move in the same direction. On the other hand, if parliamentary involvement were firmly limited to the formal amendments of international treaties, parliaments would be unnecessarily disconnected from the development of international law. Here again, an important function of judicial review would be to re-formalize informal political action.

3. Judicial advisory powers

This leads us to the issue of judicial review. No court can fully disregard the consequences of its decisions. This is even more the case when these consequences are not nebulous social implications but legally well defined. The objection to an international commitment based on a breach of domestic constitutional law voiced through a national court can lead to a violation of exactly this international commitment. Undoubtedly, it is also because of this perfectly reasonable consideration that courts tend to monitor international commitments rather hesitantly. How can this be rectified?

A relatively simple remedy would be to postpone the moment when the international commitment takes effect after judicial review has been exercized. Commitments come into being only after the head of state ratifies an agreement, when all other procedural steps have been taken. It should

---

[50] Federal Constitutional Court, *Strategisches Konzept der NATO*, BVerfGE 104, 151 (199).

[51] J. Klabbers, *An Introduction to International Institutional Law* (Cambridge: Cambridge University Press, 2nd ed 2009), 213–20.

generally be possible to carry out judicial review during this phase. In practice, the head of state could suspend the ratification until after a judicial review. But this informal solution depends on the cooperation of the actors involved and requires institutional safeguards. Bringing a legal action against an agreement in court usually requires that the agreement has acquired a certain domestic legal form, such as through the approval of parliament. This requirement conforms to the criteria identified above, according to which judicial review is appropriate only if the reviewed decision has been completed.[52] By this point, however, there may be hardly any time left.

Therefore, another solution could lie in an anticipation of judicial review. One way to institutionalize this would be to give courts the power to give legal advice in advance; the option to obtain a legal opinion before a reviewable legal act comes into force. Constitutional courts tend to be suspicious of such a power because it places an additional burden on them and could promote a certain degree of irresolution among the other branches. The US Supreme Court considers judicial advisory powers to be unconstitutional in American law.[53] Germany's Federal Constitutional Court statute originally included such a power, but it was unpopular with the court and, therefore, soon abolished by the legislator.[54] The French Conseil Constitutionnel is basically an institution that gives such advice but has consequently been considered to be not a 'real' court for quite a while. Advisory power should therefore not be introduced without good cause. International commitments could be an instance of it. Interestingly, the procedural law of the European Court of Justice provides for an advisory power. Article 218 (11) TFEU and, notably, the ECJ is much more active than national courts are in reviewing the EU's foreign actions. Unlike the German Federal Constitutional Court and the US Supreme Court, the ECJ has already adjudicated plenty of legal acts in the area of foreign affairs and even invalidated some of them for breach of European law.[55]

The introduction of advisory power removes the pressure of subsequent costs from courts, which the *ex post* review of international commitments otherwise entails. It represents a workable mechanism for channelling foreign commitments back into a system of separated powers.[56]

---

[52] See Chapter 3, III.

[53] Last held in *Clinton v Jones*, 520 U.S. 681, 699 (1997).

[54] § 97 Federal Statute for the Constitutional Court (previous version); Federal Constitutional Court, Plenargutachten Heuss, BVerfGE 2, 79 (86).

[55] See for example European Court of Justice, Advisory Opinion 2/94, *ECHR*, Slg. 1996, I-1759; Advisory Opinion 1/94, *WTO*, Slg. 1994,I-5267; Advisory Opinion, C-2/00, *Cartagena-Protocol*, Slg. 2001, I-9713.

[56] See Chapter 2, III., 3.

4. Referenda

National referenda have been subject to manifold criticism from democratic theory, which quite often rejects them in favour of representative democracy.[57] This criticism, which at times overstates its case, should nonetheless be taken seriously.[58] Referenda tend to privilege those who initiate the process and put a certain issue to the public vote. They also privilege certain specific topics over the general political decision-making process and tend to radicalize the public debate, as they are not designed for compromise. As a result, the instrument of plebiscites seems often somewhat misplaced in the general context of parliamentary legislation. But even supposing that all these objections to referenda are correct, we also have to accept that they equally apply to *parliamentary* participation in foreign relations: here, too, parliament has no choice but to answer a question raised from outside negatively or affirmatively. Compromise and deliberation with an open result are not part of the procedure.

In this respect, parliamentary approval *ex post* and referenda are similar in their short-comings. But what would then be a positive argument for a referendum over parliamentary involvement in foreign affairs? Certainly, there is the lack of publicity that still accompanies foreign policy and could also be linked to the structure of international law-making. The effects of foreign commitments challenge the mechanisms of democratic accountability only if they impact concrete legal positions: if in the form of national rules, for example, they affect domestic firms or individual actions. But when this happens, it is already too late. In this sense, referenda serve as a democratic reminder of the importance of international commitments. In domestic law, the possibility of new legal regulations is democratically processed by political programmes in national elections and by the parliamentary debate. International relations has no such mechanisms, particularly since even national governments typically do not follow the political patterns of 'right' and 'left' at the international level.[59] Furthermore, the introduction of referenda does not necessarily contradict the parliamentarization of foreign relations. This is because any form of parliamentary involvement in the preparation of international agreements will never

[57] See Chapter 2, III., 2.

[58] For a critical perspective on referenda: W. Riker, *Liberalism Against Populism* (San Francisco: W. H. Freeman, 1982); D. Lacy, M.S. Niou, 'A Problem with Referendums', *12 Journal of Theoretical Politics* (2000), 5; H. Nurmi, 'Voting Paradoxes and Referenda', *15 Social Choice and Welfare* (1998), 333. For a good analysis of the debate: S. Hug, G. Tsebelis, 'Veto Players and Referendums Around the World', *14 Journal of Theoretical Politics* (2002), 465; S. Hug, 'Some thoughts about referendums, representative democracy, and separation of powers', *20 Constitutional Political Economy* (2009), 251.

[59] I. Ley, *Opposition im Völkerrecht* (Heidelberg: Springer, 2014).

generate the legitimacy of an open, unbiased legislative consultation. To this extent, there is a need for additional democratic participation.

One might wonder whether the sensitive area of foreign policy is suited to such a politicization or whether the options of approval or rejection would not be better placed within a parliament. However, we have to compare the dangers of politicizing foreign policy with the more imminent dangers of its de-politicization. The ideal of intergovernmental cooperation, which under-pinned, for instance, early European integration, becomes less plausible the more intensely international law defines the individual legal positions of citizens. The more international law concerns traditional issues of domestic policy—from security issues to the alignment of education systems—the more demanding are the standards of legitimacy. Even the referenda in France and the Netherlands, which rejected the European constitutional treaty, should be seen as a step towards normalizing a democratic foreign and European policy, in which international and supranational cooperation is the consequence of a democratic decision, not of a technical necessity. Obviously, moments of crisis like the reaction to 9/11 or reactions to the European financial crisis undermine this approach but wrongly so: no crisis has a self-evident answer that does not deserve democratic debate and judicial control. The introduction of plebiscites into foreign affairs could be one attempt to address these problems, especially in parliamentary systems that tend to have less politically independent control. One workable constitutional rule could be an obligation to hold a plebiscite in cases in which a foreign commitment also requires a constitutional amendment.[60]

5. Conclusion: alignments of domestic and foreign constitutional law

Although two of the three institutional options addressed here introduce special rules for foreign commitments, all three should be understood as an attempt to align the legitimacy standards of foreign-policy action with those of domestic constitutionalism. The fact that differentiations occur in our analysis is simply a result of the existing institutional asymmetry between domestic and foreign affairs, from the perspective of national constitutional law. Constitutional theory must take seriously the demand for a higher juridified protection of the legitimacy of foreign politics. The notion of a special status for foreign policy, the 'high politics' that has been dragged from the early modern period into the constitutional law of the 20th century, is no longer tenable in the face of the broad regulatory scope of contemporary international law. Nevertheless, it is widely and correctly accepted that

---

[60] Compare H. Abromeit, 'Volkssouveränität in komplexen Gesellschaften', in H. Brunkhorst, P. Niesen (eds.), *Das Recht der Republik* (Frankfurt am Main: Suhrkamp, 1999), 17.

the system of separated powers of democratic nation-states is unsuited to foreign affairs. Therefore, the problem of legitimacy cannot be approached on the state level only. We must also turn our sights towards the structure of public organizations beyond the state.

III. EUROPEAN INTEGRATION

We cannot understand the institutions of the European Union without a brief look at their development. First of all, there was the political will among member states to harmonize certain areas of their politics and thereby break from the clutch of nation-states. The first member states decided to design a depoliticized form of public authority in order to achieve the political goal of a peaceful Europe.[61] In this sense, the early European institutions, especially the 'High Authority', the predecessor of the European Commission, was very similar to an independent administrative agency, subject to judicial review and limited by a specific mandate.[62]

From the beginning, one central, substantial principle of the European legal system was a ban on discrimination between the member states. In particular, this ban prohibited any differentiation of transnational market behaviour with regard to its national origin. So the member states were committed to removing certain transnational economic barriers. This process included the review of national rules, which indirectly justified such barriers, like, for example, the payment of subsidies and the presence of monopolistic businesses.

Using this non-discrimination doctrine will help to introduce us to the central problems of the legitimacy of European integration.[63] We have already noted the core dilemma of all international organizations: they are constituted by and legitimized through their member states, but at the same time, they should act independently of their members' political preferences. The goal of the European ban on discrimination was the establishment of a European common market.[64] However, this goal inevitably points beyond itself. Powers to regulate economic issues are difficult to delineate because

---

[61] The British government had doubts concerning the compatibility of the English parliamentary doctrine with European integration from the beginning: K. Adenauer, *Erinnerungen 1945–1953* (Stuttgart: DVA, 1965), 499.

[62] See Chapter 3, I., 4. For more on the European Commission, see this Chapter, II., 4. For an understanding of the European integration that still sticks to this scheme: P. Lindseth, *Power and legitimacy* (Oxford: Oxford University Press 2010).

[63] Also see this Chapter, preliminary considerations, 1.

[64] T. Schubert, *Der Gemeinsame Markt als Rechtsbegriff—Die allgemeine Wirtschaftsfreiheit des EG-Vertrages* (München: Beck, 1999), 133. Historically: G. Grin, *The Battle of the European Single Market* (London: Kegan Paul, 2003).

every public action potentially has an economic element. Environmental regulations or even the regulation of education could impact the traffic of goods or services, and the removal of trade barriers generates a comprehensive need for follow-up regulation.[65] Consequently, in the European Treaties as well as in the jurisdiction of the ECJ, the concept of discrimination has, over time, discarded its economic element.[66] This also confirms our observation that supranational levels favour structures of regulation that work against discrimination in a general sense.[67] But expanding the concept of discrimination creates a demand for legitimacy beyond the political participation of member states within the EU.

The development of European integration raises specific difficulties for an analysis that uses the concept of separated powers as a benchmark because the different European institutions played different roles in different phases of the process of integration. Furthermore, what significance the different institutions have actually held for European integration remains an empirically contested question. Was integration the work of the member state governments, or rather that of the Commission, the courts, and, particularly, the ECJ?

For our analysis, we can start by distinguishing three types of legitimacy for the European Union.[68] These forms can be carefully assigned to the EU's different institutions: *intergovernmentalism* uses the national democracies to legitimize the European polity. The shortcomings of intergovernmentalism have already been explored above.[69] Within the organization of the EU, it is the Council and the European Council that claim this form of legitimacy. Secondly, the very own democratic legitimacy of the EU we may call *federal* legitimacy. It should fulfil the requirements of democratic self-determination at the European level. Whether this type is either possible or desirable for the EU, whether it is convincing to speak of a separate European democratic subject, remains politically and theoretically contested.[70] As an

---

[65] See this Chapter, preliminary considerations, 1.

[66] European Court of Justice, Case C-85/96, *Martinez Sala*, European Court reports 1998, I-2691, para 62; European Court of Justice, Case C-184/99, *Grzelczyk*, European Court reports 2001, I-6193, para 34.

[67] See this Chapter, preliminary considerations, 1.

[68] From a point of view of legal scholarship, see M. Kaufmann, *Demokratieprinzip und Europäische Integration* (Baden-Baden: Nomos, 1997), 103. From a point of view of political science, see M. Höreth, *Europäische Union im Legitimationstrilemma* (Baden-Baden: Nomos, 1999), 104.

[69] See this Chapter, preliminary considerations, 1.

[70] The most important arguments can still be found in at Dieter Grimm, 'Does Europe need a Constitution?', 1 *European Law Journal* (1995), 282–302.

institution, the European Parliament calls for this kind of legitimacy within the EU.

Intergovernmental and federal concepts of legitimacy modify classic democratic theory, but they do not depart from its egalitarian foundation. Yet another form of legitimacy may be called *supranational*. This specifically European mode could either replace or complement the other types. It describes the specific forms of European law-making, particularly through the European Commission and the ECJ. There is no coherent theoretical concept behind the term 'supranational'. Rather, it results from the assumption that European integration cannot, or at least cannot exclusively, be justified by traditional democratic models. That is why quite different concepts—not all of which are compatible with one another—call themselves 'supranational': a technocratic justification of the Commission;[71] a liberal theory of increasing welfare by removing trade restrictions;[72] a version of discourse theory that sees supranational institutions as a means of creating deliberative rationality;[73] a theory of civil society interpreting integration as an instrument to facilitate transnational social understanding;[74] or a theory of supranational jurisdiction geared towards the ECJ and which may come close to our model of individual legitimacy.[75] We will have to discuss how these theories fit in with our concept of separated powers. However, it is evident from the start that this concept has no need for additional types of legitimacy, in particular when they compromise the mechanisms endorsed here. Examining the European Commission will illustrate this point best.[76]

1. Separation of powers in the European Union?

Can a tripartite institutional structure be found within the EU? This is debated frequently and in a variety of ways, not least with the conceptually rather unconvincing reference to the novelty and originality of the European Union.[77] One formal reason that could be held against an application of any

---

[71] See G.-D. Majone, *Regulating Europe* (London: Routledge, 1996), 9.

[72] F. Scharpf, *Governing in Europe* (Oxford: Oxford University Press, 1999).

[73] R. Schmalz-Bruns, 'Deliberativer Supranationalismus', 6 *Zeitschrift für Internationale Beziehungen* (1999), 185 (204, 212).

[74] D. Curtin, *Postnational Democracy* (The Hague: Kluwer Law International, 1997), 45.

[75] L. H. Helfer, A.-M. Slaughter, 'Toward a Theory of Effective Supranational Adjudication', *107 Yale Law Journal* (1997), 273 (287, 290).

[76] See this Chapter, III., 4 (treats the European Commission).

[77] From the constructive part of the debate: K. Lenaerts, 'Some Reflections on Separation of Powers in the European Community' 28 *Common Market Law Review*, (1991), 11 (13); P. Dann, 'The Political Institutions', in A. v. Bogdandy, J. Bast (eds.), *Principles of European Constitutional Law* (Oxford: Hart,

model of separated powers is that the European Treaties, unlike most national constitutions, do not explicitly recognize this distinction. The common scheme of naming three powers without defining them but ascribing to them the actions of certain institutions is not found in the Treaties. Article 13, Paragraph 1 of the Treaty of the European Union merely lists the institutions without giving them a proper 'function'. At least Article 16 (1) TEU allocates legislative and budgetary functions jointly in the Council and Parliament. Article 17 (1) refers to executive functions of the European Commission, yet adds these to its coordinating and management functions. A further note on this: in national constitutional systems, certain legal forms ensure that the three powers remain discernible. This is particularly true for the democratic statute as the epitome of legislative action. This attribution was missing in European Union law, though the Treaty of Lisbon has since changed this.[78] Though there is still no European law in the sense of a defined form that deserves the name by resulting from a general political procedure, there is at least a default procedure: Article 17 (2) TEU, though weakened by many 'exceptional' law-making procedures for particular policies.[79] Looking at these procedures vividly indicates just how fragmented EU law is.[80]

These objections sound a note of caution regarding the unreflective application of any model of separated powers to the EU, but they do no more than that. Even so, elements of a modified concept of separated powers can also be found in the jurisprudence of the ECJ: the notion of an autonomy of powers has been used by the ECJ in its case law in order to ensure that the different institutions can work autonomously whilst relating to one another.[81] Alongside this idea of a certain degree of institutional division, the notion of a balance of powers plays a central role in the rulings of the ECJ. The court has even nominally developed its own doctrine of separated powers: the principle of 'institutional balance'. In accordance with

---

2nd rev. ed 2010), 237–72; G. Conway, 'Recovering a separation of powers in the European Union', 17 *European Law Journal* (2011), 304.

[78] P. P. Craig, 'The Treaty of Lisbon', *33 European Law Review* (2008), 137 (160); see also the in-depth analysis in J. Bast, 'New Categories of Acts after the Lisbon Reform—Legal Regimes and Institutional Practice', *49 Common Market Law Review* (2012), 885–928.

[79] J. Bast: 'European Union: Legal instruments and judicial protection', in A. v. Bogdandy, J. Bast (eds.), *Principles of European Constitutional Law* (Oxford: Hart, 2nd rev. ed 2010), 345.

[80] P. P. Craig, 'The Treaty of Lisbon', *33 European Law Review* (2008), 137 (156).

[81] For the autonomy of Parliament with rather ambivalent results, see European Court of Justice, Case 230/81, *Luxemburg v Parliament*, European Court reports 1983, 255, para 9; European Court of Justice, Case C-345/95, *France v Parliament*, European Court reports 1997, I-5215, para 32. For the Commission, see European Court of Justice, Case C-1/00 SA, *Cotecna v Commission*, European Court reports 2001, I-4219, para 9 (no seizure at the Commission).

this principle, the court has attempted to define an institutional blueprint of the European organization and to assess European legal acts.[82] The court's main concern was to strip the simple (then predominantly intergovernmental) lawmaker of his control over the treaty rules.[83] The Council, in particular, should not decide by itself on what legal basis and through which procedure a legal act may be passed. As a result, most decisions referring to institutional balance have concerned the role of the European Parliament. It was important for the ECJ to make sure that the Parliament would be involved in the law-making procedures. With the idea of institutional balance, the ECJ had developed a concept that restricted the authority of the member states represented in the Council in order to strengthen the political organs of the EU.

This interpretation of the idea of the separation of powers does not seem too unusual. It invites—but does not yet urge us—to apply the traditional tripartite division to the European institutions. However, can the European institutions be accurately described this way? Does not the singular fact that the Council, the Commission, and the Parliament regulate their relations with one another through agreements already prove the uniqueness of European institutions?[84] Where should we to start to apply our concept? Not with the institutions themselves, which—like the Commission—are relatively unique, but rather with the powers, ie with the question of where we can find legislative, executive, and judicial law-making within the European institutions.

2. *Judicial law-making*

The judicial function of the EU is the easiest to define: it is performed by the EU courts in cooperation with the national courts. The latter have to bring open questions of EU law before the European courts for their judgment. The preliminary ruling power, Article 267 TFEU, is perhaps the instrument through which national and European courts are institutionally linked.[85]

---

[82] K. Lenaerts, A. Verhoeven, 'Institutional Balance and Democracy', in C. Joerges, R. Dehousse (eds.), *Good Governance in Europe's Integrated Market* (Oxford: Oxford University Press, 2002), 42.

[83] European Court of Justice, Case 9/56, *Meroni v High Authority*, European Court reports 1958, 1 (11); Case 10/56, *Meroni v High Authority*, European Court reports 1958, 51 (75).

[84] For further information and a different approach, which is opposed to the application of the separation of powers doctrine with regard to the EU: F. von Alemann, *Die Handlungsform der interinstitutionellen Vereinbarung* (Heidelberg: Springer, 2006), 407.

[85] K. J. Alter, *The European Court's political power* (Oxford: Oxford University Press, 2009), 185.

a) The ECJ as a quasi-federal high court

In order to understand and to evaluate the function of the European Court of Justice, one has to regard its double function as a supreme court in a quasi-federal order that has to protect the integrity of European law against the member states on the one hand, and as a constitutional court that implements the supremacy of the European Treaties on the other, if needed, against the European organs.[86] There is a certain asymmetry between these two functions in the ECJ's jurisprudence.

The ECJ launched this jurisprudence with a characteristic and now famous strategy: very early on, it began interpreting the European Treaty law as granting subjective rights to participants in the market. With this strategy, market participants became guardians of European law, which could initiate reviews with the help of national courts.[87] This case law, along with the postulated supremacy of European law, constituted a considerable institutional shift that was set in motion by the court, though it is open to debate in how far the original political decision to include a preliminary ruling procedure into the European Treaties paved the way. As a result, European law began to differ categorically from international law.[88] A legal system beyond the state, which granted citizens comprehensive legal protection, evolved. One can hardly overestimate the singularity of this process, and the legitimacy of this institutional shift is certainly questionable. For it is not only the most important example of the thesis established above, that a surplus of judicial as opposed to democratic lawmaking is typical for supranational legal systems.[89] Rather, there is much to suggest that this case law can be explained only by the fact that the political intergovernmental legislative process was stagnating and the ECJ stepped in to substitute a political process.[90] The creation of subjective rights by courts without legislative involvement, however, is, as we have seen, highly problematic.[91] Yet, we have also noted that after having placed legal questions into the hands of a court, the appeal to the concept of separated powers

---

[86] See Chapter 3, II., 3 for an analysis of those different functions; see also E. Sharpston, G. de Baere, 'The Court of Justice as a constitutional adjudicator', in A. Arnull (ed.): *A constitutional order of states?* (Oxford: Hart, 2011), 123; with regards to the protection of the federal balance between the EU and the member states, see K. Lenaerts, 'Federalism and the rule of law', 33 *Fordham International Law Journal* (2010), 1338.

[87] J. Masing, *Die Mobilisierung des Bürgers für die Durchsetzung des Rechts* (Berlin: Duncker & Humblot, 1997).

[88] See J. H. H. Weiler, *The Constitution of Europe* (Cambridge: Cambridge University Press, 1999), 26.

[89] See this Chapter, preliminary considerations, 3.

[90] Again J. H. H. Weiler, 'The Transformation of Europe', 100 Yale Law Journal (1991), 2403.

[91] See Chapter 3, II., 4.

creates only procedural but no workable material limits for their action.[92] It is finally important to consider that institutional resistance to this development within the European system of courts came almost exclusively from national *constitutional* courts.[93] Reasons might be that most constitutional courts are relatively far removed from the individual affairs of a citizen and that they see themselves as guardians of national legal identities. While regular courts are among the winners of European integration, as they can apply European law, specialized constitutional courts that can only apply national constitutional law are clear losers of this process. To assess the expansion of subjective rights in the ECJ's jurisprudence, one must also bear in mind that any control of the member states' application of European law is particularly difficult because of the heterogeneous structure of the European executive. We will come back to this point in a moment.[94]

The methods of the ECJ, especially its often very sweeping interpretation of EU standards and competences, have frequently been criticized.[95] One prominent complaint points out that the ECJ generally privileges the EU institutions over the member states. But this complaint may miss the important distinction between the different functions of a high court in a quasi-federal system and a constitutional court in the first place. As we saw above, it is an important task of federal high courts to protect the integrity of a federal structure by applying common rules. Furthermore, many standards of EU law, such as the different bans on discrimination, are primarily directed against the member states. For the ECJ, actions of the EU are potentially authoritative definitions of the European common good, whereas individual actions of member states may give voice to national special interests.[96] This is less an expression of a political suspicion than an inherent element of material European law and the institutional logic of federal or quasi-federal integration. As a result, the rulings of the ECJ are more often directed against the member states than against the EU itself. However, this neither stems from a lack of method by the court nor is it untypical of federal systems.

The same argument is also true for the judicial review of the European competences. As shown above, the concept of a legally determinate and

---

[92] See Chapter 2., II.

[93] For a comparative approach, see K. J. Alter, *Establishing the Supremacy of European Law* (Oxford: Oxford University Press, 2001), 64, 124.

[94] See this Chapter, III., 4. and 5.

[95] C. Hillgruber, 'Grenzen der Rechtsfortbildung durch den EuGH—Hat Europarecht Methode?', in T. v. Danwitz (ed.), *Auf dem Wege zu einer europäischen Staatlichkeit* (Stuttgart: Boorberg, 1993), 31 (39); H. Rasmussen, *On Law and Policy in the European Court of Justice* (Dordrecht: Nijhoff, 1986); I. Solanke, 'Stop the ECJ? An empirical analysis of activism at the Court', 17 *European Law Journal* (2011), 764.

[96] See this Chapter, III.,1.

judicially reviewable catalogue of federal powers, applied for example, in Germany, is not feasible for all federal systems.[97] Federal powers, even if they are well defined in a written constitution, are situated at the crossroads of legislative action and judicial control. Particularly in cases in which the distribution of competences between the levels is politically contested, a court will be reluctant to intervene in the decisions of the legislator of its own level, that is, from the perspective of the ECJ, the European legislator. This is especially true in an international context, in which the consensus of the states typically expresses the highest political as well as legal authority. Within the context of a legal integration through transnational subjective rights, which is so typical for the process of the European integration, this judiciary is also backed by a strong version of what we have here called individual legitimacy.

One might, however, argue that the ECJ, far from restricting itself to hesitantly supervising the powers of the European legislator, even establishes new powers for the legislator.[98] The exercise of basic freedoms against domestic statutes often entails the need for standardization on a European level. Wherever the ECJ affirms the need to protect these basic freedoms, the European legislator is empowered to regulate. By determining the scope of a transnational subjective right, such as to free trade within the EU, the court defines the powers of the European legislator in relation to the member states. The ability to institute legal action on economic freedoms before the ECJ directly extends the influence of the European legislator.

b) The ECJ as constitutional protector of fundamental rights?

Compared with this jurisprudence the court has been, and still is, quite reluctant to apply European standards to the European organs, which would mean to serve as a real *constitutional* court at the European level. We have already noticed that it takes up this role to adjudicate legal conflicts between European organs. Here, the court has no choice than to decide—and it tends to side with the supranational, not with the intergovernmental organs. A different story is the protection of basic rights. The ECJ began early on to flesh out a jurisprudence of European basic rights[99] and after some

---

[97] See Chapter 3, II., 3.

[98] See M. P. Maduro, *We the Court* (Oxford: Hart, 1999), 78.

[99] European Court of Justice, Case 44/79, *Hauer*, European Court Reports 1979, I-03727; more recently European Court of Justice, Case C-112/00, *Schmidberger*, European Court Reports 2003 I-05659; European Court of Justice, Case C-36/02, *Omega*, European Court Reports 2004 I-09609; T. Ackermann, 'Case law— Case C-36/02, Omega Spielhallen- und Automatenaufstellungs-GmbH v. Oberbürgermeisterin der Bundesstadt Bonn', 42 *Common Market Law Review* (2005), 1107; European Court of Justice, Joined cases C-399/06 P and C-403/06 P, *Hassan et al.*, European Court Reports 2009 I-11393; H. Abbott, 'The European Court of Justice and the protection of fundamental rights', 15 *Irish Journal of European Law* (2008), 79.

struggles, recently managed to more or less align this jurisprudence with the case law of the European Court of Human Rights.[100] Still, the protection of basic rights against actions of the European Union is about to become the central problem of the court for three reasons. The European legislator is no longer just a distributor of trans-national negative freedoms, as enshrined in the original Treaties, but also a political actor who passes anti-terrorism measures and comparable rules that abridge individual freedom. The EU executive, though elusive to define as a legal actor, as we will see, is increasingly directly addressing European citizens' sphere of individual freedom. Finally, through the Treaty of Lisbon, the European Union will enter into the European Convention on Human Rights, allowing the European Court of Human Rights to review European Union law directly.[101] This process may pose problems of its own for the ECtHR[102], but it may also push the ECJ to take the review of fundamental rights more seriously than it had before. From the point of view of our model, this seems desirable for two reasons, even if we remain generally sceptical about this kind of judicial review. The first reason is that the application of trans-national freedoms by the court against the member state had both a federal and a political effect: it gave trans-national rights privilege over domestically functioning rights, effectively meaning economic rights over political rights such as freedom of association.[103] Entering into a general rights review could end this asymmetry. If the court does not do so, this role could be assumed by national courts. Though there is a serious case against the fragmentation that could follow from this, it is obvious that fragmentation is better than no judicial protection of individual rights at all. The current approach of courts—national, supranational, and regional international levels—to step in to review infringements made by authorities of other levels if, and only if, there is no review at this level, seems to be

[100] A. Haratsch, 'Die Solange-Rechtsprechung des EGMR', 66 *Zeitschrift für ausländisches öffentliches Recht und Völkerrecht* (2006), 927.

[101] T. Lock, 'Walking on a tightrope—the draft ECHR accession agreement and the autonomy of the EU legal order', 48 *Common Market Law Review* (2011), 1025; O. Quirico, 'Substantive and procedural issues raised by the accession of the EU to the ECHR', 20 *Italian Yearbook of International Law* (2011), 31; J. Vondung, *Die Architektur des europäischen Grundrechtsschutzes nach dem Beitritt der EU zur EMRK* (Tübingen: Mohr Siebeck, 2012).

[102] See N. O'Meara, '"A More Secure Europe of Rights?" The European Court of Human Rights, the Court of Justice of the European Union and EU Accession to the ECHR', 12 *German Law Journal* (2011), 1813; J.-P. Jacqué, 'The Accession of the European Union to the European Convention on Human Rights and Fundamental Freedoms', 48 *Common Market Law Review* (2011), 995.

[103] C. Joerges, F. Rödl: 'Informal politics, formalised law and the "social deficit" of European integration. Reflections after the judgments of the ECJ in Viking and Laval', 15 *European Law Journal* (2009), 1–19; J. Krzeminska-Vamvaka, 'Horizontal effect of fundamental rights and freedoms much ado about nothing? German, Polish and EU theories compared after Viking Line', *Jean Monnet Working Paper* 11/2009 (New York, NY: NYU School of Law).

relatively consolidated. It is the doctrine of national courts with regard to the ECJ,[104] the doctrine of the ECtHR with regard to the ECJ,[105] and the doctrine of the ECJ with regard to the United Nations.[106] To be sure, from the perspective of our model, this doctrine is nothing more than makeshift. It looks only at a structural loss of judicial review but not at individual infringements. This seems necessary as a matter of division of labour, mutual respect among the different levels of public authority, and their democratic legitimacy. But the deficits in the protection of individual freedom remain undeniable.

The other reason in favour of a more extended review of rights by the ECJ concerns the legitimacy of European legislation. If the critique of judicial review rests on the democratic legitimacy of the legislator, we will have to check this legitimacy for the European case. This leads us to European legislation.

3. Legislation

Legislative law has a comparably wide scope and an orientation towards the future. It should be the result of a political procedure, which is defined by constitutional rules but open with regard to content.[107] In EU law, this kind of law is called 'secondary law', meaning those legal acts passed by the political institutions of the EU through the process set out in the Treaties. Secondary law is distinguished from the primary law in the Treaties. In addition, one could identify a layer of (mostly delegated) tertiary law, which the Commission is authorized to set.[108] The difference between European secondary and tertiary law resembles the distinction between a parliamentary statute and an executive rule in national legal systems.

In the old European Economic Community, the Council unanimously passed 'basic legal acts' on the initiative of the Commission, which were later reviewed by the ECJ. This division of labour was called the 'Community method'. Built on member state consensus, the Commission was the

---

[104] Federal Constitutional Court, *Solange I*, BVerfGE 37, 271; *Solange II*, BVerfGE 73, 339.

[105] European Court of Human Rights, Judgment of 30 June 2005, *Bosphorus Hava Yollari Turizm v Ireland*, App. No. 45036/98; see F. Schorkopf, 'The European Court of Human Rights' Judgment in the Case of Bosphorus Hava Yollari Turizm v. Ireland', 6 *German Law Journal* (2005), 1255.

[106] European Court of Justice, Cases C-402/05 P and C-415/05 P, *Yassin Abdullah Kadi and Al Barakaat International Foundation v Council of the European Union and Commission of the European Communities*; see D. Halberstam, E. Stein, 'The United Nations, the European Union, and the King of Sweden: Economic Sanctions and Individual Rights in a Plural World Order', 46 *Common Market Law Review* (2009), 13.

[107] See Chapter 2, III., 2.

[108] See K. Lenaerts, P. van Nuffel, *Constitutional Law of the EU* (London: Thomson, Sweet & Maxwell, 2nd ed 2005), paras. 11-001-003.

independent and apolitical actor responsible for progress; for agenda-setting in the process of integration. Gradually, the European Parliament gained first an advisory and then a co-decision-making role. In the process of co-decision-making, the Council and the Parliament, on the initiative of the Commission, must agree on a legislative act. How should we evaluate this procedure in accordance with our model?

a) The European Parliament

For a long while, the European Parliament had an institutional position that was irreconcilable with its status as a proper parliament.[109] To date, it is composed according to electoral rules, which take into account the different populations of the member states by prescribing strongly weighted votes. This raises the question of who is the subject of legitimacy that actually creates the EP. For some time, moreover, the members of the EP understood themselves to be representatives of their respective national electorates. They felt politically closer to their compatriots than to their political affiliates from other states. This has changed. One can observe a noticeable politicization and de-nationalization of the political discourse within the EP.[110] To date, however, the parliament suffers from very weak voter participation, which does not do justice to the Parliament's newly achieved, dramatically enhanced institutional role. In terms of democratic theory, what conclusions can we draw from these developments?

One answer could point out that there simply is not a 'European people' and, therefore, that it is no coincidence if democratic representation does not work within the EP.[111] From this perspective, introducing strictly egalitarian electoral rules for the EP would imply a loss of legitimacy, as it would introduce a structure of representation with nothing to represent. The low voter turnout vividly corroborates this position. Nonetheless, after what has been elaborated above, it remains doubtful whether this reconstruction is adequate. A different interpretation could point out that the establishment of the EP by the member states is in itself an expression of a democratically consented demand for a European platform of discourse with legislative competences. Those Europeans who fail to participate in elections for the EP are—paradoxically—the same ones to have voted for the national governments and parliaments that established the EP. In any case, the internal development of the EP towards a forum for European political competition beyond member state affiliation, as well as its many competences, are good

---

[109] For the following compare Christoph Möllers, 'Multi-Level Democracy', 24 *Ratio Juris* (2011), 247.

[110] H. Maurer, 'Das föderative Verfassungsorgan im europäischen Vergleich', in *Verfassung im Diskurs der Welt. Festschrift für Peter Häberle* (Tübingen: Mohr 2004), 551–78.

[111] Federal Constitutional Court, *Lissabon-Vertrag*, BVerfGE 123, 267 (358).

arguments for greater political interest in its elections. In other words, in a democratic polity, the electorate also has a democratic responsibility to actively accompany institutional change and to get involved. It is understandable, in this respect, that a certain amount of time needs to pass between the institutional innovation, on the one hand, and its recognition by a politically active European public sphere on the other. It is against this background, too, that the Council of Ministers' extent of *factual* political power, which for the time being exceeds the power of the EP, remains justified. The Council prevents the EP from acting as a legislator without a subject of legitimacy. At the same time, the remarkable circumstance that the first introduction of both—majority decisions in the Council and the co-decision procedure—occurred simultaneously and pertained to the same political field,[112] elucidates the close relationship between the two procedures. If the EP becomes an institution perceived as relevant by the European public, the weights should shift. Again, though there can be a temporal delay between institutional developments and their perception by the democratic public, there is no guarantee that this experiment in supranational democracy will be successful.

In any case, the problem cannot be solved by means of institutional law alone. The Parliament can gain political clout only when it develops its own political identity without the institutional legal framework having to be changed. Institutional law should simply establish an equilibrium between the two legislative institutions, the Council and the Parliament, in which shifting political influences can balance out and develop.

b) Co-decision-making

However, in their current form, the Treaties have never included a truly general law-making procedure. Instead, they provided different decision-making rules for different political spheres, in a few of which the Parliament still has only an advisory function. Though the co-decisional process of what is now Article 294 TFEU is most commonly used, including many political fields thought to be crucial to the member states, there remains a distinct lack of parliamentary decision-making power.[113] However, the making of a true legislative equilibrium requires that the EP is included into co-decisional procedures in all legislative areas. If the member states believe that certain political areas are particularly sensitive, this can have an impact on the decision-

---

[112] By way of Art. 100a Treaty of the European Economic Communities according to the Single European Act.

[113] P.P. Craig, 'Treaty of Lisbon', *33 European Law Review* (2008), 137 (156). For a critique from a democratic theory point of view, see J. v. Achenbach, 'Vorschläge zu einer Demokratietheorie der dualen demokratischen Legitimation europäischer Hoheitsgewalt', in S. Kirste, A. van Aaken (eds.), *Interdisciplinary research in jurisprudence and constitutionalism* (Stuttgart: Steiner, 2012), 205.

making rules in the Council (demand for unanimity), but it does not legitimize the exclusion of the Parliament.

In the standard European legislative procedure, neither the Council nor the Parliament has a formal right of initiative. This right rests with the Commission.[114] In the classic concept, the Commission was intended to be the stimulator for European integration. Its initiatives can be amended or rejected only by member state consensus. However, the Council possesses a practically significant, soft right of initiative when it requests that the Commission consider a particular issue. Equipping the Parliament at least with such a right would be adequate, as we expect legislative organs to be able to act spontaneously on their own initiative; an option that is necessarily entailed in our understanding of democratic legitimacy of the legislator. Even if the legislator does not actually make use of this right, it creates his responsibility for action as well as for inaction. This may be one reason why the European Parliament itself is hesitant to claim such a competence.

What other implications could our concept have for the mechanisms of European legislation? We have seen that the inner organization of a parliament must be left as far as possible to the parliament itself, the only exceptions being the public nature of parliamentary sessions, the final say of the plenum, and the majority rule.[115] In this sense, the European Parliament is organized like a legitimate legislature. This will be confirmed by a closer look at the relationship of the Parliament with the Commission.

Does the *composition* of the Parliament suggest another reading? We noticed that the EP does not reflect the democratic equality of the European citizens. Rather, the process is skewed towards proportional representation of member states, which favours smaller states. On the one hand, this is not totally unusual. For a long time, there was an over-representation of Scotland in the House of Commons, and comparable asymmetries still exist in many other parliaments. Democratic representation does not work like a naturalistic photograph of a given political will. On the other hand, the existing over-representation is drastic and does not seem necessary to protect small member states. Every state should have some members in the EP. That said, the place where Luxembourgers are represented in the EU not as citizens of the Union, but rather as Luxembourgers as such, is not the Parliament but the Council. Under an institutional arrangement in which both legislative institutions must agree to every law, the danger of being outvoted is not a compelling argument.

---

[114] See Article 293 (1) TFEU. [115] See Chapter 2, III., 2.

c) Council and European Council

The internal organization of the Council raises more questions than the Parliament. We discussed the lack of intergovernmental legitimacy earlier on.[116] To a certain extent, this problem cannot be solved if one insists (for good reasons) on national legitimacy in international law. However, there are more specific questions: though the Council has begun to meet in public, according to the Treaty of Lisbon its work is still far from transparent.[117] Even though, as in parliaments, a certain informal pre-decision-making process may take place behind closed doors, a binding *legislative* decision must always be accompanied by an open debate and the knowledge of who voted how. Moreover, in its function as a legislative institution the Council mostly meets as a congregation of specialized ministers. There is no higher, more general level that could balance different departmental interests where, for example, the ministers for the environment would meet with those for agriculture. This results in what has been called a sectoralization of the decision-making procedure. Different regimes with different interests do not communicate. This leaves the whole legislative process more open to asymmetric lobbying efforts. Ultimately, the Council branches out into a rather confusing jungle of different committees because of its vast variety of competences. But these committees—unlike parliamentary committees—do not consist of legitimate members of the legislative institution but of officials.[118] As a result, the Council is an institution that debates only within its respective sectors. It makes non-public decisions, which are cleared at the level of officials to a fairly large extent.

How can these problems be solved? Beyond the issue of transparency, reform is needed: as a legislative institution the Council should have a general legislative responsibility in accordance with our requirement of a general democratic forum.[119] This would be possible if all member states nominated European ministers who were the only representatives of their country in the Council.[120] Moreover, such a structure could also protect organizational resources and would reduce the pressure to form committees. The special role of the European Council as the truly general, yet highly problematic super-organ of the EU will have to be considered later.

---

[116] See this Chapter I.

[117] On Article 16 (8): D. Curtin, *Executive power of the European Union* (Oxford: Oxford University Press, 2009), 228–32.

[118] F. Hayes Renshaw, H. Wallace, *The Council of Ministers* (Basingstoke, Hampshire: MacMillan, 1997), 97.

[119] See Chapter 2.

[120] F. C. Mayer, 'Nationale Regierungsstrukturen und europäische Integration', *29 Europäische Grundrechte-Zeitschrift* (2002), 111.

In democratic constitutional states, legislation is the core of collective self-determination. Although the Treaty of Lisbon for the first time introduces the concept of the democratic statute or law as a legal form into the European legal order, it still seems unsuitable to speak of democratic European legislation in an emphatic sense. This is due not least to the structure of the Treaties, which do not establish a constitution in the sense of a general, all-encompassing political procedure but instead regulate individual policies very specifically and precisely, not allowing for the regular legislative bodies to take part in their general formation. A more general design of legislative procedures could enhance the legislative organs' democratic legitimacy.

4. The Commission: government or agency?

In national constitutional orders the legislature works in close cooperation with the government. Some cooperation seems even necessary in presidential systems. However, is there a government of the European Union? This is a controversial issue.[121] The responsibilities of the government in national constitutional orders are relatively similar. In foreign affairs, the government represents a country. In parliamentary systems, it defines the political agenda—either single-handedly or with parliament. The government implements parliamentary statutes through rules and regulations, and, in federal systems, it has certain supervisory powers over the members of the federation. Is there any organ with such powers within the EU?

One candidate could be the European Council, which consists of the Heads of State or Governments of the member states, its President, and the President of the Commission. The European Council gives the EU programmatic impulses through legally non-binding but politically very influential resolutions.[122] Today, it serves as the most important agenda-setter in the EU; a position even reinforced through the new office of a President of the Council who prepares and chairs European Council meetings and has certain competencies to represent the EU externally. The rotating presidency of the Council of Ministers plays a similar role in that the respective presiding member state defines a political agenda while also representing the EU externally in certain contexts. We shall return to the function of the European Council and the different presidencies at the end of this section. In

---

[121] For further information on that discussion, see P. Dann, 'The Political Institutions', in A. v. Bogdandy, J. Bast (eds.), *Principles of European Constitutional Law* (Oxford: Hart, 2nd rev. ed 2010), 237.

[122] Critically A. v. Bogdandy, J. Bast, F. Arndt, 'Handlungsformen im Unionsrecht', 62 *Zeitschrift für ausländisches öffentliches Recht und Völkerrecht* (2002), 126.

any case, both are intergovernmental institutions that undoubtedly take on central *political* governmental functions.

There is still another institution which exercises many of governmental functions for the EU: the European Commission. The Commission holds the monopoly of initiative over European legislation. In many practically important fields, such as in world trade law, it represents the EU externally. The Commission oversees the member states in their implementation of EU law and enacts further implementing rules, which apply secondary legislation in the same way that regulations specify parliamentary laws in national legal orders.

So the Commission actually possesses many legal powers that resemble those of a national government. It certainly does not have the corresponding political heft, however. This raises the question of how the legislative and the Commission relate to one another. A government, just like a legislature, holds a general political mandate. Therefore, the government needs a general democratic legitimacy, whether conveyed through the legislature or directly, through the democratic electorate. Governmental action remains tethered for good reason to some kind of direct political accountability, by parliamentary or general election. But such accountability exists for the Commission only indirectly: the President of the Commission is appointed by the European Council and approved by the European Parliament. The President of the Commission and Council appoint the other members of the Commission that are subject to parliamentary approval. The Parliament has the right to interrogate the Commission and to access information from it. The Parliament can also appoint commissions of enquiry. The Commission must annually report to the Parliament on the implementation of specific policies. Finally, the Commission can, as a body, be ousted from office by a parliamentary resolution with a two-thirds majority. Both, Parliament and the Council, thus formally legitimize the Commission. Nevertheless, the Commission lacks the political influence of a national government. This corresponds with the fact that the intergovernmental process between the member states is decisive in choosing the President of the Commission.

As a result, the Commission cannot actually be compared with a majority government accountable to parliament, though as a matter of a more recent, unwritten convention, it is the strongest political faction in the European Parliament to which the President of the Commission shall belong. However, the Commission is not fully constituted by this majority, but rather consists of a double proportional representation of political affiliation and national origin. Moreover, the appointment of the Commission is detached from the elections to Parliament. The Commission does not define its work in relation to the political majorities in Parliament. There is no parliamentary opposition that keeps a critical eye on the Commission. Instead, the whole Parliament considers itself as a form of counter-institution to the Commission and to the Council. The most similar national constitutional system may be the proportional membership of the Swiss government, the Bundesrat. Here, the different political parties agree on their proportional representation in the highest governmental body with respect to the latest election results.[123] The consensual design of this setting, the only indirect implications of general elections for the makeup of the government and, therefore, for the general political direction of the country, as well as the strongly federal design of the whole political system, might indeed serve as a role model for the progress of European integration. This is all the more the case as Switzerland is a land with four national languages and a multi-denominational religious culture.

All in all, evaluating the legitimacy of the Commission is not easy. On the one hand, it is hardly possible to measure the Commission against the very specific ideal of a parliamentary system of government, although the parliamentary accountability of the Commission has developed enormously in recent years, precisely because of the strong political evolution of the European Parliament. Yet the Commission not only performs the duties of a government, and governmental functions are not performed by the Commission alone but also by the different forms of the Council. Ultimately, the institutional self-image of the Commission, as we shall see, has developed out of quite different circumstances. Nevertheless, the far-reaching powers of the Commission can only be legitimized when they are democratically programmed. In this sense, the emerging relationship between Parliament and Commission seems wholly appropriate, even though the destination of this development will more likely be a concordant-democratic system such as in Switzerland, rather than in a majoritarian parliamentary system.[124]

The Commission was not traditionally considered a governmental entity. Its legitimacy was not meant to stem from a political process, but rather from its absence, from the expertise of the organization, and its commitment to the substantial goals of the Treaties, namely a standardized market and the welfare gain associated with it.[125] The Commission was originally—as the High Authority of the European Coal and Steel Community—a strange

---

[123] The principle of proportional representation is not a constitutional order, however. The Swiss Constitution would also allow for a majority government; see Article 175 of the Federal Constitution; U. Klöti, 'Consensual Government in a Heterogeneous Polity', in J.-E. Lane, *The Swiss Labyrinth* (London: Frank Cass, 2001), 19 (22).

[124] G. Lehmbruch, *Proporzdemokratie* (Tübingen: Mohr, 1976); A. Lijphart, *Democracies: patterns of majoritarian and consensus government in twenty-one countries* (New Haven: Yale University Press, 1984).

[125] See this Chapter, III., 1.

combination of a technocratic, independent administrative agency and the secretary of an international organization. What was new was its independent regulatory capacity, particularly its monopoly on legislative initiative. From the outset, there loomed the question of how the Commission could achieve a political balance of interests that legitimizes a binding legislative proposal. During the development of the internal market, that is until the early 1990s, this question was not a pressing one because the demolition of market restrictions did not call for any further political legitimacy—it was explicitly established in the European Treaties and supported by the individual legitimacy of subjective, transnational freedom. But with the liberalization there arose the necessity of readjustments by regulation, for example in the area of environmental protection. This entailed restrictions on freedom, which were more difficult to justify. When the expansion of the powers of the European polity led to a more pronounced need for legitimacy, such as with the Treaty of Maastricht, the Commission was faced with a problem. By this point at the latest, it was no longer the guardian of transnational freedoms but an authority with the power to abridge individual rights.

How can the Commission obtain legitimacy under these conditions? To anticipate the answer: it cannot and, formally, there is no such need as long as the Commission only proposes legislative decisions but does not enact them. Nonetheless, one may identify some tendencies in the institutional development of the EU that also hint at its legitimization problem. First, there is the enhanced accountability of the Commission towards the European Parliament, as described above. Apparently, the Commission has never wanted it. Secondly, since the Treaty of Maastricht, even formal political agenda-setting has shifted to the intergovernmental organs. Paradoxically, today the Commission is less political but more politically accountable than ever before. The increase of indirect legal initiatives by the Council or the European Council and the formation of the domestic and foreign policy powers of the EU, in which the Commission has less of a role, confirm this finding. But also in the ongoing euro crisis, the Commission rather seems to have fallen back into the role of a problem-solving secretariat, whereas the presidency and some member states are the leading political actors.

In addition, even the classic technocratic self-image of the Commission as a competent broker of legitimate interests seems in crisis. This could also serve as evidence for our introductory assumption that the Commission has no genuine supranational legitimacy. Despite this, the Commission frequently tries to deploy its former self-image as a competent, apolitical, technocratic organization. The question remains: how does the Commission manage the balance of interests in order to justify its own legislative initiatives? In practice, the Commission attempts to enter into a conversation with those actors that might be affected by a potential regulation; it launches an organized dialogue with interest groups. However, as this is not a dialogue based on the principle of democratic equality mediated through political parties, the Commission must induce a corporatist-lobbyist environment. Empirical findings show that the Commission is more susceptible to the influence of special interests than national governments.[126] It has developed its own culture of cooperation and corruption. However, the Commission does attempt to counteract this impression through the inclusion of interests and through transparency initiatives. Among the most prominent of these initiatives was the 'White Paper on European Governance', in which the Commission promoted informal structures of dialogue between the Commission and 'civil society'.[127] This concept suggested the view, not uncommon in both legal and political science, that traditional forms of democratic representation are not sufficient for the European project. Instead, it advocated new forms of legitimacy under the heading of 'governance'. Without looking to pre-empt our more fundamental critique of this concept at the end of this book,[128] one can assert that the politically weakened Commission is currently not a suitable candidate for the illustration of such new forms. The Commission has not been able to bring transparency to the influences that affect its decision-making. Furthermore, the Commission is not perceived by anyone outside academic discourse as an agent possessing a level of legitimacy that could compete with national governments or the European Parliament. Its unintended development towards classical forms of politicization via parliamentary control and party politics, along with the lack of much sense for democratic representation in its own documents, make the future of an innovative Commission now look rather bleak. However, despite this sceptical assessment, we will see that the Commission remains the most plausible candidate to fill the position of a future European government.

5. The complex administration

Both temporally and in its scope, executive law-making stands in between the legislature and the judiciary. It implements legislative decisions at different levels to such an extent that they can become the object of judicial

---

[126] P. Bouwen, 'A Comparative Study of Business Lobbying in the European Parliament, the European Commission and the Council of Ministers', *Max-Planck Institut für Gesellschaftsforschung Discussion Paper* (Köln, 2002); P. Bouwen, 'Exchanging access goods for access: a comparative study of business lobbying in the European Union institutions', 43 *European Journal of Political Research* (2004), 337.

[127] Commission White Paper on European Governance, COM (2001), 428. For a critique, see C. Joerges, Y. Mény, J. H. H. Weiler (eds.), *Mountain or Molehill? A Critical Appraisal of the Commission White Paper on Governance* (New York: NYU School of Law, 2001).

[128] See in this work, Outlook.

review. But how is the EU executive actually structured? The wide scope of executive action can, in an idealized manner, be divided into two parts. The first element consists of executive rule-making—the implementation of legislative decisions through more specific standards, codified in rules and regulations. The second element is the application of these rules to legal subjects—citizens, enterprises, and in the case of the EU even member states: the Council and the European Parliament can reach a legislative decision by issuing a directive, e.g., which regulates general standards for drinking water. On the basis of this, more specific standards are established. Then, based upon these specific standards, certain orders and bans can be imposed, for example against an individual farmer who uses nitrate fertilizer.

Who is responsible for these different stages of concretization? To answer this question, let us start with a basic model. As a rule, the European Commission is entitled to substantiate a basic legislative act by issuing tertiary legislation. The member states are then responsible for applying these standards to individual cases. Thus, executive action is divided into at least two different stages between the Commission and the member states. However, in order to get a complete picture, we will have to modify this model slightly.

First, committees, consisting of one representative for each member state and one for the Commission, are involved when tertiary legislation is being enacted. Here, the member states can voice objections, delay, or even prevent the implementing rules.[129] These committees are also needed to exchange information, for the member state administrations will subsequently enforce the standards. In such 'comitology committees', the member states return to the European executive at quite an early stage. Comitology has become a much-disputed topic of the academic discussion in recent years. For some, comitology is the epitome of an intransparent bureaucratic rule by committees behind closed doors that should be tightly controlled by the European Parliament. For others, it is a system with particularly high deliberative standards, in which Commission and member states can voice their arguments and improve regulation.[130] According to the standards developed here, both assumptions seem exaggerated. First, it is important to see that the function of the committees is to ensure the participation of the member state administrations in EU *executive*

---

[129] H. Hofmann (ed.), *Administrative law and policy of the European Union* (Oxford: Oxford University Press, 2011), 281, 386.

[130] For further information on Comitology Committees, see C. Joerges, E. Vos (eds.), *EU Committees* (Oxford: Hart, 1999); K. Lenaerts, A. Verhoeven, 'Towards a legal framework for executive rulemaking in the EU?: The contribution of the new comitology decision', *37 Common Market Law Review* (2000), 645.

rule-making. It is obvious that the member states should have a look at the rules that they will have to implement later on. Such structures are familiar from other systems of executive federalism, in which the lower level has the power and the duty to apply law that was made on the higher level.[131] Therefore, according to our model of parliamentary control, formal interventions of the European Parliament cannot enhance the legitimacy of this procedure. As we have seen above, this form of parliamentary control does make adequate use of the institutional virtues of a parliamentary body.[132] There is an effort—mostly by the European Parliament—to limit the participation of comitology committees under the Treaty of Lisbon.[133] However, it is not yet clear how these rules will play out in practice. The practical need for horizontal coordination between the Commission and the member state administrations at this stage of executive rule-making makes it probable that there will be informal cooperation anyway.

Secondly, the Commission has a remarkable influence on the member states' further implementation of executive rules. General rules concerning this matter do not exist in the European Treaties. However, though the Commission does not have the right to give individual instructions to the member states' administrations, there is a vast range of different administrative procedures for every regulatory field, which makes European administrative law very opaque.[134] In most cases, the Commission can demand information and reports from the member states, check accounts, and, in some cases, even issue individual instructions, although no kind of general administrative scheme is discernible.

Thirdly, in some areas the Commission directly applies European administrative law and addresses individual legal subjects. This is the case in competition law, including the imposition of individual sanctions, in which the Commission acts both as a policy-maker and the administrative actor. In these rather exceptional but very important cases, the European polity directly faces its subjects instead of hiding behind the member states' administrations.

---

[131] G. Biaggini, *Theorie und Praxis des Verwaltungsrechts im Bundesstaat* (Basel: Helbing und Lichtenhahn, 1996.

[132] See Chapter 3, I.

[133] H. Hofmann, 'Legislation, delegation and implementation under the Treaty of Lisbon', 15 *European Law Journal* (2009), 482 (494); C. Möllers, J. v. Achenbach, 'Die Mitwirkung des Europäischen Parlaments an der abgeleiteten Rechtsetzung der Europäischen Kommission nach dem Lissabonner Vertrag', 46 *Europarecht* (2011), 39.

[134] For specific analysis, see E. Schmidt-Aßmann, B. Schöndorf-Haubold (eds.), *Der europäische Verwaltungsverbund: Formen und Verfahren der Verwaltungszusammenarbeit in der EU* (Tübingen: Mohr-Siebeck, 2005); T. v. Danwitz, *Europäisches Verwaltungsrecht* (Heidelberg: Springer, 2008), 609–48.

For the European Commission, the administrations of the member states are distant, complex, and very heterogeneous entities in a vast administrative space. In order to oversee the correct implementation of European law, the Commission must first learn what twenty-seven very different member states with completely different administrative cultures actually do with it. The Commission potentially suffers from great deficits in information. For this reason, European law traditionally includes many duties to provide information to both the Commission and also to citizens.[135] The citizen's right to information from national administrations is new to some national administrative law traditions. For the Commission these rights are, if nothing else, an additional way to control the member state administrations.

The most effective but also most cumbersome instrument of forcing member states to obey European law is the right of the European Commission to sue a state before the ECJ. Such procedures are frequent but represent a less than efficient method, as they require plenty of resources. Not least because of this, European law recognizes a variety of subjective rights through which citizens of the member states can take legal action even before national courts to claim a violation of EU law. The creativity of the ECJ in devising such subjective rights has been criticized above.[136] But we can now also understand this move as an instrument to secure control over the administration in a heterogeneous, quasi-federal polity. With the help of subjective rights, citizens and businesses become agents of the Commission, observing and monitoring the member states. If a state illicitly levies tariffs, the Commission must take notice, object, and take legal action. If the ban is also understood as a violation of the subjective right of a corporation, it can file a lawsuit. In doing so, the enterprise relieves the Commission of its monitoring duty and becomes part of a decentralized control effort.

Along with the number of its member states, the duties of the EU have been multiplying. This also increases the need for the Commission to keep abreast of affairs. Since the Commission, unlike national governments, has very little influence over its own financial budget, it suffers from a constant lack of resources. The Commission could monitor most closely if it implemented all of the standards itself, but that is both costly and goes against the wishes of member states, which see their powers to implement European

---

[135] A. v. Bogdandy, 'Information und Kommunikation in der Europäischen Union: föderale Strukturen in supranationalem Umfeld', in W. Hoffmann-Riem, E. Schmidt-Aßmann (eds.), *Verwaltungsrecht in der Informationsgesellschaft* (Baden-Baden: Nomos, 2000), 133; K. Heußner, *Informationssysteme im Europäischen Verwaltungsverbund* (Tübingen: Mohr Siebeck, 2007).

[136] See this Chapter, III., 2.

law as one residual element of their sovereignty. Still, the Commission cannot simply abandon its duty to review the member states.

To help solve this problem, new administrative structures have emerged, two of which are of particular interest. First, European agencies have been founded. Agencies are European authorities that have gained a certain independence from the Commission and hold specific administrative responsibilities, such as the study of environmental data or drug safety. The first generation of European agencies were limited to collecting information and technically preparing decisions of the Commission, and had no law-making powers. More recent agencies such as those in the field of flight safety possess their own regulatory power.[137] Within the agency organization, the antagonism—so characteristic of the European executive—between the Commission and the member states recurs: officers from the Commission and representatives from the member states are represented in the agency institutions. Therefore, the organization of agencies can once again be understood as a compromise between the Commission's need to control implementation of European law and the member states' participatory demands.[138]

But are European administrative agencies a new form of an unchecked super-bureaucracy, merging legislative and judicial powers into an illegitimate fourth branch of government? It still seems safe to say that this is not the case. As we have seen above, the notion of administrative autonomy itself depends on many procedural and substantial parameters.[139] European agencies still only implement rules of a well-defined and narrow regulatory scope. The Commission and, in some cases, the European Parliament closely monitor them. Underdefined open-phrased regulatory schemes that concern important markets, as is the case in US administrative law, are unusual in European law.[140] The rise of agencies in the EU backs our assumption that this type of organization is established in constitutional structures with competing strands of democratic legitimacy. In this case, they express the competing claims of the Commission and the member states to represent the executive branch of the EU.

A second, more recent instrument for controlling the member states is the *horizontal* connection of national administrative authorities with one

[137] D. Curtin, *Executive power of the European Union* (Oxford: Oxford University Press, 2009), 146; D. Riedel, 'Die europäische Flugsicherheitsagentur', in E. Schmidt-Aßmann, B. Schöndorf-Haubold (eds.), *Der europäische Verwaltungsverbund* (Tübingen: Mohr Siebeck, 2005), 103.

[138] E. Chiti, 'Decentralisation and Integration into the Community: A New Perspective on European Agencies', 10 *European Law Journal* (2004), 402.

[139] See Chapter 3.

[140] D. Curtin, *Executive power of the European Union* (Oxford: Oxford University Press, 2009), 146.

another under the supervision of the Commission.[141] In such a constellation, European law obliges national authorities to take the decisions of other national authorities into consideration before making a decision. In a regulatory act concerning the German telecommunications market, the responsible German authority must, according to European law, observe both the standards of the Commission and the corresponding decisions of the authorities of other member states.[142] This requirement, though technical-sounding, is quite revolutionary and highlights particular problems of administrative legitimacy in the EU: if national authorities were previously committed to German and European standards, they are now—through European law—also committed to the actions of other member states. The Commission reserves certain rights to make an ultimate decision in this horizontal procedure. Thus, the Commission is in the best position to leave its costly everyday business to national authorities and restrict itself to regulating standards and assessing important individual issues. As a matter of organizational prudence this seems to be a promising scheme, which has so far been implemented in certain types of market regulation, e.g., concerning financial markets.[143] This kind of procedure respects the member states' preference for avoiding centralized European authorities. As a matter of legitimacy, though, this setting seems dubious. Any form of horizontal coordination is especially difficult to track, and the path of democratic accountability becomes even more complex than when European authorities act directly.

All in all, the picture of a European administration remains complex. Its three basic elements are the Commission, the individual member state administrations, and the body of all member states, which apply EU law in different configurations—at times in horizontal, cooperative structures and sometimes in rather vertical, hierarchical ones. Classically, legal literature used to identify two basic mechanisms for implementing EU law: indirect implementation, which leaves the implementation to the member states, and direct implementation, in which the Commission executes European law

---

[141] For example, in competition and telecommunications law, see M. d. Visser, *Network-based governance in EC law. The example of EC Competition and EC Communications law* (Oxford: Hart, 2009); H.-H. Trute, 'Der europäische Regulierungsverbund in der Telekommunikation', in L. Osterloh, K. Schmidt, H. Weber (eds.), *Staat—Wirtschaft—Finanzverfassung: Festschrift für Peter Selmer* (Berlin: Duncker & Humblot, 2004), 585.

[142] For the role of national authorities, see M. d. Visser, *Network-based governance in EC law. The example of EC Competition and EC Communications law* (Oxford: Hart, 2009), 41.

[143] N. Moloney, 'EU financial market regulation after the global financial crisis', 47 *Common Market Law Review* (2010), 1317; A. Kern, 'Reforming European financial supervision', in *Europäische Rechtsakademie Trier: ERA-Forum* (2011), 229; M. Eckardt, W. Ebert, 'Wirtschafts- und finanzpolitische Koordinierung in der Europäischen Union', in W. Schäfer (ed.), *Aktuelle Probleme der europäischen Integration* (Baden-Baden: Nomos, 2012), 43.

without any recourse to the member state administrations. Supposedly, the former is the general rule and the latter the exception. However, the specificity of the European executive is lost in this basic distinction: in almost every European administrative decision both the Commission and either an affected member state or a committee of all member states assembled are involved.

How do these structures fit into our model of separated powers? In the federal structures of the EU, as in the German system, higher and lower levels (Federation and federal states, Union and member states) exercise their executive powers in a cooperative manner. Usually, the lower level implements the legislative acts enacted at the higher level.

In this format, two issues of legitimacy arise, both of which can be linked to our two models of legitimacy. *Democratic* accountability requires that, through the electoral process, each citizen can hold the public authority politically responsible for every decision that concerns him or her. *Legal* accountability, on the other hand, requires that this citizen can challenge decisions of the public authority in court. The fusion of different executives in a federal structure may disrupt both lines of accountability. This can be illustrated by examples typical of both national and supra-national federal administrative structures. A member state department of commerce issues a subsidy in favour of a business. Later, the European Commission instructs the national authority to withdraw this subsidy. The national administrator obeys. An administrative or judicial complaint of the business must be formally directed at the national authority because this is the only entity the business entertained a legal relation with. The complaint cannot be addressed to the European Commission, which defined the substance of the decision. In addition, there are more uncertainties regarding the question which courts, national or European, are empowered to review which element of a typically compound administrative decision.[144] Finally, although it was the actual decision-maker, the European Commission cannot even be directly held to account politically.

In federal systems, in which the higher level sets legislative rules that are implemented by the lower level, such deficits are difficult to avoid. They would be straightforwardly solved in the US model, in which the political levels act separately from one another with their own distinct legislative and administrative branches.[145] Implemented in the European Union,

---

[144] In detail: J. Hofmann, *Rechtschutz und Haftung im europäischen Verwaltungsverbund* (Berlin: Duncker & Humblot, 2004).

[145] See Chapter I, I., 5.

this would require that the European Commission to build a structure of field offices all over Europe, which would be responsible for the direct implementation of European law and accountable to the Commission and the European Parliament. This would be politically risky, for the EU would suddenly become visible as a public authority on the ground and as the author of many contested decisions, whereas at the moment, when European law is regularly implemented by the national legislator and applied by national authorities, it usually vanishes behind the administrative action of the member states. Such a solution can only serve as a thought experiment in the analysis of the European administration. It is impossible to realize for practical reasons and because of the reservations of the member states, which do not simply want to relinquish the power to implement European law. The actions of the executive may be more politically sensitive than those of the legislature. It may be more important to know the police officer than the police legislator. Still, this kind of visibility would allow for a considerably higher degree of democratic accountability for the European executive.

What instruments are available to enhance the legitimacy of the cooperative administrative structure of the EU, instead? First of all, it is evident that in such intricate structures, judicial review plays an especially important role. Therefore, one important principle should be that the availability of judicial review must not depend on the complexity of the executive organization and its decision-making procedures. Citizens must not bear the practical costs of a polymorphous administrative organization. This is in no way self-evident and, in European law, there are many examples in which the administrative division of labour between the Commission and the member states actually restricts the ability to take legal action against an administrative act. The traditional concept of separated administrative spheres, which originates from a classical concept of sovereignty and immunity in international public law, asserts that courts may only check the sovereign acts of their own public authorities against their own legal standards.[146] As administrations in Europe intertwine more and more, it might be necessary to abandon this principle.

Secondly, increased accountability may also develop through a formalization of executive action that helps to specify which part of a certain decision has been made by which authority. The different shares in joint decisions must be clearly attributable to one administrative body. In this sense, the form of the directive in European law, for instance, must be understood as a mere framework that has to be implemented by national legislators ascribing enough room for political discretion to them. In the practice of

---

[146] M. N. Shaw, *International Law* (Cambridge: Cambridge University Press, 6th ed 2008), 701, 708–14.

European law, by contrast, even the smallest details are regulated in directives. A similar point can be developed against the introduction of powers to give direct orders from one administrative level to another. The public authority made responsible for a certain decision must have its own discretion to actually make this decision.

Finally, in multi-level structures as in a presidential system, it is preferable for the executive and the legislature to be separately democratically legitimized. This better justifies shared action in structures of executive co-operation. It also leads us back to the problem of a European government.

6. Conclusion: lack of government and para-constitutionalism

Democratic legitimacy needs defined actors that bear responsibility for democratic actions. In democratic states, governments, and especially government heads, take on this role. As we have already seen, it is not possible to find the one governmental actor of the European Union. While the European Commission can fill this void in areas that are not fundamentally contested between the member states, an amazing plurality of different emanations of the joint member state governments, the Council, the European Council, the presidency, the President, or even less formal meetings of some powerful member states claim governmental political leadership with regard to different issues. There is no solution to this problem. It is a consequence of the state of political integration. Still, it seems safe to say that the competition between inter-governmental and supra-national institutions should not be given a too explicit institutional form. For this reason, the Treaty of Lisbon's invention of the office of a President of the Council seems to be a step in the wrong direction. This office makes the institutional schizophrenia of the EU explicit. But from the point of view of legitimacy, a weak government or a government in the very slow making—like the European Commission—is still better than two governments. The conflict between supra-national and inter-governmental organs will persist for a long time. But it must be understood as an asymmetric conflict in which the member states do not try to introduce *ad hoc* offices and institutions, controlled by them in order to bypass the development of the European organs.

This is true for the integration of national parliaments into European structures by the Treaty of Lisbon. In such a procedure in which national parliaments may initiate the review of a European act with regard to subsidiarity, the involved parliaments act not as parliaments but rather as corporatist participants in a rather particular class action procedure. They cannot deliver democratic legitimacy in this kind of procedure. Again, it seems as if this kind of procedure served as a means to bypass a coherent parliamentarization of the EU that could only function through the European Parliament.

The same problem becomes apparent with regard to the European Council. Intergovernmentality, as we have seen, suffers from serious democratic limitations. These are especially apparent when the European Council—the assembly of the heads of state or government with the Presidents of the Commission and the Council—meets. This assembly has no formal powers and, therefore, does not have to abide by the procedural rules of EU law. Behind this council stands, for all intents and purposes, the body of the member states; the political power that creates and amends the Treaties and is therefore not bound by them. In practice, the political resolutions of the European Council have strong binding force, although this is not disclosed in any official journal and no one can formally seek judicial review of them. Every attempt to rationalize European politics and to open it up to judicial review is thereby undermined. To be sure, our approach is explicitly not to identify democratic law-making with rationality.[147] But for law-making to become democratic, it cannot end up in intergovernmental *ad hoc* decisions that bypass an already established procedure whenever convenient.

Through the euro crisis, this problem has become even more dramatic, because the new para-constitutional forms of actions do not even include all the member states, but seem to claim a treaty-amendment power beyond the formal amendment procedure. The so-called fiscal pact was created by a treaty signed by twenty-five of twenty-seven member states, but it addresses EU institutions like the Commission and the ECJ. One may well doubt that this is possible under European law.[148] In any case, it undermines the participation of the European Parliament and does not even bother to create any serious substitute for that deficiency.

European integration has reached the point where, though it is not yet possible to work with properly European mechanisms of political justification, the lack of intergovernmental legitimacy is obvious. As a result, the discussion about the scope of EU competences should be separated from the discussion about viable democratic procedures. The two are often conflated under the misleading image of a 'deeper' integration. Perhaps the European level could return responsibilities to the member states, though this has become less probable after the currency crisis. At the same time, the European level needs to justify its action more consistently. The first part of the Treaty of Lisbon includes many elements that are well in line with our

---

[147] See Chapter 2, I.

[148] J.-C. Piris, *The Future of Europe. Towards a Two-Speed EU?* (Cambridge: Cambridge University Press, 2012), 116 et seq.

considerations here, but which are weakened by many exceptions[149] for specific policies in the later parts of the text. For a functioning system of legitimacy, especially one which makes claim to the title of a constitutional order, a consistent and open procedural structure is indispensable.

IV. INTERNATIONAL LAW

1. Basic elements of international organizations

Is it possible to apply a concept of separated powers to international law that is more concrete to the internal structure of international organizations? This is a relatively rare topic of academic debate. And when it is, it is usually denied, although the recourse to these categories seems to play an intuitive role even in international law when we talk about international legislation or administration. Two points, at first glance, speak against the suitability of our concept. First, the states are still of central importance in international law. An international organization can emerge only through their international cooperation. The organization is mostly subject to their political will. Through their joint action, states can bypass its procedures and forms, and they do so. Secondly, international organizations are generally not very differentiated. Very few of them seem to be powerful and complex enough to lay claim to a full set of three different powers.

With the help of international organizations, states try—as we have seen—to pursue a common goal. The establishment of an organization represents a more intensive form of mutual commitment than a simple treaty. Again, the above-mentioned paradox emerges: on the one hand, states want to pursue their own interests; on the other hand, it seems reasonable to them to do that by establishing an organization that is independent of their will—be it simply because they can; be it because the states want to withdraw a decision from the domestic democratic process and prevail domestically by citing international obligations.[150] This dilemma has repercussions for the legitimacy of international organizations, which depends on the member states from which the international organizations must simultaneously dissociate themselves.

If one tries to describe international organizations by categories of state constitutional law, many of them begin to resemble independent

---

[149] To the idea of constitutional honesty with regard to the European Treaties: C. Möllers, 'Pouvoir Constituant—Constitution—Constitutionalization', in A. v. Bogdandy, J. Bast (eds.), *Principles of European Constitutional Law* (Oxford: Hart, 2nd ed 2009), 169–203 (203).

[150] For more on this paradox from a point of view of international law, see J. Klabbers, *An Introduction into International Institutional Law* (Cambridge: Cambridge University Press, 2002), 39. For more on the duplicity of the states' strategy, see K. D. Wolf, *Die neue Staatsräson* (Baden-Baden: Nomos, 2000).

administrative agencies. Like agencies, international organizations aim to achieve a defined limited goal with a certain degree of independence from a political law-making process. As with agencies, there may even be an authorization for certain law-making powers as a means to better pursue their specific objective. The agency floats between the co-decision-making power of the democratically legitimate members and its own independent approach to fulfilling its purpose. International law creates a hierarchy between both forms of legitimacy as clearly as does domestic constitutional law. This does not solve the problem, however: just as the domestic agency is subordinate to the legislator, the states, as parties to the international agreement establishing the organization, are the organization's masters. Whilst the details differ considerably, most international organizations exhibit a very similar organizational structure.[151] Ideally, they consist of three basic organs that do *not* represent the tripartite power structure in state constitutions.

First, most international organizations have a representative body of all member states. This assembly must be distinguished from the contracting parties of the treaty themselves, which established the organization in the first place, even though both of them are representatives of the same sovereign states. The representative body of the member states is a mere part of the organization and is not authorized to make amendments to the treaties. It is, in many cases, the highest institution of the organization. It can address all possible issues and also gives special focus to debates on the further development of the organization. Decisions are usually passed by consensus according to the principle of sovereign equality. Though the body cannot formally amend the treaties, it may in certain circumstances produce regulations, which are of lower normative rank than the treaties but which, nevertheless, bind the contracting parties and develop and *de facto* change the mission of the organization. One might speak of this body as a deliberating legislative institution, even if it is confined to passing secondary laws by consensus.

Secondly, the organization often has a political executive organ, in which representatives of the member states are again represented. Compared with the assembly of the member states, the powers of this institution are different: in some organizations, the executive organ is simply an executive committee, which is elected by the assembly in order to improve its effectiveness. In other cases, the executive organ is an institution with legally binding powers. Its composition of certain powerful member states is already determined in the treaties. It thereby qualifies the formal sovereign

---

[151] H. G. Schermers, N. M. Blokker, *International Institutional Law* (The Hague: Nijhoff, 3rd ed 1995), para 384.

equality of the states—which is expressed in the founding treaties—for the internal area of the organization. Depending on the specific structure of the organization, this institution usually works exclusively on current administrative affairs. However, in some cases, the executive organ is also the institution that gives the organization its political direction and defines its agenda.

Both types of institutions are composed of member state representatives. By contrast, the third typical organ[152] of an international organization is meant to protect the identity of the organization in relation to its members. It is no coincidence that this institution is called the 'secretariat'. In almost all international organizations, the secretariat is solely tied to the goals of the organization and expressly exempt from any direct instruction by its member states.[153] The importance of the secretariat lies just in this independence since the secretariat does not possess any legal power to bind the member states. Its importance is rather its informal influence, which can arise from two factors: its neutrality with respect to the contradictory interests of the members, as a result of which the secretariat stands up for the 'common good' of the organization, and its continuous experience within the organization, set against an ever-changing group of governmental representatives. How precarious this power really is, will become apparent when we consider the role of the UN Secretary-General.

This basic organizational structure reveals elements familiar to us from the EU. Since the EU can be seen as an especially well-developed international organization, we may now, in response, characterize the features of the EU from this perspective. The EU has become independent from the states that created it by developing its own specific mechanisms of legitimacy: the EU achieves a specific democratic legitimacy through the elections to the European Parliament and individual legitimacy through independent judicial review of European law. Standard international organizations, on the other hand, are purely executive entities. Nevertheless, the juxtaposition of a member state executive (the Council) and the organization's very own executive (the Commission) has always remained a feature of the EU.

The legitimacy of international organizations, or more precisely, their acceptability as public actors, is thus largely based on the fact that they cannot formally oblige their members, and individual citizens even less so. Beyond the triad of powers, international organizations function as centres of coordination of governmental responsibilities, which keep one political and one technical administrative branch. Only in particular cases may the

[152] In many cases, the secretariat is considered to be a proper organ of the international organization.
[153] H. G. Schermers, N. M. Blokker, *International Institutional Law* (The Hague: Nijhoff, 3rd ed 1995), para. 524.

assembly of member states also have powers similar to legislation, but even if the assembly does not have the right to legislate, it does function as a general political forum for political deliberation.

It seems consistent with the primacy of the sovereign member states that judicial review of the international organizations' actions, in particular concerning the scope of their competences, also remains the exception. Those actions of international organizations, which fall outside of their defined competences, are ineffective. They are *ultra vires*.[154] However, the assignment of competences is normally a matter of political consensus. Only very rarely are international courts empowered to authoritatively judge even consensual actions of the member states within a specific organization.[155] It is also for this reason that the national parliaments' complementary involvement in the evolution of international organizations seems so important.[156] Nevertheless, the growth of international jurisdiction, which defines rights and duties, even those of states, is, as we have seen, an important trend. Such courts, however, less importantly define the legality of the organization's action (as is the case with the ECJ in EU law), but rather form another independent type of international organization that we may call international judiciaries.[157] The International Court of Justice, which mainly judges international issues between states—provided that they have accepted its jurisdiction—does not require consideration in this context. So far, we have seen that the typical structure of international organizations gives them a foremost executive character, which does not pose a fundamental problem as long as their powers remain dependent on their member states. Whether there is more to be learned from our model for international organizations remains an open question. In order to answer it, we have to take a closer look at specific organizations.

2. The United Nations

a) Political organs

Applying the idea of the separation of powers to the United Nations is counter-intuitive even in the version of the concept developed here. Can we speak of democracy and judicial review in this case? The United Nations is a

---

[154] For this doctrine, see H. G. Schermers, N. M. Blokker, *International Institutional Law* (The Hague: Nijhoff, 3rd ed 1995), para 232; C. F. Amerasinghe, *Principles of the institutional law of international organizations* (Cambridge: Cambridge University Press, 2005), 179.

[155] International Court of Justice, *Certain expenses of the United Nations (Article 17, paragraph 2, of the Charter)*, Advisory Opinion of 20 July 1962: ICJ Reports 1962, 151 (168).

[156] See this Chapter, II., 1.

[157] See this Chapter, IV., 3.

complex organization, which hands many duties over to subsidiary organizations.[158] Three features, to which I will limit the following considerations, make it distinctive: universal membership; the goal of peacekeeping; and the UN Charter, which claims supremacy over other international legal obligations.

At first glance, one could perceive the assembly of all UN member states as a seed kernel for the development of a new global legislature. In line with the principle of sovereign equality, all member states would need to have equal voting rights. However, the United Nations is not organized in such a way. The assembly of member states, the General Assembly, does not have the right to make decisions that bind its members. At the same time, the General Assembly's interventions in some internal UN procedures have had a rather notorious effect on the organization's ability to function.[159] At best, the decisions of the General Assembly give an indication of a comprehensive consensus, which may then find recognition as international customary law.[160]

By contrast, the UN Security Council does have the right to make binding decisions. It consists of five permanent members with a right of veto and ten elected members, which are appointed by the General Assembly. The Security Council has increased its law-making activities in recent years. It has also begun to make decisions that could be termed 'legislative', since they not only relate to a political statement in a specific case but have a regulatory content.[161] The powers of the Security Council are formally restricted to keeping peace and security, but neither from a legal nor from a political point of view is it clear where the boundaries of this competence actually run, though some academic effort has been invested in drawing a legal line.[162] The most effective limit to its power is the political difficulty of reaching agreement among its members.

The composition of the Security Council has been heavily criticized and remains to date the subject of many unfulfilled plans for reform,[163] as it

---

[158] For a tentative balance sheet, see J. Habermas, 'Hat die Konstitutionalisierung des Völkerrechts noch eine Chance?', in J. Habermas, *Der gespaltene Westen* (Frankfurt am Main: Suhrkamp, 2004), 172.

[159] See M. Bertrand, 'Lehren aus einer gescheiterten Reform', *Vereinte Nationen* (2005), 174.

[160] J. A. Frowein, 'Der Beitrag der internationalen Organisationen zur Entwicklung des Völkerrechts' 36 *Zeitschrift für ausländisches öffentliches Recht und Völkerrecht* (1976), 147 (149).

[161] S. Talmon, 'The Security Council as World Legislature', 99 *American Journal of International Law* (2005), 175.

[162] See on the legal limits of United Nations Security Council Resolution S/Res/1373 (2001) L. M. H. Martínez, 'The legislative role of the Security Council in its fight against terrorism: Legal, political and practical limits', 57 *International and Comparative Law Quarterly* (2008), 333.

[163] E. C. Luck, 'How not to reform the United Nations', 11 *Global Governance* (2005), 407.

evidently does not meet any democratic standards, even if one looked for rather soft rules of global regional representation.

However, does this lack of legitimacy on the universal level of international law show the imperialism of large states or perhaps rather the ambivalence of representative authority, which also needs to have political power? To put it differently: Political legitimacy needs as an object a political power structure that has to be legitimized. Only if the enforcement mechanisms of international law, its executive branch, worked as effectively as they do in some constitutional states would it be possible to design international decision-making bodies independently from the individual executive, especially military power of their member states. Political power, however, is just as decisive for the composition of the Security Council— at least with regard to its permanent members—as the enforcement of international law is central to the UN mission when it comes to peacekeeping. This permits a different interpretation of the Security Council's composition. As the UN has no executive power of its own, the Security Council does not serve to make politically powerful states even more powerful but rather to formalize their independently existent power within a structure of organization and procedure. There seems to be a certain dialectic at work, in which only the inclusion of politically powerful states could help to produce a rule that could finally yield a more legitimate composition of the organization itself.

Can we incorporate this reflection into our general line of argument? The fact that the UN Charter has been adopted by state consensus is certainly not helpful in this regard. From our perspective, sovereign equality, unlike democratic equality, does not constitute a fundamental principle of legitimacy, for states require legitimacy themselves. Therefore, it seems more appropriate to evaluate member states with reference to the services they can provide to the organization. In the case of the UN, this service is tied to peacekeeping and, therefore, must also be calculated according to economic power and military strength.

Consequently, neither a differentiation in formal powers between member states nor the organization of the Security Council in particular should be rejected. Contrary to widespread criticism, it is not obvious that the Security Council is a weak institution. For one thing, this is demonstrated by the Council's increasing legislative activity. Furthermore, its symbolic power was even revealed during the Iraq crisis, when the Security Council was globally recognized as the forum which *should* decide on the course of action and whose unwillingness to legalize a military intervention ultimately allowed for a judgment of that war. The fact that this judgment was not needed says as little about the weakness of the Security Council as any other breach of law can tell about the legitimacy of a legislator. No functioning legal system can exclude breaches of law, but it can always give actions a certain meaning by defining them as unlawful. The fact that the Security Council has difficulty acting on the basis of consensus may be seen as a functional defect, but it does not necessarily express a lack of legitimacy.[164] As in legislative blockades in US constitutional law, there may be a case for inaction. At any rate, the Security Council fulfils one central function of a legislature: to constitute a forum in which matters of universal political importance are discussed.

These considerations do not ignore the urgent need for reform, but they put this need in a certain perspective. Any reform that would preclude the willingness of the permanent members to cooperate will prove impossible. Therefore, the right of veto makes sense. The question of which states should be represented in the Security Council cannot be determined by the set of arguments we have developed here, but any institutional reform should consider the following three points.

First, the question of which states deserve a seat in the Security Council is subject to political evaluation, which may change over time. Thus, in the best case, there should be a mechanism that authorizes changes, even for qualified Security Council membership, without having to amend the Charter itself. Even permanent members should have to deserve their permanent membership politically. Permanent membership cannot be decided upon by a simple vote of the General Assembly, however, for this would overturn the basic institutional principle of the Security Council. Rather, the process of selecting the Security Council's members must incorporate a variety of aspects creating new incentives to commit to the United Nations. In any case, the result of a Security Council reform should not just be the inclusion of new or more members but rather a procedure for appointing new members. That way a formalized political process could be created at the level of the United Nations.

Secondly, Security Council membership for regional organizations will be the most important option for reform in the long run.[165] However, if it is true that the willingness of an organization to reform cannot be stronger than that of its most willing members, it would be appropriate to take another look at the most developed regional organization: the EU. As long as France and Britain cannot agree on Europeanizing their mandate, regionalization cannot progress much further. In this respect, reform of the UN Security Council is also a matter of internal European politics.

---

[164] I. Hurd, *After Anarchy. Legitimacy and Power in the United Nations Security Council* (Princeton: Princeton University Press, 2007), 190–3.

[165] J. Habermas, 'Eine politische Verfassung für die pluralistische Weltgesellschaft?' in J. Habermas, *Zwischen Naturalismus und Religion* (Frankfurt am Main: Suhrkamp, 2005), 324 (338).

Finally, the Security Council's modus operandi does not even meet the absolute minimum of procedural legitimacy. The five permanent members organize their process of opinion-making like members of a club. The civilizing effect of a minimal amount of transparency could greatly improve the Security Council's reputation at little cost.

According to our criteria, the urgency for designing stricter formalized legal controls on the action of the Security Council increases when the Council's decisions begin to interfere more directly with individual rights. Two phenomena demonstrate that this connection both exists and exerts influence. The first is the Council's decision to compile lists of people suspected of being terrorists.[166] Hence, every UN member state has been obliged to freeze the assets of the listed persons without providing legal protection.[167] Such a decision is as illegitimate as a punitive sentence handed down by a parliament: a universal political institution passes judgment on individual rights in an individual case without any procedure of implementation. There is neither an inclusive procedure nor legal protection. Within the framework of our theory of legitimacy, if not in the decision's actual impact, such a deprivation of rights by the Security Council is reminiscent of Guantánamo. Not even the Security Council is entitled to single out individuals without proper procedure and legal protection. The courts are beginning to recognize this problem. As we saw above in the context of the European administration, the complexity of an administrative organization cannot justify any exemption from judicial review. Therefore, national and supra-national courts should not hesitate to apply human rights standards to the actions of the United Nations.[168] The immunity of states and international organizations against external judicial review was a legitimate part of a system that separated the international and national spheres. In this way, individual persons could expect to be directly addressed only by their own state. However, when this line is crossed by international organizations directly impinging on individual rights, there was no reason left to uphold the traditional notion of immunity either.

---

[166] See C. Tomuschat, 'Internationale Terrorismusbekämpfung als Herausforderung an das Völkerrecht', 85 *Speyerer Vorträge* (2006), 7. For attempts to control these measures internally, see E. Rosand, 'The Security Council's Effort to Monitor the Implementation of Al Quaeda/Taliban Sanctions', 98 *American Journal of International Law* (2004), 745.

[167] I. Ley, 'Legal Protection against the UN-Security Council between European and International Law: A Kafkaesque Situation? Report on the Fall Conference of the Graduate Program', 8 *German Law Journal* (2007), 279.

[168] D. Halberstam, E. Stein, 'The United Nations, the European Union, and the King of Sweden: Economic Sanctions and Individual Rights in a Plural World Order', 46 *Common Market Law Review* (2009), 13–72.

Still, such a form of judicial review involves one institutional danger and one weakness. The danger is a possible fragmentation of the UN regime when it is subjected to certain human rights standards only in some states or regions of the world. The weakness lies in the fact that a functioning judicial review of executive action always needs some institutional contact to the administration, whose actions must be reviewed. A European or national court with no access to the factual basis of decisions made by the Security Council can decide only on the basis of presumptions. Therefore, any decentralized review can only be a first step towards judicial review at the international level. By itself, reforming the administrative procedure now implemented will not be sufficient.[169]

There is a second area in which decisions by the Security Council directly touch upon individual rights. In territories under UN administration, Security Council decisions replace the constitutional foundations of public authority. Again, international organizations tend to immunize themselves against any independent review of constitutional standards, the observance of which they expect by their member states.[170] And again, the deficit of egalitarian democratic legitimacy of such administrative structures urgently calls for compensation, through a framework of legality and subsequent judicial review. The fact that the United Nations serves goals including peace and security cannot provide such compensation. Instead, minimum standards of delegation and legal protection for transitional administrations will have to be developed. There is a need for a particular form of international administrative law. Unlike egalitarian representative politics, organizing such forms of control where they are needed should not be too difficult.

b) Secretary-General
The office of the Secretary-General of the United Nations makes apparent the uncertain position of the secretariat of an international organization.[171] Formally, the Secretary is the 'highest administrative officer' of the United Nations. He has to perform the duties assigned to him by the political organs. He is elected by the General Assembly after a crucial nomination through the Security Council. So the Security Council, even here, enjoys some kind of veto power. The Secretary-General can formally direct the

---

[169] European General Court, Case T-85/09 *Kadi v Commission* [2010] (*Kadi II*), para. 128.

[170] For problems concerning this matter, see S. Chesterman, *You, the People: The United Nations, Transitional Administration, and State-Building* (Oxford: Oxford University Press, 2004), 154. For legal protection in Kosovo, see R. Everly, 'Reviewing Governmental Acts of the United Nations in Kosovo', 8 *German Law Journal* (2007), 21.

[171] See this Chapter, IV., 2.

attention of the Security Council towards certain issues.[172] Although it could seem appropriate with respect to the Secretary-General's legitimacy to restrict his duties to matters of internal organization, in practice this seems neither possible nor desirable. It is the classic duty of the secretariat to protect the identity of the organization in relation to its member states. This inevitably entails a political dimension when powerful member states try to redefine the organization's mission. Conversely, to take a much more trivially-sounding but practically important problem, when it comes to appointing officials, the UN suffers from patronage by states. Smaller states thereby seek to defend their interests against reinforcing the Secretary-General's appointment powers, ie centralizing the internal organization. Both phenomena illustrate how member states may try to politicize an administration originally conceived to be 'neutral'. The phenomena are certainly not equally illegitimate. It is the right of all members to take a stand against a certain course of the organization. Furthermore, it is neither avoidable nor wrongful that some states are more assertive than others in doing so, and thereby call the legitimacy of certain actions of the Secretary-General into question, while any individual intervention in the appointment of lower administrative ranks seems problematic.[173]

Despite all differences between the offices of the President of the European Commission and the UN Secretary-General, both depend on the specific power constellations among the members of their organization. They differ in the European Commission's strong formal law-making and review powers. Therefore, the question of how one can recognize the organization apart from its members remains fundamentally open in international institutional law. As long as international organizations are unable to create procedures of legitimacy on their own, their institutional identity will remain relatively weak and this is not necessarily a problem. But the protection of the neutrality of the office designed to be independent from the actual preferences of the member states remains the minimum requirement for a degree of institutional independence that justifies the existence of the organization in the first place.

3. *The World Trade Organization*

Critics of globalization often speak out against international economic organizations such as the World Bank, the International Monetary Fund, and the World Trade Organization. The first two mainly work as

---

[172] A. Orford, *International Authority and the Responsibility to Protect* (Cambridge: Cambridge University Press, 2011), 11.

[173] See Chapter 2.

credit grantors. They are organized like public banks, but in fact, they have a political mission.[174] For our purposes, however, the WTO is of greater interest.

Its predecessor, the General Agreement on Trade and Tariffs, was an international regime with the unusual quirk of deciding conflicts between the members in a court-like procedure, which nevertheless required political consensus among the contracting parties.[175] This could work only because the representatives of the member states acted relatively independent of their respective governments.[176] International trade diplomacy was conducted in a small world of its own, which had distanced itself from general, more politically-minded diplomacy. Therefore, it is still up to debate whether the old GATT system was a regime of international *law* or one of pure political consensus. After a period of institutional stagnation, a newly defined organizational framework emerged for this regime in 1994: the WTO.[177]

Through the founding of the WTO, the old system of diplomatic consensus-building has been formalized and juridified. In case of conflict over a certain commitment, member states can call upon a procedure that clearly displays judicial features. It is characterized by the individualizing and retrospective judgment of a specific case. In two quasi-judicial instances, a Panel and then an Appellate Body decide the complaint of one member against another. The validity of such judgments no longer requires member state consensus. The member states are, however, entitled to repeal a judgment by consensus. Although the Dispute Settlement Bodies cannot formally be described as courts, they do act largely independently and, in their nearly two decades of activity, have created a surprisingly large body of case law.[178]

We observe what, in the terminology of separated powers, might be called a successful intergovernmental judiciary. We also observe a certain lack of counter-institutions within the WTO. The other 'branches' of the WTO seem under-developed: a legislature cannot be found.[179] The WTO,

[174] S. Killinger, *The World Bank's non-political mandate* (Köln: Heymann, 2003).

[175] For an analysis, see R. Hudec, 'The GATT Legal System: A Diplomat's Jurisprudence [1970]', in R. Hudec, *Essays on the nature of International Trade Law* (London: Cameron May, 1999), 17 (41).

[176] Described as 'external legitimacy' by J. H. H. Weiler, 'The Rule of Lawyers and the Ethos of Diplomats', *35 Journal of World Trade* (2001), 191 (194).

[177] For an overview, see P.-T. Stoll, 'Die WTO: Neue Handelsorganisation, neue Welthandelsordnung, Ergebnisse der Uruguay-Runde des GATT', *54 Zeitschrift für ausländisches öffentliches Recht und Völkerrecht* (1994), 241 (257).

[178] Statistics can be found at: <http://www.wto.org/>.

[179] A. v. Bogdandy, 'Law and Politics in the WTO—Strategies to Cope with a Deficient Relationship', *5 Max-Planck Yearbook of United Nations Law* (2001), 618.

like most international organizations, does indeed provide a forum for the further development of its treaties. The Ministerial Conference, the WTO's highest institution, meets for this very purpose every two years. Still, political attempts to develop the treaties have been failing now for many years. In any case, in theoretical categories, these negotiations address a constitution-amending rather than a legislative process. Between the Ministerial Conferences, the assembly of the member state representatives to the WTO—the General Council—sits permanently. Various sub-councils, sorted according to theme, are attached to this General Council. Decisions of these institutions are usually made unanimously.

The same is also true for the organization's executive elements. The WTO Secretariat plays a significant role as mediator between member states during the deliberation of a treaty amendment. In addition, the Secretariat gives technical advice and support to the Dispute Settlement Bodies. Its relevance has nevertheless decreased in comparison to the old GATT as a consequence of the judicialization of the decision-making process. If the strength of the WTO lies in the independence and rule-bound character of its dispute settlement procedures, the need for powerful informality is not evident.

If the WTO actually represents an intergovernmental economic court of law, its decisions must gain their legitimacy, according to our model of separated powers, from a procedure of exclusive, retrospective decision-making, which is obtained on a case-by-case basis. Yet this procedural exclusivity is highly controversial.[180] Criticism centres on the fact that WTO law does not give enough consideration to non-economic issues such as environmental protection, occupational safety, and human rights. Furthermore, dispute settlement procedures are allegedly too exclusive, so that relevant interests by non-state actors cannot properly be voiced. Only the second objection is relevant for our problem of separated powers. Addressing it will also give us the opportunity to take a look at the first one.

If WTO dispute settlement works by and large like a court procedure between two states, then it would have to provide an individual and exclusive analysis of the disputed subject as well as reasoning derived from the applicable law.[181] In fact, WTO dispute settlement bodies rely on reasoning based as closely as possible on the actual wording of the Treaty text and—unlike many constitutional courts—on a close reading of the facts of the case

---

[180]   L. Wallach, *The WTO. Five Years of Reasons to Resist Corporate Globalization* (New York, NY: Seven Stories Press, 1999).

[181]   See Chapter 2, III., 3.

in question. But is such a close reading actually possible? Critics who want to organize the process of dispute settlement in a more inclusive way presume that every WTO report would ineluctably affect basic conflicts over relations between world trade and, for instance, environmental and work protection or health.[182] Considered in this way, the procedural characteristic of individualizing cases is part of the problem and not the solution. Instead, everyone with a substantiated interest in the outcome should be included in the decision-making process.[183] This would amount to the right to a hearing for non-governmental organizations (NGOs). At present, the Panels do take into consideration the briefs of the *amicus curiae* of the NGOs.[184]

However, this line of argument is hardly convincing. To start with, why should a judgment in international trade law concerning a ban on tuna fish caught with nets that endanger dolphins be seen as an issue of such general scope? Do decisions concerning import restrictions on meat treated with hormones actually define the relationship between world trade and health protection in a broad sense? The Appellate Body especially, the second instance, regularly tries to develop a legal argument that is carefully designed to decide only one specific case at a time.[185] Even if one wanted to view the dispute settlement procedure, against the evidence, as a crypto-political enterprise, its extension through the participation of NGOs would hardly add any fresh legitimacy to bind democratic member states. NGOs function as lobbies for certain, albeit benevolent interests. Yet they have no egalitarian, democratic mandate. As seen in Chapter 2, they may be necessary for a democratic process, but they are not democratic in themselves. In search of a legitimate political process one might, therefore, find oneself again at the heart of the unregulated diplomacy of the member states, the very process the institutions have tried to leave behind. In this respect, a higher level of participation in the dispute settlement procedure would not grant any surplus of legitimacy. Indeed, it might call it into question by overturning the individualizing effect of the procedure and reconstructing a narrowly defined mechanism as a universal forum of globalization.[186]

[182] J. Trachtman, 'Trade and . . . Problems, Cost-Benefit Analysis and Subsidiarity', 9 *European Journal of International Law* (1998), 32.

[183] R. G. Shell, 'The Trade Stakeholders Model and Participation by Nonstate Parties in WTO', 17 *Universitiy of Pennsylvania Journal of International Economic Law* (1996), 359.

[184] For the overrated significance of this practice, see P. C. Mavroidis, 'Amicus Curiae Briefs Before The WTO', in A. v. Bogdandy (ed.), *European integration and international co-ordination* (The Hague: Kluwer Law International, 2002), 317.

[185] A. Yanovich, T. Voon, 'Completing the Analysis in WTO Appeals: The Practice and its Limitations', 9 *Journal of International Economic Law* (2006), 933.

[186] With good reasons more positively towards NGOs: H. Brunkhorst, *Solidarity* (Cambridge/London: MIT Press, 2005), 157.

In addition, it is sometimes discussed whether individuals should be given direct access to the dispute settlement process. Though hardly a realistic perspective, such a proposal may serve as a thought experiment that teaches us something about the legitimacy of the system. And, as one famous case constellation shows, indirect access for individuals to WTO law may even be practically feasible.[187] A German banana importer was affected by a European import ban. A decision by the WTO dispute settlement body found this ban in violation of WTO law. Can the importer refer this breach of law to a European court and take legal action against the European regulation? At first sight, and from the perspective of many legal scholars, doing so would be quite plausible.[188] Why should the EU, or indeed any other member of the WTO, be able to act towards its citizens in defiance of WTO regulations or other international law? The ECJ, however, has refused to provide the trader with legal protection against the import ban.[189] Similarly, US legislators have explicitly ruled out the possibility of taking any action against the US because of a violation of WTO law.[190] How can this be justified? Apart from specific legal arguments, in light of our model of legitimacy, there is a strong case for denying the WTO provisions of any individual enforcement mechanism. If every affected citizen were able to sue WTO member states claiming a violation of WTO law, power within the organization and among its members would shift considerably. The members of the WTO would lose any room for political discretion in defining their obligations on the domestic front. For it is one thing to be convicted of a breach of international commitments externally by another state; it is quite another to have one's own scope of action restricted by domestic actors that claim their share of international law. Direct effect of WTO law would extend a certain form of judicialization into a very heterogeneous global sphere of influence, for which—unlike in the case of European integration—there are no legislative processes to unify and regulate the granted transnational exercise of economic freedom. In addition, differences in national and regional judicial standards would establish incongruities between the members. The more generous its system of judicial

---

[187] J. H. Jackson, P. Grane, 'The Saga Continues: An Update of the Banana Dispute', *4 Journal of International Economic Law* (2001), 581 (592).

[188] On the one hand: T. v. Danwitz, 'Der EuGH und das Wirtschaftsvölkerrecht', *56 Juristenzeitung* (2001), 721; on the other hand: A. v. Bogdandy, 'Legal Equality, Legal certainty and Subsidiarity in Transnational Economic Law', in A. v. Bogdandy (ed.), *European integration and international co-ordination* (Den Haag: Kluwer, 2002), 13.

[189] European Court of Justice, Case C-149/96 *Portugal v Commission*, paras. 42–46; European Court of Justice, Joined cases C-300/98 and C-392/98 *Dior et al.*, para. 44; European Court of Justice, Joined Cases C-120/06 P and C-121/06 *FIAMM et al.*, paras. 120; 127–29.

[190] 19 U.S.C. § 3512(c)(1).

review, the less powerful the concerned member will be. This would create a negative incentive for domestic rule of law. The system of the WTO would shift from a system of state reciprocity granted by governments to a system of protection of transnational individual rights. The balance between individual and democratic self-determination would further shift to the side of individual negative freedom. The real problem of any international jurisdiction, that is, the intergovernmental provenance of its decision-making basis, would become even more dramatic.

This leads us back to our first point of criticism mentioned above: the bias of the WTO legal system towards economic issues. This problem remains unsolved. There is much to suggest that the WTO constitutes a key element in the development of global economic liberalization, against which many political and ethical arguments can be made. That is not the issue here, however. The economic bias of the WTO cannot be resolved at the level of the dispute settlement *procedure*.[191] As we have seen, this would only exacerbate the question of legitimacy. Rather, the member states will have to address the problem on a political level. Yet another point must be taken into account: if one were to give individuals the right to claim a violation of WTO law, this would further privilege free trade as a matter of particular concern.

The legitimacy of the WTO dispute settlement procedure derives from the interaction of politically legitimate parties in a judicial procedure. Both of these elements have to be preserved. The dispute settlement bodies must come to their decisions in a judicial fashion and in a narrow and depoliticized way. The Dispute Settlement Bodies are therefore not allowed to assess the relationship between free trade and environmental protection as such but may only answer a narrowly defined legal question. For this reason, involvement of non-state actors in the formal dispute settlement process does not seem appropriate to enhance the legitimacy of the organization. The role of non-state actors has to play out in the political assessment of the decisions and in the debate about a reform of the whole system. This also applies to individual claims based directly on WTO law before the courts of a member state. Since there are no mechanisms of democratic self-determination on a global level beyond those of nation-state politics, even the establishment of subjective rights, which bind the decision-making in democratic member states, requires justification. This is even true of human rights, as we shall now see.

---

[191] It is a question outside the scope of this book if some of these problems may be solved by means of interpretation of the substantial WTO-rules, e.g., with regard to patents law: H. Hestermeyer, *Human Rights and the WTO* (Oxford: Oxford University Press 2012), 276–92.

4. The international protection of human rights

The international protection of human rights has been one of the great themes of international law since 1989, or even 1948.[192] In our approach, though, it is not self-evident that individual rights should be protected without an accompanying political process.[193] Nevertheless, we must recognize that there is a minimum catalogue of personal rights, which systematically precede every democratic decision precisely because collective self-determination cannot function without them.[194] Moreover, considering the abuse of rights in the 20th century, this minimum catalogue clearly deserves protection that cannot wait for international democratic institutions to come about. Evidently, the protection of human rights is a significant regulative idea in an international community of democratic and perhaps even non-democratic states.[195] On the other hand, however, this idea can quickly become an empty self-description of a certain group of nations, just as in the 19th century, when European colonial powers described (only) themselves as being 'civilized'.[196] Yet, if protection of human rights is to be taken seriously, this does not preclude us from taking a closer look at different forms of its institutionalization and analysing their respective legitimacy and the relationship between human rights protection and other international political processes. In the last few decades, many different regional human rights pacts have emerged,[197] the strongest of which is still the European Convention on Human Rights. Other relevant forms of human rights protection include political mechanisms and the internationalization of criminal law.

a) The European Court of Human Rights

The regional protection of human rights in Europe is based on an international treaty among the member states of the European Council. Its current organizational structure is relatively simple. After having exhausted all instances of national judicial review, plaintiffs can turn to the European

---

[192] For some researchers it even begins considerably later: S. Moyn, *The Last Utopia: Human Rights in History* (Cambridge, Mass: Harvard University Press, 2012).

[193] U. K. Preuß, 'Der politische Charakter der Menschenrechte', 31 *Europäische Grundrechte Zeitschrift* (2004), 611; C. R. Beitz, *The Idea of Human Rights* (Oxford: Oxford University Press, 2009), Chap. 5.

[194] See Chapter 2, II., 2.

[195] A. Paulus, *Die internationale Gemeinschaft* (München: Beck, 2001).

[196] M. Koskenniemi, *The Gentle Civilizer of Nations* (Cambridge: Cambridge University Press, 2002), 98.

[197] For an overview, see C. Tomuschat, *Human Rights* (Oxford: Oxford University Press, 2nd ed, 2008).

Court of Human Rights in Strasbourg. Its judgments oblige the charged member state to reverse its infringement of Convention rights. The basis of this judgment is the European Convention on Human Rights—a human rights catalogue that is formulated similarly to the catalogues of national constitutions. It not only contains human rights in an emphatic sense of the word but also other rights, which require the context of a legal order, such as property rights or certain procedural guarantees. The Court in Strasbourg aims to ensure a certain minimum standard of human rights protection in the member states.

By and large, then, the European protection of human rights functions like a constitutional court, whose jurisdiction extends across different nations and which has the power to decide upon individual claims. As we have seen, it is unclear to what extent the review of constitutional rights by national constitutional courts has to respect legislative decisions on the distribution of freedom.[198] In supranational human rights protection, there is no supranational legislator. Indeed, there is not even a supranational political subject.

This problem appears rarely in the legal literature concerning the Convention, yet increasingly often in the political deliberation of the Convention's member states: political protest against decisions of the ECtHR by national governments has become more and more common. But how can we evaluate the legitimacy of the court? On the one hand, protection of human rights is often perceived as a goal, which is an end in itself. On the other, the ECtHR has developed various juridical strategies to mitigate the conflict between its jurisprudence and national political decisions, for example by granting a certain degree of discretion to the member states, as expressed in the Court's margin of appreciation doctrine.[199] Both perspectives provide the system with a relatively high level of functionality and—despite all protests—acceptance. Still, one might wonder if this line of reasoning seems plausible only for a certain minimal standard of protection addressing the pre-political personality of an individual, whereas far-reaching, universal basic rights protection that generally redefines spheres of freedom may call for more legitimacy than a court could claim.

To give an example: in its *Caroline Hannover* decision case, the ECtHR had to balance the plaintiff's right to privacy against freedom of expression on the part of certain tabloid magazines. The ECtHR privileged its own interpretation of the relationship between the concerned spheres of freedom

---

[198] See Chapter 3, II., 4

[199] G. Letsas, 'Two Concepts of the Margin of Appreciation', *26 Oxford Journal of Legal Studies* (2006), 705. For a recent case definition, see European Court of Human Rights, *Stübing v Germany*, App. No. 43547/08 (2012), paras. 59–60.

over that of the German Federal Constitutional Court.[200] In a particular set of circumstances, it gave the protection of a public figure's personality precedence over a newspaper's freedom of communication to report about that person.[201]

The court's assumption that the relationship between freedom of expression and libel can be deduced purely from the content of the Convention implies that there is only one permissible resolution to this question. Protecting freedom of expression is, however, not only a prerequisite for a democracy.[202] Balancing conflicting spheres of freedom also requires the form of democratic legitimacy that does not exist at a supranational level. There is no evident reason why different democracies should not admit different levels of protection for freedom of expression, as can be seen, for example, in comparing freedom of speech doctrines in Germany and the US.[203] To look for a better or worse solution in this context seems methodically demanding and hardly tenable from the perspective of democratic theory. Due to the universality of human rights, a juridical line of argument, which operates without the intervention of a democratic legislator, quickly turns into an ethical argument that unduly homogenizes the legitimate variety of democratic political orders. The claim to universal rights prevents the possibility of establishing different degrees of freedom of expression in different democracies. From this perspective, *Caroline* is not necessarily a wrong judgment, but it certainly expresses the institutional deficits of a human rights court that lacks a political counterbalance. That this argument is open to abuse by authoritarian governments with an individualist political stance cannot change its systematic value, though it remains a strategic political consideration, which is unfortunately also common in much of the academic human rights discourse. But the threat by governments (like the EU presidency of the European Council in 2012) to curtail the jurisdiction of the ECtHR can only be overcome when the underlying problem is accepted.

Another interesting feature of our case example is that private individuals were on both sides of the proceedings: Caroline and a private newspaper. In such constellations, recourse to the human rights catalogue without

---

[200] European Court of Human Rights, *Von Hannover v Germany*, App. No. 59320/00; N. Krisch, *Beyond Constitutionalism* (Oxford: Oxford University Press), 139–42.

[201] For a good critical analysis, see C. Grabenwarter, 'Schutz der Privatsphäre versus Pressefreiheit: Europäische Korrektur eines deutschen Sonderweges?', 4 *Archiv für Presserecht* (2004), 309.

[202] See the parallel lines of reasoning in the German Federal Constitutional Court, *Lüth*, BVerfGE 7, 198 (208), and in the U.S. Supreme Court, *New York Times Co. v Sullivan*, 376 U.S. 254, 299 (1966); for a comparison Vicki C. Jackson, M. Tushnet, *Comparative Constitutional Law* (Foundation Press: and in the U.S. Supreme Court, New York, 2nd ed. 2006), 1605–37.

[203] D. P. Kommers, 'The Jurisprudence of Free Speech in the United States and the Federal Republic of Germany', 53 *Southern California Law Review*, 657.

democratic support seems particularly problematic.[204] Unlike in a national constitutional order, the Convention obliges only states directly while the interpretative practice of the ECtHR in such cases necessarily creates obligations for individuals. By using balancing tests and creating duties to protect, international law is starting to abridge individual rights in specific cases.

This is not a general criticism of the system of the Convention on Human Rights, which has in fact served very well in propagating citizens' rights throughout Europe. From the point of view of a theory of separated powers, however, this structure must at least also be seen as a restriction on democratic decision-making from within a democratic vacuum. Recent developments have demonstrated that the ECtHR would be well-advised to cushion these democratic objections by acting with care and political sensitivity. Otherwise, the political process in the member states might address the issue in a much more problematic way.[205]

b) Political human rights protection

It may be convincing to accept a universal core of every individual personality, be it called dignity or autonomy, which is worthy of protection and should be exempted from every democratic process. However, there is no corresponding universal judicial procedure of human rights protection; no international court of human rights. At the universal international level, human rights are protected by political procedures.[206] These include procedures of surveillance and reporting, such as in the Human Rights Council of the United Nations. In this forum, certain nations must justify particular practices and can be politically reprimanded.[207] But apart from the fact that even the new Human Rights Council leaves its own politically dubious mark,[208] it seems clear that a negotiation process between states cannot be a suitable way of addressing and sanctioning an *individual* loss of rights— at least not in the demanding sense of what here has been labelled individual legitimacy. For in examining individual matters, other aspects of political

---

[204] See the articles in: *17/18 Europäische Grundrechte Zeitschrift* (2006).

[205] A. Stone Sweet, H. Keller, *A Europe of Rights: The Impact of the ECHR on National Legal Systems* (Oxford: Oxford University Press, 2008), Chap. 11.

[206] C. R. Beitz, *The Idea of Human Rights* (Oxford: Oxford University Press, 2009), Chap. 2.

[207] C. Tomuschat, *Universal Periodic Review: A new system of international law with specific ground rules?*, in U. Fastenrath et al. (eds.), *From Bilateralism to Community Interest—Essays in Honour of Judge Bruno Simma* (Oxford: Oxford University Press, 2011), 609. On the negotiation history and the process leading up to the Universal Periodic Review, see F. D. Gaer, 'A Voice Not an Echo: Universal Periodic Review and the UN Treaty Body System', *7 Human Rights Law Review*, 109. For the previous model, see C. Tomuschat, *Human Rights* (Oxford: Oxford University Press, 2nd ed 2008), 175-7.

[208] Among the members of the Council were China, Cuba, Russia, and Saudi-Arabia in 2011–2012.

expediency constantly interfere and become part of the agenda. Individual violations are therefore both addressed selectively and de-individualized in these kinds of procedures. For these reasons, institutions that debate human rights practices at an international level may be politically welcome, but they cannot meet the requirements of a serious model of normative justification.

To date, there is no effective protection of human rights outside of democratic states. This holds true even for the member states of the most effective regional system of international human rights protection: the European Convention on Human Rights. To the citizens of its members, it makes considerably more of a difference whether they live in Russia or in Sweden than whether they live within or beyond the ECHR system.[209] This sobering insight is in line with our systematic claim that functioning protection of individual rights requires democratic structures. As it seems, only a system in which the minority has the normative potential to become the majority, can minorities and individuals be adequately protected. It reflects the experiences as well as the systematic insight of Hannah Arendt, who as a political refugee famously noted that the elementary 'right to rights' is the right to membership in a political community.[210] This might suggest that the ultimate instrument of international human rights protection should be the enforcement of democracy all over the world.[211] However, this idea is obviously very problematic for several reasons—beginning with the failed experiments with democratic state-building in recent years and ending with the normative insight that forcing people into democracy is not democratic. In any case, it becomes clear that every theory of international human rights that ignores the political legitimacy of its own implementation is both theoretically and practically incomplete.[212] The mere postulation of human rights catalogues as a sort of global system of values remains not only politically useless, it cannot even claim legitimacy. The formal recognition of human rights by certain states, on the other hand, has often almost no implications for the actual protection of human rights in these states, either.[213] The problems surrounding international enforcement

---

[209] Compare Human Rights Watch, 'World Report 2012' (2012), 479 (485 on Russian cooperation with the European Court of Human Rights).

[210] H. Arendt, *The Origins of Totalitarianism* (New York/London: Harcourt Inc., 1976), 296–7.

[211] See the rejecting, yet careful discussion of the US invasion in Iraq by J. Habermas, 'Hat die Konstitutionalisierung des Völkerrechts noch eine Chance?', in J. Habermas, *Der gespaltene Westen* (Frankfurt am Main: Suhrkamp, 2004), 178.

[212] For different reasons also see M. Ignatieff, *Human Rights as Politics and as Idolatry* (Princeton: Princeton University Press, 1999); A. Orford, *Reading Humanitarian Intervention* (Cambridge: Cambridge University Press, 2003).

[213] See the disillusioning listing by J. Goldsmith, E. Posner, *The Limits of International Law* (Oxford: Oxford University Press, 2005), 107.

of human rights point to institutional questions, especially regarding the structure of the United Nations and, therefore, to the necessity of political justification. These are questions, however, that the human rights discourse generally prefers to avoid.

c) International criminal law

Through the establishment of the International Criminal Court, another international institution has emerged that can be seen as an instrument of human rights protection. International criminal prosecution devotes itself to crimes that have violated the lives and personalities of human beings on a massive scale.[214] However, it is not self-evident to justify international criminal jurisdiction by reference to human rights protection.[215]

We have already seen that a judicial criminal procedure primarily serves to protect the rights of the defendant.[216] The procedure is tailored to individualize their actions and to establish their personal responsibility for a concrete event. If one wanted to optimally *protect* people from crime, one could do away with the judicial procedure. The establishment of a prosecutorial police force would suffice. However, the judicial procedure is essential for examining the individual culpability of an alleged perpetrator. That means: the sanctioning of a crime does not serve the rights of the victim. Judicial or quasi-judicial procedures that deal with political crimes may, as in South Africa or Guatemala, be established at the behest of surviving victims after a period of political authoritarianism.[217] There are no objections to setting them up, especially on the basis of a democratic decision. But such structures cannot claim what we call individual legitimacy. They serve different goals, especially to establish historical truth and internal political peace.[218] They take the perspective of the victims, a legitimate perspective to be sure, though as such not sufficiently legitimate for punishing a wrongdoer. Therefore, the justification of an international system of criminal jurisdiction with reference to the human rights of victims of massacres and genocide seems not unproblematic.

---

[214] K. Ambos, *Internationales Strafrecht* (München: Beck, 2006), 184.

[215] For example: M. Lutz-Bachmann, 'The Sovereignty Principle and Global Democracy' in H.-G. Justenhoven, J. Turner (eds.), *Rethinking the State in the Age of Globalization* (Münster: LIT Verlag, 2003), 217 (230).

[216] See Chapter 2, III., 3.

[217] For example: C. Tomuschat, 'Clarification Commission in Guatemala', *23 Human Rights Quarterly* (2001), 233.

[218] For the differences and for the problems to establish historical truth through legal means, see Y. Thomas, 'La verité, le temps, le juge et l'historien', in *Les Opérations du Droit* (Paris: Hautes Études Gallimard Seuil, 2011), 255–81.

From the *perspective of the defendant* and disregarding, for a moment, his actual responsibility for unspeakable atrocities, such trials may look like ad hoc political procedures tailored to particular persons, which, therefore, precisely do not bring forth the individualization of a case that is necessary for a truly independent legal judgment. Just consider the institutional implications for the Yugoslavia Tribunal had it acquitted Slobodan Miloseviç for lack of evidence. The introduction of the International Criminal Court by the Statute of Rome is an adequate answer to this kind of objection because now there is a judicial institution responsible for a field of law in its entirety in place of ad hoc tribunals that deal only with politically selected, individual cases. The greater the variety of cases before the ICC, the less dependent the court's reasoning is on the political context of a specific constellation. Nonetheless, the basic problem remains that the penalization of individual defendants seems to be a political matter. Finally, when the Yugoslavia Tribunal extensively construes the relevant statutory offences in light of the statute's 'humanitarian goals',[219] it draws attention to a concrete element of our general objection: the politicized interpretation of a criminal statute, which is the form of law generally expected to be most strictly interpreted and most neutrally applied.

There are, likewise, objections from the perspective of a democratic nation-state. The definition of criminal offences in international agreements suffers from the democratic deficiencies of all intergovernmentally negoti-ated legal provisions.[220] But for a democratic community, the codification of criminal law may be an important instrument for defining its moral and political preferences. Sharply contrasting views of the death penalty between the United States and the European states are a case in point. There seems to be no universally acceptable international solution, even within the com-munity of democratic states, for how to treat capital punishment. The same could be said for many other major or minor offences. Perhaps even more than private law, criminal law serves as the expression of a political identity, as the benchmark for what is acceptable behaviour in a specific community. The Rome Statute has different substantial and procedural means to solve this problem. On a procedural level, there is the subsidiarity of the whole procedure, which accepts that the affected states would be the first to prosecute the crimes in question. On the substantial level, it is the quality and especially the transnational effect of the crimes that fall under the ICC procedures. One might argue that these crimes define the lowest behav-ioural standards of the international community and, therefore, serve the

---

[219] International Criminal Tribunal for Former Yugoslavia, Case IT-94-1-A, *Prosecutor v Tadić*, 124 *International Law Reports* (2003), 176 (284).

[220] See Chapter 4, I., 2.

same function as domestic criminal law. Still, this argument cuts both ways. When the ICC begins to accept 'terrorism' as an international crime,[221] it is far from clear whether this standard can be met. Put differently: as in the case of the ECtHR, the ICC may show the inclination to legal reasoning comparable to the reasoning of domestic courts. And as in the case of the ECtHR, this may stretch the institution's fragile legitimacy too far.

As a matter of separated powers, finally we shall have to look at prosecutorial power. The institutional setting of criminal prosecution is a difficult and perhaps unsolvable problem, even within domestic constitutional orders. On the one hand, prosecution is part of a judicial process. It should, therefore, follow a principle of legality and not of political opportunity. On the other hand, strictest legality would, as a consequence, require quasi-judicial independence. But the office of an independent prosecutor seems to represent a dangerous combination of an independent administration agency with a strong power to intervene in basic rights, without political accountability. This problem is multiplied on the level of the ICC for several reasons. First, there is no legitimate political process available on the international level. Secondly, it seems quite obvious that the ICC must have a prudent perspective on the political implications of its actions. The possibility of provoking a violent uproar or civil war cannot be completely irrelevant for an institution that seeks to protect human rights. Thirdly, unlike the prosecution of many domestic issues, the crimes in question do not seem open to any prosecutorial deference, as they concern the violation of universal human rights. This creates a true dilemma, in which a politically unaccountable official is forced to make political compromises in a field that normatively does not allow for such compromise. One might argue that it is better to prosecute some of these crimes instead of none. But this renders human rights mere privileges in a given political landscape.[222] A defendant in the ICC may legitimately ask why he is being prosecuted but no one, say, responsible from North Korea. That is because one part of the defendant's individual status should be a claim to equal treatment under the rules. None of these arguments require us to renounce international criminal jurisdiction. But they could at least demonstrate that the democratic decision of certain states not to take part in this system has normative arguments in its favour and that this kind of protection of human rights has a price that is sometimes even paid in human rights.

---

[221] A. Cassesse, 'The Multifaceted Criminal Notion of Terrorism in International Law', 4 *Journal of International Criminal Justice* (2006), 933 (950).

[222] See A. M. Danner, 'Enhancing the legitimacy and accountability of prosecutorial discretion at the International Criminal Court', 97 *American Journal of International Law* (2003), 510.

5. Hybrid organizations

The phenomena examined thus far are all more or less part of a traditional institutional framework, within the distinctions between private and state action, national and international law-making, binding law, and non-law. Whether such conceptual matrices are appropriate for describing current international law is a matter of dispute that cannot be solved here and probably eludes universal answers, but as a general observation, it seems that distinctions like the mentioned ones are not rendered useless only because an institutional reality does not correspond to them. They may serve to describe the hybridity and ambiguity of new institutional phenomena. In the following, we will explore three forms of law-making that can be described as hybrid with regard to these distinctions. They also represent an interesting challenge to our concept of separated powers.

a) Soft law through international organizations

International law has long been recognizing a vast and growing number of other international organizations alongside the United Nations and the WTO. These mostly constitute forums for international deliberation of certain topics or for the further development of multilateral agreements, as well as structures to monitor their compliance. In most cases, these organizations, as we have seen, have no independent powers to impose legal duties on their members.[223] Only a few organizations have their own regulatory powers, most frequently for cases in which the need for decisions could be urgent, such as in flight safety or protection against epidemics. In some, more recent organizations, especially in international environmental law, representatives of the contracting parties work permanently on amending the respective treaty.[224] In general, however, international organizations with binding regulatory powers remain the exception.

Nonetheless, international organizations have a large variety of mechanisms to implement non-binding obligations, ie 'soft law', for member states. How successful these are is the subject of an on-going discussion[225] from which we may distil some insights. The standard of compliance with international law is high, and the central reasons for that may lie precisely in

---

[223] J. E. Alvárez, *International Organizations as Law-makers* (Oxford: Oxford University Press, 2005), 273.

[224] R. Churchill, G. Ulfstein, 'Autonomous Institutional Arrangements in Multilateral Environmental Agreements: A Little-Noticed Phenomenon in International Law', 94 *American Journal of International Law* (2000), 623.

[225] Sceptically, J. Goldsmith, E. Posner, *The Limits of International Law* (Oxford: Oxford University Press, 2005). More optimistically: O. Hathaway, 'Do Human Rights Treaties Make a Difference?', 111 *Yale Law Journal* (2002), 1935.

the consensus that has to be reached to create an obligation.[226] This consensus even seems often to be relevant when international rules are violated because the obligated states either do not know or cannot obey the rules for reasons of resources, even though they would be willing to do so in principle. But if there is no opposing political will, there is no reason not to create mechanisms to remind the obligated states of their duties, to make them aware of their offences, and to support them in honouring their commitments.[227] Duties relating to this kind of procedure, which at least reminds a state to confront its non-compliance, seem unobjectionable. The International Labour Organization, for example, has a mechanism by which the member states' parliaments must debate conventions, even though they are under no obligation to turn them into domestic law.[228] International organizations regularly try to implement their concerns through such soft means—compliance measures—by providing information or by raising political awareness.[229]

Although these mechanisms seem unproblematic, non-binding means of international law may have an unexpectedly great and not always legitimate impact on domestic democratic decisions. Two examples of the power of international informality come from the field of education. In the so-called Bologna Process, the EU member states agreed together with others to standardize their systems of university degrees.[230] The agreement, which had revolutionary implications for European universities, was non-binding under both European and international law. Nevertheless, it was adopted and implemented by all participant states. Regardless of how one actually judges the policies in question, it is clear that after the informal agreement was made, there was no longer any scope for making a derogating political decision. The factually homogenizing force of the agreement left no practical space: the practical danger of excluding the domestic university system from supply and demand of students from abroad was factually too strong. And, precisely because this form of agreement had no binding force, it was

---

[226] This is one of the central insights in T. Franck, *The Power of Legitimacy among Nations* (New York/Oxford: Oxford University Press, 1990).

[227] A. Chayes, A. Chayes, *The New Sovereignty* (Cambridge: Harvard University Press, 1995).

[228] C. Möllers, *Gewaltengliederung* (Tübingen: Mohr-Siebeck, 2005), 303.

[229] Critically: M. Koskenniemi, 'Formalism, Fragmentation, Freedom: Kantian Themes in Today's International Law', 4 *No Foundations. Journal of Extreme Legal Positivism* (2007), available at <http://www.helsinki.fi/nofo/NoFo4Koskenniemi.pdf>.

[230] L. S. Terry, 'The Bologna Process and Its Impact in Europe: It's So Much More than Degree Changes', 41 *Vanderbilt Journal of Transnational Law* (2008), 107; A. v. Bogdandy, M. Goldmann, 'The Exercise of International Public Authority through National Policy Assessment—The OECD's PISA Policy as a Paradigm for a New International Standard Instrument', 5 *International Organizations Law Review* (2008), 241.

not subjected to parliamentary approval. The public debate came too late. Paradoxically, then, while soft law does not need formal parliamentary approval because it is not binding, the absence of democratic procedures make it so effective that it needs democratic legitimacy.

A comparable phenomenon took place within the so-called PISA Process.[231] The Organization for Economic Co-operation and Development is an international organization active in many different areas, but with hardly any formal regulatory powers itself.[232] The PISA study is an on-going comparative study of the schooling achievements of OECD member states, ranked by their quality in different areas. It has met widely varying responses in different countries. At first glance, such a study, undertaken by an agency that is independent from the member states, highlights the advantages of informally operating international organizations. Systematic comparisons with other states are an important instrument for providing national societies with rationally based self-assessments, on the basis of which they can decide for themselves how they should grow and develop. But at the same time, it is important to check whether the comparisons initiated by the OECD can simply be interpreted as the findings of expertise without taking into account its liberal political and economic agenda and the meaning of quantified methodologies in the area of education. Obviously, contradictions can arise between this orientation and a suitable reform of the school system: whether education should serve as a purveyor of growth is a political decision. The instrument of comparison by quantified parameters that in the end creates rankings may be biased in itself, as it creates an obvious asymmetry between better quantifiable and worse quantifiable parameters. Solutions to these deficiencies would not necessarily end these kinds of soft regulatory schemes. The main institutional deficit may not even lie in international law but in the national political processes unprepared to take a critical perspective on this kind of international law; all too ready to receive certain comparative standards and, thereby, to accept the cognitive as the normative. Obviously, it is not impossible to improve participation and to debate these kinds of comparisons before they are implemented. This means that national parliaments must learn to better get involved in the procedures of soft standardization. This requires formal rights of information vis-à-vis governments but also a political sensitivity and internal organization that can only be created by means of self-organization.

---

[231] M. Goldmann, 'The Accountability of Private vs. Public Governance by Information. A Comparison of the Assessment Activities of the OECD and the IEA in the Field of Education', *58 Rivista trimestrale di diritto pubblico* (2008), 43.

[232] See J. Salzman, 'Decentralized Administrative Law in the OECD', *68 Law & Contemporary Problems* (2005), 190.

Finally, even for this kind of soft law, some formalization seems necessary. We shall return to this point in the following section.

b) Transnational administrative networks

Traditionally, sovereign states organize their relations with other states centrally via their governments and, especially, their foreign offices. The foreign ministry monopolizes foreign relations. Public authorities subordinated to the government are not permitted to develop a foreign policy of their own. They do not work together with the corresponding authorities in other countries, unless through the foreign office.

There are different reasons for this kind of centralization.[233] From the perspective of international law, necessity dictates that a state whose action has international legal implications appears as a unitary actor on the scene. Constitutionally, it seems reasonable that the head of the executive monopolizes foreign actions that could potentially affect the whole state. As James Madison declared (with regard to the federal aspect of it but in general terms): 'If we are to be one nation in many respects, it clearly ought to be in respect to other nations.'[234] But despite these arguments, the centralization of national foreign relations has been contested for some time. National authorities subordinated to their government have begun to nurture relationships with their counterparts in other states. They exchange information about mutually regulated issues, find common informal organizations, and define uniform standards for the implementation of regulatory schemes. These phenomena have not emerged throughout governmental organizations but only in certain areas in which authorities handle transnational issues, such as overseeing stock exchanges, banks, and insurance companies.

One key characteristic of this cooperation is its informality. Organizations such as the meetings of security commissioners, the International Organization of Security Commissions or selected national bank supervisors like the Basel Committee on Banking Supervision are not international organizations in the sense of public international law. They set informal standards by consensus without any legally binding effect. Nevertheless, these standards are almost always complied with, and they represent an important benchmark for the decisions of national and some supra-national authorities. Such standards always develop in non-public negotiations, in which certain states have an unequally greater weight in relation to others, and in which the international professional associations of the regulated industries also play a powerful and some times problematic role. The Basel Committee on Banking Supervision shows how important

---

[233] See this Chapter, preliminary considerations, 1.

[234] Federalist Papers, No. 42 (Madison).

these standards can be. Here, the banking supervision authorities of selected states work out standards for the lending policy of banks and for their minimum capitalization. Needless to say, they are of great importance to the entire economy. These non-binding standards (Basel I and II) were adopted by many national legislatures, even by those that were not involved in the negotiations, and they form the basis of some important crucial elements of current banking law, like standards of capitalization, in the United States, the European Union, and many other states.[235]

Even though these phenomena appear only in certain policy areas, they are frequently interpreted as evidence for a fundamental change in transnational relations: among a system of 'disaggregated' states,[236] authority networks develop that are arranged according to policy topics and which tackle certain regulatory tasks more technically than politically. Some legal scholars welcome this development as a specific form of deliberative democracy.[237] But a meeting of experts who discuss a problem has to be distinguished from the concept of deliberative legitimacy. Not all of those who are potentially affected will be granted the opportunity of having a say. Neither do all those who are actually involved have the same opportunity of involvement. Rather, it seems that states or groups of states also use their networks to present their own regulatory philosophies to—or even impose them on—other states.[238]

It is, however, true that this kind of cooperation is a reaction to the necessity of regulating transnational economic activity and other emanations of globalization. A less-than-convincing alternative would be the establishment of an international super-agency, for instance for the supervision of banks. This model seems difficult to establish even within the European Union.[239] Still, the questions of legitimacy remain unanswered: informal standards are barely democratically legitimate, and even though states may deviate from them, they practically never do. Such standards emerge obscurely and exclude affected interests. The fragmentation of

---

[235] C. Möllers, 'Transnationale Behördenkooperation', *65 Zeitschrift für ausländisches öffentliches Recht und Völkerrecht* (2005), 351.

[236] A.-M. Slaughter, *A New World Order* (Princeton: Princeton University Press, 2004), 36, 131.

[237] A.-M. Slaughter, *A New World Order* (Princeton: Princeton University Press, 2004), 203–8 seems to confuse moral peer pressure for a benevolent end and deliberative democracy as an example of youths that urge a peer to quit smoking. One might wonder if the discussions between banking regulators correspond to neither or both.

[238] K. Raustiala, 'The Architecture of International Cooperation: Transgovernmental Networks and the Future of International Law', *43 Virginia Journal of International Law* (2002), 1.

[239] R. M. Lastra, 'The Governance Structure for Financial Regulation and Supervision in Europe', *10 Columbia Journal of Transnational Law* (2003), 49 (58); Regulation (EC) No. 1093/2010 of the European Parliament and of the Council of 24 November 2010.

international law-making in different regimes does not allow for a balancing of different regulatory concerns;[240] banking regulation remains the business of banking regulators and banks and so on. The cognitive virtues of a general political process[241] are lost. Furthermore, with the establishment of their own foreign policy agenda, national regulatory authorities also gain independence from their own domestic sources of democratic legitimacy.

Solutions could consist of more intense political observation of administrative networks by national parliaments and governments. Something else to consider would be a partial legal formalization of these structures, possibly through the establishment of international framework organizations. Such a framework could be associated with the development of procedural standards that would permit public participation at least during the decisive phase of standard-setting. Evidently little of this seems feasible for the addressed administrations, which tend to value flexibility over political legitimacy. The development of networks may, in this respect, be neither a blessing nor a threat but rather a functionally appropriate reaction to the internationalization of markets, which are indeed difficult to coordinate by national mechanisms alone. Still, as in the case of territorial administration, general minimum standards for the consistency of framework legislation, administrative procedures, and legal protection should be developed as part of this form of international administrative law.[242]

c) Private law-making

Whether a key feature of the state is a monopoly on the legitimate exercise of physical force—as is often suggested in the continental European tradition—seems questionable at least.[243] Ultimately, all legal systems also recognize legitimate private force, for instance the right to self-defence. But if needed, states may at least attempt to monopolize the answer to the question of which kind of force is legal and which is not. States indeed claim a monopoly on law-making, even if they explicitly accept other forms of law, whether religious or indigenous. But the identification of law-making and state authority is a relatively young phenomenon.[244] In European states,

---

[240] Though one may argue that the fragmentation of international organizations enables a new political process of mutual political control between the regimes, especially when they provide parliamentary structures: I. Ley, 'Opposition im Völkerrecht', 2012 (forthcoming).

[241] See Chapter 2, II.

[242] 'The Emergence of Global Administrative Law', 68 *Law & Contemporary Problems* (2005), 3, 4; B. Kingsbury, N. Krisch, R. B. Stewart, J. B. Wiener (eds.), *Internationales Verwaltungsrecht. Eine Analyse anhand von Referenzgebieten* C. Möllers, A. Voßkuhle, C. Walter, (eds.), (Tübingen: Mohr, 2007).

[243] This formula goes back to R. v. Ihering, *Der Zweck im Recht [1877], Vol I* (Leipzig: Breitkopf & Härtel, 1905), 247.

[244] W. Reinhardt, *Geschichte der Staatsgewalt* (München: Beck, 1999), 291.

as recently as the late 19th century, there were corporations, universities, and professions with their own legal systems, which were only slowly replaced by state control.

Even today, all state legal systems have reserves of private law-making. For example, most states do not set standards for medical practice themselves, but instead incorporate them from doctors and, thus, only formally make them a part of the state legal system. Today, again, it seems the etatization of law-making is once again in decline. Legal theory has started to recognize private law-making as a central development and some theorists are even starting to speak of the emergence of stateless legal systems.[245] How should this development be judged against the background of our model of separated powers?

Two immediate examples may be considered. The first is the so-called *lex mercatoria*.[246] This name denotes a legal system that is developed by transnationally operating corporations for its transactions with other businesses. What is key is that civil disputes in such cases are no longer judged by state courts but rather by private tribunals to which the parties have agreed to submit. In this way, there emerges a law of transnational trade relations that is not based on state legislation and not judged by state courts. The second example is the standardization of products.[247] Products that go on sale must abide by defined technical standards. Although there is no coherent global regime for such standards, they are usually devised by private standardizing committees that finance themselves and are composed of engineers and representatives of the companies producing the relevant goods.[248] Though not introduced by states, state law acknowledges them, for example by legally presuming that a certain action is lawful as long as it adheres to these standards. Therefore, such standards are law, even though they are not state-set law.

The first question to be answered in order to assess such phenomena could ask: whose spheres of freedom are affected by these private regulations? If the *lex mercatoria* were only a matter of bilateral agreements between equally powerful businesses, such a mechanism would seem completely acceptable.[249] In this case, the renunciation of state legal enforcement mechanisms and the reliance on incentives and sanctions that the

---

[245]   G. Teubner (ed.), *Global Law without a State* (Aldershot: Dartmouth, 1997).

[246]   G. Teubner, 'Globale Bukowina', *15 Rechtshistorisches Journal* (1996), 255 (264).

[247]   For a detailed description, see: H. Schepel, *The Constitution of Private Governance* (Oxford: Hart, 2005).

[248]   For their history: M. Vec, 'Alle Weltworte streben nach Standardisierung. Vereinheitlichung und Vereinheitlichungskritik in historischer Perspektive', in H.-D. Assmann, F. Baasner, J. Wertheimer (eds.), *Normen, Standards, Werte* (Baden-Baden: Nomos, 2012), 11–34.

[249]   For a parallel argument see Chapter 2, III., 3.

contracting parties can inflict on one another cannot be assessed differently from any other private legal transaction between free and equal legal persons. That does not rule out the possibility that a state might step in, for instance, when the framework of these agreements includes plans to commit crimes. Furthermore, in many cases it can be questioned whether a contract affects the rights of a third party. The most important example would be competition law that cannot be waived by contract. Lastly, employees have to be employed in accordance with state rules. All in all, such forms of private law-making seem legitimate as long as there is no externalization of constraints to the autonomy of third parties. This also means that the states involved must have the power to regulate such external effects. For this reason, purely private forms of transaction seem to be much less dubious than regulatory models in which private parties and states are bound together by means of public international law, as in the case of investment protection agreements.[250] Here, a national democratic process is limited by privileged property rights that are effectively protected by other states.

More problematic than *lex mercatoria* is the law of standardization. Product standards potentially address all those who can produce or buy a certain product, regardless of their ability to directly influence the respective standard-setting procedure. Does private law-making require democratic legitimacy when it creates rules that potentially affect everyone?[251] If one considered private standard-setting an overstretched delegation of law-making power by the legislator to private individuals, this would indeed call for more state involvement.[252] However, this interpretation is not entirely convincing for different reasons. First, standardizing procedures depend on private initiative. This is always a good indication that they should not be treated as state action.[253] Secondly, an etatization of the procedure in most cases effectively amounts to the state formally approving standards, or courts just applying them, but hardly ever to a deliberate re-definition by a state administration. Thirdly, a decisive, though rarely addressed question is what type of norms do standards actually represent?[254] Standards function not as agreements but as constitutive rules, which also

---

[250] For a critical appraisal: M. Renner, *Transnationales zwingendes Recht* (Baden-Baden: Nomos, 2011).

[251] For more on this issue, see O. Lepsius, in C. Möllers et al (eds.), *Internationales Verwaltungsrecht* (Tübingen: Mohr 2007), 345.

[252] L. Jaffe, 'Law Making by Private Groups', *51 Harvard L. Rev.* 201, (1937).

[253] C. Möllers, *Staat als Argument* (München: Beck 2000, 326).

[254] See, for example, the omission in this regard in H. Schepel, *The Constitution of Private Governance* (Oxford: Hart, 2005) who also misses this point despite a comprehensive analysis.

affect the rights of third parties, as they *define* a product.[255] This means that standards often fulfil their purpose simply *by* regulating something, regardless of *how* they regulate it—just like certain traffic regulations. So standards help by identifying products as such and thereby making them marketable— a task which does not necessarily require democratic legitimacy as long as competition rules prevent standards from being misused to create barriers to competition through new products. In this respect, standard setting is also a special form of market selection. Only on a secondary—and perhaps overrated—level does the question of a political content of standards arise, for example when certain economic interests come into conflict with ecological or security issues, such as in the case of genetically modified crops. But it is clear that, as they hardly escape the attention of the political process, if the political process itself is open, these kinds of decisions almost never take place totally outside the context of public regulations. They are, for example, often subject to approval procedures that monitor standardization without replacing them with separate state decisions.

Still, certain procedural requirements that guarantee transparency and an appropriate representation of interests seem necessary.[256] Putting such procedures in place is the duty of the democratic legislator. In a pattern typical for contemporary public law, the legal system responds to the privatization of state duties—among which standard-setting can be seen— by imposing organizational and procedural duties on private companies resembling those for public organizations.

One has to be careful of generalizing these and similar phenomena to make fundamental assertions about the development of the 'law in a globalized world'. Certainly, the fact that not all law is set by the state has been given short shrift in 20th century legal theory.[257] However, this also demonstrates that, historically, the coexistence of private and state law-making is a normal state of affairs.

---

[255] J. Rawls, 'Two Concepts of Rules', 64 *Philosophical Review* (1955), 64, 3–32.

[256] H. Schepel, *Constitution of Private Governance* (Oxford: Hart, 2005), 406.

[257] But see K. C. Culver, M. Giudice, *Legality's Border* (Oxford: Oxford University Press, 2011).

Outlook: Governance—Constitutionalization— Fourth Branches?

At the beginning of the 21st century, the principle of the separation of powers seems like an attractive idea, but one in steady decline, drawn from the arsenal of a classical political modernity that has grown old. The prevailing impression is that public authority has been centralized in executive organizations and that the internationalization of the legal system has outpaced the classical structure of separated powers. In this book, we have attempted to offer a model of legitimacy in reply to this flawed narrative, which tends to petrify a certain idea of statehood that has probably never been historically true in the first place.

At the end of this book, we shall summarize a few tendencies that run across the path of the argument, yet figure significantly in the discussion. Incidentally, one long-bemoaned phenomenon, the de-parliamentarization of legal systems, will not be considered in this final section. The assumption of a general loss of parliamentary power is built neither on correct theoretical nor compelling historical premises.[1] Moreover, the alleged decline of parliamentary power does not apply to some important parliaments, such as the US Congress or even the European Parliament. Sometimes the stories about the decline of parliaments seem to evoke the end of parliamentary systems rather than to describe it.[2]

INFORMALITY

Mandatory provisions of positive law may restrict us, but they may also widen our scope of action and free us from informal power.[3] Where

---

[1] See Chapter 3, I., 1.

[2] Particularly evident with the continuously imprecise G. Agamben, *State of exception* (Chicago: University of Chicago Press, 2005).

[3] A. L. Stinchcombe, *When Formality Works, Authority and Abstraction in Law and Organizations* (Chicago: The University of Chicago Press, 2001), Chapters 2, 6.

enforceable rules between agents apply, these rules are not necessarily limiting, they also define the relationship between these agents in an egalitarian, explicit, and therefore potentially liberating way. This is especially the case when social power among the agents is unequally distributed.[4] The intervention of state law in family or labour relations can, at once, be both hierarchical and liberating. However, the context of these rules can change and their effect may disappear. When collective labour law gives employees a stronger position in negotiations with their employers, the liberating effect may be diminished by the fact that employment relationships individualize. Then, unemployment, rather than exploitation in the workplace, becomes the main threat. In short: enforceable rules replace informal relationships, and this can possibly lead to more freedom, but not necessarily so.

Informal, non-binding rules are a key challenge for the separation of powers in national and international law. They appear in the most diverse forms: as a voluntary commitment of private organizations not to show a certain pornographic film; as an informal pact between a country and its universities to achieve budget stability in return for defined but limited spending cuts; as the non-binding convention of an international organization; or as an agreement on a certain standard between the banking regulation authorities of different states.

Against a background of widespread criticism of state regulation, informal regulations seem to have the charm of liberality and flexibility; an attraction whose justification cannot be completely denied. However, one can also identify specific dangers of informality for a legitimate system of separated powers. Voluntary private agreements—such as the refusal of private movie theatres to show a certain film—may lead to a regulatory monopoly. This might circumvent certain guarantees, which are only directed at the state, such as the freedom of expression. As long as courts cannot apply basic rights in such cases,[5] the increasingly important function of competition law for the whole legal order becomes evident, especially if one tries to avoid a complete reformalization of informal practices. Competition law is an alternative tool against specific threats to modern democracies, such as the guarantee of democratic publicity through an open media market. Moreover, even private self-regulations must meet certain procedural standards, as we have seen.

Even more questionable structures emerge when the state or any other public authority with the power of setting binding standards makes use of informality. For these actors regularly do so in order to bypass binding

---

[4] This aspect is consequently ignored in J. Tully's critique of western constitutionalism: J. Tully, *Strange Multiplicity. Constitutionalism in an age of diversity* (Cambridge: Cambridge University Press, 1995).

[5] For Germany: German Federal Constitutional Court, *Blinkfüer*, BVerfGE 25, 256.

procedural duties. Over the course of this book, we have seen some examples of that. The EU has no authority to standardize university degrees, so the member states arrange the standardization informally. The United Nations is not allowed to overrule criminal sentences, so it compiles a list of terror suspects to guide the member states. National banking supervision authorities do not have the authority to conduct foreign relations, so they internationally coordinate their implementation practice informally. The informality of the bypassed procedural requirements threatens both our basic types of legitimacy: informality is obscure and allows the formal definition of responsibility and the real authorship of democratic decisions to disintegrate. It also has negative implications for judicial review. Concerned subjects often have no specific starting point to address a formal complaint.

When binding procedural rules are circumvented in this way, informal conflict resolution or consultation mechanisms are often established in their place because even informal procedures require information from the parties involved. Here a dilemma arises, which we already know from the practice of the European Commission.[6] Informality either fails to win acceptance or fails to make plausible that all affected interests are appropriately represented.[7] That is why these kind of procedures have begun, bit by bit, to be reformalized, a trend that can be observed both in alternative dispute settlement procedures and standard-setting involving public authorities.

GOVERNANCE

In academic discussion, new institutional arrangements are often discussed under the heading 'governance'. This category serves as a fairly underdefined collective term for different possible 'new' forms of public authority, meant no longer to be subsumed under the classical term of 'government'.[8] It was the World Bank that introduced 'governance' to the internal debate of public institutions. Knowing the source of the notion might help us to define it more accurately.[9] If organizations such as the World Bank monitor the institutional situation of supported countries, they act as external entities, which are not democratically accountable to that country. They are oriented towards efficiency criteria and make no categorical distinction between private and public contributions to the general welfare. This covers many

[6] S. Smismans, *Law, Legitimacy, and European Governance* (Oxford: Oxford University Press, 2004).

[7] For the dilemma of informality, see R. Abel, 'Delegalization—A Critical Review of its Ideology, Manifestations, and Social Consequences', *6 Jahrbuch für Rechtssoziologie und Rechtstheorie* (1980), 27.

[8] For the origins, see C. Theobald, *Zur Ökonomik des Staates* (Baden-Baden: Nomos, 2000).

[9] C. Möllers, 'European Governance—Meaning and Value of a Concept', *43 Common Market Law Review* (2006), 314.

significant elements of 'governance', not simply by adopting the World Bank terminology, but by observing it in action. These features also characterize the practice of other institutions, such as the European Commission or the OECD: the term 'governance' refers to institutional constellations in which technocratic agents of international law try to informally influence the institutional organization of states.

Governance structures can support democratic states in their decision-making. But they also tend to replace a political balancing of interests with the result of an allegedly independent analysis of practical constraints. Moreover, the term 'governance' transports a dubious narrative. New terms frequently serve to declare and to justify very different developments as general paradigm shifts, without making clear what is actually new and what is actually outdated. The term 'governance', too, is in danger of becoming a self-fulfilling prophecy, which legitimizes itself by realizing itself. But the idea that the output of democratic states can be assessed in a non-political procedure is, as we have seen, neither new nor compelling.

CONSTITUTIONALIZATION

In international law, the idea of constitutionalization is in growing demand. It refers to the increasing legalization of international relations, in which sovereign states no longer solely define the rules but must submit to universally recognized rules, such as the prohibition of aggression or certain humanitarian standards.[10] The idea of constitutionalization is a response to the history of the 20th century and the horrors that emanated from sovereign states. Therefore, the two basic elements of the concept are the recognition of universal rules, which bind states even against their will, and the recognition of rights and duties of individual persons. Both elements tend to perceive state sovereignty as a problem and both aim to de-politicize international relations. The model of international constitutionalism is frequently nourished by the fear of unregulated international politics, which has the means to wage war and is just focused on the exercise of power. This view identifies constitutionalism with the juridification of politics.

However, there is also the other tradition of political constitutionalism; the revolutionary idea that identifies constitutionalism with the democratic politicization of the legislator. According to this reading, the legitimacy of international law directly depends on the internal political composition of

---

[10] For a representative account see J. A. Frowein, 'Konstitutionalisierung des Völkerrechts', *39 Berichte der Deutschen Gesellschaft für Völkerrecht* (2000), 427. In contrast, with democratic concerns like here: H. Brunkhorst, 'Demokratie in der globalen Rechtsgenossenschaft', *Special Edition Zeitschrift für Soziologie* (2005), 330 (332).

the states, which create it. Thus, besides the development of universal rules, which bind all sovereign states, one could also view the democratization of the participating states as a key element of constitutionalization. A constitution-alization through democratization would then add to a constitutionalization through juridification. Such an understanding of constitutionalization does, however, break even more resolutely with the doctrine of sovereignty, for it has a great impact on the inner constitution of affected states. Furthermore, there is a higher potential for conflict, since, properly thought through, it is tantamount to a forced democratization of states. Elements of such an understanding can easily be found in the foreign policy of the United States.[11]

However, the discussion of international constitutionalism is mostly limited to the former and, thereby, suffers from the problems already discussed here with regard to the protection of international human rights. In the terminology of separated powers, constitutionalism must develop through both judicial and legislative law-making. Therefore, it is no coinci-dence that legally binding international institutions mostly deal with the retrospective sanctioning of human rights violations.

Especially in Europe, where constitutionalism through law is particularly important, a confusing accumulation of basic rights layers (four levels in Germany: state and federal basic rights; EU fundamental rights; and those of the European Convention on Human Rights) demonstrates the risks of an over-juridification of democratic politics. A well-defined concept of constitu-tionalism requires more democratic decision-making, not just more judicial review. In the long run, every form of international constitutionalization that deserves that name has to take on the cumbersome quest for insti-tutions that add political legitimacy to international law-making.

THE DIFFUSION OF ACCOUNTABILITY

Overlapping layers of law-making make it more difficult to attribute deci-sions to an accountable legal subject. The latter, however, is a condition for democratic politics as well as for judicial review. Within the EU, one can easily witness the difficulty in defining political and legal responsibilities. Who do I have to sue when I am up against a decision in which both the Commission and the member-states were involved? This problem also applies to political decisions: the negative referenda in France and the Netherlands against the European Constitutional Treaty in 2005 were quickly dismissed as being of purely domestic nature. The recognition of

---

[11] Thought through in N. Krisch, 'Amerikanische Hegemonie und liberale Revolution im Völkerrecht', 43 *Der Staat* (2004), 267; N. Krisch, 'International Law in Times of Hegemony', 16 *European Journal of International Law* (2005), 369.

democratic processes, however, prohibits such a reinterpretation of a clearly phrased question to the democratic subject. Indeed, it seems dubious whether a neat distinction between national and European politics is viable at all, when a European treaty is decided upon at a national level.

In multilayered legal systems, this ambiguity of democratic decisions is inevitable. It is also an expression of the openness of democratic will formation; democratic votes do not necessarily tally with the specific issue that is put to the vote. The law can do little more than structure accountability by creating legal forms, which make decisions attributable to the respective levels of government. The definition of 'formally responsible' remains the legal condition of the possibility of freedom. Only a legal system that allows for responsible contributions by both the individual and democratic subjects when creating legal commitments can convey legitimacy.

FREEDOM, REGIME, AND FOURTH POWER

The institutional diversity of public institutions at the beginning of the 21st century, which has evidently brought about sophisticated alternatives to the traditional nation-state, does not imply the uselessness of our triadic concept of separated powers. If our reconstruction proves coherent, whether the concept of separated powers is still worthwhile would depend on our own expectations of the legitimacy of public action. Hence, it seems intellectually lazy to characterize every new form of public organization as a 'fourth power' and to declare the end of a 'classical idea' of separated powers that nobody has ever advocated in the first place, time and again.

But of course, our expectations of legitimacy can change. Indeed, the very demand for justifying public authority might dwindle. Ultimately, it remains an open question whether constitutional systems expected to be legitimate are in decline compared with others, which are essentially run by experts or systemic necessities.[12] Such a supposition, which views a parallel development of economic, ecological, and other regulatory regimes as a natural and necessary future for national and international constitutional law, would, if true, make the standards identified here obsolete. If it were correct, one should face it uncompromisingly and, in the description as in the assessment of such new patterns, forsake the concept of autonomy.

---

[12] G. Teubner, *Constitutional Fragments* (Oxford: Oxford University Press, 2011); sceptically M. Koskenniemmi, 'The Fate of Public International Law', 70 *The Modern Law Review* (2007), 1. Arguing for a broader theoretic context for such assumptions, which associates the concept of separated powers with the expiring era of balance, see D. Baecker, *Studien zur nächsten Gesellschaft* (Frankfurt am Main: Suhrkamp, 2007), 147.

Bibliography

Abbott, Henry. 2008. The European Court of Justice and the protection of fundamental rights. *Irish Journal of European Law* 15: 79.

Abel, Richard. 1980. Delegalization—A Critical Review of its Ideology, Manifestations, and Social Consequences. *Jahrbuch für Rechtssoziologie und Rechtstheorie* 6: 27.

Abromeit, Heidrun. 1999. Volkssouveränität in komplexen Gesellschaften. In *Das Recht der Republik*, ed. Brunkhorst, Hauke / Niesen, Peter, 17. Frankfurt am Main: Suhrkamp.

von Achenbach, Jelena. 2012. *Das Mitentscheidungsverfahren des Art. 294 AEUV als demokratisches Gesetzgebungsverfahren der Europäischen Union, insbesondere im Bereich der Biomedizin und Humanbiotechnologie*, Diss. jur. Heidelberg.

——. 2012. Vorschläge zu einer Demokratietheorie der dualen demokratischen Legitimation europäischer Hoheitsgewalt. In *Interdisciplinary research in jurisprudence and constitutionalism*, ed. Kirste, Stephan / van Aaken, Anne et.al., 205. Stuttgart: Steiner.

Achterberg, Norbert. 1970. *Probleme der Funktionenlehre*. München: Beck.

Ackerman, Bruce A. 1991. *We the People*. Volume 1. Cambridge, Mass.: Harvard University Press.

——. 2000. The New Separation of Powers. *Harvard Law Review* 113: 634.

——. 2005. *The Failure of the Founding Fathers*. Cambridge, Mass.: Harvard University Press.

Adenauer, Konrad. 1965. *Erinnerungen 1945–1953*. Stuttgart: DVA.

Agamben, Giorgio. 2005. *State of Exception*. Chicago: University of Chicago Press.

Albert, Hans. 1998. *Marktsoziologie und Entscheidungslogik*. Tübingen: Mohr Siebeck.

Albert, Richard. 2010. Presidential Values in Parliamentary Democracies. *International Journal of Constitutional Law* 8: 207.

——. 2009. The Fusion of Presidentialism and Parliamentarism. *American Journal of Constitutional Law* 57: 531.

von Alemann, Florian. 2006. *Die Handlungsform der interinstitutionellen Vereinbarung*. Heidelberg: Springer.

Alexander, Kern. 2011. Reforming European financial supervision. *ERA Forum - Journal of the Academy of European Law: adapting EU institutions to market structures* 12: 229.

Alexy, Robert. 2002. *A Theory of Constitutional Rights*. Oxford: Oxford University Press.

———. 1983. *Theorie der juristischen Argumentation*. Frankfurt am Main: Suhrkamp.

Allison, John W. F. 1997. *A Continental Distinction in the Common Law*. Oxford: Clarendon Press.

Alter, Karen J. 2001. *Establishing the Supremacy of European Law*. Oxford: Oxford University Press.

———. 2009. *The European Court's political power*. Oxford: Oxford University Press.

Alvárez, José E. 2005. *International Organizations as Law-makers*. Oxford: Oxford University Press.

Ambos, Kai. 2006. *Internationales Strafrecht*. München: Beck.

Amerasinghe, Chittharanjan F. 2005. *Principles of the institutional law of international organizations*. Cambridge: Cambridge University Press.

Andenas, Mads (ed). 2000. *Judicial Review in International Perspective*. Den Haag: Kluwer.

Arendt, Hannah. 1976. *The Origins of Totalitarianism*. New York/London: Harcourt Inc.

———. 2005. Introduction into Politics. In *The Promise of Politics*. New York: Random House.

———. [1963] 2006. *On Revolution*. New York: Penguin Books.

———. 1949. Es gibt nur ein einziges Menschenrecht. In *Die Wandlung*, 754.

———. 2005. Introduction into Politics. In *The Promise of Politics*. New York: Schocken.

Aristotle. 1905. *Politics*. Trans. B. Jowett. Oxford: Oxford University Press.

Badie, Bertrand. 1992. *L'État importé*. Paris: Fayard.

Constant, Benjamin. [1819] 1980. De la liberté des anciens comparée à celle des modernes. In *De la liberté chez les modernes*, ed. Marcel Gauchet. Paris: Hachette/Pluriel.

Baecker, Dirk. 2007. *Studien zur nächsten Gesellschaft*. Frankfurt am Main: Suhrkamp.

Bagehot, Walter. [1867] 1966. *The English Constitution*. Ithaca: Cornell University Press.

Baranger, Denis. 2008. *Écrire la constitution non-écrite*. Paris: Presses Universitaires de France.

Barber, Nicholas W. 2001. Prelude to the Separation of Powers. *Cambridge Law Journal* 60: 59.

Bast, Jürgen. 2003. Handlungsformen. In *Europäisches Verfassungsrecht*, ed. Armin von Bogdandy, 479. Berlin: Springer.

———. 2010. European Union: Legal instruments and judicial protection. In *Principles of European constitutional law*, ed. von Bogdandy, Armin/Bast, Jürgen, 345. Oxford: Hart.

———. 2012. New Categories of Acts after the Lisbon Reform—Legal Regimes and Institutional Practice. *Common Market Law Review* 49: 885.

Bates, David. 2005. Political Unity and the Spirit of the Law: Juridical Concepts of the State in the Late Third Republic. *French Historical Studies* 28: 69.

Beaud, Olivier. 1999. *Le sang contaminé. Essai critique sur la criminalisation de la responsabilité des gouvernants.* Paris: P.U.F., coll. 'Béhémoth'.

——. 2005. De quelques particularités de la justice constitutionelle dans un système federal. In *La notion de la justice constitutionelle,* ed. Grewe, Constance/Jouanjan, Olivier/Maulin, Eric/Wachsmann, Patrick, 49. Paris: Dalloz.

——. 2009. *Théorie de la Fédération.* Paris: Presses Universitaires de France.

Beetham, David. 1991. *The Legitimation of Power.* Macmillan: London.

Beitz, Charles R. 2009. *The Idea of Human Rights.* Oxford: Oxford University Press.

Bellamy, Richard. 2007. *Political Constitutionalism.* Cambridge: Cambridge University Press.

Bentham, Jeremy. 1998. *An Introduction to the Principles of Morals and Legislation.* 4th Edition, ed. James H. Burns and Herbert L.A. Hart. Oxford: Oxford University Press.

Berat, Lynn. 2005. The Constitutional Court of South-Africa and jurisdictional questions: In the Interest of Justice? International Journal of Constitutional Law 3: 39.

Berlin, Isaiah. 2005. Two Concepts of Liberty. In *Liberty.* 5th Edition, ed. Henry Hardy, 166. Oxford: Oxford University Press.

Bertrand, Maurice. 2005. Lehren aus einer gescheiterten Reform. *Vereinte Nationen* 2005: 174.

Bessette, Joseph M. 1994. *The Mild Voice of Reason.* Chicago: University of Chicago Press.

von Beyme, Klaus. 1968. *Die verfassunggebende Gewalt des Volkes.* Tübingen: Mohr Siebeck.

——. 1997. *Der Gesetzgeber.* Opladen: Westdeutscher Verlag.

Biaggini, Giovanni. 1996. *Theorie und Praxis des Verwaltungsrechts im Bundesstaat.* Basel: Helbing und Lichtenhahn.

Blackstone, William. 1765–1769. *Commentaries to the Laws of England I.* Oxford: Clarendon Press.

Blum, P. Wege zu besserer Gesetzgebung. Gutachten für den 65. Deutschen Juristentag, *Verhandlungen des 65. Deutschen Juristentages. Gutachten. Volume 1.* (München: C.H. Beck, 2004).

Bobbitt, Philip. 1994. War Powers: An Essay on John Hart Ely's 'War And Responsibility: Constitutional Lessons of Vietnam and Its Aftermath'. *Michigan Law Review* 92: 1364.

Böckenförde, Ernst-Wolfgang. 1982. Sozialer Bundesstaat und parlamentarische Demokratie In *Politik als gelebte Verfassung,* ed. J. Jekewitz. Opladen: Westdeutscher Verlag.

———. 1987. Demokratie als Verfassungsprinzip. In *Handbuch des Staatsrechts*. 1st
Edition. Volume 1, ed. Josef Isensee and Paul Kirchhof, § 22. Heidelberg:
C. F. Müller.

von Bogdandy, Armin and Jürgen Bast, Felix Arndt. 2002. Handlungsformen im
Unionsrecht. *Zeitschrift für ausländisches öffentliches Recht und Völkerrecht* 62: 126.

von Bogdandy, Armin and Matthias Goldmann. 2008. The Exercise of International
Public Authority through National Policy Assessment—The OECD's PISA Policy
as a Paradigm for a New International Standard Instrument. *International
Organizations Law Review* 5: 241.

von Bogdandy, Armin. 2000. *Gubernative Rechtsetzung*. Tübingen: Mohr Siebeck.

———. 2000. Information und Kommunikation in der Europäischen Union: föderale
Strukturen in supranationalem Umfeld. In *Verwaltungsrecht in der
Informationsgesellschaft*, ed. Hoffmann-Riem, Wolfgang Schmidt-Aßmann,
Eberhard, 133. Baden-Baden: Nomos.

———. 2001. Law and Politics in the WTO—Strategies to Cope with a Deficient
Relationship. *Max-Planck Yearbook of United Nations Law* 5: 609, 618.

———. 2002. Legal Equality, Legal certainty and Subsidiarity in Transnational
Economic Law. In *European integration and international co-ordination*, ed. Armin
von Bogdandy, 13. Den Haag: Kluwer.

———. 2004. Globalization and Europe: How to Square Democracy, Globalization,
and International Law. *European Journal of International Law* 15: 885.

———. 2005. Parlamentarismus in Europa: eine Verfalls- oder Erfolgsgeschichte?
Archiv des Öffentlichen Rechts 130: 445.

Brandt, Reinhard. 1998. *D'Artagnan und die Urteilstafel*. München: dtv.

Brinktrine, Ralf. 1998. *Verwaltungsermessen in Deutschland und England*. Heidelberg:
C.F. Müller.

Brunkhorst, Hauke 2005. *Solidarity—From Civic Friendship to a Global Legal
Community*. Cambridge / London: MIT Press.

———. 2005. Demokratie in der globalen Rechtsgenossenschaft. *Zeitschrift für
Soziologie* 2005: 330.

Burke, Edmund. 2000. Speech to the Electors of Bristol (3 November 1774). In
On Empire Liberty and Reform. Speeches and Letters of Edmund Burke, ed. Bromwich,
David. New Haven: Yale University Press.

Busch, Andreas. 1999. Das oft geänderte Grundgesetz. In *Demokratie in Ost und West*,
ed. Merkel, Wolfgang / Busch, Andreas, 549. Frankfurt am Main: Suhrkamp.

Calabresi, Guido. 1982. *A Common Law for the Age of Statutes*. Cambridge, Mass.:
Harvard University Press.

Caldwell, Peter C. 1997. *Popular Sovereignty and The Crisis of German Constitutional
Law*. Durham: Duke University Press.

Calliess, Christian. 1999. *Subsidiaritäts- und Solidaritätsprinzip in der Europäischen Union*. 2nd Edition. Baden-Baden: Nomos.

Cappelletti, Mauro. 1989. *The Judicial Process in Comparative Perspective*. Oxford et. al.: Clarendon Press.

Caranta, Robert / Andenas, Mads / Fairgrieve, Duncan (eds.). 2004. *Independent Administrative Authorities*. London: British Institute of International and Comparative Law.

Carolan, Eoin. 2009. *The New Separation of Powers*. Oxford: Oxford University Press.

Carré de Malberg, Raymond. [1931] 1984. *La Loi, expression de la volonté générale*. Paris: Economica.

Casper, Gerhard. 1997. *Separating Powers*. Cambridge, Mass.: Harvard University Press.

Cassesse, Antonio. 2006. The Multifaceted Criminal Notion of Terrorism in International. *Journal of International Criminal Justice* 4: 933.

Cassese, Sabino. 2010. Die Entfaltung des Verwaltungsstaates in Europa. In *Ius Publicum Europaeum*. Vol. II, von Bogdandy, Arnim / Cassese, Sabino / Huber, Peter M. (eds.), 19. Heidelberg: C.F. Müller.

Charney, Jonathan L. 1998. Is International Law Threatened by Multiple International Tribunals? *Recueil des Cours* 271: 101.

Chayes, Abram and Antonia H. Chayes. 1995. *The New Sovereignty*. Cambridge, Mass.: Harvard University Press.

Chesterman, Simon. 2004. *You, the People: The United Nations, Transitional Administration, and State-Building*. Oxford: Oxford University Press.

Chiti, Edoardo. 2004. Decentralisation and Integration into the Community: A New Perspective on European Agencies. *European Law Journal* 10: 402.

Christie, George C. 2012. *Philosopher Kings? The Adjudication of Conflicting Human Rights and Social Values*. Oxford: Oxford University Press.

Churchill, Robin and Geir Ulfstein. 2000. Autonomous Institutional Arrangements in Multilateral Environmental Agreements: A Little-Noticed Phenomenon in International Law. *American Journal of International Law* 94: 623.

Cohen, Jean L. 2010. Sovereignty in the Context of Globalization: A Constitutional Pluralist Perspective. In *The Philosophy of International Law*, Besson, Samantha / Tasioulas, John (eds.), 261. Oxford: Oxford University Press.

Cohen, Joshua. 2011. *Rousseau. A Free Community of Equals*. Oxford: Oxford University Press.

Conway, Gerard. 2011. Recovering a separation of powers in the European Union. *European Law Journal* 17: 304.

Craig, Paul P. 1991. *Public Law and Democracy in the United Kingdom and the United States of America*. Oxford: Oxford University Press.

———. 2008. The Treaty of Lisbon *European Law Review* 33: 137.

Craig, Paul P. and Tomkins, Adam. 2006. *The Executive and Public Law*. Oxford: Oxford University Press.

Craiutu, Aurelian. 2012. *A Virtue for Courageous Minds. Moderation in French Political Thought, 1748–1830.* Princeton: Princeton University Press.

Cremer, Wolfram. 1977. Art. 80 Abs. 1 S. 2 GG und Parlamentsvorbehalt. *Archiv des öffentlichen Rechts* 122: 248.

Crouch, Colin. 2004. *Post-democracy.* Cambridge: Polity Press.

Culver, Keith C. and Michael Giudice. 2011. *Legality's Borders.* Oxford: Oxford University Press.

Currie, David P. 1997. *The Constitution in Congress: The Federalist Period 1789–1801.* Chicago: University of Chicago Press.

Curtin, Deirdre. 1997. *Postnational Democracy.* The Hague: Kluwer Law International.

———. 2009. *Executive power of the European Union.* Oxford: Oxford University Press.

Cushman, Robert E. 1972. *The independent regulatory commissions (1941).* New York: Octagon Books.

Dann, Philipp. 2006. The Political Institutions. In *Principles of European Constitutional Law,* von Bogdandy, Arnim/Bast, Jürgen (eds.), 229. Oxford: Hart.

———. 2011. Federal Democracy in India and the European Union: Towards Transcontinental Comparison of Constitutional Law. *Verfassung und Recht in Übersee* 44: 160.

Danner, Marston A. 2003. Enhancing the legitimacy and accountability of prosecutorial discretion at the International Criminal Court. *American Journal of International Law* 97: 510.

von Danwitz, Thomas. 2001. Der EuGH und das Wirtschaftsvölkerrecht. *Juristenzeitung* 2001: 721.

Davidson, Donald. [1963] 2001. Actions, Reasons and Causes. In *Essays on Actions and Events,* Davidson, Donald et. al. (eds.), 3. Oxford: Clarendon Press.

Davies, Gareth. 2006. Subsidiarity, the wrong idea, in the wrong time, at the wrong place. *Common Market Law Review* 43: 63.

Davis, Dennis M. 2008. Socioeconomic rights: Do they deliver the goods? *International Journal of Constitutional Law* 6: 687 (South-Africa).

De Tocqueville, Alexis. [1835] 1992. De la démocratie en Amérique. In *Œuvres Tome II,* ed. André Jardin. Paris: Gallimard.

de Visser, Maartje. 2009. *Network-based governance in EC law. The example of EC Competition and EC Communications law.* Oxford: Hart.

Derrida, Jacques. 1992. Force of Law. In *Deconstruction and the possibility of justice,* 3. New York: Routledge.

Derrida, Jacques. 1994. *Force de Loi.* Paris: Galilée.

Dewey, John. 1954. *The public and its problems.* Athens: Ohio University Press.

Dicey, Albert V. 1920. *Introduction to the Study of Law of the Constitution.* 8th Edition. London: Macmillan.

Dorsen, Norman, Michel Rosenfeld, Andras Sajo, and Susanne Baer. 2011. *Comparative Constitutionalism. Cases and Materials.* 2nd Edition. St. Paul: West.

Duxbury, Neil. 1995. *Patterns of American Jurisprudence.* Oxford: Clarendon Press.

Dworkin, Ronald. 1977. *Taking Rights Seriously.* Cambridge, Mass.: Harvard University Press.

——. 1984. Rights as Trumps. In *Theories of Rights*, Waldron, Jeremy (ed.), 153. New York: Oxford University Press.

——. 1986. *Law's Empire.* Cambridge, Mass: Harvard University Press.

Eckardt, Martina and Werner Ebert. 2012. Wirtschafts- und finanzpolitische Koordinierung in der Europäischen Union. In *Aktuelle Probleme der europäischen Integration*, Schäfer, Wolf (ed.), 43. Baden-Baden: Nomos.

Edwards, Paul N. and Stephen H. Schneider. 2001. Self-Governance and Peer Review in Science-for-Policy: The Case of the IPCC Second Assessment Report. In *Changing the Atmosphere: Expert Knowledge and Environmental Governance*, Miller, Clark/Edwards, Paul N. (eds.), 219. Cambridge: MIT Press.

Elkins, Stanley M. and Eric L. McKittrick. 1993. *The Age of Federalism.* Oxford: Oxford University Press.

Ellickson, Robert C. 1991. *Order without Law.* Cambridge, Mass.: Harvard University Press.

Ellwein, Thomas. 1954. *Das Erbe der Monarchie in der deutschen Staatskrise.* München: Isar Verlag.

Elster, Jon. 1998. Deliberation and Constitution Making. In *Deliberative Democracy*, Elster, Jon et al. (eds.), 97. Cambridge: Cambridge University Press.

——. 1998. Introduction. In *Deliberative Democracy.* Cambridge: Cambridge University Press.

Ely, John. H. 1980. *Democracy and Distrust.* Cambridge, Mass.: Harvard University Press.

Emde, Ernst. T. 1991. *Die demokratische der funktionalen Selbstverwaltung.* Berlin: Duncker & Humblot.

Epstein, David and Sharyn O'Halloran. 1999. *Delegating Powers.* Cambridge: Cambridge University Press.

Everly, Rebecca. 2007. Reviewing Governmental Acts of the United Nations in Kosovo. *German Law Journal* 8: 21.

Farber, Daniel A. and Philip P. Frickey. 1991. *Law and Public Choice.* Chicago: University of Chicago Press.

Fenske, Hans. 1982. Gewaltenteilung. In *Geschichtliche Grundbegriffe Band 3*, Brunner, Otto/Conze, Werner/Koselleck, Reinhard (eds.), 923. Stuttgart: Klett-Cotta.

Finer, Herman. 1941. Administrative Responsibility in Democratic Government. *Public Administration Review* 1: 335.

Fischer-Lescano, Andreas. 2005. *Globalverfassung.* Weilerswist: Velbrück Wissenschaft.

Fish, Stanley. 1995. The Law Wishes to Have a Formal Existence. In *There's No Such Thing as Free Speech: And It's a Good Thing, Too*, 141. Oxford: Oxford University Press.

Foley, Michael. 1989. *The Silence of the Constitutions*. London: Routledge.

Fraenkel, Ernst. 1976. *Das amerikanische Regierungssystem*. 3rd Edition. Opladen: Westdeutscher Verlag.

Franck, Thomas. 1990. *The Power of Legitimacy among Nations*. New York/Oxford: Oxford University Press.

Frankenberg, Günter. 1985. Critical Comparisons: Re-thinking Comparative Law. *Harvard Law Review* 26: 411.

Frowein, Jochen A. 1976. Der Beitrag der internationalen Organisationen zur Entwicklung des Völkerrechts. *Zeitschrift für ausländisches öffentliches Recht und Völkerrecht* 36: 147.

——. 2000. Konstitutionalisierung des Völkerrechts. *Berichte der Deutschen Gesellschaft für Völkerrecht* 39: 427.

Gaer, Felice D. 2007. A Voice Not an Echo: Universal Periodic Review and the UN Treaty Body System. *Human Rights Law Review* 7: 109.

Gauchet, Marcel. 1995. *Révolution des pouvoirs*. Paris: Gallimard.

Gaudemet, Yves and Olivier Gohin. 2004. *La République décentralisée*. Paris: LGDJ.

Gee, Graham, and Grégoire C. N. Webber. 2010. What is a Political Constitution? *Oxford Journal of Legal Studies* 30: 273.

Glénard, Guillaume. 2004. La doctrine publiciste française et la faculté d'empêcher. *Revue d'histoire des facultés de droit et de la science juridique* 24: 99.

Goldmann, Matthias. 2008. The Accountability of Private vs. Public Governance by Information. A Comparison of the Assessment Activities of the OECD and the IEA in the Field of Education (2008). *Rivista trimestrale di diritto pubblico* 58: 43.

Goldsmith, Jack L. and Eric A. Posner. 2005. *The Limits of International Law*. Oxford: Oxford University Press.

Goldsworthy, Jeffrey (ed.). 2006. *Interpreting Constitutions*. Oxford: Oxford University Press.

Gough, John W. 1955. *Fundamental Law in English Constitutional History*. Oxford: Clarendon Press.

Grabenwarter, Christoph. 2004. Schutz der Privatsphäre versus Pressefreiheit: Europäische Korrektur eines deutschen Sonderweges? *Archiv für Presserecht* 4: 309.

Graf von Kielmannsegg, Peter. 1971. Legitimität als analytische Kategorie. *Politische Vierteljahresschrift* 12: 393.

Greber, Anton R. 2000. *Die vorpositiven Grundlagen des Bundesstaates*. Basel: Helbing & Lichtenhahn.

Grimm, Dieter. 1991. Die Gegenwartsprobleme der Verfassungspolitik und der Beitrag der Politikwissenschaft. In *Die Zukunft der Verfassung*, 352. Frankfurt am Main: Suhrkamp.

——. 1995. Does Europe need a Constitution? *European Law Journal* 1: 282.

Bibliography ∽ 241

——. 2000. Constitutional Adjudication and Democracy, 108–109. In *Judicial Review in International Perspective*, Mads Andenas, (ed.). 103. Den Haag: Kluwer.

——. 2002. Die Politische Parteien. In *Die Zukunft der Verfassung*. 3rd Edition, 265. Frankfurt am Main: Suhrkamp.

——. 2005. The protective function of the state. In *European and US Constitutionalism*, Georg Nolteed (ed.), 137. Cambridge: Cambridge University Press.

Guéhenno, Jean-Marie. 1995. *The End of the Nation-State*. Minneapolis: University of Minnesota Press.

Günther, Klaus. 1992. *Der Sinn für Angemessenheit*. Frankfurt am Main: Suhrkamp.

Gutmann, Amy and Dennis Thompson. 2002. *Deliberative democracy beyond process*. *Journal of Political Philosophy* 10/2: 153.

Rasmussen, Hjalte. 1986. *On Law and Policy in the European Court of Justice*. Dordrecht: Nijhoff.

Habermas, Jürgen. 1983. Wahrheitstheorien. In *Vorstudien und Ergänzungen zur Theorie des kommunikativen Handelns*, 127. Frankfurt am Main: Suhrkamp.

——. 1996. *Between Facts and Norms*. Cambridge: MIT Press.

——. 1998. On the internal relation between the rule of law and democracy. In *The Inclusion of the Other*, 253. Cambridge: MIT Press.

——. 2003. Rightness versus truth: On the sense of normative validity in moral judgments and norms. In *Truth and justification*, 237. Cambridge: MIT Press.

——. 2004. Hat die Konstitutionalisierung des Völkerrechts noch eine Chance?. In *Der gespaltene Westen*, 113. Frankfurt am Main: Suhrkamp.

——. 2004. *Wahrheit und Rechtfertigung*. Frankfurt am Main: Suhrkamp.

——. 2005. Eine politische Verfassung für die pluralistische Weltgesellschaft?. In *Zwischen Naturalismus und Religion*, 324. Frankfurt am Main: Suhrkamp.

——. 2008. *Between Naturalism and Religion*. Cambridge: Polity Press.

Häge, Frank Michael. 2012. *Bureaucrats as law-makers*. London: Routledge (forthcoming).

Halberstam, Daniel. 2012. Systems Pluralism and Institutional Pluralism in Constitutional Law: National, Supranational, and Global Governance. In *Constitutional Pluralism in the European Union and Beyond*, Avbelj, Matej/Komárek, Jan (eds.).

——. 2001. Comparative Federalism and the Issue of Commandeering. In *The Federal Vision*, Nicolaidis, Kalypso/Howse, Robert (eds.), 213. Oxford: Oxford University Press.

Halberstam, Daniel and Eric Stein. 2009. The United Nations, the European Union, and the King of Sweden: Economic Sanctions and Individual Rights in a Plural World Order. *Common Market Law Review* 46: 13.

Halbig, Christoph 2006. Varieties of Nature in Hegel and McDowell. *European Journal of Philosophy* 14: 222.

Halfmann, Ralf. 2000. *Entwicklungen des deutschen Staatsorganisationsrechts im Kraftfeld der europäischen Integration*. Berlin: Duncker & Humblot.

Hansen, Mogens H. 1983. *Initiative und Entscheidung: Überlegungen über die Gewaltenteilung im Athen des 4. Jahrhunderts.* Konstanz: Universitätsverlag.

Haratsch, Andreas. 2006. Die Solange-Rechtsprechung des EGMR. *Zeitschrift für ausländisches öffentliches Recht und Völkerrecht* 66: 927.

Hart, Herbert L.A. and Tony Honoré. 1985. *Causation in the Law.* 2nd Edition. Oxford: Clarendon.

Hart, Herbert L. A. 1994. *The Concept of Law.* 2nd Edition. Oxford: Oxford University Press.

Hathaway, Oona A. 2002. Do Human Rights Treaties Make a Difference? *Yale Law Journal* III: 1935.

Hayes-Renshaw, Fiona and Helen Wallace. 1997. *The Council of Ministers.* Basingstoke, Hampshire: MacMillan.

Hegel, Georg W. F. [1820] 2010. *Elements of the Philosophy of Right.* 14th reprint. Trans. Hugh B. Nisbet. Cambridge: Cambridge University Press.

——. [1821] 2006. Grundlinien der Philosophie des Rechts. In *Werke,* Wilhelm Weischedel, (ed.). Frankfurt am Main: Suhrkamp.

Held, David. 1987. *Models of Democracy.* Oxford: Polity Press.

Helfer, Laurence. H. and Anne-Marie Slaughter. 1997. Toward a Theory of Effective Supranational Adjudication. *Yale Law Journal* 107: 273.

Hershovitz, Scott. 2002. Wittgenstein on Rules: The Phantom Menace. *Oxford Journal of Legal Studies* 22: 619.

Hesse, Konrad. 1995. *Grundzüge des Verfassungsrechts.* 20th Edition. Heidelberg: C. F. Müller.

Heun, Werner. 1992. *Funktionell-rechtliche Schranken der Verfassungsgerichtsbarkeit.* Baden-Baden: Nomos.

——. 2002. Verfassungsrecht und einfaches Recht—Verfassungsgerichtbarkeit und Fachgerichtsbarkeit. *Veröffentlichung der Vereinigung der Deutschen Staatsrechtslehrer* 61: 80.

——. 2006. Freiheit und Gleichheit. In *Handbuch der Grundrechte.* Volume II/1., Merten, Detlef/Papier, Hans-Jürgen (eds.), § 34. Heidelberg: Müller.

——. 2006. Rechtliche Wirkungen verfassungsgerichtlicher Entscheidungen. In *Fortschritte der Verfassungsgerichtsbarkeit II,* Christian Starck (ed.), 173. Baden-Baden: Nomos.

Heuschling, Luc. 2002. *Etat de droit, Rechtsstaat, Rule of Law.* Paris: Dalloz.

Heußner, Kristina. 2007. *Informationssysteme im Europäischen Verwaltungsverbund.* Tübingen: Mohr Siebeck.

Hillgruber, Christian. 1993. Grenzen der Rechtsfortbildung durch den EuGH—Hat Europarecht Methode?. In *Auf dem Wege zu einer europäischen Staatlichkeit,* Thomas von Danwitz et al. (eds.), 31. Stuttgart: Boorberg.

Hirschman, Albert O. 1970. *Exit, Voice, and Loyalty.* Cambridge, Mass.: Harvard University Press.

Hirshl, Ran. 2004. *Towards Juristocracy. The Origins and Consequences of the New Constitutionalism*, Introduction. Cambridge, Mass.: Harvard University Press.

——. 2006. On the blurred methodological matrix in comparative constitutional law. In *The Migration of Constitutional Ideas*, Choudry, Sujit (ed.), 39. Cambridge, Cambridge University Press.

Hoebeke, Christopher. H. 1995. *The Road to Mass Democracy*. New Brunswick: Transaction Publishers.

Hofmann, Hasso. 1987. Das Postulat der Allgemeinheit des Gesetzes. In *Die Allgemeinheit des Gesetzes*, Starck, Christian (ed.), 9. Göttingen: Vandenhoeck & Ruprecht.

——. 1998. *Das Recht des Rechts, das Recht der Herrschaft und die Einheit der Verfassung*. Berlin: Duncker & Humblot.

Hofmann, Herwig, Gerard C. Rowe, and Alexander H. Turk. 2011. *Administrative law and policy of the European Union*. Oxford: Oxford University Press.

Hofmann, Herwig. 2009. Legislation, delegation and implementation under the Treaty of Lisbon. *European Law Lournal* 15: 482.

Hofmann, Jens. 2004. *Rechtschutz und Haftung im europäischen Verwaltungsverbund*. Berlin: Duncker & Humblot.

Hohfeld, Wesley N. 1913. Some fundamental legal conceptions as applied in judicial reasoning. *Yale Law Journal* 23: 16.

Holmes, Oliver W. 1897. The Path of the Law. *Harvard Law Review* 10: 457.

——. [1913, 1920] 1990. Law and the Court. In *Collected Legal Papers*. Gloucester, Mass. : Peter Smith Publisher Inc.

Holmes, S. 'Precommitment and the Paradox of Democracy', in: Passions and Constraints (Chicago: The University of Chicago Press: 1995), 134–77.

Höreth, Marcus. 1999. *Europäische Union im Legitimationstrilemma*. Baden-Baden: Nomos.

Hudec, Robert E. 1999. The GATT Legal System: A Diplomat´s Jurisprudence (1970). In *Essays on the nature of International Trade Law*, 17. London: Cameron May.

Hug, Simon and George Tsebelis. 2002. Veto Players and Referendums Around the World. *Journal of Theoretical Politics* 14: 465.

Hug, Simon. 2009. Some thoughts about referendums, representative democracy, and separation of powers. *Constitutional Political Economy* 20: 251.

Hume, David. [1741] 1994. On the First of Principles of Government. In *Hume. Political Essays*, Haakonssen, Knud (ed.) 16. Cambridge: Cambridge University Press.

——. [1739–40] 1978. *A Treatise of Human Nature*. Oxford: Oxford University Press.

Hurd, Ian. 2007. *After Anarchy. Legitimacy and Power in the United Nations Security Council*. Princeton: Princeton University Press.

Husserl, Gerhart. 1955. *Recht und Zeit*. Frankfurt am Main: Klostermann.

Ignatieff, Michael. 1999. *Human Rights as Politics and as Idolatry*. Princeton: Princeton University Press.

von Ihering, Rudolf. [1877] 1905. *Der Zweck im Recht*. Volume 1. Leipzig: Breitkopf & Härtel.

Irons, Peter H. 1982. *The New Deal Lawyers*. Princeton: Princeton University Press.

Jackson, John. H. and Patricia Grane. 2001. The Saga Continues: An Update of the Banana Dispute. *Journal of International Economic Law* 4: 581.

Jackson, Vicki C. and Mark Tushnet. 2006. *Comparative Constitutional Law*. 2nd Edition. New York: Foundation Press.

Jackson, Vicki C. 2009. *Constitutional Engagement in a Transnational Era*. Oxford: Oxford University Press.

Jaffe, Louis L. 1937. Law Making by Private Groups. *Harvard Law Review*. 51: 201.

Jäger, Wolfgang. 1978. Opposition. In *Geschichtliche Grundbegriffe*. Volume 4, Brunner, Otto/Conze, Werner/Koselleck, Reinhard (eds.), 469. Stuttgart: Klett-Cotta.

Jarass, Hans Dieter. 1975. *Politik und Bürokratie als Elemente der Gewaltenteilung*. München: Beck.

Jaume, Lucien. 2000. Le gaullisme et la crise de l'Etat. *Modern and Contemporary France* 8: 7.

Jesch, Dietrich. 1968. *Gesetz und Verwaltung*. 2nd Edition. Tübingen: Mohr Siebeck.

Jestaedt, Matthias, Oliver Lepsius, Christoph Möllers, and Christoph Schönberger. 2011. *Das entgrenzte Gericht*. Frankfurt am Main: Suhrkamp.

Joerges, Christian, Yves Mény, and J. H. H. Weiler. 2001. *Mountain or Molehill? A Critical Appraisal of the Commission White Paper on Governance*. New York: NYU School of Law.

Joerges, Christian and Florian Rödl. 2009. Informal politics, formalised law and the 'social deficit' of European integration. Reflections after the judgments of the ECJ in Viking and Laval. *European Law Journal* 15: 1.

Kagan, Elena. 2001. Presidential Administration. *Harvard Law Review* 114: 2245.

Kahn, Paul W. 2000. Speaking Law to Power: Popular Sovereignty, Human Rights, and the New International Order. *Chicago Journal of International Law* 1: 1.

Kant, Immanuel. [1788] 1983. Kritik der praktischen Vernunft. In *Werke*, ed. Wilhelm Weischedel. Darmstadt: Wissenschaftliche Buchgesellschaft.

———. [1790] 1983. Kritik der Urteilskraft, In *Werke*, ed. Wilhelm Weischedel. Darmstadt: Wissenschaftliche Buchgesellschaft.

———. [1797] 1983. Metaphysik der Sitten, In *Werke*, ed. Wilhelm Weischedel. Darmstadt: Wissenschaftliche Buchgesellschaft.

———. [1793] 1983. Über den Gemeinspruch: Das mag in der Theorie richtig sein, taugt aber nicht für die Praxis. In *Werke*, ed. Weischedel. Darmstadt: Wissenschaftliche Buchgesellschaft.

Kany, Roland. 2007. *Augustins Trinitätsdenken*. Tübingen: Mohr Siebeck.

Kaiser, Frederick, Walter Oleszek, and Todd Tatelmann. 2011. Congressional Research Service. *Congressional Oversight Manual*, Document RL 30240.

Kaufmann, Marcel. 1997. *Europäische Integration und Demokratieprinzip*. Baden-Baden: Nomos.

Kelman, Mark. 1987. *A Guide to Critical Legal Studies*. Cambridge, Mass.: Harvard University Press.

Kelsen, Hans. 1925. *Allgemeine Staatslehre*. Berlin: Springer.

———. 1928. Wesen und Entwicklung der Staatsgerichtsbarkeit. *Veröffentlichungen der Vereinigung der Deutschen Staatsrechtslehrer* 5: 30.

———. 1929. *Vom Wesen und Wert der Demokratie*. 2nd Edition. Tübingen: Mohr Siebeck.

Kersting, Wolfgang. 2004. *Kant über Recht*. Paderborn: Mentis.

Khosla, Madhav. 2010. Making social rights conditional: Lessons from India. *International Journal of Constitutional Law* 8: 739.

Kiiver, Philipp. 2006. *National Parliaments in the European Union: A Critical View on EU Constitution-building*. The Hague: Kluwer Law International.

Killinger, Stefanie. 2003. *The World Bank's non-political mandate*. Köln: Heymann.

Kingsbury, Benedict, Nico Krisch, Richard B Stewart, and Jonathan B. Wiener (eds.). 2005. Symposium on The Emergence of Global Administrative Law. *Law & Contemporary Problems* 68: 3–4.

Kirchhof, Paul. 1997. Demokratischer Rechtsstaat—Staatsform der Zugehörigen. In *Handbuch des Staatsrechts*. Volume 9, Isensee, Josef/Kirchhof, Paul (eds.). Heidelberg: C. F. Müller.

Kirsch, Martin. 1999. *Monarch und Parlament im 19. Jahrhundert*. Göttingen: Vandenhoeck & Ruprecht.

Klabbers, Jan. 2009. *An Introduction to International Institutional Law*. 2nd Edition. Cambridge: Cambridge University Press.

Klatt, Matthias. 2008. *Making the Law Explicit*. Oxford: Hart.

Kloepfer, Michael. 1984. Der Vorbehalt des Gesetzes im Wandel. *Juristenzeitung* 1984: 685.

Klöti, Ulrich. 2001. Consensual Government in a Heterogeneous Polity. In *The Swiss Labyrinth*, Lane Jan-Erik (ed.). London: Frank Cass.

Knoll, Gabriele. 2002. *Grundzüge eines europäischen Standards für den einstweiligen Rechtsschutz gegen Verwaltungsakte*. Berlin: Duncker & Humblot.

Koh, Harold H. 1992. The Fast Track and United States Trade Policy. *Brooklyn Journal of International Law* 18: 143.

———. 2002. The case against military commissions. *American Journal of International Law* 96/2: 337.

Komesar, Neil K. 1994. *Imperfect Alternatives*. Chicago: University of Chicago Press.

———. 2001. *Law's Limits*. Cambridge: Cambridge University Press.

Kommers, Donald P. 1979. The Jurisprudence of Free Speech in the United States and the Federal Republic of Germany. *Southern California Law Review* 53: 657.

Korn, Jessica. 1996. *The Power of Separation*. Princeton: Princeton University Press.

Koskenniemi, Martti. 2002. *The Gentle Civilizer of Nations*. Cambridge: Cambridge University Press.

———. 2007. Formalism, Fragmentation, Freedom: Kantian Themes in Today's International Law. *No Foundations: Journal of Extreme Legal Positivism* 4: 7.

———. 2007. The Fate of Public International Law. *The Modern Law Review* 70: 1.

Kramer, Larry D. 2001. Foreword: We the Court. *Harvard Law Review* 115: 5.

———. 2004. *The People Themselves*. Oxford: Oxford University Press.

Krisch, Nico. 2004. Amerikanische Hegemonie und liberale Revolution im Völkerrecht. *Der Staat* 43: 267.

———. 2005. International Law in Times of Hegemony. *European Journal of International Law* 16: 369.

———. 2011. *Beyond Constitutionalism*. Oxford: Oxford University Press.

Krynen, Jacques. 2011. *L'emprise contemporaine des juges*. Paris: Gallimard.

Krzeminska-Vamvaka, Joanna. 2009. Horizontal effect of fundamental rights and freedoms much ado about nothing? German, Polish and EU theories compared after Viking Line. *Jean Monnet working paper* 2009: 11. New York, NY: NYU School of Law.

Kübler, Friedrich. 2005. Demokratische Justiz?. In *Festschrift Simon*, Kiesow, Rainer Maria / Ogorek, Regina / Simitis, Spiros (eds.). Frankfurt am Main: Vittorio Klostermann.

Laclau, Ernesto. 2005. *On Populist Reason*. London / New York: Verso.

Lacy, Dean and Emerson M.S. Niou. 2000. A Problem with Referendums. *Journal of Theoretical Politics* 12: 5.

Lafont, Cristina. 2006. Is the ideal of a deliberative democracy coherent? In *Deliberative Democracy and its discontents*, Besson, Samantha / Marti, Jose Luis (eds.), 3. Aldershot: Ashgate.

Landis, James M. 1938. *The Administrative Process*. New Haven: Yale University Press.

Lastra, Rosa. M. and Geoffrey P. Miller. 2001. Central Bank Independence in Ordinary and Extraordinary Times. In *Central Bank Independence*, Kleinemann, Jan (ed.), 31. The Hague: Kluwer Law International.

———. 2003. The Governance Structure for Financial Regulation and Supervision in Europe. *Columbia Journal of Transnational Law* 10: 49.

Latour, Bruno. 1999. *Politiques de la Nature*. Paris: La Découverte.

———. 2002. *La Fabrique du Droit*. Paris: La Découverte.

Leggewie, Claus. 2003. *Die Globalisierung und ihre Gegner*. München: Beck.

Lehmbruch, Gerhard. 1976. *Proporzdemokratie*. Tübingen: Mohr Siebeck.

Lehoucq, Fabrice. 2005. Constitutional Design and Democratic Performance in Latin America, *Verfassung und Recht in Übersee* 38: 370.

Leiter, Brian. 2007. *Naturalizing Jurisprudence*. Oxford: Oxford University Press.

Lenaerts, Koen. 1991. Some Reflections on Separation of Powers in the European Community. *Common Market Law Review* 28: 11.

———. 2010. Federalism and the rule of law. *Fordham International Law Journal* 33: 1338.

Lenaerts, Koen and Amaryllis Verhoeven. 2000. Towards a legal framework for executive rulemaking in the EU? The contribution of the new comitology decision. *Common Market Law Review* 37: 645.

———. 2002. Institutional Balance and Democracy. In *Good Governance in Europe's Integrated Market*, Joerges, Christian/Dehousse, Richard (eds.), 42. Oxford: Oxford University Press.

Lenaerts, Koen and Piet van Nuffel. 2005. *Constitutional Law of the EU*. 2nd Edition. London: Thomson, Sweet & Maxwell.

Lentsch, Justus and Peter Weingart (eds.). 2011. *The Politics of Scientific Advice: Institutional Design for Quality Assurance*. Cambridge: Cambridge University Press.

Lepsius, Oliver. 1997. *Verwaltungsrecht unter dem Common Law*. Tübingen: Mohr Siebeck.

———. 2007. Standardsetzung und Legitimation. In *Internationales Verwaltungsrecht*, Möllers, Christoph/Voßkuhle, Andreas/Walter, Christian (eds.), 345. Tübingen: Mohr Siebeck.

Lessig, Lawrence and Cass R. Sunstein. 1994. The President and the Administration. *Columbia Law Review* 94: 1.

Lessig, Lawrence. 1998. The New Chicago School. *Journal of Legal Studies* 27: 66.

Letsas, George. 2006. Two Concepts of the Margin of Appreciation. *Oxford Journal of Legal Studies* 26: 705.

Levin, Remy Z. and Paul Chen. 2012. Rethinking the Constitution-treaty relationship. *International Journal of Constitutional Law* 10: 242.

Levinson, Daryl and Richard Pildes. 2006. Separation of Parties not Powers. *Harvard Law Review* 119: 2311.

Ley, Isabelle. 2007. Legal Protection against the UN-Security Council between European and International Law: A Kafkaesque Situation? Report on the Fall Conference of the Graduate Program. *German Law Journal* 8: 279.

———. 2012. *Opposition im Völkerrecht*. Manuscript 2012.

Lieber, Tobias. 2007. *Diskursive Vernunft und formelle Gleichheit*. Tübingen: Mohr Siebeck.

Lijphart, Arend. 1984. *Democracies: patterns of majoritarian and consensus government in twenty-one countries*. New Haven: Yale University Press.

Lindseth, Peter L. 2010. *Power and legitimacy*. Oxford: Oxford University Press.

Linz, Juan J. and Arturo Valenzuela. 1994. *The Failure of Presidential Democracy*. Baltimore: Johns Hopkins University Press.

Llewellyn, Karl. 1942. American Common Law Tradition, and American Democracy. *Journal of Law and Political Sociology* 1: 14.

Lock, Tobias. 2011. Walking on a tightrope—the draft ECHR accession agreement and the autonomy of the EU legal order. *Common Market Law Review* 48: 1025.

Locke, John. 1698. *Two Treatises of Government*. London: Black Swan.

Loewenstein, Karl. 1957. *Political Power and the Governmental Process*. Chicago: University of Chicago Press.

Lombard, Martine. 2010. Warum bedient man sich im Bereich der Wirtschaft unabhängiger Behörden? In *Unabhängige Regulierungsbehörden*, Masing, Johannes / Marcou, Gerard (eds.), 143. Tübingen: Mohr Siebeck.

Loughlin, Martin. 1992. *Public Law and Political Theory*. Oxford: Clarendon Press.

———. 2003. *The Idea of Public Law*. Oxford: Oxford University Press.

Lowi, Theodore J. 1979. *The End of Liberalism*. 2nd Edition. New York: Norton

Luck, Edward. C. 2005. How not to reform the United Nations. *Global Governance* 11: 407.

Luhmann, Niklas. 1975. *Legitimität durch Verfahren*. Darmstadt: Luchterhand.

———. 2000. *Organisation und Entscheidung*. Opladen: Westdeutsche Verlag.

Lutz-Bachmann, Matthias. 2003. The Sovereignty Principle and Global Democracy. In *Rethinking the State in the Age of Globalization*, Justenhoven, Heinz-Gerhard / Turner, James (eds.), 217. Münster: LIT Verlag.

MacDowell, John. 1994. *Mind and World*. Cambridge, Mass.: Harvard University Press.

Maduro, Miguel P. 1999. *We the Court*. Oxford: Hart.

Magill, Elizabeth M. 2000. The Real Separation in Separation of Powers Law. *Virginia Law Review* 86: 1127.

Maitland, Frederic W. [1908] 1961. *The Constitutional History of England*. Cambridge: Cambridge University Press.

Majone, Giandomenico. 1993. The European Union between Social Policy and Social Regulation. *Journal of Common Market Studies* 31: 153.

———. 1996. *Regulating Europe*. London: Routledge.

Malleson, Kate and Peter H. Russell. 2006. *Appointing Judges in an Age of Judicial Power*. Toronto: University of Toronto Press.

Manin, Bernard. 1994. Checks, balances and boundaries: The separation of powers in the constitutional debate of 1787. In *The Invention of the Modern Republic*, Fontana, Biancamaria (ed.), 27. Cambridge: Cambridge University Press.

Manin, Bernard. 1995. *Principes Du Gouvernement Représentatif*. Paris: Flammarion.

March, James G. and Johan P. Olsen. 1995. *Democratic Governance*. New York: Free Press.

Martínez, Hinojosa L.M. 2008. The legislative role of the Security Council in its fight against terrorism: Legal, political and practical limits. *International and Comparative Law Quarterly* 57: 333.

Masing, Johannes. 1997. *Die Mobilisierung des Bürgers für die Durchsetzung des Rechts.* Berlin: Duncker & Humblot.

Masterman, Roger. 2011. *The Separation of Powers in the Contemporary Constitution. Judicial Competence and Independence in the United Kingdom.* Cambridge: Cambridge University Press, 2011.

Maulin, Éric. 2003. *La théorie de l'état de Carré de Malberg.* Paris: Presses Universitaires de France.

Maurer, Hartmut. 2004. Das föderative Verfassungsorgan im europäischen Vergleich, *Verfassung im Diskurs der Welt. Festschrift für Peter Häberle.* Tübingen: Mohr Siebeck.

———. 2007. *Staatsrecht I.* 5th Edition. München: Beck.

Maus, Ingeborg. 1986. Entwicklung und Funktionswandel der Theorie des Bürgerlichen Rechtsstaats. In *Rechtstheorie und politische Theorie im Industriekapitalismus,* Maus, Ingeborg (ed.), 11. München: Fink.

———. 1992. *Zur Aufklärung der Demokratietheorie.* Frankfurt am Main: Suhrkamp.

Mavroidis, Petros C. 2002. Amicus Curiae Briefs Before The WTO. In *European integration and international co-ordination,* von Bogdandy, Arnim (ed.), 317. Den Haag: Kluwer.

Mayer, Franz C. 2002. Nationale Regierungsstrukturen und europäische Integration. *Europäische Grundrechte-Zeitschrift* 2002, 111.

McCormick, Neil and Robert Summers (eds.). 1991. *Interpreting Statutes.* Aldershot: Dartmouth.

Meder, Stephan. 1999. *Urteilen.* Frankfurt am Main: Klostermann.

Merkl, Adolf. 1923. *Die Lehre von der Rechtskraft entwickelt aus dem Rechtsbegriff.* Leipzig: Deuticke.

———. 1927. *Allgemeines Verwaltungsrecht.* Wien: Springer.

Meyer, John W. 2000. *Die Politik der Gesellschaft.* Frankfurt am Main: Suhrkamp.

Michelman, Frank I. 2005. The protective function of the state in the United States and Europe: the constitutional question. In *European and US Constitutionalism,* Nolte, Georg (ed.), 156. Cambridge: Cambridge University Press.

Millgram, Elijah. 1995. Was Hume a Humean?. In *Hume Studies* 21: 75.

Möllers, Christoph and Andreas Voßkuhle and Christian Walter (eds.). 2007. *Internationales Verwaltungsrecht. Eine Analyse anhand von Referenzgebieten.* Tübingen: Mohr Siebeck.

Möllers, Christoph and Jelena von Achenbach. 2011. Die Mitwirkung des Europäischen Parlaments an der abgeleiteten Rechtsetzung der Europäischen Kommission nach dem Lissabonner Vertrag. *Europarecht* 46: 1.

Möllers, Christoph. 1997. Der parlamentarische Bundesstaat. In *Föderalismus,* Aulehner, Josef (ed.), 81. Stuttgart: Boorberg.

———. 2000. *Staat als Argument.* München: Beck.

——. 2001. Globalisierte Jurisprudenz. *Archiv für Rechts- und Sozialphilosophie/Beiheft* 79: 41.

——. 2005. *Gewaltengliederung.* Tübingen: Mohr Siebeck.

——. 2005. Transnationale Behördenkooperation. *Zeitschrift für ausländisches öffentliches Recht und Völkerrecht* 65: 351.

——. 2006. European Governance—Meaning and Value of a Concept. *Common Market Law Review* 43: 314.

——. 2007. Globalisierte Verwaltungen zwischen Verselbständigung und Übervernetzung. In *Weltrecht*, Schulte, Martin/Stichweh, Rudolf (eds.). Berlin: Duncker & Humblot.

——. 2007. Expressive versus repräsentative Demokratie. In *Internationale Verrechtlichung und Demokratie*, ed. Regina Kreide. Frankfurt am Main: Campus.

——. 2007. Willensfreiheit durch Verfassungsrecht. In *Willensfreiheit und rechtliche Ordnung*, ed. Ernst-Joachim Lampe and Michael Pauen. Frankfurt a.M.: Suhrkamp.

——. 2010. Pouvoir constituant—Constitution—Constitutionalisation. In *Principles of European Constitutional Law.* 2nd revised Edition, von Bogdandy, Arnim/Bast, Jürgen (eds.), 169. London: Hart.

——. 2011. Multi-Level Democracy. *Ratio Juris* 24: 247.

——. 2012. Les Gardiennes d'une séparation: Les constitutions comme instruments de protection des différences entre le droit et la politique. *Ius Politicum* (forthcoming).

——. 2012. Politik und Verwaltung. In *Ius Publicum Europaeum*, von Bogdandy, Arnim/Cassese, Sabino/Huber, Peter M. (eds.), § 94. Heidelberg: C. F. Müller.

——. 2012. *Why there is no Governing with Judges.* Manuscript 2012.

Moloney, Niamh. 2010. EU financial market regulation after the global financial crisis. *Common Market Law Review* 47: 1317.

Montesquieu. [1748] 1777. *The Spirit of Laws.* Complete Works. Volume 1. London: T. Evans.

Moore, Michael S. 2009. *Causation and Responsibility.* Oxford: Oxford University Press.

Mouffe, Chantal. 2000. *The Democratic Paradox.* London, New York: Verso.

——. 2002. For an Agonistic Public Sphere. In *Democracy Unrealized*, ed. Enwezor, Okwui (2002), 87. Ostfildern: Hatje Cantz Verlag.

Moyn, Samuel. 2010. *The Last Utopia—Human Rights in History.* Cambridge/Massachusetts/London: The Belknap Press of Harvard University Press.

Von Münch, Ingo. 1998. Minister und Abgeordneter in einer Person: die andauernde Verhöhnung der Gewaltenteilung. *Neue Juristische Wochenschrift* 1/2: 34.

Neuborne, Burt. 2003. The Supreme Court of India. *International Journal of Constitutional Law* 1: 476.

Neurath, Otto. 1922/23. Protokollsätze. *Erkenntnis* 3: 204.

Neves, Marcelo. 1992. *Verfassung und Positivität des Rechts in der peripheren Moderne.* Berlin: Duncker & Humblot.

——. 2000. *Zwischen Themis und Leviathan: Eine schwierige Beziehung.* Baden-Baden: Nomos.

Nipperdey, Thomas. 1995. *Deutsche Geschichte 1866–1918.* Volume 2. München: Beck.

Nozick, Robert. 1974. *Anarchy, State, and Utopia.* New York: Basic Books.

Nurmi, Hannu. 1998. Voting Paradoxes and Referenda. *Social Choice and Welfare* 15: 333.

O'Meara, Noreen. 2011. 'A More Secure Europe of Rights?' The European Court of Human Rights, the Court of Justice of the European Union and EU Accession to the ECHR. *German Law Journal* 12: 1813.

Oeter, Stefan. 1998. *Integration und Subsidiarität im deutschen Bundesstaatsrecht.* Tübingen: Mohr Siebeck.

Ogorek, Regina. 1991. *Richterkönig oder Subsumtionsautomat.* Frankfurt am Main: Klostermann.

Olsen, Johan P. 2006. Maybe it is Time to Rediscover Bureaucracy. *Journal of Public Administration Research and Theory* 16: 1.

Orford, Anne 2003. *Reading Humanitarian Intervention.* Cambridge: Cambridge University Press.

——. 2011. *International Authority and the Responsibility to Protect.* Cambridge: Cambridge University Press.

Ost, François. 1999. *Le Temps du Droit.* Paris: Éditions Odile Jacob.

Ost, François and Michel van der Kerchove. 2002. *De la pyramide au réseau.* Brussels: Facultés universitaires Saint-Louis.

Pacteau, Bernard. 2003. *Le conseil d'Etat et la fondation de la justice administrative française au XIXe siècle.* Paris: Presse Universitaire de France.

Page, Edward. C. 1992. *Political Authority and Bureaucratic Power.* 2nd Edition. New York: Harvester Wheatsheaf.

Pahlow, Louis. 2000. *Justiz und Verwaltung.* Goldbach: Keip.

Pasquino, Pasquale. 1997. Constitutional Adjudication and democracy. *Ratio Juris* 11: 28.

——. 2002. *What is Constitutional Adjudication about?* NYU School of Law Working Paper.

Pauen, Michael. 2001. *Grundprobleme der Philosophie des Geistes.* Frankfurt am Main: Fischer Taschenbuchverlag.

Paulus, Andreas. 2001. *Die internationale Gemeinschaft im Völkerrecht.* München: Beck.

Petersmann, Ernst.-Ulrich. 1991. *Constitutional Functions and Constitutional Problems of International Economic Law.* Fribourg: University Press.

von der Pfordten, Dietmar. 2000. Rechtsethische Rechtfertigung—material oder prozedural? In *Verantwortung zwischen materialer und prozeduraler Zurechnung*, Schulz, Lorenz (ed.), 17. Stuttgart: Steiner.

——. 2004. Normativer Individualismus. *Zeitschrift für philosophische Forschung* 58: 321.

Pierce, Richard. J. Jr. 1992–1993. Lujan v. Defenders of Wildlife: Standing as A Judicially Imposed Limit on Legislative Power. *Duke Law Journal* 42: 1170.

Pippin, Robert B. 2008. *Hegel's Practical Philosophy.* Cambridge: University Press.

Piris, Jean-Claude. 2012. *The Future of Europe. Towards a Two-Speed EU?* Cambridge: Cambridge University Press.

Pitkin, Hanna Fenichel. 1967. *The Concept of Representation.* Berkeley, California: University of California Press.

Plato. 1996. The Euthyphro. In *The Works of Plato*, 5–23. Volume V. Trans. Thomas Taylor and Floyer Sydenham. Westbury: Prometheus Trust.

Pollmann, Hans J. 1969. *Repräsentation und Organschaft.* Berlin: Duncker & Humblot.

Ponthoreau, Marie-Claire. 1999. Pour une réforme de la responsabilité politique du Président de la République française. In *La résponsabilité des gouvernants*, Olivier Beaud et al. (eds.). Paris: Descartes et Cie.

Posner, Eric A., and Adrian Vermeule. 2010. *The Executive Unbound.* Oxford: Oxford University Press.

Posner, Richard. 2003. *Law, Pragmatism, and Democracy.* Cambridge, Mass.: Harvard University Press.

Postema, Gerald J. 1986. *Bentham and the Common law Tradition.* Oxford: Clarendon Press.

Power, Michael. 1999. *The Audit Society.* New York: Oxford University Press.

Prakash, Saikrishna B. 1993. Field Office Federalism. *Virginia Law Review* 79: 1957.

Prempeh, H. Kwasi. 2007. Africa's 'constitutionalism revival': False start or new dawn? *International Journal of Constitutional Law* 5: 469.

Preuß, Ulrich K. 2004. Der politische Charakter der Menschenrechte. *Europäische Grundrechte Zeitschrift* 2004: 611.

Putnam, Hilary. 2002. *The Collapse of the Fact/Value Dichotomy.* Cambridge, Mass.: Harvard University Press.

Quante, Michael. 2011. *Die Wirklichkeit des Geistes.* Berlin: Suhrkamp.

Quine, Willard V. O. 2000. Epistemology Naturalized. In *Epistemology: An Anthology*, Sosa, Ernest/Kim, Jaegwon (eds.), 292. London: Blackwell.

Quirico, Ottavio. 2010. Substantive an procedural issues raised by the accession of the EU to the ECHR. *The Italian yearbook of international law* 20: 31.

Ramelow, Art. 2004. Wille. In *Historisches Wörterbuch der Philosophie*. Volume 12, Ritter, Joachim/Gründer, Karlfried/Gabriel, Gottfried (eds.), 770. Basel: Schwabe.

Raustiala, Kal. 2002. The Architecture of International Cooperation: Transgovernmental Networks and the Future of International Law. *Virginia Journal of International Law* 43: 1.

Rawls, John. 1971. *A Theory of Justice*. Cambridge, Mass.: Harvard University Press.

Raz, Joseph. 1986. *The Morality of Freedom*. Oxford: Clarendon Press.

Reinhardt, Wolfgang. 1999. *Geschichte der Staatsgewalt*. München: Beck.

Reisman, William M. 1999. *Law in Brief Encounters*. New Haven: Yale University Press.

Renner, Moritz. 2011. *Transnationales zwingendes Recht*. Baden-Baden: Nomos.

Riedel, Daniel. 2005. Die europäische Flugsicherheitsagentur. In *Der europäische Verwaltungsverbund*, Eberhard Schmidt-Aßmann et al. (eds.). Tübingen: Mohr Siebeck.

Riker, William H. 1982. *Liberalism Against Populism*. San Francisco: W.H. Freeman.

Riles, Annelise. 2001. *Rethinking the Masters of Comparative Law*. Oxford: Hart.

Roellecke, Ines S. 1999. *Gerechte Einwanderungs- und Staatsangehörigkeitskriterien*. Baden-Baden: Nomos.

Ronsanvallon, Pierre. 2006. *La contre-démocratie*. Paris: Éditions du Seuil.

Rosand, Eric. 2004. The Security Council's Effort to Monitor the Implementation of Al Quaeda/Taliban Sanctions. *American Journal of International Law* 98: 745.

Rosenberg, Gerard N. 1991. *The Hollow Hope*. Chicago: University of Chicago.

Rosenn, Keith. S. 2011. Procedural Protection of Constitutional Rights in Brazil. *The American Journal of Comparative Law* 59: 1009.

Rousseau, Dominique. 2010. *Droit de Contentieux Constitutionnel*. 9th Edition. Paris: Montchrestien.

Rousseau, Jean-Jacques. [1762] 1969. *Contrat Social*. Paris: Gallimard.

——. 1969. Lettres écrites de la Montagne No. 8. In *Œuvres Complètes Tome III*, ed. Marcel Raymond and Bernard Gagnebin, 842. Paris: Gallimard.

Roux, Theunis. 2009. Principle and Pragmatism on the Constitutional Court of South-Africa. In *International Journal of Constitutional Law* 7: 106.

Rusteberg, Benjamin. 2012. *Grundrechtsdogmatik als Schlüssel für das Verhältnis von Individuum und Gemeinschaft*. Talk (forthcoming).

Sadurski, Wojciech. 2008. *Equality and Legitimacy*. Oxford: Oxford University Press.

Salzman, James. 2005. Decentralized Administrative Law in the OECD. *Law & Contemporary Problems* 68:190.

Samuels, David J. and Matthew S. Shugart. 2011. *Presidents, Parties, and Prime Ministers. How the Separation of Powers affects Party Organization and Behaviour*. Cambridge: Cambridge University Press.

Sartori, Giovanni. 1965. *Democratic Theory*. New York: Praeger.

Saurer, Johannes. 2005. *Die Funktionen der Rechtsverordnung*. Berlin: Duncker & Humblot.

Scalia, Antonin. 1983. The Doctrine of Standing as an Essential Element of Separation of Powers. *Suffolk University Law Review* 17: 881.

Scharpf, Fritz. W. 1970. *Die politischen Kosten des Rechtsstaats*. Tübingen: Mohr Siebeck.

———. 1999. *Governing in Europe*. Oxford: Oxford University Press.

Schelling, Thomas. 1960. *The Strategy of Conflict*. Cambridge, Mass.: Harvard University Press.

Schepel, Harm. 2005. *Constitution of Private Governance*. Oxford: Hart.

Scheppele, Kim L. 2006. The migration of anti-constitutional ideas: the post-globalization of public law and the international state of emergency. In *The Migration of Constitutional Ideas*, Choudry, Sujit (ed.). Cambridge: Cambridge University Press.

Schermers, Henry G. 2000. Weighted Voting. In *Encyclopaedia of Public International Law*. Vol. 4, Rudolf Bernhardt (eds.), 1446. Amsterdam: Elsevier.

Schermers, Henry G. and Niels M. Blokker. 1995. *International Institutional Law*. 3rd Edition. The Hague: Nijhoff.

Schmalz-Bruns, Rainer. 1999. Deliberativer Supranationalismus. *Zeitschrift für Internationale Beziehungen* 6: 185.

Schmidt-Aßmann, Eberhard. 1997. Gefährdungen der Rechts- und Gesetzesbindung der Exekutive In *Festschrift Stern*, Burmeister, Joachim (ed.), 745. München: Beck.

———. 2001. *Grundrechtspositionen und Legitimationsfragen im öffentlichen Gesundheitswesen*. Berlin: de Gruyter.

Schmidt-Aßmann, Eberhard and Bettina Schöndorf-Haubold. 2005. *Der europäische Verwaltungsverbund: Formen und Verfahren der Verwaltungszusammenarbeit in der EU*. Tübingen: Mohr-Siebeck.

Schmitt, Carl. 1912. *Gesetz und Urteil*. Berlin: Liebmann.

———. [1923] 1991. *Die geistesgeschichtliche Lage des heutigen Parlamentarismus*. 7th Edition. Berlin: Duncker & Humblot.

———. 1928. *Verfassungslehre*. München: Duncker & Humblot.

———. [1932] 1958. Legalität und Legitimität. In *Verfassungsrechtliche Aufsätze*, 263. Berlin: Duncker & Humblot.

———. 1936. Vergleichender Überblick über die neueste Entwicklung des Problems der gesetzgeberischen Ermächtigungen (Legislative Delegationen). *Zeitschrift für ausländisches öffentliches Recht und Völkerrecht* 6: 252.

———. 1963. *Der Begriff des Politischen*. Berlin: Duncker & Humblot.

Schnapper, Dominique. *Une Sociologue au Conseil Constitutionel*. Paris: Éditions Gallimard, 2010.

Schneewind, Jerome B. 1998. *The Invention of Autonomy*. Cambridge: Cambridge University Press.

Schönberger, Christoph. 2001. Die überholte Parlamentarisierung. Einflußgewinn und fehlende Herrschaftsfähigkeit des Reichstags im sich demokratisierenden Kaiserreich. *Historische Zeitung* 272: 623.

——. 2004. Die Europäische Union als Bund. *Archiv des öffentlichen Rechts* 129: 81.

——. 2005. *Unionsbürger.* Tübingen: Mohr Siebeck.

——. 2012. Höchstrichterliche Rechtsfindung und Auslegung gerichtlicher Entscheidungen. *Veröffentlichungen der Vereinigung der Deutschen Staatsrechtslehrer* 71: 296.

Schorkopf, Frank. 2005. The European Court of Human Rights' Judgment in the Case of Bosphorus Hava Yollari Turizm v. Ireland. *German Law Journal* 6: 1255.

Schubert, Thure. 1999. *Der Gemeinsame Markt als Rechtsbegriff—Die allgemeine Wirtschaftsfreiheit des EG-Vertrages.* München: Beck.

Schulz-Schaeffer, Ingo. 2004. Rechtsdogmatik als Gegenstand der Rechtssoziologie. *Zeitschrift für Rechtssoziologie* 25: 141.

Schwöbel, Christine E. J. 2010. Situating the Debate on Global Constitutionalism. *International Journal of Constitutional Law* 8: 611.

Shapiro, Hal and Lael Brainard. 2003. Trade Promotion Authority formerly known as Fast Track: Building Common Ground on Trade Demands more than a Name Change. *The George Washington International Law Review* 35: 1.

Shapiro, Ian. 2004. *The State of Democratic Theory.* Princeton: Princeton University Press.

Shapiro, Martin M. 1981. *Courts.* Chicago : University of Chicago Press.

Sharp, Malcolm P. 1935. The Classical American Doctrine of 'The Separation of Powers'. *University of Chicago Law Review* 3: 385.

Sharpston, Eleanor and Geert de Baere. 2011. The Court of Justice as a constitutional adjudicator. In *A constitutional order of states?*, Anthony Arnull et al. (eds.), 123. Oxford: Hart.

Shell, Richard. G. 1996. The Trade Stakeholders Model and Participation by Nonstate Parties in WTO. *Universitiy of Pennsylvania Journal of International Economic Law* 17: 359.

Sieyès, Emmanuel J. 1795. *Du jury constitutionnaire.*

——. [1791] 2003. An essay on privileges. In *Political writings*. Indianapolis: Hackett.

Simon, Dieter. 1975. *Die Unabhängigkeit des Richters.* Darmstadt: Wiss. Buchgesellschaft.

Simon, Herbert A. [1947] 1997. *Administrative Behavior.* 4th Edition. New York: The Free Press.

Skach, Cindy. 2005. *Borrowing Constitutional Designs.* Princeton: Princeton University Press

——. 2007. The 'newest' separation of powers: Semipresidentialism. *International Journal of Constitutional Law* 5: 93.

Skinner, Quentin. 2008. *Hobbes and Republican Liberty.* Cambridge: Cambridge University Press.

Skowronek, Stephen. 1982. *Building a new American State.* Cambridge: Cambridge University Press.

Slaughter, Anne-Marie. 2004. *A New World Order*. Princeton: Princeton University Press.

Sloterdijk, Peter and Gesa Mueller von der Hagen. 2005. Instant Democracy: The Pneumatic Parliament. In *Making Things Public: Atmospheres of Democracy*, Latour, Bruno/Weibel, Peter (eds.), 952. Cambridge: MIT Press.

Smend, Rudolph. 1928. Das Recht der freien Meinungsäußerung. *Veröffentlichungen der Vereinigung Deutscher Staatsrechtslehrer* 4: 44.

Smismans, Stijn. 2004. *Law, Legitimacy, and European Governance*. Oxford: Oxford University Press.

Solanke, Iyiola. 2011. Stop the ECJ? An empirical analysis of activism at the Court. *European Law Journal* 17: 764.

Stahlberg, Tim and Henning Lahmann. 2011. Humpty-Dumpty, the War on Terror, and the Power of Preventive Detention in the United States, Israel, and Europe. *The American Journal of Comparative Law* 59: 1051.

Stein, Eric. 2001. International Law and Democracy: No Love at First Sight. *American Journal of International Law* 95: 489.

Steinberg, Rudolf. 1979. *Politik und Verwaltungsorganisation*. Baden-Baden: Nomos.

Stigler, George J. and Gary S. Becker. 1977. De Gustibus Non est Disputandum. *American Economic Review* 67: 76.

Stinchcombe, Arthur L. 2001. *When Formality Works, Authority and Abstraction in Law and Organizations*. Chicago: The University of Chicago Press.

Stoll, Peter-Tobias. 1994. Die WTO: Neue Handelsorganisation, neue Welthandelsordnung, Ergebnisse der Uruguay-Runde des GATT. *Zeitschrift für ausländisches öffentliches Recht und Völkerrecht* 54: 241.

Stolleis, Michael. 1989. Die Entstehung des Interventionsstaats und das öffentliche Recht. *Zeitschrift für neuere Rechtsgeschichte* 11: 129.

——. 1990. Condere leges et interpretari. Gesetzgebungsmacht und Staatsbildung in der frühen Neuzeit. In *Staat und Staatsräson in der frühen Neuzeit*. Frankfurt am Main: Suhrkamp.

——. 2003. Judicial Review, Administrative Review, and Constitutional Review in the Weimar Republic. *Ratio Juris* 16: 266.

Stone, Geoffrey R. 2007. National security v. civil liberties. *California Law Review* 95/6: 2203.

Stone Sweet, Alec. 1992. *The Birth of Judicial Politics in France*. New York: Oxford University Press.

——. 2000. *Governing with Judges. Constitutional Politics in Europe*. Oxford: Oxford University Press.

Stone Sweet, Alec and Helen Keller. 2008. *A Europe of Rights: The Impact of the ECHR on National Legal Systems*. Oxford: Oxford University Press.

Stone Sweet, Alec and Jud Mathews. 2008. Proportionality Balancing and Global Constitutionalism. *Columbia Journal of Transnational Law* 47: 73.

Strauss, David A. 1966. Common Law Constitutional Interpretation. *University of Chicago Law Review* 63: 877.

Strauss, Peter F. 1984. The Place of Agencies in Government: Separation of Powers and the Fourth Branch. *Columbia Law Review* 84: 573.

——. 1987. Formal and Functional Approaches to Separation of Powers Questions—A Foolish Inconsistency? *Cornell Law Review* 72: 488.

Streeck, Wolfgang and Kathleen Thelen. 2005. Introduction: Institutional Change in Advanced Political Economies. In *Beyond Continuity*, Streeck, Wolfgang/Thelen, Kathleen (eds.). Oxford: Oxford University Press.

Stürmer, Michael. 1967. *Koalition und Opposition in der Weimarer Republik 1924–1928*, Droste: Düsseldorf.

Sunstein, Cass R. 1985. Interest Groups in American Public Law. *Stanford Law Review* 38: 29.

——. 1995–1996. On the Expressive Function of Law. *University of Pennsylvania Law Review* 144: 2021.

——. 1997. *Free Markets and Social Justice*. New York: Oxford University Press.

——. 1999. *One Case at a Time*. Cambridge, Mass.: Harvard University Press.

——. 2000. Nondelegation Canons. *The University of Chicago Law Review* 67: 315.

——. 2000. Deliberative Trouble, Why Groups go to Extremes. *Yale Law Journal* 110: 71.

Svarez, Carl G. [1791/1792] 2000. *Die Kronprinzenvorlesungen 1791/1792. Erster Teil: Staatsrecht. Zweiter Teil: Das positive preußische Recht*, Krause, Peter (ed.). Stuttgart-Bad Cannstatt: Fromann-Holzboog.

Talmon, Stefan. 2005. The Security Council as World Legislature. *American Journal of International Law* 99: 175.

Taylor, Charles. 1992. *Sources of the Self*. Cambridge, Mass.: Harvard University Press.

Terry, Laurel. S. 2008. The Bologna Process and Its Impact in Europe: It's So Much More than Degree Changes. *Vanderbilt Journal of Transnational Law* 41: 107.

Teubner, Gunther. 1996. Globale Bukowina, 264. *Rechtshistorisches Journal* 15: 255.

——. 1997. *Global Law without a State*. Aldershot: Dartmouth.

——. 2011. *Constitutional Fragments*. Oxford: Oxford University Press.

Theobald, Christian. 2000. *Zur Ökonomik des Staates*. Baden-Baden: Nomos.

Tomkins, Adam. 2005. The Struggle to Delimit Executive Power in Britain. In *The Executive and Public Law*, 16. Oxford: Oxford University Press.

Tomuschat, Christian. 2001. Clarification Commission in Guatemala. *Human Rights Quarterly* 23: 233.

——. 2006. Internationale Terrorismusbekämpfung als Herausforderung an das Völkerrecht. *Speyerer Vorträge* 85: 7.

——. 2008. *Human Rights*. 2nd Edition. Oxford: Oxford University Press.

Tomuschat, Christian. 2011. Universal Periodic Review: A new system of international law with specific ground rules? In *From Bilateralism to Community Interest—Essays in Honour of Judge Bruno Simma*, Ulrich Fastenrath et al. (eds.), 609. Oxford: Oxford University Press.

Toniolo, Gianni. 1988. *Central Banks' Independence in Historical Perspective*. Berlin: de Gruyter.

Trachtman, Joel P. 1998. Trade and . . . Problems, Cost-Benefit Analysis and Subsidiarity. *European Journal of International Law* 9: 32.

———. 2000. Regulatory Competition and Regulatory Jurisdiction. *Journal of International Economic Law* 3: 331.

Tribe, Laurence H. 2000. *American Constitutional Law*. 3rd Edition. New York: Foundation Press.

Troper, Michel. 1973. *La séparation des pouvoirs*. Paris: Pichon et Durand-Auzias.

———. 1997. Le monopole de la contrainte légitime—Légitimité et légalité dans l' Etat moderne. In *Festschrift für Günther Winkler*, Haller, Herbert (ed.), 1195. Wien, New York: Springer.

———. 2001. Les rélations exterieur dans la constitution de l'an III. In *La Théorie, Le Droit, L'État*, 129 (Paris: P.U.F.)

———. 2003. The Logic of Justification of Judicial Review. *International Constitutional Law* 1: 99.

Trute, Hans-Heinrich. 2002. Regulierung—am Beispiel des Telekommunikationsrechts. In *Der Wandel des Staates vor den Herausforderungen der Gegenwart: Festschrift für Winfried Brohm*, Eberle, Carl-Eugen/Ibler, Martin/Lorenz, Dieter (eds.), 169. München: Beck.

———. 2004. Der europäische Regulierungsverbund in der Telekommunikation. In *Festschrift Selmer*, Lerke Osterloh et al. (eds.), 585. Berlin: Duncker & Humblot.

———. 2006. Die demokratische der Verwaltung. In *Grundlagen des Verwaltungsrechts*, Hoffmann-Riem, Wolfgang/Schmidt-Aßmann, Eberhard/Voßkuhle, Andreas (eds.), § 6. München: Beck.

Tschentscher, Alex. 2001. Indienstnahme der Gerichte für die Effizienz der Verwaltung. In *Funktionen und Kontrolle der Gewalten*, Demel, Michael et al. (eds.), 165. Stuttgart: Boorberg.

———. 2002. Der Konsensbegriff in Vertrags- und Diskurstheorien. *Rechtstheorie* 34: 43.

Tsebelis, George. 2002. *Veto Players: How Political Institutions Work*. Princeton: Princeton University Press.

Tugendhat, Ernst. 1992. Der Begriff der Willensfreiheit. In *Philosophische Aufsätze*, 334. Frankfurt am Main: Suhrkamp.

Tully, James. 1995. *Strange Multiplicity. Constitutionalism in an age of diversity*. Cambridge: Cambridge University Press.

Tuori, Kaarlo. 2009. *Ratio and Voluntas: The Tension between Reason and Will in Law*. Farnham: Ashgate.

Tushnet, M. 1999. *Taking the Constitution Away From The Courts*. Princeton: Princeton University Press.

——. 2008. *Weak Courts, Strong Rights*. Princeton: Princeton University Press.

Urbinati, Nadia. 2006. *Representative Democracy*. Chicago: The University of Chicago Press.

Van Caenegem, Raul. 1987. *Judges, Legislators & Professors*. Cambridge: Cambridge University Press.

Vec, Miloš. 2012. Alle Weltworte streben nach Standardisierung. Vereinheitlichung und Vereinheitlichungskritik in historischer Perspektive. In *Normen, Standards, Werte*, Assmann, Heinz-Dieter/Baasner, Frank/Wertheimer, Jürgen (eds.). Nomos: Baden-Baden.

Vilbert, Frank. 2007. *The Rise of the Unelected*. Cambridge: Cambridge University Press.

Vile, Maurice J. C. 1967. *Constitutionalism and the separation of powers*. Oxford: Clarendon Press.

Vogenauer, Stefan. 2006. Sources of Law and Legal Method in Comparative Law. In *Oxford Handbook of Comparative Law*, Mathias Reimann and Reinhard Zimmermann (eds.), 894. Oxford: Oxford University Press.

Vondung, Julie. 2012. *Die Architektur des europäischen Grundrechtsschutzes nach dem Beitritt der EU zur EMRK*. Tübingen: Mohr Siebeck.

Voßkuhle, Andreas. 2005. Sachverständige Beratung des Staates. In *Handbuch des Staatsrechts*, § 43. Volume 3, 3rd Edition, Isensee, Josef/Kirchhof, Paul (eds.). Heidelberg: C.F. Müller.

Wahl, Rainer. 1981. Der Vorrang der Verfassung. *Der Staat* 20: 485.

——. 2004. Die objektiv-rechtliche Dimension der Grundrechte im internationalen Vergleich. In *Handbuch der Grundrechte*. Volume 1, Merten, Detlef/Papier, Hans-Jürgen (eds.), § 19. Heidelberg: C. F. Müller.

Waldron, Jeremy. 2006. The Core of the Case against Judicial Review. *Yale Law Journal* 115: 1346.

Walen, Alec D. 2011. A unified theory of detention, with application to preventive detention of suspected terrorists. *Maryland Law Journal* 70: 871.

Wallach, Lori. 1999. *The WTO. Five Years of Reasons to Resist Corporate Globalization*. New York, NY: Seven Stories Press.

Walzer, Michael. 1987. *Interpretation and Social Criticism*. Cambridge, Mass.: Harvard University Press.

Weber, Max. [1918] 1988. Regierung und Parlament im neugeordneten Deutschland. In *Gesammelte Politische Schriften*. 5th Edition, Winckelmann, Johannes (ed.), 306. Tübingen: Mohr Siebeck.

——. [1920/21] 1980. *Wirtschaft und Gesellschaft*. 5th Edition. Tübingen: Mohr Siebeck.

Weick, Karl E. 1995. *Sensemaking in Organizations*. Thousand Oaks: Sage.

Weiler, Joseph H. H. 1999. *The Constitution of Europe*. Cambridge: Cambridge University Press.

Weiler, Joseph H. H. 2001. The Rule of Lawyers and the Ethos of Diplomats, 194. *Journal of World Trade* 35: 191.

Weingart, Peter. 2001. *Die Stunde der Wahrheit?* Weilerswist: Velbrück Wissenschaft.

Wilson, Woodrow. 1885. *Congressional Government: A Study in American* Politics. Boston, New York: Houghton Mifflin Co.

Witt, Peter-Christian. 1983. Kontinuität und Diskontinuität im politischen System der Weimarer Republik. In *Regierung, Bürokratie und Parlament in Preußen und Deutschland*, Ritter, Gerhard A. (ed.), 117. Düsseldorf: Droste.

Wittgenstein, Ludwig. 2009. *Philosophische Untersuchungen*. Frankfurt am Main: Suhrkamp.

Wolf, Klaus D. 2000. *Die neue Staatsräson*. Baden-Baden: Nomos.

Wood, Gordon S. 1969. *The Creation of the American Republic 1776–1787*. Chapel Hill: University of North Carolina Press.

Yanovich, Alan and Tania Voon. 2006. Completing the Analysis in WTO Appeals: The Practice and its Limitations. *Journal of International Economic Law* 9: 933.

Ypi, Lea. 2011. Self-Ownership and the State: A Democratic Critique. *Ratio* 24: 91.

———. 2012. *Global Justice and Avant-Garde Political Agency*. Oxford: Oxford University Press.

Zoller, Elisabeth. 1999. *Droit constitutionel*. 2nd Edition. Paris: Presses Universitaires de France.

Zürn, Michael. 2006. Globalizing Interests—An Introduction. In *Globalizing Interests, Pressure Groups and Denationalization*, Zürn, Michael/Walter, Gregor (eds.), 200. Albany: State University of New York Press.

Index

Note: Page numbers in bold represent main discussion of the topic.

262   Index

Germany 32–7, 37–8, 41, 44, 50, 93, 98, 101, 105,
    107, 114, 127, 129, 133–4, 137–8, 141, 174, 191, 231
  Basic Law 5, 34–6, 47, 115
  Basic Rights 35, 37, 105
  Constitution of the Weimar Republic 34
  Federal Constitutional Court 36, 37, 39, 46,
    105, 117, 164, 212
  Federal Council 38, 39
  Freirechtsschule 83
  Parliament 33–5, 38
  Rechtsstaatlichkeit 33–4
  Weimar Republic 34, 36, 112
Globalization 3, 158–9
Government 10, 21, 25–8, 40–5, 53, 62, 96–7, 105,
    110–13, 119, 148, 181, 229
Great Britain 89, 114, 201
  see also England
Guatemala 215

Habermas, Jürgen 58–9, 65
Hamilton, Alexander 18, 30, 31
Hart, H. L. A. 24
Hegel, Georg Wilhelm Friedrich 12–13, 55
Hobbes, Thomas, 3, 22, 51, 63
Holmes, Oliver 131
Human rights 58–9, 210–17, 231
Hume, David 58
Hungary 36, 127

India 73, 117, 146
International Court of Justice 198
International Criminal Court 215–17
International Labour Organisation 219
International Monetary Fund 204
International Organisation of Security
    Commissions 221
Iraq 200
Israel 137
Italy 36, 114, 127, 138

Jefferson, Thomas 27, 30
Judicial Review 21, 26, 36, 77, 82, 98, 110,
    130, 142–8, 160, 163–4, 173–6, 192, 198,
    202–3, 231
Judiciary 89–96, 99, 106–9, 148

Kant, Immanuel 4, 34, 50, 57, 64, 83, 107, 112
Kelsen, Hans 1, 49, 83, 129

Latin America 112
Legislature / legislative 45, 84–9, 94, 97, 99,
    106–9, 148
Legitimacy 4–6, 13, 20, 29, 34, 34, 42, 45, 50, 52,
    54, 58–60, 62–3, 67–73, 79–80, 108, 128–9,
    142, 150, 152, 157–9, 168–9, 191, 231
  Democratic 67, 69–70, 71–6, 78, 87, 108,
    153–6, 159–60

Individual 67–71, 76–7, 79–80, 103, 108,
    156–7, 169, 174, 215
Lincoln, Abraham 53
Locke, John 17, 22, 24, 26, 40–1, 44, 45, 47
Luhmann, Niklas 92
Luxembourg 179

Madison, Jamas 28–9, 221
  Federalist Papers 28
Comte de Mirabeau, Gabriel de Riqueti 22
de Malberg, Raymond Carré 1
Mill, John Stuart 88
Milošević, Slobodan 216
Montesquieu, Charles de Secondat, Baron de
    17–20, 22, 25, 28, 31, 32, 40–1, 42, 44, 45, 46, 47

Napoleon 21
NATO 162
Necker, Jaques 22
Netherlands 127, 166, 231
Nixon, Richard Milhous 44
North Korea 217

Organisation for Economic Co-Operation and
    Development 220, 230

Parliament 1, 14, 45, 48, 81–2, 85–9, 102, 107,
    110–13, 148, 161
Parliamentary control 45, 46, 118–19
Plato 6
Plebiscite 88–9, 165–6
Poland 36, 127, 137
Political parties 8, 103–6
Presidentialism 14, 110, 112
Property 30, 31, 33, 68
Parliamentarism 8, 14, 85, 110–13
Public authority 5, 42, 51–3, 62–3, 68, 71, 79, 81,
    228, 232

Rawls, John 1, 3, 5, 10, 58
Referendum see Plebiscite
Romania 112
Rousseau, Jean Jaques 4, 19–20, 50, 57, 108
Roosevelt, Franklin D. 37
Russia 112, 214

Schmitt, Carl 1, 44, 58, 83, 114
Separation of powers 3–5, 9–10, 14, 22, 26, 28–9,
    32, 35, 36–7, 39, 40–50, 62, 81, 84, 94–5, 108,
    148, 160, 169–71, 191, 206, 224, 228, 231
  Checks and balances 5, 28, 43, 45–6, 50
  Differentiation of powers 44
  Division of powers 5, 16, 33, 43
South Africa 36, 48, 117, 127, 215
Spain 35, 127, 137
Statute of Rome 216
Sweden 214

9 780198 738084